AF675425

ARTIFICIAL INTELLIGENCE AND COMPUTER SCIENCE

ARTIFICIAL INTELLIGENCE AND COMPUTER SCIENCE

SUSAN SHANNON
EDITOR

Nova Science Publishers, Inc.
New York

For permission to use material from this book please contact us:
Telephone 631-231-7269; Fax 631-231-8175
Web Site: http://www.novapublishers.com

LIBRARY OF CONGRESS CATALOGING-IN-PUBLICATION DATA

Artificial Intelligence and Computer Science / Susan Shannon, editor.
p. cm.
Includes index.
ISBN 1-59454-411-5 (hardcover)
1. Artificial Intelligence and Computer Science. Susan Shannon.
QC173.7.T74 2005
530.14'072--dc22 2004024758

Published by Nova Science Publishers, Inc. ✣ New York

CONTENTS

PREFACE

We are living in a world where complexity of systems created and studied by people grows beyond all imaginable limits. Computers, their software and their networks are among the most complicated systems of our time. Science is the only efficient tool for dealing with this overwhelming complexity. One of the methodologies developed in science is the axiomatic approach. It proved to be very powerful in mathematics. In Chapter 1, we develop further an axiomatic approach in computer science initiated by Floyd, Manna, Blum and other researchers. In the traditional constructive setting, different classes of algorithms (programs, processes or automata) are studied separately, with some indication of relations between these classes. In such a way, the constructive approach gave birth to the theory of Turing machines, theory of partial recursive functions, theory of finite automata, and other theories of constructive models of algorithms. The axiomatic context allows one to research collections of classes of algorithms, automata, and processes. These classes are united in a collection by common properties in a form of axioms. As a result, axiomatic approach goes higher in the hierarchy of computer and network models, reducing in such a way complexity of their study. The suggested axiomatic methodology is applied to evaluation of possibilities of computers and their networks. People more and more rely on computers and other information processing systems. So, it is vital to know better than we know now what computers and other information processing systems can do and what they can't do. The main emphasis in this paper is done on such properties as computability, decidability, and acceptability. These properties are important for the further development of artificial intelligence.

Chapter 2 reviews current algorithms for distributed, asynchronous control of data networks. Different problem formulations are considered: from the simplest shortestpath approach, without Quality of Service (QoS) constraints, via total flow cost minimization for given traffic quality equations, until dynamic flow control with influencing users through transmission prices. These different formulations are presented in a unified way and compared from the possible application area point of view.

In order to solve complex configuration tasks in technical domains, various knowledge based methods have been developed. However, their applicability is often unsuccessful due to their low efficiency. One of the reasons for this is that (parts of the) problems have to be solved again and again, instead of being "learnt" from preceding processes. However, learning processes bring with them the problem of conservatism, for in technical domains *innovation* is a deciding factor. On the other hand, a certain amount of conservatism is often desired since uncontrolled innovation as a rule is also detrimental.

Chapter 3 proposes the heuristic RKF (Relevant Knowledge First) for making decisions in configuration processes, based on the so-called *relevance* of objects in a knowledge base. The underlying relevance-function has two components, one based on reinforcement learning and the other based on forgetting (fading). The relevance of an object increases with its successful use and decreases with age, when it is not used. RKF has been developed to speed up the configuration process and to improve the quality of the solutions in relation to the user's rating of the solutions.

An algorithm for managing a portfolio of stocks using a trading agent is presented in Chapter 4. A simulation game inspired by history-based Parrondo games is described. A performance measure is defined, with which various strategy mixes can be judged. Even when transaction costs are taken into account, active portfolio management (as opposed to Buy and Hold) is shown to be profitable.

In Chapter 5 the authors propose a novel criterion for support vector machine (SVM) learning: maximizing the margin in the input space, not in the feature space like the original SVM. This criterion is appropriate in particular when some prior knowledge is given by a metric in the input space. We derive an algorithm that consists of two alternating steps to estimate the dual sets of parameters, where those parameters are first initialized by the original SVM. The first step is to update one set of parameters by a Newton-like procedure, and the second step is to update the dual set by solving a quadratic programming (QP) problem. The algorithm converges to a local optimum in a few steps under mild conditions, and it preserves the sparsity of support vectors. Although the complexity for calculating temporal variables becomes large, the complexity for the QP problem does not change. It is also shown that the original SVM can be seen as a special case of this framework. We further derive a simplified algorithm which enables us to use existing codes for the original SVM.

In a state-update protocol for a system of L asynchronous parallel processes that communicate only with nearest neighbors, global desynchronization in operation times can be deduced from kinetic roughening of the corresponding virtual-time horizon (VTH). The utilization of the parallel processing environment can be deduced by analyzing the microscopic structure of the VTH. In Chapter 6 we give an overview of how the methods of non-equilibrium surface growth (physics of complex systems) can be applied to uncover some properties of state update algorithms used in distributed parallel discrete-event simulations (PDES). In particular, we focus on the asynchronous conservative PDES algorithm in a ring communication topology. The time evolution of its VTH is simulated numerically as asynchronous cellular automaton whose update rule corresponds to the update rule followed by this algorithm. There are two cases of a balanced load considered: (1) the case of the minimal load per processor, which is expected to produce the lowest utilization (the so-called worst-case performance scenario); and, (2) the case of a general finite load per processor. In both cases, we give theoretical estimates of the performance as a function of L and the load per processor, i.e., approximate formulas for the utilization (thus, the mean speedup) and for the desynchronization (thus, the mean memory request per processor). It is established that the memory request per processor, required for state savings, does not grow without limit for a finite number of processors and a finite load per processor but varies as the conservative PDES evolve. For a given simulation size, there is a theoretical upper bound for the desynchronization and a theoretical non-zero lower bound for the utilization. We show that the conservative PDES are generally scalable in the ring communication topology. The new approach to performance studies, outlined in this chapter, is particularly useful in the search for the design of a new-generation of algorithms that would efficiently carry out an autonomous or tunable synchronization.

Chapter 7 explores a new robust approach for Semantic Parsing of unrestricted texts. Our approach formalizes Semantic Parsing as a Consistent Labelling Problem (CLP), allowing the integration of several knowledge types (syntactic and semantic) obtained from different sources (linguistic and statistical). The current implementation obtains 95% accuracy in model identification and 72% in case-role filling.

In Chapter 8 the description of the language model of data, offered by the author, responding the purposes of storage and retrieval of complicatedly structured data and initiation of control operations, according to recursive rules, having the same structure, as the data, is given. In the model, as it is accepted, the structural, manipulation and integrity parts are allocated, the features of implementation are considered. The possibilities of formulation and realization of the tasks of teaching and semantic search of information on natural language within the framework of the model are discussed also.

In Chapter 9 we investigate the relation between decisions, deliberation and agent types. In particular, we are interested how deliberation leads to decisions, and how agent types classify patterns of deliberation. We therefore consider Classical and Qualitative Decision Theories (CDT and QDT), the Beliefs-Desire-Intention (BDI) model, 3APL systems, and Belief-Obligation-Intention-Desire (BOID) systems. The first two are based on a decision rule which expresses a notion of rationality, whereas the latter three are based on deliberation processes and agent types.

In: Artificial Intelligence and Computer Science
Editor: Susan Shannon, pp. 1-61

ISBN: 1-59454-411-5

Chapter 1

MEASURING POWER OF ALGORITHMS, PROGRAMS AND AUTOMATA

Mark Burgin
Department of Mathematics, University of California, Los Angeles
405 Hilgard Ave., Los Angeles, CA 90095

Abstract

We are living in a world where complexity of systems created and studied by people grows beyond all imaginable limits. Computers, their software and their networks are among the most complicated systems of our time. Science is the only efficient tool for dealing with this overwhelming complexity. One of the methodologies developed in science is the axiomatic approach. It proved to be very powerful in mathematics. In this paper, we develop further an axiomatic approach in computer science initiated by Floyd, Manna, Blum and other researchers. In the traditional constructive setting, different classes of algorithms (programs, processes or automata) are studied separately, with some indication of relations between these classes. In such a way, the constructive approach gave birth to the theory of Turing machines, theory of partial recursive functions, theory of finite automata, and other theories of constructive models of algorithms. The axiomatic context allows one to research collections of classes of algorithms, automata, and processes. These classes are united in a collection by common properties in a form of axioms. As a result, axiomatic approach goes higher in the hierarchy of computer and network models, reducing in such a way complexity of their study. The suggested axiomatic methodology is applied to evaluation of possibilities of computers and their networks. People more and more rely on computers and other information processing systems. So, it is vital to know better than we know now what computers and other information processing systems can do and what they can't do. The main emphasis in this paper is done on such properties as computability, decidability, and acceptability. These properties are important for the further development of artificial intelligence.

Key words: computation, computing power, acceppting power, axiom, solvability, computability, decidability, acceptability

1 Introduction

Mathematical methods play more and more important role in society. Mathematics is applied to a diversity of other fields. Mathematics provides a variety of methods for description, modeling, computation, reasoning, constructing, etc. This extensive variety of methods is traditionally divided into two directions: constructive and axiomatic. Beginning from Euclid's "*Elements*," which present geometry as an axiomatic discipline, axiomatic methods have demonstrated their power in mathematics. As Burton (1997) writes, generation after generation regarded the "*Elements*" as the summit and crown of logic and mathematics, and its study as the best way of developing facility of exact reasoning. Abraham Lincoln at the age of forty, while still a struggling lawyer, mastered the first six books of Euclid, solely as training for his mind. Even now, in spite of the discovery of non-Euclidean geometries and improvements of the system of Euclid, "Elements" largely remains the supreme model of a book in mathematics, demonstrating the power of the axiomatic approach.

The main goal of this paper is to show that axiomatic methods are also very efficient for computer science. When computers were created and utilized, the theory of algorithms formed a core of computer science and till now this is the most developed mathematical discipline of computer science. Methods and technique developed in this paper for the theory of algorithms and computation are oriented at various applications in computer science and technology. Examples of practical problems that benefit from this approach are debugging and testing computer software, design of software metrics, and comparison of computational power for different systems.

It is possible to consider three levels of axiomatization: local, global, and multiglobal.

Local or *object oriented axiomatization* gives axioms for a description/determination of a single object, e.g., a separate program or algorithm. As an example, we can take the axiomatic theory of programs originated in (Naur, 1966; Floyd, 1967) and developed further in (Hoare, 1969; Milner, 1978) and many other books and papers.

Global or *class oriented axiomatization* gives axioms for a description/determination of a definite class of objects, e.g., Euclidean geometry, the class of all vector spaces, and the class of all groups. Axiomatic definitions of programming languages give other examples of global or class oriented axiomatization (Hoare and Wirth, 1973; Schwartz, 1978; Meyer and Halpern, 1980).

Multiglobal or *feature oriented axiomatization* gives axioms for a description/determination of a system of definite classes that have some specific features in common, e.g., all set theories in which the Axiom of Choice is valid or all classes of finite groups.

In the global approach, a system of axioms is taken (built or selected) for a description of some system. Then these axioms are used for deduction of properties of this system. This is the standard mathematical way of axiomatic studies. It is embodied in such classical works as Euclid's *Elements*, Hilbert's axiomatization of the Euclidean geometry, and axiomatic set theories (cf. Fraenkel and Bar-Hillel, 1958): **ZF** of Zermelo-Fraenkel, **VN** of von Neumann, **BG** of Bernays-Godel, and two theories of Quine – **NF** and **ML**. The problem that is solved by a global axiomatization is what are basic properties of a given system that allow one to deduce all other properties.

In contrast to this, the multiglobal approach is oriented not at a system of objects but at definite properties of such systems. The aim of multiglobal axiomatization is to characterize by simple properties $P_1, \dots, P_m$ such classes of systems in which some important results $R_1, \dots, R_n$ are valid. Properties $P_1, \dots, P_m$ are formulated as axioms and conditions $A_1, \dots, A_m$ and the necessary results $R_1, \dots, R_n$ are deduced from these axioms and conditions as theorems $T_1, \dots, T_n$. Usually, the initial properties $P_1, \dots, P_m$ in the form of axioms and conditions $A_1, \dots, A_m$ are transparent and easy to test, while the deduced properties $R_1, \dots, R_n$ are complicated and hidden from direct comprehension.

This allows one not to prove the same result, for example, R_i, for each class from a diverse variety of classes separately, but to check for each of those classes only initial axioms, which are much simpler, and then to deduce this result R_i from a general theorem T_i proved in the axiomatic setting. Axiomatic form of concept introduction in modern mathematics, such as rings, fields, Hilbert spaces, Banach spaces etc., gives classical examples of such a technique. Another example of this approach is Blum's (1967) concept of the size of a machine, which synthesized many measures of algorithms and software metrics. Another his concept is computational complexity, which in the axiomatic form synthesized such concepts as time complexity and space complexity of computation (Blum, 1967a). The further development of this approach resulted in axiomatic development of the theory of complexity of algorithms and computation (Burgin, 1982; 1992) and its application to software measures (Burgin and Debnath, 2003).

The first Godel's incompleteness theorem (1931) shows that the problem of global axiomatization cannot be completely solved for sufficiently rich mathematical systems. Axioms cannot present all properties of such systems, given traditional means of inference. Thus, it becomes more efficient to consider partial systems of axioms that define systems of classes in the context of multiglobal axiomatization. According to the modern methodology of science, such systems of axioms become laws of the second order (Burgin and Kuznetsov, 1994).

The reason why we need multiglobal axiomatization in computer science is existence of a huge diversity of computer and network systems, programs and program systems, as well as their theoretical models. Axiomatics allows one to compress information about all these devices and systems, providing efficient means for their study and development.

An extreme case of the multiglobal axiomatization is *reverse mathematics* aimed at finding minimal conditions for a possibility to prove some result or a system of results. Multiglobal axiomatization is also closely related to reverse mathematics, which strives to obtain the simplest conditions under which a given result (mathematical theorem) is valid. Namely, reverse mathematics is the branch of mathematics concerned with what are the minimal axioms needed to prove the particular theorem (Friedman and Hirst, 1990; Giusto and Simpson, 2000). It turns out that over a weak base theory, many mathematical statements are equivalent to the particular additional axiom needed to prove them.

Axiomatic approach brings the theory of algorithms to a new level. Historically, this theory appeared when models of algorithms were constructed to prove absolute undecidability of some mathematical problems. Such ultimate undecidability demanded to show that there is no algorithm for problem solution. In other words, it was necessary to give an exact description of all possible algorithms. The goal was achieved by constructing such ultimate classes of recursive algorithms as Turing machines, partial recursive functions, and many other models of algorithms. However, recent development of computer science demonstrated that these classes are not absolute and there are more powerful algorithms (cf., for example, Burgin, 2001). Thus, we have come to the situation when it is impossible to reduce decidability problems to one universal class of algorithms. Axiomatic setting allows one to eliminate this obstacle and to prove undecidability without constructive models of algorithms. Many other properties are also obtained from axioms and simple conditions.

In this paper, we consider the most conventional class of reactive algorithms and abstract automata. These algorithms and automata react to a given input by producing some output or coming to some state. Active, interactive, and proactive algorithms and automata are considered elsewhere.

Our advent in a new realm of multiglobal axiomatics of algorithms, automata, and programs, we begin (Section 2) with an analysis of such basic for computer science concepts as algorithms, programs, and abstract automata. The suggested approach allows us to eliminate some contradictions and inconsistencies in the conceptual system of computer science.

In Section 3, types of algorithms and functioning of automata and algorithms are analyzed and formalized. A multifaceted typology is developed for algorithms aimed at axiomatizing computer science.

In Section 4, basic axioms for algorithms are considered in three forms: *postulates* as the most basic assumptions, *axioms* as global assumptions that represent important properties, and *conditions* as local assumptions that represent specific properties.

An example of computer science postulates is the Deterministic Computation Postulate **PDC**, which states that any algorithm A that takes inputs from a set X and gives outputs that belong to a set Y determines a function f_A from X into Y.

An example of computer science axioms is the Universality Axiom **AU**, which states that for a class **K** of automata/algorithms and some coding $\mathbf{c} : \mathbf{K} \rightarrow V^+$, there is a universal algorithm/automaton in **K**.

An example of computer science conditions is the Switching Condition **SW**, which states that for any x and y from X, there is a switching for x and y algorithm/automaton in a class **K**.

In Section 5, power of algorithms and automata is investigated. Exact mathematical methods are developed for comparison and evaluation of algorithms and automata.

In Section 6, properties and related problems of algorithms and automata are classified and studied. All properties and problems are separated into several classes: linguistic, functional, description, operational, etc. Some of these classes have been intensively studied for different models of algorithms, such as finite automata, Turing machines, and some others. Here these properties and problems are considered in axiomatic setting, allowing one to essentially expand the scope of applications. Other studied here properties and problems have been beyond the scope of conventional computer science although they are important for practice.

In Section 7, boundaries for algorithms and computation are found. In particular, it is proved that all non-trivial linguistic (Theorem 7.5) and functional (Theorem 7.6) properties are undecidable for a lot of classes of algorithms. This implies classical results of Rice (1951) for Turing machines and some results from (Adleman and Blum, 1991) for inductive inference. At the same time, for other kinds of properties (e.g., operational properties), there are both decidable and undecidable non-trivial properties.

Applications of the theoretical results to software and hardware verification and testing are considered in Section 8.

Denotations and Basic Definitions:

N is the set of all natural numbers;

ω is the sequence of all natural numbers;

$\varnothing$ is the *empty set*;

The logical symbol $\forall$ means "for any";

The logical symbol $\exists$ means "there exists";

If **P** is a property, then $\neg$**P** is the *complementary property*, i.e., an object x has the property **P** if and only if it does not have the property $\neg$**P**.

R is the set of all real numbers;

A *binary relation* T between sets X and Y is a subset of the direct product $X \times Y$. The set X is called the *domain* of T ($X = \mathrm{D}(T)$) and Y is called the *codomain* of T ($Y = \mathrm{CD}(T)$). The *range* of the relation T is $\mathrm{R}(T) = \{ y ; \exists\, x \in X\ ((x, y) \in T) \}$. The *definability domain* of the relation T is $\mathrm{DD}(T) = \{ x ; \exists\, y \in Y\ ((x, y) \in T) \}$.

A *function* or *total function* from X to Y is a binary relation between sets X and Y in which there are no elements from X which are corresponded to more than one element from Y and to any element from X is corresponded some element from Y. Often total functions are also called everywhere defined functions.

A *partial function* f from X to Y is a binary relation in which there are no elements from X which are corresponded to more than one element from Y.

For a partial function f, its *definability domain* $\mathrm{DD}(f)$ is the set of all elements for which f is defined.

A function $f_{\varnothing}$ is called *empty* or *nowhere defined* if $\mathrm{DD}(f) = \varnothing$.

For any set, S, $\chi_S(x)$ is its *characteristic function*, that is, $\chi_S(x)$ is equal to 1 when $x \in S$ and is equal to 0 when $x \notin S$, and $\mathrm{C}_S(x)$ is its partial characteristic function, that is, $\mathrm{C}_S(x)$ is equal to 1 when $x \in S$ and is undefined when $x \notin S$.

An *alphabet* or vocabulary A of a *formal language* is a set consisting of some symbols or letters. A vocabulary is an alphabet on a higher level of hierarchy because words of a vocabulary play the same role for building sentences as symbols in an alphabet for building words. Traditionally any alphabet is a set. However, a more consistent point of view is that an alphabet is a multiset (Knuth, 1981), containing an unbounded number of identical copies of each symbol.

A *string* or *word* is a sequence of elements from the alphabet. A^* denotes the set of all finite words in the alphabet A. Usually there is no difference between strings and words. However, having a language, we speak about words of this language and not about its strings. A^{**} denotes the set of all (finite and infinite) words in the alphabet A. A^+ denotes the set of all non-empty finite words in the alphabet A. A^{++} denotes the set of all non-empty (finite and infinite) words in the alphabet A.

A *formal language* L is any subset of A^*.

The *length* $\mathrm{l}(w)$ of a word w is the number of letters in the word w.

ε is the *empty word*.

Λ is the *empty symbol*.

When an algorithm/automaton A gives y as the result being applied to x, it is denoted by $A(x) = y$. When an algorithm/automaton A gives no result being applied to x, it is denoted by $A(x) = *$.

D(A) is the *domain* of an algorithm A, i.e., the set X of such elements that are processed by A.

DD(A) is the *definability domain* of an algorithm A, i.e., is the set X of such elements that if any of them is given as input to A, then A gives a result/output.

C(A) is the *codomain* of an algorithm A, i.e., the set Y of such elements that are tentative outputs of A.

2 Algorithms, Programs, Procedures, and Abstract Automata

We begin with clarification of relations between such basic concepts of computer science as algorithms, programs, and automata.

In many cases, these terms are used interchangeably. However, computing practice and research experience show that these concepts are different. For instance, programmers and computer scientists are aware that the same algorithm can be expressed in a variety of forms. Texts are conventional forms of algorithm representation. For many algorithms, a representing text can be practically in any language, from natural languages like English or Spanish to programming languages like C^{++} or Java. That is why, as it is stressed by Shore in (Buss *et al*, 2001), it is important to know that algorithm is different from its representation and to make a distinction between algorithms and their representations. In a similar way, Cleland (2001) emphasizes that "it is important to distinguish instruction-expressions from instructions." Instructions are the simplest algorithms. The same instruction may be expressed in many different ways, including in different languages and in different terminology in the same language. Also, some instruction may be communicated non-verbally, e.g., when one computer sends a program to another computer in a form of electrical signals.

However, advanced languages provide more means for algorithm representation. As a result, not all algorithms that can be described in English have a representation Zulu. It would be an interesting problem to compare natural languages by those means that they provide for algorithm representation. The same is true for mathematical models of algorithms. As we know Turing machines allow one to represent much more algorithms than finite automata. For instance, addition of arbitrary binary numbers can be represented in many models: by a Turing machine, by a formal grammar, by a neural network, or by a finite automaton. At the same time, it is possible to realize multiplication of arbitrary binary numbers by a Turing machine, neural network or formal grammar. No finite automaton can multiply arbitrary binary numbers.

In addition, an algorithm can be represented not only in a symbolic form but also by hardware. For instance, in computer memory, programs and consequently, algorithms, are represented by states of memory cells. Another type of algorithm representation by hardware gives digital arithmetic. Digital arithmetic encompasses study of symbolic number representations, algorithms for operations on numbers, implementations of arithmetic units in hardware, and their use in general-purpose and application-specific systems (Ercegovac, M.D. and Lang, 2002; Wakerly, 2001). Numerical algorithms are represented by (embodied in) integrated circuits of arithmetical units (processors) of computers.

Moreover, neural networks realize dynamic storage of information, utilizing a part of the network. To preserve its state, a neuron can be initiated to go into a self-sustaining loop that keeps the neuron firing even when the top input is no longer active. The stored binary bit is continuously accessible by looking at the output. This configuration is called a latch. The part of a network that used only for dynamical storage plays the role of the short-term memory of people or primary memory of computers: random access memory (RAM) and read only memory (ROM). Experimental evidence shows existence of such a dynamic memory in the brain (Suppes and Han, 2000). When we store a program in this dynamic memory, we have a representation of an algorithm by a process.

Consequently, we come to two forms of algorithm representation: *iconic*, *symbolic*, and *physical*.

Definition 2.1. *An algorithm representation by means of structures is called iconic.*

A neural network or a cellular automaton in graphical form is an example of an iconic algorithm representation.

Definition 2.2. *An algorithm representation by means of symbols is called symbolic or an algorithm description.*

A program printed on paper is an example of a symbolic algorithm representation.

Definition 2.3. *An algorithm representation by means of a physical entity (hardware) is called physical.*

A program stored in computer memory is an example of a system algorithm representation.

In turn, physical algorithm representation can be subdivided into three classes: *system*, *state*, and *process* physical algorithm representation.

Chips of arithmetic units form system algorithm representation. A program written in a CD is a state algorithm representation. Specific processes in the brain form process algorithm representation.

It is also possible to divide physical representations by types of systems and processes. It gives us mechanical, electronic, and quantum representations of algorithms. Here it is necessary to remark that in the case of information, it is more correct to write about quantum representation of information and not about quantum information.

There are three main classes of symbolic representations for algorithms and procedures:

Automaton representations. Turing machines and finite automata give the most known examples of such representations.

Instruction representations. Formal grammars, rules for inference, and Post productions give the most known examples of such representations.

Equation representations. Here an example of such recursive equation is given.

$$\text{Fact}\,(n) = \begin{cases} 1 & \text{when} \quad n = 1, \\ n\cdot\text{Fact}\,(n-1) & \text{when} \quad n > 1 \end{cases}$$

The fixed point of this recursive equation defines a program for computation of the factorial n!

We frequently encounter similar situations of multiple representations in nature and society. For instance, it emerges in the case of numbers. For instance, the same rational number may be represented by the following fractions 1/5 , 2/10 or 3/15, as well as by decimals 0.2, 0.20 or 0.19999... Number seven is represented by the Arab (or more exactly,

Hindu) numeral 7 in the decimal system, the sequence 111 in the binary number system, and by three symbols VII in the Roman number system.

There are, at least, three natural ways for separation of algorithms from their descriptions such as programs or systems of instructions.

The model approach:

Some type **D** of algorithm representations (for example, Turing machines) is taken as a model description, in which there is a one-to-one correspondence between algorithms and their representations. Then we introduce an equivalence relation R between different representations of algorithms. This relation has to satisfy two axioms:

(**DA1**) Any representation of an algorithm is equivalent to some element from the model class **D**.

(**DA2**) Any two elements from the model class **D** belong to different equivalence classes.

Such an approach is applied by Moschovakis, who considers the problem of unique representation for algorithms in his paper "What is an Algorithm?' (2001). He demonstrates that machine models of algorithms, such as Turing machines, are only models but not algorithms themselves. The main argument is that there are many models for one and the same algorithm. To remedy this, he defines algorithms as systems of mappings, building insuch a way a new model for algorithm, which is defined by recursive equations and called *recursor*. This is a progress in understanding and mathematical modeling algorithms. However, this does not solve the problem of separating algorithms as something invariant from their representations. This type of representation is on higher level of abstraction than traditional representations, such as Turing machines or partial recursive functions. Nevertheless, a *recursor* (in the sense of Moschovakis) is only a new model for algorithm but not algorithm itself.

The relational approach:

An equivalence relation R between different descriptions of algorithms is chosen. With this relation, we define algorithm as a class of equivalent descriptions. Equivalence of descriptions can be determined by some natural axioms, describing, for example, properties of operations:

Composition Axiom. Composition (sequential, parallel, etc.) of descriptions represents the corresponding composition of algorithms.

Decomposition Axiom. If a description H represents a sequential composition of algorithms A and B, a description K represents a sequential composition of algorithms C and B, and $A = C$, then H is equivalent to K.

At the same time, the equivalence relation R between descriptions can be formed on the base of computational processes. Namely, two descriptions define the same algorithm if these descriptions generate the same sets of computational processes. This definition depends on our understanding of equal processes. For example, in some cases it is natural to consider processes on different computing devices as different, while in other cases it might be better to treat some processes on different computing devices as equal.

An example of such a relation R is obtained by modification of the rule suggested by Cleland (2001) for instructions:

Different algorithm descriptions, i.e., representations of algorithms, express the same algorithm only if they prescribe the same type of functioning.

Such a definition of algorithm is not unique and depends on organization of computational processes. For example, let us consider some Turing machine **T** and another Turing machine **Q**. The only difference between **T** and **Q** is that **Q** contains all instruction of **T** and one more instruction that is never used in computations of the machine **Q**. Then, on one hand, it is possible to assume that this additional instruction has no influence on computational processes and thus, **T** and **Q** *algorithm* one and the same algorithm. On the other hand, if a Turing machine in a course of computation always go through all instructions to choose the one to be performed, then the processes are different and consequently, **T** and **Q** represent different algorithms.

The structural approach:

In it, a specific invariant (structure) is extracted from different representations. This structure is called an algorithm. Here we understand structures in the sense of (Burgin, 1997). It results in the following understanding, which separates algorithm from its descriptions.

Definition 2.4. *An algorithm is a (finite) structure with exact effective information (instructions) for some performer (class of performers) that allows this performer(s) to perform operations (actions) in order to achieve a definite goal.*

This shows that algorithms are compressed constructive, i.e., giving enough information for realization, representations of processes. In particular, they represent intrinsic structures of computer programs. Hence, algorithm is an essence that is independent of how it happens to be represented and is similar to mathematical objects. Once the concept of algorithm is so rendered, its broader connotations virtually spell themselves out. As a result, algorithm appears as consisting of three components: *structure*, *representation* (linguistic, mechanical, electronic etc.), and *interpretation*.

It is important to understand that not all systems of rules represent algorithms. For example, you want to give a book to your friend Johns, who often comes to your office. So, you decide to take the book to your office (the first rule) and to give it to Johns when he comes to your office (the second rule). While these simple rules are fine for you, they are much too ambiguous for a computer. In order for a system of rules to be applicable to a computer, it must have certain characteristics. We specify these characteristics later in formal definitions of an algorithm. Now we only state that formalized functioning of complex systems (such as people) is mostly described and controlled by more general systems of rules than algorithmic structures. They are called procedures.

Definition 2.5. *A procedure is a compressed operational representation of a process in the form of a structure.*

For instance, you have a set of instructions for planting a garden where the first step instructed you to remove all large stones from the soil. This instruction may not be effective if there is a ten-ton rock buried just below ground level. So, this is not an algorithm, but only a procedure. However, if you have means to destroy this rock, this system of rules becomes an algorithm.

Definition 2.5 describes procedure in the theoretical sense because there is also a notion of procedure in the sense of programming. Namely, a *procedure in a program*, or *subroutine*, is a specifically organized sequence of instructions for performing a separate task. This allows the subroutine code to be called from multiple places of the program, even from within itself, in which case the form of computation is called recursive. Most programming languages allow programmers to define subroutines. Subroutines, or procedures in this sense, are also representations of algorithms by means of programming languages.

Algorithms are connected to procedures in a general sense, being special cases of procedures. If we consider algorithms as rigid procedures, then there are also soft procedures, which have recently become very popular in the field of soft computing.

To discern algorithms from procedures, it is usually assumed that algorithms satisfy specific conditions:

1. *Operational decomposition*: There is a system of effective basic operations that are performed in a simple way with some basic constructive objects, while all other operations can be reduced to the basic operations.
2. *Purposefulness*: Execution of algorithms is aimed at some purpose.
3. *Discreteness*: Operations are performed in a discrete time, that is, step by step and each such step is separated from the others.

Some experts demand additional conditions that are not always satisfied both in the theory of algorithms and practice of computation:

4. *Substantial finiteness*: All objects of operation in algorithm and the number of objects involved into operation on each step are finite.
5. *Operational finiteness*: The number of operations in algorithm and operations themselves are finite.
6. *Temporal finiteness*: The result of the algorithm functioning/execution is obtained in finite time.
7. *Demonstrativeness*: Algorithm provides explicit information when it obtains the necessary result.
8. *Definability*: Given a relevant input, algorithm always obtains the result.

It is possible to formalize all these conditions in the context of a multiglobal axiomatic approach.

Like algorithms, procedures (in a general sense) are also different from their descriptions.

Definition 2.6. *A description of a procedure/algorithm is a symbolic materialization of this procedure/algorithm in form of a text.*

According to this understanding, algorithms and procedures are similar to mathematical objects because, as it is demonstrated in Burgin (1998), all mathematical objects are structures. This explains why algorithms in a strict sense appeared in mathematics, were named after a mathematician, and have been developed into a powerful and advanced mathematical theory – the theory of algorithms and computation.

However, in the theory of algorithms and computation there is no distinction between algorithms and their descriptions. In what follows, we follow this tradition to make comprehension easier.

Going from more abstract and implicit to more concrete and explicit, it is natural to consider three levels of algorithm descriptions:

1. *An analytical description.*
2. *A prescriptive description.*
3. *An embodied description.*

An analytical description represents an algorithm in form of some formulas, e.g., a set of equations, regular expressions, recursive functions, formulas of the λ–calculus etc. Formulas represent relations in sets of processed/computed data. It is an implicit form because it is necessary to derive rules for computation from these formulas.

A prescriptive description provides rules for computation in an explicit form. The most popular examples of this form are computer programs, formal or generative grammars, deduction rules in logical calculi, finite automata, and inference rules in expert systems.

An embodied description provides not only rules for computation but also a description of a device that performs these computations. Usually this form is called an abstract machine or automaton. The most popular examples of this form are different versions of Turing machines, random access machines, Boolean circuits, etc.

Any kind of representation of algorithms must include, implicitly or explicitly, *metarules*. These metarules define how an algorithm starts functioning, where from it takes its input, how the rules from the algorithm are applied to data, in what cases the algorithm stops, how and where it gives its output, and what is the result of its functioning. As a result, the same hardware and software allow one to define automata of different types. For example, metarules for result determination can give three different types of automata: *computing*, *accepting* or *deciding*. Thus, we have computing and accepting finite automata, computing, accepting, and deciding Turing machines and so on. The same structure (hardware) of a Turing machine and the same rules (software) allows one to define ordinary Turing machines, inductive Turing machines (Burgin, 1983), infinite time Turing machines (Hamkins and Lewis, 2000) or persistent Turing machines (Goldin and Wegner, 1988).

It is possible to call metarules from an algorithm representation by the name *metasoftware*. Computers also have metasoftware in the form of user instructions. There are many kinds of such instructions: instructions to the computer as a whole, instructions to different program systems and separate programs, instructions to separate devices (printer, scanner, etc.) and so on.

We begin with an abstract automaton as the most complete representation of algorithm. The first abstract automaton was Turing machine created by Turing (1936). Von Nemann (1951) introduced a general concept of an abstract automaton. Finite automata were formalized, modified and studied by Mealy (1953), Kleene (1956), and Moore (1956). Potentially infinite automata were formalized, modified and studied by Church (1957).

Abstract automata and algorithms work with symbols, words, and other symbolic configurations, transforming them into other configurations of the same type. For example, words are transformed into words. While words and strings are linear configurations, there are many useful abstract automata and algorithms work with such configurations as graphs, vectors, arrays, etc. (cf., for example, Kolmogorov, 1953; Rabin, 1969; Pratt, Rabin, and Stockmeyer, 1974; Burgin and Karasik, 1975; Burgin, 1982a; Van Leeuwen and Wiedermann, 1985).

An abstract automaton consists of an abstract information processing device (*abstract hardware*), an algorithm/program of its functioning (*abstract software*), and description/specification of information which is processed (*abstract infware*).

In a general case, the hardware of an abstract automaton, consists of three main parts: abstract *input device*, abstract *information processor*, and abstract *output device*, which are presented in Figure 1. For example, Turing machine can have special input and output tapes or one and the same tape works as an input/output device and a part of the processor. Neural networks also have these parts: the input device that comprises all input neurons, output device that consists of all output neurons, and information processor that includes all hidden neurons. In some cases, input and output neurons are combined into one group of visible neurons. In some cases, as for example, for finite automata, input and output devices are not specified.

Accordingly, we have a *structural classification* of automata (Fisher, 1965):

1. A *generator* is an abstract automaton without input device.
2. An *acceptor* is an abstract automaton without output device.
3. A *transducer* is an abstract automaton with both input and output devices.

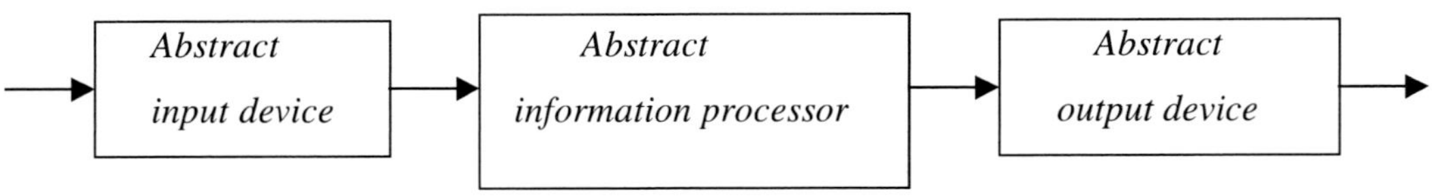

Figure 1. The structure of an abstract automaton

A finite state machine with a read-only input and a write-only output is, for example, a finite state transducer. In this case, the input and output cannot be reread or changed. Decision tables (Humby, 1973) represent the simplest case of transducers that have no memory. Basically any abstract automaton can be considered as a transducer because we can add, if necessary, both input and output devices.

At the same time, any transducer can also work only either as an acceptor or as a generator. For example, very often Turing machines are often considered as acceptors (cf. Hopckroft *et al*, 2001), although they produce some output, which is written in their tapes at the time when they stop. In some cases, it is assumed that Turing machines always start from the initial state with empty input. It means that they work as generators. However, it is possible to prove that theoretically both only accepting and only generating Turing machines are equivalent with respect to their power to Turing machines that work as transducers.

Let us consider some examples of different representations of algorithms.

Example 2.1. A finite automaton *A*.

Infware of *A* is the *linguistic structure* L = (Σ, Q, Ω) in which Σ is a finite set of *input symbols*, Q is a finite *set of states*, and Ω is a finite set of *output symbols* of the automaton *A*.

Hardware of *A* is the *structure* $S = (Q, q_0 , F)$ where q_0 is an element from *Q* that is called the *start state* and *F* is a subset of *Q* that is called the set of *final* (in some cases, *accepting*) states of the automaton *A*.

Software or program of *A* is the *transition function*

$$\delta_A : \Sigma \times Q \to Q \times \Omega$$

For a deterministic finite automaton *A*, δ is a function. For a nondeterministic finite automaton *A*, δ is a binary relation or correspondence from Σ×Q to Q×Ω. For an ε-nondeterministic finite automaton *A*, δ is a binary relation or correspondence from $\Sigma_\varepsilon \times Q$ to Q×Ω where $\Sigma_\varepsilon = \Sigma \cup \{\varepsilon\}$.

A finite automaton C without output, or an accepting finite automaton, does not have output symbols in its linguistic structure and therefore its *transition function* is simpler:

$$\delta_C : \Sigma \times Q \to Q$$

Example 2.2. A Turing machine T.

Infware of the Turing machine T consists of languages $\boldsymbol{L} = (L_I , L_W , L_O)$ where L_I is the *input* language, L_W is the *working* language, and L_O is the *output* language of T.

Hardware or device of the Turing machine T. What is the hardware of a computer? It consists of all devices (processor, system of memory, display, keyboard, etc.) that constitute the computer. In a similar way, a Turing machine T has three abstract devices: a finite automaton A, which we may the controller of T and which controls performance of the Turing machine T; a processor or operating device h, which is traditionally called the head of the Turing machine T; and the memory L, which is traditionally called the tape or tapes of the Turing machine T.

Software of the Turing machine T is a single program in a form of simple rules. In the traditional representation, these rules have the following form.

$$q_h a_i \to a_j q_k \, , \; q_h a_i \to \mathrm{R} q_k , \; q_h a_i \to \mathrm{L} q_k$$

Each rule directs one step of computation of the corresponding Turing machine.

If such rules are given without any specified hardware, we have the second type of algorithms representation: a program. Examples of programs that represent algorithms are computer programs in any programming language: LISP, ALGOL, C^{++}, Java, etc.

Analytical representations of algorithms does not contain all information presented in a program. For example, analytical representation does not necessarily include data types. Analytical, prescriptive, and embodied representations are divided into two classes: *formal* and *informal*. Examples of formal analytical representations are formal grammars, primitive recursive, recursive and partial recursive functions. Examples of informal prescriptive representations are different block schemes and flow charts.

Algorithms are often represented by computer programs. However, the concept of a program is more general.

Definition 2.7. *A program is a (finite) description of actions for pursuing a definite goal.*

While, in general, program, are less exact than algorithms, computer programs are more exact and contain more specific information than algorithms in general.

3 Functioning of Automata and Algorithms

Processes represented by algorithms have different types. This implies the corresponding classification of algorithms.

Transformation algorithms describe how to transform some input into a definite output, for example, how to calculate 375 + 573.

Performance algorithms describe some activity or functioning, for example, algorithms of functioning of a plane or algorithms of human-computer interaction. Performance algorithms also describe organized mental activity and organization functioning.

Construction algorithms describe how to build/construct objects.

Decision algorithms describe decision-making. They are kinds of construction algorithms because their goal is to construct decisions.

Algorithms are also classified by objects involved in the processes they describe. In such a way, we have:

1. *Material algorithms*, which work with material objects (for example, algorithm of a vending machine or algorithms of pay phone functioning);
2. *Symbolic algorithms*, which work with symbols (for example, computational algorithms are symbolic algorithms that control computing processes);
3. *Mixed algorithms*, which work both with material and symbolic objects (for example, algorithms that control production processes or algorithms of robot functioning).

All mathematical models of algorithms are symbolic algorithms. Thus, in computer science and mathematics, only symbolic algorithms, i.e., algorithms with symbolic input, working material, and output are studied.

Algorithms that work with finite words in some alphabet X are the most popular in the theory of algorithms. As a rule, only finite alphabets are utilized. For example, natural numbers in the decimal form are represented by words in the alphabet $X = \{0, 1, 2, 3, 4, 5, 6, 7, 8, 9\}$, while in binary form they are represented by words in the alphabet $X = \{0, 1\}$. The words in X may represent natural numbers or other entities, but in any way there is a natural procedure to enumerate all such words. This makes it possible, when it is necessary, to assume that algorithms work with natural numbers. In such a way, through enumeration of words, any algorithm A defines a partial function $f_A : N \rightarrow N$ (cf., (Burgin, 1985)). However, there are many reasons to consider algorithms that work with infinite words or streams or ω-words (Thomas, 1990; Vardi and Wolper, 1994; Staiger, 1997) or with such infinite objects as real numbers (Shannon, 1941; Abramson, 1971; Moore, 1996; Blum, *et al.* 1998). In addition, there are algorithms that work with abstract data (Tucker and Zukker, 1988; 1992; 2002; Feferman, 1992; 1996) and arbitrary structures (Bournez, et al, 1003).

Computer algorithms, i.e., such algorithms that are or may be performed by computers, form an important class of all algorithms. Thus, we come to the concept of *computation*. There are different approaches to this concept. According to an engineer, computation is any thing computer can do. On one hand, this restricts computation to computers that exist at a given time. Each program that solves a new problem extends the scope of computation. On the other hand, not everything that computers do is computation. For example, interaction with users or with other computers, sending e-mails, and connecting to the Internet are not computations. Mathematical approach reduces dependence on computers. According to a mathematician, computation is a sequence of symbolic transformations that are performed according to some algorithm. From the mathematical point of view, computers function under the control of algorithms, which are embodied in computer programs. So, to understand possibilities of computers and their boundaries, we have to study algorithms.

To form an algorithm, a system of rules must have a description how these rules are applied. This description consists of metarules for an algorithm, given in a form of some abstract machine. Metarules have often the form of an abstract automaton.

Taking the most general case of automata with input and output devices, we see that there are three main types of automata with respect to their connection with environment.

1. *Reactive automata* that need to be given some input, to produce output.
2. *Proactive automata* that themselves find initial information to produce output.
3. *Interactive automata* can work both as reactive and proactive automata.

Reactive automata represent the classical approach to computation (cf., for example, (Turing, 1936)). Proactive automata represent the intelligent agent approach to computation (cf., for example, (Russel and Norvig, 1995)). Interactive automata represent the interactive approach to computation (cf., for example, (Wegner, 1998)).

The general idea of abstract automaton implies that there are three main modes of processing input data by an abstract or real information processing system:

1. The *computing* mode when an automaton produces (computes or outputs) some words (its output or configuration) as a result of its activity.
2. The *deciding* mode when an automaton, given a word/configuration u and a set X of words/configurations, indicates (decides) whether this word/configuration belongs to X or not.
3. The *accepting* mode when an automaton, given a word/configuration u, either accepts this word/configuration or rejects it.

Remark 3.1. Automata without output device can work only in the accepting mode. Automata without input device can work only in the computing mode. Automata with all three devices can work in all three modes.

In addition, there are two partial deciding modes:

4. The *positive deciding* mode when an automaton, given a word/configuration u and a set X of words/configurations, indicates (decides) whether this word/configuration belongs to X.
5. The *deciding* mode when an automaton, given a word/configuration u and a set X of words/configurations, indicates (decides) whether this word/configuration does not belong to X.

Sometimes (cf., for example, (Hamkins and Lewis, 2000)), the positive deciding mode is called a *semi-decidable* mode.

These types not only reflect the principal modes of computer functioning, but also define the main utilization modes for algorithms and programs. There are several kinds of each mode. For example, there is acceptation by a state and by a result.

Definition 3.1. An automaton A *accepts* a word u *by a result* if A gives some result, or gives a definite result (e.g., the symbol 1 or the word *yes*), when u is its input.

For example, a Turing machine T accepts a word u if and only if: 1) T gives some output when u is its input; after producing the output T halts. At the same time, it is possible to demand that a Turing machine *T* accepts a word *u* if and only if the produced result is equal to 1. It is possible to show that both ways of acceptation are equivalent.

Remark 3.2. As a rule it is possible to reduce acceptation by some result to acceptation by a definite result.

To define acceptation by a state, some states of the automaton are labeled as final or accepting.

Definition 3.2. An automaton *A* *accepts* a word *u* *by a state* if to accept *u*, *A* has to come to a final or accepting state when *u* is given as its input.

Remark 3.3. For many classes of algorithms or abstract automata, acceptance of a word *u* means that the automaton/algorithm that works with the input *u* comes to an inner state that is an accepting state for this algorithm or automaton. Finite automata give an example of such a class. However, for such algorithms that produce output, the acceptance assumption means that whenever an algorithm comes to an inner accepting state it produces some chosen result (e.g., the number 1) as its output. In such a way, this algorithm informs that it has reached an inner accepting state.

Another way to define an accepting state is to consider a state of some component of an abstract automaton. For example, pushdown automata accept words not only by an accepting inner state, but also by an empty stack, that is, by a definite state of their stack, which is an external state for these automata.

Definition 3.3. An automaton *A* *accepts* a word *u* *by a component state* if a chosen component of *A* comes to a final or accepting state when *u* is the input of *A*.

For a Turing machine, such accepting component is its control device, while for push down automaton such accepting component is either its stack or its control device (Hopcroft *et al*, 2001).

Remark 3.4. For finite automata (Trahtenbrot and Barzdin, 1970) and for pushdown automata (Hopcroft *et al*, 2001), it is proved that acceptance by a result is functionally equivalent to acceptance by a state.

It is possible to prove the following general result.

Theorem 3.1. If a class **K** of automata allows one to enhance each automaton from **K** with an output that informs about the inner state of this automaton, without changing the process (result) of acceptation, then acceptance by a state is reducible to acceptance by a result.

On the other hand, it is possible to do the inverse reduction.

Theorem 3.2. If a class **K** of automata allows one to enhance each automaton from **K** with an output register that stores output, without changing the process (result) of acceptation, then acceptance by a result is reducible to acceptance by a state.

All considered above forms of acceptation are *static*. At the same time, there are dynamic forms of acceptation. They depend on the behavior of the automaton. For example, a finite automaton *A* accepts infinite strings when *A* comes to an accepting state infinitely many times. Such automata are called Büchi automata (Büchi, 1960). Another example is inductive Turing machine (Burgin, 2003). It produces a result or accepts a word when its output stabilizes.

An important distinction exists between *deterministic* and *non-deterministic* algorithms. At first, such condition as complete determination of each step of an algorithm was considered as necessary for a general model of algorithm. For a long time, all models were strictly deterministic. However, necessity to reflect real situations and model computational processes influenced introduction of non-deterministic algorithms (Rabin and Scott, 1959).

Thus, it is possible to have an impression that the extensive diversity of models results in a similar diversity for the concepts of algorithm, computation and computable function. Nevertheless, mathematicians and computer scientists found that the algorithmic reality is well organized. They have found a unification law for this reality, which was called the Church-Turing Thesis. This Thesis, or better to say, Conjecture postulates existence of the most powerful, absolute in this sense model of computation – Turing machine or partial recursive function.

Different definitions of algorithm bring us to the conclusion that algorithms consist of rules or instructions. As a rule, it is supposed that each instruction is performed in one step. This implies several features of algorithms:

1. *Algorithms function in a discrete time.*
2. *All instructions are sufficiently simple.*
3. *Relations between operational steps of algorithm determine topology (organization) of computation.*

These properties look very natural. However, some researchers suggest models of computation with continuous time. Examples are given by real number computations in the sense of Shannon (1941) and Moore (1996). Instructions in these models may look simple, but their realization may be very complex. For example, even addition with infinite precision of two transcendental numbers in numerical form is, as a rule, impossible, in spite that its description in an algebraic form is really simple.

Besides, there are descriptions of algorithms that do not have instructions. Examples are: analytical representations (e.g., a regular expression), programs in functional programming languages, and equation representations (e.g., minimization or recursion equations).

Algorithms for computers generate and direct a diversity of computations. These computations have different characteristics. One of the most important of them is the computation topology. The most popular types of the computation topology with the corresponding computing architecture are:

1. *Sequential computation.*
2. *Parallel or synchronous computation.*
3. *Concurrent or asynchronous computation.*

Each of these types has several subtypes:

1. **Sequential computation** may be:
   1.1. *Acyclic*, i.e., such that it has no cycles;
   1.2. *Cyclic*, i.e., organized in one cycle;
   1.3. *Incyclic*, i.e., it is not one cycle, but contains cycles.

2. **Parallel computation** may be:
   2.1. *Branching*, which means parallel processing of different data from one package of data;

2.2. *Pipeline*, which means synchronous processing of similar elements from different packages of data (Kogge, 1981);
2.3. *Extending pipeline*, which combines properties both of branching and pipeline computations (Burgin, Liu, and Karplus, 2001a).

3. According to the control system for computation, **concurrent computation** may be:
3.1. *Instruction controlled*, which means parallel processing of different data from one package of data;
3.2. *Data controlled*, which means synchronous processing of similar elements from different packages of data;
3.3. *Agent controlled*, which means that another program controls computation.

While two first approaches are well known and popular, the third type exists without recognition and is not considered as a separate approach. However, even now the third approach is often used implicitly for organization of computation. Examples of agent controlled computations are utilization of an interpreter, which taking instructions from the program, transforms them into machine code, and then this code is executed by the computer. Interpreter is the agent that controls the process. Universal Turing machine is a theoretical example of agent controlled computations. In this case, the program of the universal Turing machine is the agent that controls the process. In future the role of agent controlled computations will grow immensely.

Usually, it is assumed that algorithms satisfy specific conditions of non-ambiguity, simplicity and effectiveness of separate operations, which have to be organized for an automatic performance. Thus, each operation in an algorithm must be sufficiently clear so that it does not need to be simplified for its performance. Since an algorithm is a collection of rules or instructions, we must know the correct order in which to execute the instructions. If the order is unclear, we may perform the wrong instruction or we may be uncertain which instruction should be performed next. This characteristic is especially important for computers. A computer can only execute an algorithm if it knows the exact order of steps to perform.

Thus, it is assumed traditionally that the principal characteristics of algorithm are:

1) an algorithm consists of a finite number of rules;
2) the rules constituting an algorithm are unambiguous (definite), simple to follow (effective), and have simple finite description (are constructive);
3) an algorithm is applied to some collection of input data and aimed at a solution of some problem.

This minimal set of properties allows one to consider algorithms from a more general perspective, including those that work with real numbers or even with continuous objects; those that do not need to stop to produce a result; and those that use infinite and even continuous time for computation.

Here we are not going to discuss in more detail what algorithm is or to give a comprehensive definition. Our goal is to find some simple properties of algorithms in general, to present these properties in a form of axioms, and to deduce from these axioms theorems that describe much more profound properties of algorithms. This allows one, taking some class **A** of algorithms, not to prove these theorems but only to check if the initial axioms are valid in **A**. If this is the case, then it makes possible to conclude that all corresponding theorems are true for the class **A**. As we know, computer scientists and mathematicians study and utilize a huge variety of different classes and types of algorithms, automata, and abstract machines. Consequently, such an axiomatic approach allows them to obtain many properties of studied algorithms in a simple and easy way.

4 Basic Axioms for Algorithms

We consider three types of a priori assumptions: *postulates*, *axioms*, and *conditions*.

Postulates are the most basic assumptions. Any class that is considered satisfies, at least, one postulate.

Axioms are global assumptions that represent important properties of algorithms and are used frequently in different situations.

Conditions are local assumptions that represent specific properties of algorithms and are used only for definite results.

The **first group of postulates** defines what algorithms are doing and in what mode abstract automata are functioning.

Let **K** be a class of automata/algorithms that take inputs from a set X and give outputs that belong to a set Y.

Computation Postulate PCM. Any algorithm A from **K** determines a binary relation r_A in the direct product $X \times Y$ of all its inputs X_A and all its outputs Y_A .

Examples of classes that compute relation and not a function are: non-deterministic computing finite automata, algorithms for multiple computations (Burgin, 1983a), and interactive algorithms (Wegner, 1998; Van Leeuwen and Wiedermann, 2000).

Definition 4.1. The set X_A is called the domain of A and the set Y_A is called the codomain of A.

Definition 4.2. A relation r in the direct product $X \times Y$ is called computable in **K** if $r = r_A$ for some algorithm A from **K**.

Deterministic Computation Postulate PDC. Any algorithm A from **K** determines a function f_A from X into Y.

Informally it means that given some input, A always produces the same result

Remark 4.1. Functions may be partial and total. The latter are defined for all elements of X.

Definition 4.3. A function f from X into Y is called computable in **K** if $f = f_A$ for some algorithm A from **K**.

Totality Axiom AT. Any algorithm A from **K** determines a total function f_A from X into Y.

Informally it means that A gives output for any input.

Classes of finite automata and primitive recursive functions satisfy Totality Axiom.

Classes of Turing machines and partial recursive functions do not satisfy Totality Axiom.

This axiom brings us to the distinction between the domain and definability domain of an algorithm.

Definition 4.4. The domain D(A) of an algorithm A is the set X of elements that are processed by A.

Definition 4.5. The definability domain DD(A) of an algorithm A is the set X of elements from D(A) such that if any of them is given as input to A, then A gives a result/output.

This allows us to define domains for a class **K** of algorithms/automata.

Definition 4.6. $D_*(\mathbf{K}) = \cap_{A\in \mathbf{K}} D(A)$ is the lower domain of **K**.

Definition 4.7. $D^*(\mathbf{K}) = \cup_{A\in \mathbf{K}} D(A)$ is the upper domain of **K**.

These concepts make possible to consider classes of algorithms that work with different entities, e.g., numbers, words, graphs, etc.

Definition 4.8. $DD_*(\mathbf{K}) = \cap_{A\in \mathbf{K}} DD(A)$ is the lower definability domain of **K**.

Definition 4.9. $DD^*(\mathbf{K}) = \cup_{A\in \mathbf{K}} DD(A)$ is the upper definability domain of **K**.

Lemma 4.1. $D_*(\mathbf{K}) \subseteq D^*(\mathbf{K})$, $DD_*(\mathbf{K}) \subseteq DD^*(\mathbf{K})$, $DD_*(\mathbf{K}) \subseteq D_*(\mathbf{K})$, and $DD^*(\mathbf{K}) \subseteq D^*(\mathbf{K})$.

Lemma 4.2. If the empty, i.e., nowhere defined, function $f_\varnothing$ is realized by some algorithm from **K**, then $DD_*(\mathbf{K}) = \varnothing$.

Lemma 4.3. If the identity function is realized by some algorithm from **K**, then $DD^*(\mathbf{K}) = D^*(\mathbf{K})$.

In a similar way, we define codomains and ranges for the class **K**.

Definition 4.10. $C_*(\mathbf{K}) = \cap_{A\in \mathbf{K}} C(A)$ is the lower codomain of **K**.

Definition 4.11. $C^*(\mathbf{K}) = \cup_{A\in \mathbf{K}} C(A)$ is the upper codomain of **K**.

Definition 4.12. $R_*(\mathbf{K}) = \cap_{A\in \mathbf{K}} R(A)$ is the lower range of **K**.

Definition 4.13. $R^*(\mathbf{K}) = \cup_{A\in \mathbf{K}} R(A)$ is the upper range of **K**.

Lemma 4.4. $C_*(\mathbf{K}) \subseteq C^*(\mathbf{K})$, $R_*(\mathbf{K}) \subseteq R^*(\mathbf{K})$, $R_*(\mathbf{K}) \subseteq C_*(\mathbf{K})$, and $R^*(\mathbf{K}) \subseteq C^*(\mathbf{K})$.

Lemma 4.5. If the identity function is realized by some algorithm from **K**, then $D^*(\mathbf{K}) = R^*(\mathbf{K})$.

Acceptation Postulate PAM. Any algorithm A from **K** determines a subset $L(A)$ in the set of all its inputs X.

When $X = V^*$ is the set of all words in some alphabet V, then $L(A)$ is called the language of the algorithm A.

Finite automata and Turing machines determine such sets by final states.

Push-down automata determine such sets by final states or by empty stacks.

In general, one of the most popular ways to determine a subset Z of a set X is to define the *characteristic function* c_Z of Z in X. Traditionally (cf., for example, (Fraenkel and Bar-Hillel, 1958)) this function is defined by the following rules:

$c_Z(x) = 1$ when x is an element from Z and $c_Z(x) = 0$ when x does not belong to Z.

A *separation function* is a generalization of the characteristic function. Namely, the separation function s_Z of Z in X is defined by the following rules:

there is an element a in the range of s_Z such that $s_Z(x) = a$ when x is an element from Z and $s_Z(x) = b$ for some $b \neq a$ when x does not belong to Z.

Decision Postulate PDM. Any algorithm A from **K** determines the separation function for a subset $K(A)$ in the set of all its inputs X, giving a fixed output on all elements from $K(A)$ and another output on all elements that do not belong to $K(A)$.

A *dichotomic separation function* of Z in X is a separation function of Z in X that takes one and the same value for all elements that do not belong to Z. A characteristic function is an example of a dichotomic separation function. Usually, computability in a class **K** of a separation function for some set Z implies computability in the class **K** the dichotomic separation function for the same set.

Some classes of algorithms do satisfy PDM although they satisfy its weaker version PSM.

Semidecision Postulate PSM. Any algorithm A from **K** determines the indicator function for a subset $K(A)$ in the set of all its inputs X, giving a fixed output a for all elements from $K(A)$ as inputs and only for them.

Here a function $h(x)$ is called the *indicator function* for a set Z, if there is an element such that $h(x) = a$ if and only if $x \in Z$. An example of an indicator function is the *partial characteristic function* c_Z of Z in X defined by the following rules:

$c_Z(x) = 1$ when x is an element from Z and $c_Z(x)$ is undefined when x does not belong to Z.

Lemma 4.6. PSM implies PAM.

Lemma 4.7. PDM implies PSM if the following condition is satisfied in the class **K**:

(Z) For any algorithm A from **K** and any element a from the set Y_A, there is an algorithm B from **K** such that $B(x) = A(x)$ when $A(x) = a$ and $B(x)$ is undefined when $A(x) \neq a$.

Remark 4.2. This condition is true for many natural classes of algorithms and programs. For instance, when a Turing machine gives some $c \neq a$ as its result, it is possible to change the rules of the machine so that it goes into an infinite cycle after getting c.

Types of algorithms defined by Postulates PCM, PAM, and PDM correspond to the main modes of automaton/algorithm functioning. Given an automaton/algorithm A, we say that A:

computes a set X_A (a formal language L_A) if X_A (correspondingly, L_A) consists of all outputs of A;

accepts a set X_A (a formal language L_A) if X_A (correspondingly, L_A) consists of all elements (words) accepted by A;

decides a set X_A (a formal language L_A) if A, given a word/configuration u, indicates (decides) whether this word/configuration belongs to X_A (to L_A) or not.

It is possible to explain differences in practical meaning of these forms of information processing in the following way. Computability is a way to build objects and to find (compute) their properties. Decidability is a way to find if an object has some property or not. Thus, in a deciding mode, an automaton begins with a property and applies it to an object. In contrast to this, in a computing mode, an automaton begins with an object and derives its properties. Acceptability is a way to select (choose) objects according to their properties.

Definition 4.14. The language L_A is called the *computation (acceptation or decision) language of the algorithm/automaton A.*

Remark 4.3. Usually, when the mode of computation is fixed, L_A is called simply the language of the automaton/algorithm A. For example, in (Hopcroft *et al*, 2001) only the accepting mode is treated. This makes possible to speak about languages of finite automata, push down automata and Turing machines.

The **second group of postulates** defines objects with which algorithms are working.

Usually algorithms and abstract automata work with words in some alphabet V. An example is Turing machines. We call V the working alphabet of algorithms/automata from a given class. Sometimes it is assumed that they transform natural or whole numbers into natural or whole numbers. An example is recursive functions. These properties are formulated as postulates.

Domain Semiotic Postulate PDS. The domain D(A) of A is the set V^* of all finite words in some alphabet V.

Unrestricted Domain Semiotic Postulate PUDS. The domain D(A) of A is the set V^{**} of all strings, finite and infinite, in some alphabet V.

Domain Numeric Postulate PDN. The domain D(A) of A is a set of natural numbers.

Unrestricted Domain Numeric Postulate PUDN. The domain D(A) of A is a set of numbers.

Codomain Semiotic Postulate PCS. The codomain C(A) of A is the set V^* of all finite words in some alphabet V.

Unrestricted Codomain Semiotic Postulate PUCS. The codomain C(A) of A is the set V^{**} of all strings, finite and infinite, in some alphabet V.

Codomain Numeric Postulate PCN. The codomain C(A) of A is a set of natural numbers.

Unrestricted Codomain Numeric Postulate PUCN. The codomain C(A) of A is a set of numbers.

Remark 4.4. Many algorithms (cf., for example, (Krinitsky, 1977) or (Burgin, 1985)) work with more general entities than words. As an example, it is possible to consider as data such configurations that were utilized by Kolmogorov (1953) in his analysis of the concept of algorithm and construction of the most general definition. Configurations are sets of symbols connected by relations and may be treated as multidimensional words, arrays or hypertexts. Hypertext technology is now very important in information processing both for people and computers (Barrett, 1988; Nielsen, 1990; Landow, 1992). Discrete graphs are also examples of configurations.

The **axioms and conditions from third group** provide means for operations with algorithms and automata. These operations represent transformations, joins, and combinations of programs, computers, and networks. Finding properties of algorithmic operations, we discover regularities in such areas as software reusability and interoperability, network integration, computer clusterization and reliability.

Definition 4.15. An algorithm C is called a *computing sequential composition* of algorithms A and B if $C(x)$ is defined and equal to $B(A(x))$ when: 1) $A(x)$ is defined and belongs to the domain of B ; 2) $B(A(x))$ is defined. Otherwise, C gives no result being applied to x, i.e., $C(x) = *$.

A computing sequential composition of algorithms A and B is denoted by $A \circ B$.

Remark 4.5. In a general case, a sequential composition of algorithms A and B is not unique. For instance, we can take a Turing machine C that is a sequential composition of two Turing machines T and Q. Then we can rename some inner states of C or add to the rules of C such rules that are never performed. This will give us another Turing machine K that is functionally equivalent to C. Thus, by Definition 4.15, K is also the sequential composition of the same machines T and Q by

Sequential C-Composition Axiom ASC. For any two algorithms A and B from **K**, their computing sequential composition $A \circ B$ also belongs to **K**.

Accepting sequential compositions are *organized in a more complicated way.*

Definition 4.16. An algorithm C is called an *accepting sequential composition of the first type* of algorithms A and B when C accepts a word x if and only if there are words u and v such that $x = uv$, A accepts u, and B accepts v.

Accepting sequential compositions of the first type are used in classes of finite automata (cf., for example, (Hopcroft *et al*, 2001)).

Sequential A-Composition Axiom AAC1. For any two algorithms A and B from **K**, their accepting sequential composition $A \circ B$ of the first type also belongs to **K**.

Definition 4.17. An algorithms C is called an *accepting sequential composition of the second type* of algorithms A and B when C accepts a word x if and only if A accepts x and B accepts the word z written on the tape of A after A accepts x and stops.

Accepting sequential compositions of the first type are used in classes of Turing machines (cf., for example, (Sipser, 1997) or (Hopcroft *et al*, 2001)).

Sequential A-Composition Axiom AAC2. For any two algorithms A and B from **K**, their accepting sequential composition $A \circ B$ of the second type also belongs to **K**.

Remark 4.6. In addition to sequential compositions, there are other kinds of compositions of algorithms. An important class is formed by parallel compositions (cf., for example, (Burgin, 1983)). However, other kinds of compositions are studied elsewhere.

A specific kind of composition is related to universal automata and algorithms, which play an important role in computing and are useful for different purposes. The construction of such automata and algorithms is usually based on some codification (symbolic description) $\mathbf{c}$: $\mathbf{K} \to X$ of all automata/algorithms in **K**.

Definition 4.18. An automaton/algorithm U is *universal* for the class **K** if given a description $\mathbf{c}(A)$ of an automaton/algorithm A from **K** and some input data x for it, U gives the same result as A for the input x or gives no result when A gives no result for the input x.

In some cases, it is important not only to compute the same function, but also to simulate the behavior of other automata/algorithms. This condition is reflected in the concept of a strictly universal automaton/algorithm.

Definition 4.19. An automaton/algorithm U is *strictly universal* for the class **K** if given a description $\mathbf{c}(A)$ of an automaton/algorithm A from **K** and some input data x for it, U simulates A, working with the same input x, and gives the same result as A or gives no result when A gives no result for the input x.

Universal automata/algorithms combine together input data and automaton/algorithm descriptions like computers combine together input data and programs. Thus, descriptions of the form $\mathbf{c}(A)$ (cf. the Codification Axiom **AC**) play the role of programs for U.

Assuming the Domain Semiotic Postulate **PDS**, we have a set V^* as the domain of all algorithms in **K**. Usually algorithms from **K** are codified in the set V^+ that consists of all finite nonempty words in an alphabet V.

Codification Axiom AC. There is an injective mapping $\mathbf{c} : \mathbf{K} \to V^+$.

The word $\mathbf{c}(A)$ is the "code" or "description" of the algorithm A.

The most popular kind of such a codification is the Godel numbering or enumeration of algorithms or computable functions (cf., for example, (Rogers, 1987)).

It is possible to codify any finite system of symbols by words of equal length in a binary alphabet. This implies the following result.

Proposition 4.1. Axiom AC implies that there is an injective mapping $\mathbf{b} : \mathbf{K} \to \{1, 0\}^+$.

However, to have a codification is not enough because we have to work with it. Thus, we need stronger axioms.

Constructive Codification Axiom CAC. There is an algorithm in **K** that realizes an injective mapping $\mathbf{c} : \mathbf{K} \to V^+$.

Decidable Codification Axiom DAC. There is a decidable injective mapping **c : K →** V^+, i.e., there is an algorithm in **K** such that given a word *w* it decides whether *w* is a code for some algorithm from **K** and is able to restore this algorithm.

Usually classes of recursive algorithms, such as Turing machines, partial recursive functions or two-register push down automata, satisfy both axioms CAC and DAC. Many classes of subrecursive algorithms, such as recursive functions or polynomial time Turing machines, also satisfy both axioms CAC and DAC. In addition, Many classes of super-recursive algorithms, such as limiting partial recursive functions or inductive Turing machines, also satisfy both axioms CAC and DAC.

Universality Axiom AU. For some coding **c : K →** V^+, there is a universal algorithm in **K**.

Let the domain *X* of the algorithms in **K** contains more than one element.

Definition 4.20. An automaton/algorithm A_c is called *shifting* if for any x from X, $A_c(x) \neq x$.

For the future, we will need the following property.

Shifting Condition SH. There is a shifting algorithm in **K**.

The majority of natural classes of algorithms satisfy **SH**. In particular, we have the following result.

Proposition 4.2. Any class **K** of algorithms that contains the class **DFA** of all deterministic finite automata satisfies **SH**.

Let the lower domain D*(**K**) of **K** contains more than one element and coincides with the lower codomain C*(**K**) of **K**.

Definition 4.21. An automaton/algorithm A_{sw} is called *switching* for x and y from X if $A_{sw}(x) = y$ and $A_{sw}(y) = x$.

Switching Condition SW. For any x and y from X, there is a switching for x and y algorithm in **K**.

Local Switching Condition LSW$_{xy}$ **.** For given x and y from X, there is a switching for x and y algorithm in **K**.

It is possible to realize a switching algorithm by a simple finite automaton. This implies the following result.

Proposition 4.3. Any class **K** of automata/algorithms that includes the class of all finite automata satisfies Condition **SW**.

Condition CA2. The alphabet *V* that is used for building words processed by algorithms from **K** has, at least, two different elements.

Definition 4.22. An automaton/algorithm A_c is called *weakly switching* for x and y from X if the automaton A_w given the input y gives no output and given the input x, gives y as the output.

Weak Switching Condition WSW. For any x and y from X, there is a weakly switching for x and y algorithm in **K**.

Weak Local Switching Condition WLSW$_{xy}$ **.** For given x and y from X, there is a weakly switching for x and y algorithm in **K**.

A_c**-Composition Condition CSH.** For any algorithm *A* from **K** and the shifting algorithm A_c, their sequential composition belongs to **K**.

A_{sw}**-Composition Condition CSW.** For any algorithm *A* from **K** and the switching algorithm A_{sw}, their sequential composition belongs to **K**.

Let us assume that **K** satisfies Postulates **PCM** (or **PAM**), **PDS** (or **PDN**), and **PCS** (or **PCN**), as well as Conditions **SH** and **CSH**.

Theorem 4.1. Axioms **AT** and **AU** are mutually exclusive for the class **K**.

Proof. Let us assume that a class of algorithms **K** also satisfies Axiom **AT** and a universal algorithm U with respect to a coding $\mathbf{c} : \mathbf{K} \to V^+$ exists in **K**. Then U is everywhere defined as **K** satisfies **AT**. Conditions **SH** and **CSH** allow us to build in **K** the algorithm $D = P \circ U \circ A_c$ where P is a pairing algorithm that given a word w produces the pair (w, w) and A_c is the shifting algorithm.

Let us consider words $w = \mathbf{c}(D)$ and $x = D(w)$. The word x exists because **K** satisfies **AT**. Then we have $P(w) = (w, w) = (\mathbf{c}(D), w)$ and $U(\mathbf{c}(D), w) = D(w)$ by the definition of a universal algorithm. At the same time, $A_c(D(w)) \neq D(w)$ and we come to the contradiction that $D(w) = A_c(U(P(w))) = A_c(U(\mathbf{c}(D), w)) = A_c(D(w)) \neq D(w)$. This completes the proof of the theorem.

Informally, Theorem 4.1 means that either the class **K** has a universal algorithm but its algorithms are not everywhere defined or they are everywhere defined but the class **K** does not have a universal algorithm. In other words, universality is incompatible with totality.

Theorem 4.1 implies the following results.

Corollary 4.1. In the class of all recursive functions, there are no universal algorithms.

Corollary 4.2. In the class of all primitive recursive functions, there are no universal algorithms.

Corollary 4.3. In the class of all finite automata, there are no universal algorithms.

5 Power of Algorithms: Comparison and Evaluation

Having such a diversity of models for algorithms, we need to compare them. To do this, we introduce such concept as power of an algorithm or of a class of algorithms.

Definition 5.1. *Power* of an algorithm (of a class of algorithms) is a measure of what this algorithm (algorithms from this class) can do.

Algorithms are used to solve problems. So, it is natural to estimate power by those problems that algorithms can solve.

It is natural to consider two kinds of power for algorithms: absolute that is defined with respect to problems and relative that only compares different algorithms and different classes of algorithms.

Definition 5.2. The *absolute problem solving power* of an algorithm A (of a class **K** of algorithms) is the set of all problems solvable by this algorithm (by algorithms from this class).

Usually it is impossible to describe the absolute problem solving power of a complex algorithm or a big algorithmic class. That is why we introduce relative problem solving power of algorithms.

Definition 5.3. The *problem solving power* of an algorithm A (of a class **H** of algorithms) is *less than or equal to* (is *cognitively weaker than or equivalent to*) the *problem solving power* of an algorithm B (of a class **K** of algorithms) when the algorithm B can solve any problem that A can (any problem that can be solved by a algorithm from **H** can be also solved by some algorithm from **K**). Naturally, the algorithm B is *cognitively stronger than or equivalent to* (has *more than or the same problem solving power*) the algorithm A.

We denote these relation by $A \leq_{ps} B$, $A <_{ps} B$, $A =_{ps} B$, $\mathbf{H} \leq_{ps} \mathbf{K}$, $\mathbf{H} <_{ps} \mathbf{K}$, and $\mathbf{H} =_{ps} \mathbf{K}$.

For instance, if **T** is the class of all deterministic Turing machines and **DFA** is the class of all deterministic finite automata, then $\mathbf{DFA} <_{ps} \mathbf{T}$. If **NFA** is the class of all non-deterministic finite automata, then $\mathbf{NFA} =_{ps} \mathbf{DFA}$.

Different modes of information processing allow one to introduce special concepts: *computing power*, *accepting power*, *decision power*, and *equivalence* of algorithms and their classes.

Definition 5.4. The *computing power* of an algorithm A is *less than or equal to* (is *weaker than or equivalent to*) the *computing power* of an algorithm B when the algorithm B can compute everything that A can compute. Naturally, the algorithm B is *stronger than or equivalent to* (has *more than or the same computing power*) the algorithm A.

Let us take as an example algorithms that solve some algorithmic problem P for a class of algorithms **A**. Such problem P may be: to define whether a given algorithm from **A** gives the result for some data; to define whether a given algorithm from **A** gives the result for all possible data; or to define whether a given algorithm from **A** has more computing power than another given algorithm from **A**.

Proposition 5.1. If an algorithm A solves the problem P for the class $\mathbf{A}_1$, an algorithm B solves the problem P for the class $\mathbf{A}_2$, and $\mathbf{A}_1 \subset \mathbf{A}_2$, then the computing power of B is larger than the computing power of A.

Definition 5.5. Two algorithms A and B are *functionally equivalent* (or simply, *equivalent*) if the algorithm B can compute everything that A can compute and the algorithm A can compute everything that B can compute.

Taking into account different modes of algorithm functioning, we come to a more general concept.

Definition 5.6. Two algorithms are called *functionally equivalent with respect to computability* (*acceptability*, *positive decidability*, *negative decidability* or *decidability*) if they define in the corresponding mode the same function f_A or relation r_A .

Example 5.1. In the theory of finite automata, functional equivalence means that two finite automata accept the same language (Hopcroft *et al*, 2001). This relation is used frequently to obtain different properties of finite automata. The same is true for the theory of pushdown automata.

However, in general, functional equivalence is stronger than linguistic equivalence defined below.

Definition 5.7. Two algorithms are called *linguistically equivalent with respect to computability (acceptability, positive decidability, negative decidability or decidability)* if they define in the corresponding mode the same language L_A .

As L_A is the range of the function f_A (relation r_A), we have the following result.

Proposition 5.1. Two algorithms are linguistically equivalent with respect to computability (acceptability, positive decidability, negative decidability or decidability) if they are functionally equivalent with respect to computability (acceptability, positive decidability, negative decidability or decidability).

The inverse statement is not true in general as the following example demonstrates.

Example 5.2. Let algorithm A computes the function $f_A(n) = n + 1$ for all $n = 1, 2, 3, \dots$ and E is an identity algorithm on the set $\{2, 3, \dots \}$, i.e., $E(m) = m$ for all $n = 2, 3, \dots$. Then A

and E are linguistically equivalent with respect to computability, but they are not functionally equivalent with respect to computability.

While in practice, we usually compare individual algorithms, for theory it is even more important to compare power of different classes of algorithms.

Definition 5.8. A class of algorithms $\boldsymbol{A}$ has *less or equal computing power* than (is *weaker than or equivalent to*) a class of algorithms $\boldsymbol{B}$ when algorithms from $\boldsymbol{B}$ can compute everything that algorithms from $\boldsymbol{A}$ can compute. Naturally, the class of algorithms $\boldsymbol{B}$ is *stronger than or equivalent to* (has *more or equal computing power than*) the class of algorithms $\boldsymbol{A}$.

Remark 5.2. Any mathematical or programming model of algorithms defines some class of algorithms. Thus, comparing classes corresponding to models, we are able to compare power of these models.

For example, the class of all finite automata is weaker than the class of all Turing machines. It means that a Turing machine can compute everything that can compute finite automata. However, there are such functions that are computable by Turing machines while finite automata cannot compute them.

Remark 5.3. Definitions 5.2 - 5.4 and 5.8 are not exact because they contain such a term as *everything*, which is very imprecise. To develop a mathematical theory of algorithms and automata, we need completely formal constructions. Formalization is achieved in different ways. The first one is to relate to an algorithm the function that it computes. Such formalization is done in Definitions 5.5, 5.7, 510, and 5.11. The second approach is based on introduction of sets or languages defined by an automaton/algorithm and consideration of three modes of automaton functioning: *computation*, *acceptation*, and *decision*. Such formalization is done in Definitions 5.6 and 5.9.

As it is known, any set of words forms a *formal language*. This allows us to consider full output of algorithms, that is, the set L_A of all words that an algorithm A computes, accepts or decides.

This allows us to compare computing, accepting and deciding power of algorithms.

Definition 5.9. The *linguistic computing* (*accepting or decision*) *power* of a class of algorithms $\boldsymbol{A}$ is less than or equal to (the class $\boldsymbol{A}$ is *linguistically weaker than or equivalent to*) the *linguistic computing* (*accepting or decision*) *power* of a class of algorithms $\boldsymbol{B}$ when algorithms from $\boldsymbol{B}$ can compute (accept or decide, correspondingly) any language that algorithms from $\boldsymbol{A}$ can compute (accept or decide). Naturally, the class of algorithms $\boldsymbol{B}$ is *linguistically stronger than or linguistically equivalent to* (has *more or equal linguistic computing* (*accepting or decision*) *power than*) the class of algorithms $\boldsymbol{A}$.

Instead of using sets or languages, it is possible to use functions for comparison of computing power.

Definition 5.10. The *functional computing* (*accepting or decision*) *power* of a class of algorithms $\boldsymbol{A}$ is less than or equal to (is *functionally weaker than or equivalent to*) the functional computing (accepting or decision) power a class of algorithms $\boldsymbol{B}$ when algorithms from $\boldsymbol{B}$ can compute any function that algorithms from $\boldsymbol{A}$ can compute.

Definition 5.11. Two classes of algorithms are *functionally equivalent* (or simply, *equivalent*) if they compute the same class of functions, or relations for non-deterministic algorithms.

Remark 5.7. Linguistic equivalence of algorithms is stronger than functional equivalence because more algorithms are glued together by linguistic equivalence than by functional equivalence. Really, when two algorithms compute the same function, then they compute the same language. However, it is possible to compute the same language by computing different functions. For example, let us take the alphabet $\{a, b\}$ and two automata A and B. The first one gives as its output the word that is its input. It computes the identity function $f(x) = x$. The automaton B gives the following outputs: $B(\varepsilon) = \varepsilon$, $B(a) = b$, and $B(b) = a$. As a result, A and B are equivalent, but not functionally equivalent.

6 Problems and Related Properties of Algorithms

There are three main types of problems: *cognitive*, *constructive*, and *sustaining* or *preserational.*

A *cognitive* problem is aimed at knowledge acquisition.

A *constructive* problem is aimed at building, transforming or finding some thing.

A *sustaining* problem is aimed at preserving something (a process, data, knowledge, environment, etc.).

To define an algorithmic problem, we at first, consider parametric or class problems in classes of objects. Let us consider a class of objects X.

Definition 6.1. A *parametric* or *class problem* in a class X asks about some property (properties) of an arbitrary object from X. Such problems have one parameter with X as a range and are called unary parametric problems.

For instance, when X is a set of computers, we have following parametric problems:

What is system memory capacity for a given computer c from X ?

What is hard disk capacity for a given computer c from X ?

What is processor clock speed for a given computer c from X ?

It is possible to consider problems with several parameters that have some sets X_1 , X_2 , … , X_n as their ranges.

Definition 6.2. A *parametric problem* in classes X_1 , X_2 , … , X_n asks about a relation(s) between arbitrary objects a_1 , a_2 , … , a_n from X_1 , X_2 , … , X_n , correspondingly. Such problems are called n-ary parametric problems.

As a rule, we are interested not in solving a pararmetric problem for one value of the parameter, but in finding a possibility to solve this problem for all values of its parameters. Algorithms can provide such a possibility.

Definition 6.3. An *algorithmic* problem (in classes X_1 , X_2 , … , X_n) asks to find an algorithm for solving some a parametric problem (in these classes) for all values of its parameters.

Remark 6.1. There are parametric problems that are not algorithmic. For example, the following problems are parametric in the class X of all real continuous functions:

Find a solution of the differential equation $\mathrm{d}u/\mathrm{d}x = f(x)$ in the class $\mathbf{C}(\boldsymbol{R}, \boldsymbol{R})$ of all real continuous functions.

Find necessary and sufficient conditions for a matrix A to be invertible in the class $\mathbf{M}_n$ of all real n-dimensional matrices.

Find the mass of such subatomic particle as neutrino. Because there are many neutrino, this is also a parametric problem.

However, actually it is possible to correspond to any problem an algorithmic one. Indeed, if we have a problem A, then we can correspond to it an algorithmic problem "Find an algorithm that solves A."

Here we are mostly interested not only in finding an algorithm that solves some problem, but in having a good or, at least, reasonable algorithm for this purpose. Thus, we study here algorithmic problems with respect to chosen classes of algorithms, abstract automata, formal languages or programs.

Definition 6.4. An *algorithmic* problem (in classes X_1 , X_2 , ... , X_n) with respect to a class **K** asks to find an algorithm from **K** for solving some a parametric problem (in these classes) for all values of its parameters.

Let us consider some important algorithmic problems in a class **K** of algorithms with the input domain X and output domain Y.

1. The *Definability Problem* $\mathbf{R_D}$: given an arbitrary algorithm A from **K** and an arbitrary element x from X, find if $A(x)$ is defined.
2. The *Local Definability Problem* $\mathbf{R_{DA}}$: for a fixed algorithm A from **K** and an arbitrary element x from X, find if $A(x)$ is defined.
3. The *Fixed Output Problem* $\mathbf{R_{O\mathit{b}}}$: given an arbitrary algorithm A from **K** and an arbitrary element x from X, find for a fixed element b from Y if $A(x) = b$.
4. The *Local Output Problem* $\mathbf{L_{O\mathit{b}}}$: given an arbitrary element x from X, find for a fixed algorithm A from **K** and a fixed element b from Y if $A(x) = b$.
5. The *Free Output Problem* $\mathbf{F_{O\mathit{b}}}$: given an arbitrary algorithm A from **K**, an arbitrary element b from Y, and an arbitrary element x from X, find if $A(x) = b$.

Lemma 6.1. Decidability of $\mathbf{R_D}$ in **K** implies decidability of $\mathbf{R_{DA}}$ in **K**.

Lemma 6.2. Decidability of $\mathbf{F_{O\mathit{b}}}$ in **K** implies decidability of $\mathbf{R_{O\mathit{b}}}$ in **K** and decidability of $\mathbf{R_{O\mathit{b}}}$ in **K** implies decidability of $\mathbf{L_{O\mathit{b}}}$ in **K**.

Lemma 6.3. If Y is finite, then decidability of $\mathbf{R_{DA}}$ in **K** implies decidability of $\mathbf{R_D}$ in **K**.

Many problems are related to some properties. If we have some property **P**, then we can define two class problems:

1. The problem $\underline{\mathbf{P}}$ that demands to find if an arbitrary object from the property domain $D(\mathbf{P})$ has this property **P** or not.
2. The problem $\overline{\mathbf{P}}$ that demands to find if an arbitrary object from the property domain $D(\mathbf{P})$ has this property **P**.

The difference between problems $\underline{\mathbf{P}}$ and $\overline{\mathbf{P}}$ is that $\underline{\mathbf{P}}$ demands to give an answer in both cases - when an object has the property **P** and when an object does not have the property **P**, while in $\overline{\mathbf{P}}$ we are interested only in objects that have this property.

In addition to properties of algorithms/automata, there are relations between algorithms/automata. However, relations are kinds of properties (Burgin, 1984). Binary relations can be viewed as properties of pairs. Ternary relations can be viewed as properties of triples and so on. Thus, algorithmic problems are corresponded not only to properties but also to relations. For instance, if we have a binary relation R, then we take the property **P** "to belong to the relation R correspond to it two problems: $\underline{\mathbf{P}}$ and $\overline{\mathbf{P}}$. The first problem $\underline{\mathbf{P}}$ demands to find if a given pair belongs to R or not, while the second problem $\overline{\mathbf{P}}$ demands to find if a given pair belongs to R.

Definition 6.5. A binary relation is called trivial if it is empty or contains all pairs from its domain.

At the same time, relations induce many properties in the same domain. For instance, any binary relation R in **K** for each A from **K** determines the property R_A = "B has the property R_A if the pair (A, B) belongs to R" and the property R^A = "B has the property R^A if the pair (B, A) belongs to R." These property R_A and R^A are called a *sections* of the relation R. Sections allow us to prove different decidability results.

Definition 6.6. A property is called *trivial* if either there are no objects with this property or all objects from its domain have this property.

Lemma 6.1. A binary relation is nontrivial if and only if it has a nontrivial section.

Definition 6.7. A class/parametric problem **Q** is *solvable* in a class **K** of algorithms if there is such an algorithm $R_{\mathbf{P}}$ such that gives a solution to this problem for values of the problem parameters.

Solvability of problems in many cases is related to decidability of properties.

Definition 6.8. A property **P** is *decidable* in a class **K** of algorithms if there is an algorithm $R_{\mathbf{P}}$ such that it defines if an arbitrary object (from X) has the property **P** or not when this object or its description is given to $R_{\mathbf{P}}$ as input.

Let **H** be a class of algorithms.

Proposition 6.1. If a binary relation R has an undecidable in **H** section, then the relation R is also undecidable in **H**.

Proposition 6.2. Any section of a decidable in **H** relation is also decidable in **H**.

Let a class **K** satisfies the **Local Switching Condition** $\mathbf{LSW}_{yn}$ **.**

Proposition 6.3. A property **P** is decidable in **K** if and only if the property ¬**P** is also decidable in **K**.

Definition 6.9. A property **P** is *semidecidable* in a class **K** of algorithms if there is such an algorithm $R_{\mathbf{P}}$ such that it defines if an arbitrary object (from X) has the property **P** when this object or its description is given to $R_{\mathbf{P}}$ as input.

Any decidable property is semidecidable. At the same time, for many classes of algorithms, there are more semidecidable properties than decidable. For instance, the halting property of Turing machines is semidecidable but not decidable in the class of all Turing machines.

Proposition 6.4. A class problem $\underline{\mathbf{P}}$ with the domain X is solvable in a class **K** of algorithms if the corresponding property **P** is decidable.

Corollary 6.1. A class problem $\underline{\mathbf{P}}$ is solvable in **K** if and only if the class problem $\underline{\neg\mathbf{P}}$ is also solvable in **K**

Proposition 6.5. A class problem $\overline{\mathbf{P}}$ with the domain X is solvable in a class **K** of algorithms if the corresponding property **P** is semidecidable.

For many classes of algorithms, there are more semidecidable properties than decidable. It is known for many classes of recursive algorithms, such as Turing machines. In a general setting, we will see this in the next section.

Definition 6.10. A class/parametric problem **Q** that demands an answer *yes* or *no* is *semisolvable* in a class **K** of algorithms if there is such an algorithm $R_{\mathbf{P}}$ such that gives a correct solution to this problem in all cases when the answer is *yes*.

Any solvable problem is semisolvable. At the same time, for many classes of algorithms, there are more semisolvable problems than solvable. For instance, the halting problem for Turing machines is semisolvable but not solvable in the class of all Turing machines.

Proposition 6.6. A class problem $\underline{\mathbf{P}}$ with the domain X is semisolvable in a class **K** of algorithms if the corresponding property **P** is semidecidable.

When we consider such objects as abstract automata and algorithms, we come to specific classes of properties.

Definition 6.11. A property P of algorithms from **K** is called *linguistic* if for any two automata/algorithms A and B, $L(A) = L(B)$ implies $P(A) = P(B)$.

Linguistic Properties:

For an automaton/algorithm B:

1. $L(B) = \varnothing$, that is, the language $L(B)$ of B is empty.
2. $L(B) \neq \varnothing$, that is, the language $L(B)$ of B is not empty.
3. $b \in L(B)$, that is, a given element b belongs to the language $L(B)$.
4. $b \notin L(B)$, that is, a given element b does not belong to the language $L(B)$.

For two automata/algorithms A and B:

1. $L(A) = L(B)$, that is, languages $L(A)$ and $L(B)$ are equal.
2. $L(A) \subseteq L(B)$, that is, the languages $L(B)$ contains the languages $L(A)$.
3. $L(A) \cap L(B) = \varnothing$, that is, languages $L(A)$ and $L(B)$ do not have common elements.
4. $L(A) \cap L(B) \neq \varnothing$, that is, languages $L(A)$ and $L(B)$ have common elements

Linguistic Problems:

1. The *Linguistic Equivalence Problem* $\mathbf{R_{LE}}$: given two arbitrary algorithms A and B from **K**, find if $L(A) = L(B)$.
2. The *Linguistic Inclusion Problem* $\mathbf{R_{LI}}$: given two arbitrary algorithms A and B from **K**, find if $L(A) \subseteq L(B)$.
3. The *Linguistic Membership Problem* $\mathbf{R_{LM}}$: given an arbitrary algorithm A from **K** and an arbitrary element b from Y, find if $b \in L(B)$.
4. The *Linguistic Non-membership Problem* $\mathbf{R_{LN}}$: given an arbitrary algorithm A from **K** and an arbitrary element b from Y, find if $b \notin L(B)$.

Remark 6.2. It is possible to consider linguistic properties of algorithms as properties of languages determined by algorithms.

Linguistic properties and problems are the most popular in the theory of algorithms because algorithms and automata are usually related to formal languages (cf., for example,

(Rogers, 1987) or (Hopckroft *et al*, 2001)). However, there are other important properties of algorithms, programs, and automata.

Definition 6.12. A property P of algorithms from **K** is called *functional* if for any two automata/algorithms A and B, $A_f = B_f$ implies $P(A) = P(B)$.

Functional Properties:

For an automaton/algorithm B:

1. $B_f = f_\varnothing$, that is, the function B_f realized by B is empty.
2. $B_f \neq f_\varnothing$, that is, the function B_f realized by B is defined for some elements.
3. $DD(B_f) = V^*$, that is, the function B_f realized by B is defined for all finite words.
4. $DD(B_f) = N$, that is, the function B_f realized by B is defined for all natural numbers.

For two automata/algorithms A and B:

1. Algorithms A and B compute the same function, i.e., $A_f = B_f$;
2. $\forall x\ (A_f(x) \leq B_f(x))$.
3. Algorithms A and B have the same definability domain, i.e., $DD(A) = DD(B)$.
4. $DD(A_f) \cap DD(B_f) = \varnothing$.
5. $DD(A_f) \cap DD(B_f) \neq \varnothing$.

Functional Problems:

1. Find if algorithms A and B have the same characteristic function of the definability domain.
2. Find if algorithms A and B have the same semicharacteristic function of the definability domain.
3. Functional Equivalence Problem $\mathbf{R}_{\mathbf{FE}}$: given two arbitrary deterministic algorithms A and B from **K**, find if algorithms A and B compute the same function, i.e., $f_A = f_B$.

Remark 6.3. It is possible to consider functional properties of algorithms as properties of functions determined by algorithms.

Sometimes to demand that all results of algorithms coincide, as we do in the definition of a functional property, is too much. Thus, we introduce weak functional properties.

Let Z be a subset of the lower definability domain $DD_*(\mathbf{K})$ of **K**.

Definition 6.13. A property P of algorithms from **K** is called *weak functional* on Z if for any two automata/algorithms A and B, $P(A) = P(B)$ when the equality $A_f(x) = B_f(x)$ is true for all for all x from Z.

Weak Functional Properties:

1. *Self-application property*:

$$\mathrm{SAP}(A) = \begin{cases} 1 & \text{if being applied to } \mathbf{c}(A)\text{, the algorithm } A \text{ gives the result;} \\ 0 & \text{otherwise.} \end{cases}$$

2. *Self-acceptation property*:

$$\mathrm{SAC}(A) = \begin{cases} 1 & \text{if being applied to } \mathbf{c}(A)\text{, the algorithm } A \text{ accepts } \mathbf{c}(A)\text{;} \\ 0 & \text{otherwise.} \end{cases}$$

3. *Self-approval property*:

$$\mathrm{SAR}(A) = \begin{cases} 1 & \text{if being applied to } \mathbf{c}(A)\text{, the algorithm } A \text{ gives the result } \textit{yes}\text{;} \\ 0 & \text{if being applied to } \mathbf{c}(A)\text{, the algorithm } A \text{ gives the result } \textit{no}\text{.} \end{cases}$$

By definition, any functional property is a weak functional property. It implies the following result.

Proposition 6.7. If for some subset Z of the lower definability domain $\mathrm{DD}_*(\mathbf{K})$, all weak functional properties of algorithms/automata from **K** are decidable (undecidable, semidecidable) in **K**, then all functional properties of algorithms/automata from **K** are decidable (undecidable or semidecidable, correspondingly) in **K**.

Comparing functional and linguistic properties, we find that there is a strict correspondence between properties of both kinds. To build it, we need additional axioms and conditions.

Condition CD. C(**K**) = D(**K**).

Axiom of a pair correspondence APC. There is an injection p: D(**K**)×D(**K**) → D(**K**)

Axiom of a computable pair correspondence ACPC. There is an injection p: D(**K**)×D(**K**) → D(**K**) such that $p(R_f)$ is computable in **K** for any computable in **K** function f.

Axiom of a decidable pair correspondence ADPC. There is a decidable injection p: D(**K**)×D(**K**) → D(**K**)

Remark 6.4. In conventional set theories, such as ZF (cf. Fraenkel and Bar-Hillel, 1958), **APC** holds if and only if D(**K**) is an infinite set. As the majority of computational models works with inputs from infinite domains, usually, words or numbers, **APC** is true for almost all conventional models. For classes of recursive algorithms, such as Turing machines or partial recursive functions, these injections are decidable and thus, computable.

Axiom CL. For any algorithm/automaton A from **K**, the language L_A computed by A is equal to the image Im f_A

Let LP(**K**) and FP(**K**) be classes of all linguistic and functional properties of algorithms/automata from **K**, correspondingly.

Theorem 6.1. If the Axiom **ACPC** is true, then there are natural injections **rel**: FP(**K**) → LP(**K**) and **ch**: LP(**K**) → FP(**K**).

Proof. At first, we show that taking an arbitrary function f: D(**K**) → D(**K**) , it is possible to correspond a subset L_f of the set D(**K**) to it so that if g: D(**K**) → D(**K**) is another function, then $f = g$ if and only if $L_f = L_g$. Really, there are defined in a standard way binary relations R_f

, $R_g \subseteq$ D(**K**)×D(**K**) such that $f = g$ if and only if $R_f = R_g$. Then we put $L_f = p(R_f)$ and $L_g = p(R_g)$ where p is given in the Axiom **ACPC**. L_f and L_g are formal languages and $f = g$ if and only if $L_f = L_g$ because p is an injection.

For a property P of algorithms from **K**, we define **rel**(P) = { H; $H \in P$ and H computes the language $L_H = p(R_f)$ for the function $f = F_A$ some $A \in P$ }. Then if P is a functional property of algorithms from **K**, **rel**(P) is a linguistic property. Indeed, let us consider two algorithms H and F from **K** and assume that H has the property **rel**(P) and they both compute the same language L. It means that $L_H = L_F$. At the same time, $L_H = p(R_f)$ for the function $f = F_A$ some $A \in P$. Consequently, $L_F = p(R_f)$ for the function $f = F_A$ some $A \in P$ { A ; $A \in P$} and by the definition F also has the property **rel**(P). Thus, **rel**(P) is a linguistic property.

Let us take as **ch** the identity mapping, i.e., **ch**(Q) = Q for any property Q, and consider some linguistic property P of algorithms from **K**. We show that P is also a functional property. Indeed, let us consider two algorithms A and B from **K** and assume that A has the property P and they both realize the same function f. We know by the Axiom **CL** that the language L_A computed by A is equal to the image Im f_A and the language L_B computed by B is equal to the image Im f_B . As $f_A = f_B$, Im f_A = Im f_B. As P is a linguistic property P, B also has the property P. As A and B are arbitrary algorithms from **K**, P is a functional property.

Corollary 6.2. Any linguistic property is a functional property.

Remark 6.5. There are functional properties that are not linguistic. To show this let us consider the following property P_0 of Turing machines with the alphabet {1, 0}:

A Turing machine does not give the result for the input 0.

It is possible to define a Turing machine T that realizes the function f such that $f(0w) = w$ and $f(1w) = w$ for any nonempty word w, while $f(0)$ and $f(1)$ are undefined. If E is a Turing machine that realizes the identity function $e(x) = x$, then $f = f_T \neq f_E = e(x)$ but $L = L$. By the definition, the Turing machine T has the property P_0 , while the Turing machine E does not have this property. Consequently, P_0 is not a linguistic property.

Correspondence between functional and linguistic properties allows us to establish connections between decidability of these properties.

Corollary 6.3. If all functional properties of algorithms/automata from **K** are decidable (undecidable, semidecidable), then all linguistic properties of algorithms/automata from **K** are decidable (undecidable or semidecidable, correspondingly).

Corollary 6.4. If not all linguistic properties of algorithms/automata from **K** are decidable (undecidable, semidecidable), then not all functional properties of algorithms/automata from **K** are decidable (undecidable or semidecidable, correspondingly).

If A is an algorithm/automaton, then $\text{Tr}_A(x)$ denotes the computational trajectory of A generated by an input x. Let Z be a subset of the lower definability domain DD_*(**K**) of **K**.

Definition 6.14. A property P of algorithms from **K** is called a *performance property* (on Z) if the equality $\text{Tr}_A(x) = \text{Tr}_B(x)$ for all x (from Z) implies $P(A) = P(B)$.

Performance Properties:

1. Given input x, a Turing machine T from a class **T** starts from an empty cell.
2. Given input x, the head of a Turing machine T comes into the cell with number n.
3. Given input x, a Turing machine T uses only (n-1) cells for its computation.

4. Given input x, the head of a Turing machine T comes two times into the cell with number n.
5. A Turing machine T never stops.

Performance Problems:

1. Find if starting with input x, the head of a Turing machine T comes into the cell with number n.
2. Find if a Turing machine T from a class **T** starts from an empty cell.
3. Find if starting with input x, the head of a Turing machine T comes two times into the cell with number n.
4. Find if starting with input x, a Turing machine T from a class **T** never stops.

Definition 6.15. A property P of algorithms from **K** is called a *weak performance property* (on Z) if the equivalence $\mathrm{Tr}_A(x) \sim \mathrm{Tr}_B(x)$ for all x (from Z) implies $P(A) = P(B)$.

For instance, we assume that two trajectories are equivalent when either they are both infinite or they both bring automata to the same output result. In the case of Turing machines that either give no final result or stop functioning in the same final state, this equivalence coincides with the functional equivalence.

Remark 6.6. For non-deterministic automata, one input can result in many (sometimes even infinitely many) different trajectories. Thus, for a definition of performance properties, it is natural to consider systems of trajectories instead of separate trajectories in the case of non-deterministic automata.

If A is an algorithm/automaton, then $\mathrm{Op}_A(q, x)$ denotes the operation that A performs having input x, being in a state q. For automata with memory, the state includes the state of memory.

Definition 6.16. A property P of algorithms from **K** is called *operational* the equality $\mathrm{Op}_A(q, x) = \mathrm{Op}_B(q, x)$ for all inputs x and all states q implies $P(A) = P(B)$.

Operational Properties:

1. The head of a Turing machine moves only to the right for a given input.
2. The head of a Turing machine returns into the first cell for a given input.
3. The head of a Turing machine comes to the n-th cell, at least, two times for a given input.
4. The head of a Turing machine comes to the n-th cell for a given input.
5. The head of a Turing machine moves only to the right for all inputs.
6. The head of a Turing machine returns into the first cell for all inputs.
7. The head of a Turing machine comes to the n-th cell, at least, two times for all inputs.

Operational Problems:

1. Find if starting with input x, the head of a given Turing machine moves only to the right.

2. Find if starting with input x, the head of a given Turing machine returns into the first cell.
3. Find if starting with input x, the head of a given Turing machine returns into the first cell.
4. Find if starting with input x, the head of a given Turing machine comes to the n-th cell.

Proposition 6.8. Any operational property is a performance property.

Remark 6.7. Not all performance properties are operational properties as the following example shows.

Example 6.2. Let us take the class $\mathbf{T}_{St}$ of all automata with the same structure as Turing machines with one linear tape and one head, in which all machines are enumerated and the n-th machine starts from the n-th cell in the tape. It is possible to consider the following property P_x:

"Given an input x, a machine A from $\mathbf{T}_{St}$ starts from an empty cell."

This is a performance property as the equality $\mathrm{Tr}_A(x) = \mathrm{Tr}_B(x)$ means that given the input x, A and B start functioning with the head in the same cell. At the same time, P is not an operational property. Indeed, there are machines A and B in $\mathbf{T}_{St}$ such that have the same active performance rules, but different numbers because one of them (say A) has many passive rules, i.e., rules that are never used. Consequently, these machines start functioning with their heads in different cells. Thus, there is an input x such that A starts from an empty cell and B from a cell with some symbol. As a result, $P_x(A) \neq P_x(B)$, meaning that P_x is not an operational property.

Correspondence between performance and operational properties allows us to establish connections between decidability of these properties.

Corollary 6.5. If all operational properties of algorithms/automata from **K** are decidable (undecidable), then all performance properties of algorithms/automata from **K** are decidable (undecidable).

Corollary 6.6. If not all performance properties of algorithms/automata from **K** are decidable (undecidable), then not all operational properties of algorithms/automata from **K** are decidable (undecidable).

Proposition 6.9. Any performance property is an operational property if all algorithms from **K** start functioning from the same state q_0, given the same input x.

Corollary 6.7. For the class **T** of all Turing machines, performance and operational properties are the same.

Corollary 6.8. For the class **T** of all deterministic finite automata, performance and operational properties are the same.

Corollary 6.9. All operational properties of algorithms/automata from **K** are decidable (undecidable) if and only if all performance properties of algorithms/automata from **K** are decidable (undecidable).

Definition 6.17. Descriptive properties are properties of algorithm descriptions.

Descriptive Properties:

1. The description d(A) of an algorithm A contains the letter "a".

2. A given description d(A) of an algorithm A is minimal for all algorithms that compute the same function.
3. A given description d(A) of an algorithm A is minimal for all algorithms that compute the word x without input.

Descriptive Problems:

1. Does the description d(A) of an algorithm A contain the letter "a"?
2. Is a given description d(A) of an algorithm A is minimal for all algorithms that compute the same function?
3. Is a given description d(A) of an algorithm A is minimal for all algorithms that compute the word x without input?
4. What is the length of the description d(A) of a minimal algorithm A that computes the word x without input?

Remark 6.8. There are properties of algorithms that belong to several types. For instance, the following property P_{dnt} :

"A Turing machine T computes a total function and has a description d(T) with the length less than n," is at the same time functional and descriptive.

7 Boundaries for Algorithms and Computation

In this section, we determine what problems are algorithmically solvable and what problems are not.

Condition E. The class **K** contains an algorithm E such that for any input, it gives 1 as its output.

Condition CE. For all automata A in **K**, a sequential composition $A \circ E$ is a member of **K**.

Condition UC. If U is a universal in **K** algorithm, then for any automaton A in **K**, sequential compositions $U \circ A$ and $A \circ U$ are members of **K**.

Theorem 7.1. If a class **K** satisfies Axioms **AU** and **CAC**, and Conditions **E** and **CE**, then the problem $\mathbf{R_D}$ is semisolvable in **K**.

Proof. Let U be a universal in **K** algorithm and C be a coding algorithm for **K**, i.e., C_f : **K** $\to V^+$. Then the algorithm R defined by the sequential composition $C \circ U \circ E$ belongs to **K**. This algorithm works in the following manner. Given a pair (x, A) with $x \in V^*$ and $A \in$ **K**, R codifies A by means of C and then sends the pair (x, c(A)) to U. The algorithm U simulates functioning of A with input x. When being applied to x, A gives the result, this result goes to E and E outputs 1. Otherwise, R produces no result. This means that R computes the semicharacteristic function for all positive solutions of the problem $\mathbf{R_D}$. Consequently, $\mathbf{R_D}$ is semisolvable in **K**.

Theorem 7.1 and Lemma 6.1 imply the following result.

Theorem 7.2. If a class **K** satisfies Axioms **AU** and **CAC**, and Conditions **E** and **CE**, then the problem $\mathbf{R_{DA}}$ is semisolvable in **K**.

However, as it is demonstrated in Theorems 7.4 and 7.5, problems $\mathbf{R_D}$ and $\mathbf{R_{DA}}$ are undecidable.

Condition CA. **K** contains a converting algorithm A_C such that it checks whether a given word w is equal to $\mathbf{c}(A)$ for some A in **K** and then if this is true it converts w to $(\mathbf{c}(A)\ , w\ )$.

Condition CS. For all automata A in **K**, the sequential composition $A \circ A_C$ is a member of **K**.

Condition CC. For all automata A in **K**, the sequential composition $A_C \circ A$ is a member of **K.**

Remark 7.1. Conditions **CS** and **CC** follow from Axiom **ASC**. However, for some classes Condition **CS** may be true, while Axiom **ASC** is invalid. Inductive Turing machines of the first order (Burgin, 2003) is an example of such a class. This class does not include all sequential compositions of its members, but has all sequential compositions of its members with finite automata, while it is possible to realize algorithms A_C and C by finite automata.

Let us consider a class **A** of algorithms/automata that satisfies postulates **PDC**, **PDS**, and **PCS** (or **PDN**, and **PCN**), axioms **AT**, **AC**, and conditions **CA2**, $\mathbf{LSW}_{yn}$ (or **SW**), **CA**, **CC**, and **CS** (or axiom **ASC**).

Remark 7.2. As the working alphabet V of algorithms from **A** contains more than one element, by renaming, we can assume that $\boldsymbol{y}$ and $\boldsymbol{n}$ are elements of V.

Theorem 7.3. The Fixed Output Problem $\mathbf{R_{Oy}}$ is unsolvable in **A**, i.e., there is no automaton H in **A** such that for all algorithms A in **A**, and for all strings w in V^*, this automaton H can check if $A(w) = \boldsymbol{y}$ or not.

Proof. Let us assume that such as automaton H exists in **A**. It means that given a pair $(\mathbf{c}(A)\ , w\ )$ where $\mathbf{c}$: $\mathbf{K} \to \mathrm{V}^+$ is defined by the axiom **AC**, H produces y when $A(w) = \boldsymbol{y}$ and produces $\boldsymbol{n}$ otherwise. Properties of the class **A** provide us with the automata A_C and A_{sw}, and allow us to build the sequential composition $B = A_C \circ H \circ A_{sw}$, which also belongs to **A** and in which the automaton A_{sw} switches $\boldsymbol{y}$ and $\boldsymbol{n}$.

This composition B is presented in Figure 2.

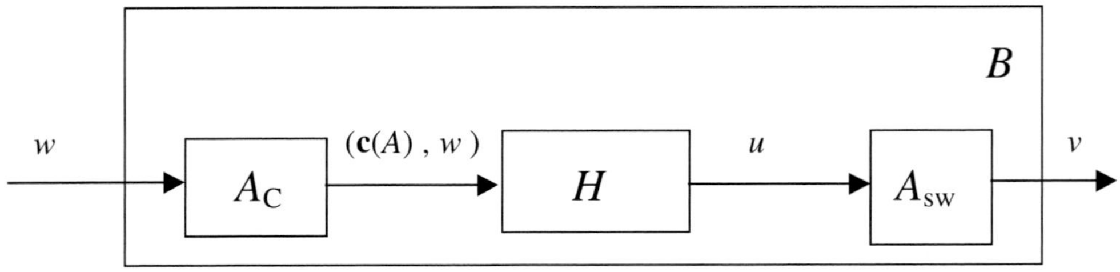

Figure 2. A hypothetical automaton B

Let us consider functioning of the automaton B when it works with the word $\mathbf{c}(B) = w$.

First, as $\mathbf{c}(B) = w$ and the output of H is equal either to $\boldsymbol{y}$ or to $\boldsymbol{n}$, the output $B(w)$ of B is also equal either to $\boldsymbol{y}$ or to $\boldsymbol{n}$.

Second, when $B(w) = \boldsymbol{y}$, the automaton H also outputs $\boldsymbol{y}$. This symbol goes to the automaton A_{sw} , which switches $\boldsymbol{y}$ and $\boldsymbol{n}$. As the result, the output of B is $\boldsymbol{n}$. This is a contradiction, which shows that it is impossible that $B(w) = \boldsymbol{y}$.

Third, when $B(w) = \boldsymbol{n}$, the automaton H also outputs $\boldsymbol{n}$. This symbol goes to the automaton A_{sw}, which switches $\boldsymbol{y}$ and $\boldsymbol{n}$. As the result, the output of B is $\boldsymbol{y}$. This is a contradiction, which shows that it is impossible that $B(w) = \boldsymbol{n}$.

Thus, we come to a situation in which B gives no output. This is impossible as the class **A** satisfies the axiom **AT**. So, Theorem 7.3 is proved by contradiction.

Theorem 7.3 and Lemma 6.2 imply the following result.

Corollary 7.1. The Free Output Problem $\mathbf{F_{Oy}}$ is unsolvable in **A**.

Let us consider a class **K** of algorithms/automata that satisfies postulates **PDC**, **PDS**, and **PCS,** axiom **AC**, and conditions **CA2, WLSW**$_{yn}$, **CA, CS,** and **CC**.

Theorem 7.4. The Decidability Problem $\mathbf{R_D}$ is unsolvable in **K**, i.e., there is no automaton H in **K** such that for all algorithms A in **K,** and for all strings w in V^*, this automaton H can check if $A(w)$ is defined or not.

Proof. Let us assume that such as automaton H exists in **K**. It means that given a pair $(\mathbf{c}(A), w)$, H produces y when $A(w) = a$ for some element a from V^*, and produces n when A gives no result. Properties of the class **K** allow us to build the sequential composition $D = A_C \circ H \circ A_w$, which also belongs to **K** and in which the automaton A_w given the input y gives no output and given the input n, gives y as the output.

This composition D is presented in Figure 3.

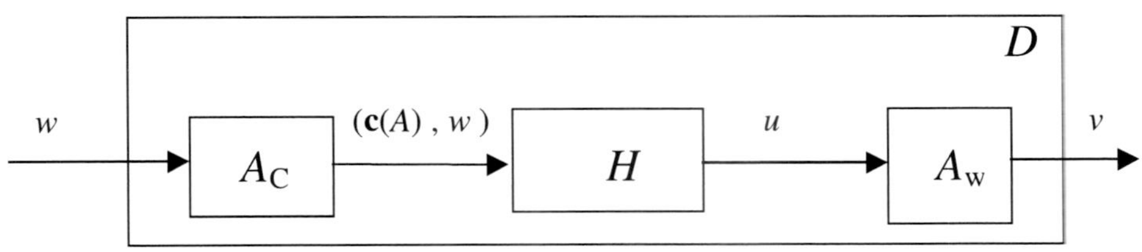

Figure 3. A hypothetical automaton D

Let us consider functioning of the automaton D when it works with the word $\mathbf{c}(D) = w$.

First, as $\mathbf{c}(D) = w$, the output of H is equal either to y or to n, and the output of A_w can be only n, the output $B(w)$ of B can also be only n.

Second, when B gives no output, the automaton H outputs n. This symbol goes to the automaton A_w, which switches y and n. As the result, the output of B is y. This is a contradiction, which shows that it is impossible that B gives no output.

Third, when $B(w) = n$, the automaton H outputs y. This symbol goes to the automaton A_{sw}, which gives no output. As the result, B also gives no output. This is a contradiction, which shows that it is impossible that $B(w) = n$.

Such automaton B that neither gives no output nor gives some output cannot exist. So, Theorem 7.4 is proved by contradiction.

Let in addition the class **K** satisfies Axiom **AU**.

Corollary 7.2. The Local Decidability Problem $\mathbf{R_{D\mathit{A}}}$ is unsolvable in **K**, i.e., there is an algorithms A in **K** such that no automaton H in **K** can check for all strings w in V^* if $A(w)$ is defined or not.

Indeed, taking a universal in **K** algorithm U as A, we see that decidability of $\mathbf{R_{D\mathit{U}}}$ is equivalent to decidability of $\mathbf{R_D}$.

Corollary 7.3. There is no finite automaton that can check for any given finite automaton if it accepts a given word, **w**.

However, Turing machines can solve this problem (cf., for example, (Hopcroft *et al*, 2001)).

Corollary 7.4. There is no recursive function that can check for any given recursive function $f(x)$ satisfiability of the condition $f(x) = n$ for a fixed number n and any given number x.

Definition 7.1. A linguistic problem $\underline{\mathbf{P}}$ (linguistic property **P**) is called *non-trivial* in **K** if there is a language L generated by some automaton from **K** that has the related property **P** and there is a language L generated by some automaton from **K** that does not have the related property **P**.

Trivial linguistic properties are such properties that either there are no computable in **K** languages with such properties or all computable in **K** languages have these properties.

Condition EL. The empty language ∅ is generated by some automaton from **K**.

Remark 7.3. Condition **EL** is inconsistent with Axiom **AT**.

Let us assume that the class **K** satisfies Postulates **PDC**, **PDS**, and **PCS,** Axioms **AC** and **AU**, and Conditions **CA2,** $\mathbf{WLSW}_{yn}$, **EL**, **CA, CS,** and **CC**.

Theorem 7.5. Any non-trivial in **K** linguistic problem $\underline{\mathbf{P}}$ is unsolvable in the class **K**.

Proof. The problem $\underline{\mathbf{P}}$ is related to a property **P**. Let us consider the class $\mathbf{L_P}$ of all languages that have the property **P** and assume that the empty language ∅ does not belong to $\mathbf{L_P}$. As the property **P** and the problem $\underline{\mathbf{P}}$ are non-trivial in **K**, there is an automaton T from **K** such that it generates some non-empty language $L = L(T)$.

Taking some algorithm A from **K** and an arbitrary word x in the alphabet V and using conditions **G** and **GC**, we can build the automaton $B_{A,x}$ in **K** that is represented by the schema in Figure 4.

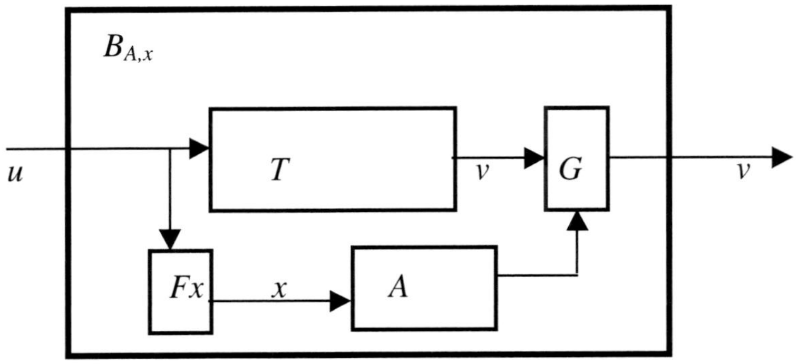

Figure 4. The structure of the machine M_Q

The automaton $B_{A,x}$ consists of four parts: T, A, Fx, and G. The automata T and A are described above. The automaton G performs the function of gates. Initially it is closed and does not let through anything. Any input that comes from A opens G and it gives as output its input v that comes from T. This output is also the output of $B_{A,x}$. The automaton Fx generates the word x, given any input, and then sends this word x to A.

This construction results in the following property of the automaton $B_{A,x}$. When A produces a result, given x as its input, the automaton $B_{A,x}$ generates the language L. When A produces no result, given x as its input, the automaton $B_{A,x}$ generates the empty language ∅. Thus, the language $L(B_{A,x})$ has the property **P** if and only if the value $A(x)$ is defined. If there is an automaton in **K** that solves the linguistic problem **P̲** for all automata $B_{A,x}$, then this automaton, or its simple modification, can solve the Decidability Problem $\mathbf{R_{D}}_A$. However, by Corollary 7.2, this problem is unsolvable when $A = U$ is a universal algorithm in **K**. Consequently, the linguistic problem **P̲** is also unsolvable.

To finish the proof, we have to consider the situation when the empty language ∅ belongs to $\mathbf{L_P}$. If the problem **P̲** is solvable in **K**, then by Corollary 6.1 the problem **¬P̲** is also solvable in **K** and ∅ does not belong to the class $\mathbf{L}_{\neg\mathbf{P}}$ of all languages that do not have the property **P**. The property **¬P** is linguistic and nontrivial because the property **P** is linguistic and nontrivial. However, it has been demonstrated that any problem related to a nontrivial linguistic property such that the empty language ∅ does not have this property is unsolvable. So, both problems **P̲** and **¬P̲** are unsolvable.

Theorem 7.5 is proved.

Remark 7.4. It is possible to prove Theorem 7.5 without Axiom AU, but with constructive forms of composition axioms. Constructive forms mean not only existence of all necessary compositions, but also that there is an algorithm in **K** that builds all these compositions.

Theorem 7.5 and Lemma 6.3 imply the following result.

Corollary 7.5. The Fixed Output Problem $\mathbf{R_{O}}_y$ is unsolvable in **K**.

Theorem 7.3 and Lemma 6.2 imply the following result.

Corollary 7.6. The Free Output Problem $\mathbf{F_{O}}_y$ is unsolvable in **K**.

Corollary 7.7. The problem whether an arbitrary given algorithm A from **K** is everywhere defined (satisfies Axiom **AT**) is unsolvable in **K**.

Corollary 7.8. The problem whether a subclass **H** of **K** satisfies Axiom **AT** is unsolvable in **K**.

Corollary 7.9 (Rice Theorem in the linguistic form, cf. (Davis, 1982; Rogers, 1987)). Any non-trivial linguistic property **P** of Turing machines (or, more general, of recursive algorithms in the sense of (Burgin, 2001)) is undecidable in the class **T** of all Turing machines (recursive algorithms).

Rice Theorem is an important result for computer science because it sets up boundaries for research in that area, as well as for software design. It informally states that only trivial properties of programs in general programming languages are algorithmically decidable.

Definition 7.2. A functional problem **P̲** (functional property **P**) is called *non-trivial* in **K** if there is a function f realized by some automaton from **K** that has the related to **P̲** property **P** and there is a function g realized by some automaton from **K** that does not have the related to **P̲** property **P**.

Trivial functional properties are such properties that either there are no computable in **K** functions with such properties or all computable in **K** functions have these properties.

Condition EF. The function $f_{\varnothing}$, which is undefined for all elements from the domain of **K**, is realized by some automaton from **K**.

Remark 7.4. Condition **EF** is inconsistent with Axiom **AT**.

Let us assume that the class **K** satisfies Postulates **PDC**, **PDS**, and **PCS,** Axioms **AC** and **AU**, and Conditions **CA2, WLSW**$_{yn}$, **EF**, **CA, CS,** and **CC**.

Theorem 7.6. Any non-trivial in **K** functional problem **P** is unsolvable in the class **K**.

Proof. The problem **P** is related to a property **P**. Let us consider the class $\mathbf{F_P}$ of all functions g: $V^* \to V^*$ that have the property **P** and assume that the empty function $f_\varnothing$ does not belong to $\mathbf{F_P}$. As the property **P** and the problem **P** are non-trivial in **K**, there is an automaton T from **K** such that it realizes some non-empty functions f: $V^* \to V^*$.

Taking some algorithm A from **K** and an arbitrary word x in the alphabet V and using conditions **G** and **GC**, we can build the automaton $B_{A,x}$ in **K** that is represented by the schema in Figure 5.

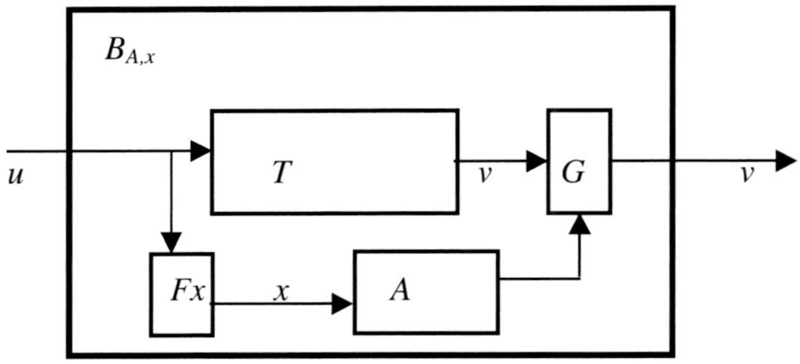

Figure 5. The structure of the machine M_Q

The automaton $B_{A,x}$ consists of four parts: T, A, Fx, and G. The automata T and A are described above. The automaton G performs the function of gates. Initially it is closed and does not let through anything. Any input that comes from A opens G and it gives as output its input v that comes from T. This output is also the output of $B_{A,x}$. The automaton Fx generates the word x, given any input, and then sends this word x to A.

This construction results in the following property of the automaton $B_{A,x}$. When A produces a result, given x as its input, the automaton $B_{A,x}$ realizes the function f. When A produces no result, given x as its input, the automaton $B_{A,x}$ realizes the empty function $f_\varnothing$. Thus, the function computed by the automaton $B_{A,x}$ has the property **P** if and only if the value $A(x)$ is defined. If there is an automaton in **K** that solves the functional problem **P** for all automata $B_{A,x}$, then this automaton, or its simple modification, can solve the Decidability Problem $\mathbf{R}_{\mathbf{D}A}$. However, by Corollary 7.2, this problem is unsolvable when $A = U$ is a universal automaton/algorithm in **K**. Consequently, the functional problem **P** is also unsolvable.

To finish the proof, we have to consider the situation when the empty function $f_\varnothing$ belongs to $\mathbf{F_P}$. If the problem **P** is solvable in **K**, then by Corollary 6.1 the problem **¬P** is also solvable in **K** and ∅ does not belong to the class $\mathbf{F}_{\neg\mathbf{P}}$ of all functions that do not have the property **P** . The property **¬P** is functional and nontrivial because the property **P** is functional and nontrivial. However, it has been demonstrated that any problem related to a nontrivial functional property such that the empty function $f_\varnothing$ does not have this property is unsolvable. So, both problems **P** and **¬P** are unsolvable.

Theorem 7.6 is proved.

Remark 7.5. It is possible to deduce Theorem 7.5 from Theorems 7.6 and 6.1. However, a direct proof gives a better insight in the situation with unsolvability.

Remark 7.6. It is possible to prove Theorem 7.6 without Axiom AU, but with constructive forms of composition axioms.

Corollary 7.7 (Rice Theorem in the functional form (Rice, 1951)). Any non-trivial functional property **P** of Turing machines (of recursive algorithms in the sense of (Burgin, 2001)) is undecidable in the class **T** of all Turing machines (recursive algorithms).

Theorem 4.1 implies that for many classes of everywhere defined algorithms (Axioms **AT**) universal algorithms do not exist (negation of Axiom **AU**). However, there are classes of everywhere defined algorithms with universal algorithms. For instance, let us take some everywhere defined Turing machine M that works with words in the alphabet $\{1, 0\}$. If a word w in this alphabet contains 0, then it is possible to represent w in the form $w = v0u$ where the word v does not contain zeroes. This allows us to correspond to each word v in this alphabet the Turing machine T_v for which $T_v(u) = M(w)$ with $w = v0u$. This Turing machine T_v is everywhere defined and M is a universal machines for the class $\mathbf{T}_M$ of all machines T_v.

Condition OF. There is an element a in V such that the set f_a that is identically equal to a is generated by some algorithm/automaton from **A**.

Let us consider a class **A** of algorithms/automata that satisfies Postulates **PT**, **PDS**, and **PCS**, Axioms **AT**, **AC** and **AU**, and conditions **CA2**, $\mathbf{LSW}_{yn}$, **CA**, **CS**, **OF**, and **CC**.

Theorem 7.7. Any non-trivial in **A** functional problem $\underline{\mathbf{P}}$ is unsolvable in the class **A**.

Condition OL. There is an element a in V such that the set $L_a = \{a\}$ is generated by some algorithm/automaton from **A**.

Theorems 7.7 and 6.1 imply the following result.

Let us consider a class **A** of algorithms/automata that satisfies Postulates **PT**, **PDS**, and **PCS**, Axioms **AT**, **AC** and **AU**, and conditions **CA2**, $\mathbf{LSW}_{yn}$, **CA**, **CS**, **OL**, and **CC**.

Theorem 7.8. Any non-trivial in **A** linguistic problem $\underline{\mathbf{P}}$ is unsolvable in the class **A**.

In contrast to functional and linguistic properties, some non-trivial operational properties are decidable in the class **T** of all Turing machines, while others are not.

The following properties are decidable (Sipser, 1997):

1. "The head of a Turing machine moves only to the right for a given input."
2. "The head of a Turing machine does not make turns."

The following properties are undecidable (Sipser, 1997):

1. "The head of a Turing machine returns into the first cell for a given input."
2. "The head of a Turing machine comes to the n-th cell, at least, two times for all inputs."

Some non-trivial descriptive properties are decidable in the class **T** of all Turing machines, while others are not.

The descriptive problem "Does the description d(A) of an algorithm A contain the letter 'a' ?" is decidable.

As results on Kolmogorov complexity and other dual complexity measures (Li and Vitanyi, 1997; Burgin, 1982) show, the following descriptive problems are undeciable:

- Is a given description d(A) of an algorithm A is minimal for all algorithms that compute the same function?
- Is a given description d(A) of an algorithm A is minimal for all algorithms that compute the word x without input?
- What is the length of the description d(A) of a minimal algorithm A that computes the word x without input?

It is interesting that although all kinds of Turing machines have the same computing power (cf., for example, (Hopckroft *et al*, 2001)), decidability of some properties of Turing machines depends on the model used. It is demonstrated by the following results.

Let us consider $n > 0$ and the property V_n:

" Given input x, the head of a Turing machine comes into the cell with number n."

Theorem 7.10. The property V_n is decidable for Turing machines with one-sided linear tape.

Proof. The property V_n is equivalent to the property U_n:

"Given input x, a Turing machine T uses only (n-1) cells for its computation."

Indeed, for Turing machines with a one-sided linear tape, the property V_n is true if and only if the property U_n is false. Thus, both of them are either decidable or undecidable.

To check the property U_n for an input x, we note that if this property is true, then T works only with words that have length less than or equal to $n - 1$. The number of such words is equal to $(p - 1)^{(n - 1)}$ where p is the number of symbols in the alphabet of the Turing machine T. Let us assume that T has r states. Then T either makes $r(p - 1)^{(n - 1)} + 1$ moves or halts. We can check both options, using universal Turing machine. If T makes $r(p - 1)^{(n - 1)} + 1$ moves, then one of the states of T repeats with the same word on the tape according to the pigeonhole principle (cf., for example, (Hopckroft *et al*, 2001)). Such a repetition means that that T goes into an infinite cycle and does not use more than (n-1) cells.

Thus, if T uses more than (n-1) cells, i.e., the head comes to the cell with number n, it is possible to find this simulating not more than $r(p - 1)^{(n - 1)} + 1$ moves of T. Consequently, the validity of U_n can be found by simulating not more than $r(p - 1)^{(n - 1)} + 1$ moves of T. It means that the property U_n is decidable.

As properties V_n and U_n are equivalent for Turing machines with a one-sided linear tape, the property U_n is also decidable.

Theorem is proved.

For a slightly changed model, the same property appears to be undecidable.

Theorem 7.11. The property V_n is undecidable for Turing machines with a two-sided linear tape.

Proof. Let T be an arbitrary Turing machine with one-sided linear tape and $\mathbf{T}_{1l}$ be the class of all such machines. As usually, we assume that the one-sided tape goes from the zero cell to the right. By the initial condition, the number n in the property V_n is larger than zero. We correspond to T a Turing machine T_2 with a two-sided linear tape and the same states as T, but working in a different manner.

The input word is written in the left part of the tape of T_2, starting with the zero cell. At the beginning, T_2 works only with the left part of its tape, i.e., with cells with numbers 0, -1, -2, -3, … , starting with its head in the zero cell. The rules of T_2 consist of two parts: R_1 and R_2. The rules of the first part R_1 are obtained from the rules of the machine T by changing all left moves of the head of T to the right moves of the head of T_2 and all right moves of the head of T to the left moves of the head of T_2. As a result, T_2 imitates all moves of the machine T, with its head going to the opposite direction.

At the same time, the machine T_2 does not have final states. To each final state q of T, there is a system of corresponding rules from R_2 that have the following form

$$qa \to \mathrm{R}q$$

Here a is an arbitrary symbol from the alphabet of T or the empty symbol Λ.

As a result, when T_2 comes to some final state of T, instead of halting, the head of T_2 starts moving to the right without stopping. Consequently, given input x', the head of T_2 comes to the cell with number n if and only if T halts given input x. Here x' is obtained from the word x by its reversion, e.g., if $x = abc$, then $x' = cba$. Thus, when the problem V_n is decidable, we can build an algorithm that decides the halting problem for all Turing machines with one-sided linear tape. As the property "to halt starting with a given input" is undecidable, the property V_n is also undecidable and theorem is proved.

8 Software and Hardware Verification and Testing

Here we show how results about abstract classes of algorithms are related to real life problems of building computers and networks, designing their software and developing information technology in general.

As an application of theoretical results obtained in previous sections, we consider problems of verification of program/device correctness and of program/device testing with the goal to eliminate bugs. At first, we reflect on software verification. As Voas and Miller (1995) write, "software verification is often the last defense against disasters caused by faulty software development. When lives and fortunes depend on software, software quality and its verification demand increased attention. As software begins to replace human decision-makers, a fundamental concern is whether a machine will be able to perform the tasks with the same level of precision as a skilled person. If not, a catastrophe may be caused by an automated system that is less reliable than a manual one."

To be able to apply theoretical results in this area, which are mostly mathematical by their nature, it is necessary to have an exact definition of software verification. Informally, verification answers the question whether a given program is correct. Although program correctness looks very simple property, experience of programmers and computer scientists demonstrates that this is a very sophisticated and complex property, which has different meanings. Programs are written to solve problems. So, a correct program p solves correctly some problem(s) P. Solving this problem is the goal of p, which is formulated to a program developer. For a long time, users simply explained what they want. Now this process is formalized, and to give an explicit and sufficiently unambiguous explanation of this goal, specifications of programs to be designed are written. There are various specification languages and different models for correctness are used (Burgin and Greibach, 2002). As a result, it is possible to define program correctness in several ways.

Definition 8.1. A program is correct if it matches the needed/demanded specification.

This is a very general and thus, not completely formalized definition of correctness because we have two undefined concepts: "to match" and "specification".

A natural way to determine a program specification in a an exact form is to correspond to a program p some function f: $X \rightarrow Y$. It is assumed that the program p has to process inputs taken from X into the outputs that belong to Y. This program representation is reflected in the Deterministic Computation Postulate **PDC.** It gives us one of the definitions of program correctness.

Definition 8.2. The program p is *functionally correct* if it realizes/computes a function f given by specification.

Usually we consider programs written in some popular programming language, such as C^{++}, Java, ALGOL, SIMULA or PROLOG, and compare them to Turing machines.

Definition 8.3. A programming language is called Turing complete if it is functionally equivalent to the class **T** of all Turing machines.

It is, as a rule, proved that the class **K** of all programs in such languages is Turing complete. That is why these languages are called *general programming languages* as the majority of programming languages satisfies this condition.

To realize some function is a nontrivial functional property P_f. Thus, by Theorem 7.6, this property is undecidable in the class **T**. As classes **T** and **K** are functionally equivalent, we have the following result.

Theorem 8.1. It is impossible to create a software system V written in a general programming language **L** such that V verifies functional correctness of all programs written in **L**.

Let us consider some system C of logical statements of the form:

If x has property P, then y has property Q.

Definition 8.4. The program p is *logically correct* with respect to the system C if all statements from C are true when x belongs to the domain X of p and x belongs to the range Y of p.

It is possible to express the property P_f in the form:

If x belongs to the domain of the function f, then $p(x) = f(x)$.

As a result, Theorem 8.1 implies the following result.

Corollary 8.1. It is impossible to create a software system V written in a general programming language **L** such that V verifies logical correctness of all programs written in **L**.

This result shows that automatic program verification cannot verify correctness for all programs. In particular, testing cannot find all bugs as the following result demonstrates.

Corollary 8.2. It is impossible to create a software system V written in a general programming language **L** such that V debugs all programs written in **L**.

Indeed, according to the conventional model of algorithms, to give a result a program must halt. So, if a program does not stop, it is a result of some bug. However, if the programming language is Turing complete, it is impossible by standard methods to check whether any given program halts or not. This implies the result of Corollary 8.2.

If it is impossible to verify all programs by program verifier, it is possible to look at logical means of program verification. There is a diverse literature on this topic (cf., for example, (Loeckx *et al*, 1985) or (Colburn *et al*, 1993)). However, results from (Lewis, 2001) imply that in a general case it is also impossible for a programmer to verify correctness of all programs by logical methods.

Consequently, automatic program verification is impossible in general and programs can be too complex for such verification. Thus, computer scientists try to find ways to do software verification, at least, partially. One way is to consider not all programs but some restricted classes, for which it might be possible to build an automatic verifier. Let us simplify the verification problem, assuming that we are dealing only with such programs that always give the result. So, for conventional programs, no infinite loops are allowed and we need to check only if the program gives a correct result. For instance, we know that for all inputs the result has to be a fixed word/number. In this case, Theorem 7.3 shows that it is impossible to check this by a general algorithm. It gives us the following result.

Theorem 8.2. It is impossible to create a software system V written in a general programming language **L** such that V verifies functional correctness of all programs in **L** that always give some result.

This result is similar to limits to software estimation established by Lewis (2001).

Another way is not to try to verify the program itself, but to build program models and to verify these models. To formalize this idea, we introduce even more general definition of program correctness.

Definition 8.5. A program p is *descriptively correct* if the program's description/model matches the needed specification.

Another way to achieve automated program verification is to make the correctness condition weaker. This is done by introduction of the concept of model program correctness.

Definition 8.6. A program p is *model correct* if the program's model matches a defined model of the needed specification.

This approach is based on the following model of program verification (Burgin and Tandon, 2003):

$$\begin{array}{ccc} M_{Sp} & \xrightarrow{\ c\ } & M_p \\ {\scriptstyle m_{Sp}}\uparrow & & \uparrow{\scriptstyle m_p} \\ Sp & \xrightarrow[\ s\ ]{} & p \end{array} \qquad (1)$$

Here p is a program (program system), Sp is its specification, M_p is its model and M_{Sp} is a model of the specification Sp. To be correct, the program p has to allow a correspondence c with specific properties.

Finite automata are natural models of programs. At the same time, abstract automata are used for program specification. They are especially useful for simulation program specification as automata give diverse models of simulated systems. In addition, automata are utilized for program synthesis. For example, Hune and Sandholm (2000) develop a method for synthesizing control programs. The method merges an existing control program with a control automaton. Different authors developed specification languages based on automata. Second, abstract automata are used for program understanding and documentation in description of the program behavior. Third, abstract automata are used for program testing and formal verification. A review of such approaches, including their system and methodological analysis, is given by Burgin and Greibach (2002).

Modeling programs and computing devices with abstract automata constitutes one of the main parts of computer science, which is effectively used in information technology.

Definition 8.7. An abstract automaton *A* is a *model* for a program (program system) *P* if some properties of *P* can be deduced from properties of *A*.

We consider here two types of automata models of programs: *descriptive* and *simulative*.

Definition 8.8. A model for a program *P* in a form of an abstract automaton *A* is called *simulative* if a correspondence between input, output and states of the program *P* and the automaton *A* is specified and transitions of *A* represent execution of the program *P* for corresponding data.

Definition 8.9. A model for a program *P* in a form of an abstract automaton *A* is called *descriptive* if the automaton *A* is completely specified by its transition diagram (function or table) and there is a structural correspondence between input, output, and states of the program *P* and the automaton *A*.

There are different ways of building descriptive automaton models for programs. A program *P* can be perceived as a collection of modules with a small, algorithmic core that expresses how the modules are used to obtain a desired effect. In a sense, the core is expressed in an application specific language, with control constructs implemented by the modules. With proper separation between core and module internals one can use a distinct language for the internals, as long as the interface is meaningful seen from either side. Rather than describe *how* the "operations" of a module work, one might describe what they achieve. In other words, we can ascribe a system of states to each module and consider possible inputs and outputs as words in some formal language. This allows us to consider transformation of data performed by a module as the transition function of this module. In such a way, an automaton is corresponded to the program module. Combining these automata, we get an automaton that represents the whole program *P*.

Since a module can be seen as implementing one or more specialized language constructs, this view on program description is closely related to programming language semantics. In ascribing meaning to the expressions in a program, it is necessary to determine both how execution of the expressions will affect the underlying computer state and how the sequence of computer state changes are related to issues of human concern. To represent these issues, it is very natural to use abstract automata. This approach is represented in the Vienna definition language (Wegner, 1972; Ollongren, 1974).

For example, it is possible to retranslate logical representation of program properties, which is used in the axiomatic theory of computer programming (Floyd, 1959; Naur, 1966; Hoare, 1969), into the automata representation of programs. As Hoare writes (1969), one of the most important properties of a program is whether or not it carries out its intended function. The intended function of a program, as well as of its parts, is specified by making general assertions about the values of input and output variables. These assertions are presented as formal expressions of the form R{*P*}Q where the precondition R and postcondition Q are some logical formulas and *P* is a program (an instruction or command). The meaning of such an expression is:

If the assertion R *is true before initiation of the program P, then the assertion* Q *is true on its termination.*

This allows us to consider logical formulas as symbols of the input and output alphabets of an automaton *A* that is corresponded to a program, while programs, commands, or instructions form the set of the states of *A*. We call this automaton the *state based automaton* of the program *P* and denote it by Ast(*P*). This is a descriptive model of *P*.

Another interpretation of the expression R{*P*}Q is given by Milner (1989):

If P is executed in a state satisfying R *and it terminates, then the terminating state will satisfy* Q.

This allows us to consider logical formulas as states of an automaton *A* that is corresponded to a program, while programs, commands, or instructions form symbols of the input alphabet of this automaton *A*. In this case, *A* is an accepting automaton. We call this automaton the *symbol based automaton* of the program *P* and denote it by Asy(*P*). This is also a descriptive model of *P*.

There are other ways to correspond automata to logical specifications of programs. For example, Hune and Sandholm (2000) utilize monadic second order logic over strings for specifying the control automata. More exactly, they use the Mona tool to translate logical specifications into automaton description.

After we build an automaton representation of both program specification and description, it is possible to use formal methods for verifying/testing their relevance and program correctness. To do this for a program *P*, we consider the automaton A_{sp} that is designed as a specification of *P* or as a model of such a specification and the automaton A_d that is built as a description of *P* when the program is already developed. We call A_{sp} a specification automaton of *P* and A_d a description automaton of *P*.

Definition 8.10. The program *P* is accepted as a correct program if a definite correspondence exists between the automata A_{sp} and A_d.

There are different kinds of natural correspondences between abstract automata. Using them, we come to different kinds of program correctness. For example, let us consider the logical correctness, to get a proof of which is the main goal of the logical or axiomatic approach to program verification (Hoare, 1969),

According to this approach, it is assumed that a program specification is done by making definite assertions about the properties of input and output data. These assertions about a program *P* are presented as formal expressions of the form R{*P*}Q where R and Q are some logical formulas. When the program *P* is created, similar expressions are corresponded to the instructions that constitute this program. Then definite logical formulas that represent rules of composition are added and from all these expressions taken as axioms, the formula R{*P*}Q representing specification is deduced.

As we have demonstrated, it is possible to interpret each formula of the form R{*C*}Q as a finite automaton. We can correspond a state based automaton Ast(*C*) and a symbol based automaton Asy(*C*) to these formulas.

As a result, we relate to the logical program specification R{*P*}Q an automaton program specification Aw(*P*), which is called the whole program automaton of *P*.

Rules of instruction composition, both in procedural and axiomatic forms, give corresponding rules for automata composition. This allows one to construct the composite program automaton Ac(*P*) of *P*. This automaton plays the role of a program description. Usually, correctness of a program is verified by establishing some equivalence relation between the specification and description automata corresponded to the program. Definition 8.10 allows us to make this idea exact.

Definition 8.11. The program *P* is A-correct (FA-correct) if the automata Aw(*P*) and Ac(*P*) are equivalent (and finite).

There are different kinds of equivalence, implying different kinds of program correctness. Here we consider algebraic forms of automata equivalence. The most evident equivalence is equality.

As it is demonstrated above, to verify program correctness, it is necessary to establish a correspondence between automata. It is natural to demand that such correspondence preserves structures of these automata. To make this concept exact, we consider here only finite automata and remind the definition of the structure of a finite automaton.

According to the traditional approach, there are three forms of representation of finite automata: *analytical*, *dynamic*, and *table* representations. We begin with the *analytical form*.

In the analytical form, a finite automaton *A* consists of three structures, i.e., $A = (L, S, \delta)$:

- The *linguistic structure* $L = (\Sigma, Q, \Omega)$ where Σ is a finite set of *input symbols*, Q is a finite *set of states*, and Ω is a finite set of *output symbols* of the automaton *A*;
- The *state structure* $S = (Q, q_0, F)$ where q_0 is an element from Q that is called the *initial* or *start state* and F is a subset of Q that is called the set of *final* (in some cases, *accepting*) states of the automaton *A*;
- The *action structure*, which consists of the *transition function*, or more exactly, *transition relation* of the automaton *A*

$$\delta: \Sigma \times Q \to Q$$

and of the *production* or *output function*, or more exactly, *production* or *output relation* of the automaton *A*

$$\sigma: \Sigma \times Q \to \Omega$$

The *dynamic form* of representation of a finite automaton *A* is different from its analytic form only in its transition function representation. The function/relation δ is given in a form of a transition diagram.

The *table form* of representation of a finite automaton A is also different from its analytic form only in its transition function representation. The function/relation δ is given in a form of a table.

Here we consider the analytical form of representation of a finite automaton A as the most appropriate for utilizing methods of modern algebra to study properties of automata models of programs.

From the algebraic perspective, it is possible to correspond a heterogeneous algebra in the sense of Birkhoff and Lipson (1970) and Mathienssen (1978) to any deterministic finite automaton A.

Definition 8.12. A *heterogeneous algebra U* is a set U (the support of U) with a system of operations Σ in which elements of U form an indexed system $U = \{A_i ; i \in I\}$ of sets and each operation is a mapping having the form $f: A_{i1} \times A_{i2} \times \ldots \times A_{ik} \to A_i$.

Other examples of heterogeneous universal algebras are modules, polygons, i.e., sets on which monoids act, polyadic or Halmos algebras (Halmos, 1962), nonhomogeniuos polyadic algebras (Leblanc, 1962), relational algebras (Beniaminov, 1979), and state machines.

Heterogeneous universal algebras were studied by several authors under different names. To mention only some of them, it is necessary to name algebras with a scheme of operators introduced by Higgins (1963; 1973), multibase universal algebras (Glushkov, et al, 1974; Shaposhnikov, 1999; Karpunin and Shaposhnikov, 2000), and many-sorted algebras studied by Plotkin (1991). The term "heterogeneous algebras" is used more often than other related terms. Heterogeneous (multibase or many-sorted) algebras represent the next level of the development of algebra. Namely, in ordinary (or homogeneous) universal algebras operations are defined on a set, while in heterogeneous algebras operations are defined on a named set (Burgin, 1990). This makes possible to develop more adequate models for many processes and systems. For example, heterogeneous algebras are extensively used for mathematical modeling information processing by computers. Such models as abstract automata and abstract states machines or evolving algebras (Gurevich, 1994) become more and more widespread in computer science. In addition, relational algebras, a special case of heterogeneous algebras, are extensively used for modeling relational databases (Beniaminov, 1979; Plotkin, 1991).

At the same time, heterogeneous algebras are particular cases of partial algebraic systems in the sense of Malcev (1954). In turn, algebraic systems and partial algebraic systems can be represented by models (Malcev, 1970). Heterogeneous models, i.e., models defined on systems of sets or on specific named sets were studied in (Schmidt, 1938; 1951; Malcev, 1959).

It is necessary to remark that transition from a set to a named set as a basic structure goes on not only for algebra but for other fields (cf. (Burgin, 1990; 2004)). Thus, in many cases fibers, which are special cases of topological named sets, replace topological spaces in topology. Multivalued and multi-sorted logics are becoming more and more popular in logic. Manifolds are used instead of Euclidean spaces in mathematical analysis. Modern combinatorics is built on multisets, which are special cases of named sets.

Finite automata and state machines are directly connected to heterogeneous algebras. A specific heterogeneous algebra Al(A) is corresponded to a deterministic finite automaton A in the following way. This algebra Al(A) has the support $\{ \Sigma, Q, \Omega \}$, two binary operations δ:

$\Sigma \times Q \to Q$, and σ: $\Sigma \times Q \to \Omega$, and several unary operations $\sigma_0, \sigma_1, \dots, \sigma_k$ on the set Q: $\sigma_0 = q_0, \sigma_1 = q_1, \dots, \sigma_k = q_k$ with $q_1, \dots, q_k \in F$.

In addition to the algebra Al(A), another heterogeneous algebra EAl(A) is also corresponded to the automaton A. This algebra EAl(A) has the support $\{ \Sigma^*, Q, \Omega^* \}$ where Σ^* and Ω^* are the sets of all finite words in the alphabets Σ and Ω, correspondingly. Operations of EAl(A) consist of two binary operations δ^*: $\Sigma^* \times Q \to Q$, and σ^*: $\Sigma^* \times Q \to \Omega^*$, and several unary operations $\sigma_0, \sigma_1, \dots, \sigma_k$ on the set Q where $\sigma_0 = q_0, \sigma_1 = q_1, \dots, \sigma_k = q_k$ with $q_1,\dots,q_k \in F$.

Usually, if an automaton A represents a program, then a state of A is a set of states of the program variables. Inputs for programs are also collections of data. Consequently, we come to the conclusion that Al(A) and EAl(A) have operations with arity higher than two.

The same constructions allow one to correspond to a nondeterministic finite automaton B an algebraic system in the sense of Malcev (1970). This system is not a (universal) algebra in a general case. Here for simplicity, we consider only deterministic automata. However, it is possible to extend the main constructions and results to the nondeterministic case.

Definition 8.13. The program P is *strictly* A-*correct* (FA-*correct*) if the automata Aw(P) and Ac(P) are (finite and) equal as heterogeneous algebras (algebraic systems).

The assumption that automata Aw(P) and Ac(P) are finite allows us to solve the problem of program verification because it is possible to check if two finite heterogeneous algebras are equal.

Theorem 8.3. The property of program strict FA-correctness is decidable.

Informally, it means that in contrast to results of Theorems 8.1 and 8.2 it is possible to build a software system such that it verifies strict program correctness for all programs.

Applying the algebraic approach, we use another popular kind of equivalence of algebraic systems, which is called isomorphism (Cohn, 1965; Kurosh, 1974).

Definition 8.14. The program P *is isomorphically* A-*correct* (FA-*correct*) if (the automata Aw(P) and Ac(P) are finite and) the algebras Al(Aw(P)) and Al(Ac(P)) of the automata Aw(P) and Ac(P) are isomorphic as heterogeneous algebras (algebraic systems).

It is possible to demand validity of a weaker condition in a definition of correctness.

Let us assume that all states of the automata Aw(P) and Ac(P) representing programs from a class **P** are distinguishable.

Theorem 8.4. The property of program isomorphic FA-correctness is decidable for the class **P**.

Indeed, if we take two finite heterogeneous algebras, there is only a finite number of mapping between them. Utilizing properties of universal algebras (cf. Kurosh, 1974), it is possible to build an algorithm that checks if any of these mapping is an isomorphism. In such a way, we can algorithmically find whether two finite heterogeneous algebras are isomorphic or not.

Corollary 8.3. If a program is equivalent as algorithm to a finite automaton, then its correctness is decidable.

Having different types of program correctness, it is possible to compare them by their verification power. This idea is formalized in the following definition.

Let us consider two types X and Z of program correctness.

Definition 8.15. X-correctness is stronger than Z-correctness if for any program P, X-correctness implies Z-correctness.

Definitions 8.13, 8.14, and15 imply the following result.

Proposition 8.1. The strict A-correctness (FA-correctness) is stronger than isomorphic A-correctness (FA-correctness).

Remark 8.1. However, if we restrict the class of possible verificators only to programs that are equivalent to finite automata, then verification becomes once more impossible. In other words, the verifying program has to be more powerful than a finite automaton.

We can apply theoretical results on problem solvability not only to software, but also to hardware, utilizing general results from computer science. A general assumption in computer science is that any general purpose computer is equivalent to a universal Turing machine (e.g., (Hopcroft *et al*, 2001)). This makes it possible to apply Theorem 8.1 to hardware and get the following statement.

Theorem 8.7. It is impossible to create a software system *V* written in a general programming language **L** such that *V* verifies for all programs whether a given program computes on a general purpose computer a given partial recursive function.

Taking some system of operations, it is possible to consider all possible computers with these operations. In this context, it is impossible to find if an arbitrary computing device is equivalent by its functions to a general purpose computer.

Theorem 8.8. It is impossible to create a software system *V* written in a general programming language **L** such that *V* verifies for all possible computers whether a given computer is a general purpose computer.

Definition 8.16. (Wikipedia) A programming language is called *Turing-complete* if it is potentially equivalent in power to the class of all Turing machines.

In a similar way, taking some system of operators, it is possible to consider all possible programming languages with these operators.

Theorem 8.9. It is impossible to create a software system *V* written in a general programming language **L** such that *V* verifies all possible programming languages whether a given programming language **C** is a Turing complete.

9 Conclusion

We explored some basic properties of the theory of algorithms and computation. In doing so, we developed an axiomatic setting for this theory. In contrast to the traditional global axiomatization prevalent in mathematics and local axiomatization developed in computer science for theory of programs, we utilize multiglobal axiomatization aimed at study of diverse classes of algorithms and automata. This axiomatization is based on postulates, axioms, and formal conditions. Postulates represent the most basic properties of algorithmic classes. Axioms describe various essential peculiarities, while conditions reflect specific features used for derivation more important and deep traits of algorithms and computation.

It is necessary to remark that there are many definitions in this paper. These definitions are not merely formal constructions their goal is structuring, organizing, and modeling the computational reality and practice for better understanding and development. Such basic definition that are given for fundamental concepts such as algorithm, procedure, and automaton form the content of computer science and artificial intelligence as scientific disciplines.

The same is true for classifications, which also structure, organize, and model the computational reality and practice for better understanding and development. According to the modern methodology of science, classifications are specific laws of science (Burgin and Kuznetsov, 1994).

Results comparing different modes of functioning and power of classes of algorithms, programs and computers are proved under very general axioms or conditions. This makes possible to apply these results to a vast variety of types and kinds of algorithms and their models. Such models may be structurally distinct like Turing machines and partial recursive functions. They may be defined by some restrictions inside the same class of models, e.g., polynomial time Turing machines, polynomial space Turing machines, and logarithmic time Turing machines. In its turn, comparing different models allows one to obtain relations between corresponding types of computers and software systems. For example, deterministic Turing machines model conventional computers, while nondeterministic Turing machines model quantum computers. As a result, properties of deterministic Turing machines reflect properties of conventional computers, while properties of nondeterministic Turing machines reflect properties of quantum computers.

In addition, axiomatic approach allows one to obtain automatically many classical results of the conventional computability, which are considered in many textbooks and monographs (cf., for example, Manna, 1974; Davis and Weyuker, 1983; Hopcroft *et al*, 2001; Rogers, 1987). Axiomatic setting is also very appropriate for the development of theory of complexity of algorithms and computation (Burgin, 1992), as well as software metrics design (Prather, 1984).

An important peculiarity of the axiomatic theory of algorithms and computation is that now its development has become more urgent than in the first period of the algorithm theory development. The main feature of the first period of the algorithm theory development was belief of the vast majority of computer scientists and mathematicians in the, so-called, Church-Turing Thesis. In one of its forms, the Thesis claims that *any problem that can be solved by an algorithm can be solved by some Turing machine and any algorithmic computation can be done by some Turing machine***.** Most of what we understand about algorithms and their limitations is based on our understanding of Turing machines and other conventional models of algorithms. The Church-Turing Thesis claims that Turing machines give a full understanding of computer possibilities. However, in spite of this Thesis, conventional models of algorithms, such as Turing machines, do not give a relevant representation of a notion of algorithm. That is why an extension of conventional models has been developed. This extension is based on the following observation. The main stereotype for algorithms states that an algorithm has to stop when it gives a result. This is the main problem that hinders the development of computers. When we understand that computation can go on but we can get what we need, then we go beyond our prejudices and immensely extend computing power.

The new models are called super-recursive algorithms. They provide for a much more computing power. This is proved mathematically for such super-recursive algorithms as inductive Turing machines (Burgin, 2003). At the same time, inductive Turing machines give more adequate models for modern computers and Internet (Burgin, 2003). These models change the essence of computation going beyond the Church-Turing Thesis and form, consequently, a base for a new computational paradigm, or metaphor as says Winograd. Problems that are unsolvable for conventional algorithmic devices become tractable for super-recursive algorithms. The new paradigm gives a better insight into the functioning of the mind, opening new perspectives for artificial intelligence.

As a result, an absolute class of algorithms disappeared and now computer scientists have to deal with a huge diversity of different classes, models, and kinds of algorithms and automata. Thus, methods that study different classes (such as multiglobal axiomatization) are more efficient than any technique (such as constructive approach or global axiomatization) that studies only one class of algorithms, even if this class is so useful and popular as the class of all Turing machines.

Being applied to program correctness, theoretical results of this paper show that, on one hand, it is impossible to find an algorithm or build a program that verifies correctness of all programs in some Turing-complete programming language. On the other hand, when a program and its specification are represented by appropriate models, such as, for example, finite automata, then it is possible to verify its correctness.

It is also necessary to remark that programs realizing inductive computations can do much more than programs realizing recursive computations (Burgin, 2001; 2003). As a consequence, it is possible to build programs that work in the inductive mode and verify correctness of much larger classes of programs than recursive verifiers. In addition, inductive verifiers can check correctness in a stronger sense.

To conclude, we formulate some open problems of the axiomatic theory of algorithms and computation.

Problem 1. What undecidability results from Section 7 is it possible to prove, utilizing the Local Universality Axiom **LAU** instead of the Universality Axiom **AU**?

Local Universality Axiom LAU. For any finite number of algorithms/automata A_1 , A_2 , … , A_n from **K** there is some coding $\mathbf{c} : \mathbf{K} \to V^+$, there is a subclass **H** of **K** such that all A_1 , A_2 , … , A_n belong to **H** and **H** satisfies the Universality Axiom **AU**.

Problem 2. What other classes of algorithms/automata, besides classes of all recursive algorithms, such as Turing machines, satisfy the Universality Axiom **AU**?

Problem 3. Characterize all those operational (performance, descriptive) properties that are decidable in the class **T** of all Turing machines.

Problem 4. What axiomatic classes of algorithms/automata have the fixed point property (cf., (Rogers, 1987))?

Problem 5. Study computable and decidable languages (sets) in axiomatic classes of algorithms/automata.

Problem 6. Study complexity of algorithms and computations in axiomatic classes of algorithms/automata.

Problem 7. Study dual complexity measures (Burgin, 1982) of algorithms and computations in axiomatic classes of algorithms/automata.

References

[1] Abramson, F.G. (1971) Effective Computation over the Real Numbers, *12th Annual Symposium on Switching and Automata Theory*, Northridge, Calif.: Institute of Electrical and Electronics Engineers

[2] Adamék, J. (1975) Automata and categories, finiteness contra minimality, *Lecture Notes in Computer Science*, **32**, Springer Verlag, Berlin/Heidelberg/ New York, pp. 160-166

[3] Adámek, J. and Trnková, V. (1990) *Automata and Algebras in Categories*, Kluwer Academic PublishersBarrett, E., ed. *Text, Context and Hypertext: Writing with and for the Computer*, Cambridge: MIT Press

[4] Adleman, L., and Blum, M. (1991) Inductive Inference and Unsolvability, *Journal of Symbolic Logic*, v. 56, No. 3, pp. 891-900

[5] Alt, F.L. (1997) End-Running Human Intelligence, in "*Beyond Calculation: The Next Fifty Years of Computing*", Copernicus, pp. 127-134

[6] Barrett, E., ed. *Text, Context and Hypertext: Writing with and for the Computer*, MIT Press, Cambridge, 1988

[7] Beniaminov, E.M. (1988) An Algebraic Approach to Models of Databases, *Semiotics and Informatics*, v. 14, 1979, pp. 44-80

[8] Birkhoff, G. and Lipson, J.D. Heterogeneous algebras, *J. Combinatorial Theory*, **8**, 1970, 115-133.

[9] Black, R. (2000) Proving Church's Thesis, *Philos. Math.,* v. 8, No. 3, pp. 244-258

[10] Blum, L., Cucker, F., Shub, M., and Smale, S. *Complexity of Real Computation*, Springer, New York, 1998

[11] Blum M. (1967) On the Size of Machines, *Information and Control*, v. 11, pp. 257-265

[12]Blum M. (1967a) A Machine-independent Theory of Complexity of Recursive Functions, *Journal of the ACM*, v. 14, No.2, pp. 322-336

[13]Bournez, O., Cucker, F., de Naurois, P.J. and Marion, J.-Y. (2003) Computability over an Arbitrary Structure. Sequential and Parallel Polynomial Time, in *Foundations of Software Science and Computation Structures - FOSSACS'03, Warsaw, Poland,* Lecture Notes in Computer Science, 2620, Springer, pp. 185-199

[14]Büchi, J.R. (1960) Weak second order arithmetic and finite automata, *Z. Math. Logic and Grudl. Math.*, v. 6, No. 1, pp. 66-92

[15] Budach, L. and Hoehnke, H.-J. (1975) *Automata und Funktoren*, Akademic Verlag, Berlin

[16] Burgin, M. S. (1982) Generalized Kolmogorov complexity and duality in theory of computations , *Notices of the Academy of Sciences of the USSR*, v. 264, No. 2, pp. 19-23 (translated from Russian, v. 25, No. 3)

[17] Burgin, M. (1982a) Products of operators of multidimensional structured model of systems, *Mathematical Social Sciences*, No.2, pp. 335-343

[18] Burgin, M. S. (1983) Inductive Turing Machines, *Notices of the Academy of Sciences of the USSR*, v. 270, No. 6, pp. 1289-1293 (translated from Russian, v. 27, No. 3)

[19] Burgin, M. S. (1983a) Multiple computations and Kolmogorov complexity for such processes, *Notices of the Academy of Sciences of the USSR*, v. 269, No. 4 , pp. 793-797 (translated from Russian, v. 27, No. 2)

[20] Burgin, M. (1984) Systems and properties, *Abstracts presented to the American Mathematical Society*, v.5, No.6

[21] Burgin, M. S. (1985) Algorithms and Algorithmic Problems, *Programming*, No. 4, pp. 3-14 (*Programming and Computer Software*, v. 11, No. 4) (translated from Russian)

[22]Burgin M.S. (1990) Theory of Named Sets as a Foundational Basis for Mathematics, in "*Structures in Mathematical Theories*", San Sebastian, pp. 417-420

[23]Burgin, M.S. (1992) Complexity measures in the axiomatic theory of algorithms, in *Methods of design of applied intellectual program systems*, Kiev, pp. 60-67 (in Russian)

[24] Burgin M.S. *Fundamental Structures of Knowledge and Information*, Ukrainian Academy of Information Sciences, Kiev, 1997 (in Russian)

[25] Burgin, M. *On the Essence and Nature of Mathematics*, Ukrainian Academy of Information Sciences, Kiev, 1998 (in Russian)

[26] Burgin, M. (2001) How We Know What Technology Can Do, *Communications of the ACM*, v. 44, No. 11, pp. 82-88

[27]Burgin, M. (2003) Nonlinear Phenomena in Spaces of Algorithms, *International Journal of Computer Mathematics*, v. 80, No. 12, pp. 1449-1476

[28]Burgin M. (2004) Algorithmic Complexity of Recursive and Inductive Algorithms, *Theoretical Computer Science*, v. 317, No. 1/3, 2004, pp. 31-60

[29]Burgin, M. *Unified Foundations of Mathematics*, Preprint Mathematics LO/0403186, 2004 (electronic edition: http://arXiv.org)

[30]Burgin, M. and Debnath, N.C. (2003) Complexity of Algorithms and Software Metrics, in Proc. ISCA 18th Int. Conf. "*Computers and their Applications*", Honolulu, pp. 259-262

[31] Burgin, M. and Greibach, S. (2002) Abstract Automata as a Tool for Developing Simulation Software, in "*Proceedings of the Business and Industry Simulation Symposium*," Society for Modeling and Simulation International, San Diego, California, pp. 176-180

[32] Burgin, M. and Karasik, A. (1975) A study of an abstract model of computers, *Programming and Computer Software*, No. **1**, pp. 72-82

[33] Burgin, M. and Kuznetsov, V. (1994) *Introduction to the Modern Exact Methodology of Science*, International Science Foundation, Moscow (in Russian)

[34] Burgin, M., Liu, D., and Karplus, W. (2001) The Problem of Time Scales in Computer Visualization, in "*Computational Science*", Lecture Notes in Computer Science, v. 2074, part II, pp.728-737

[35] Burgin, M., Liu, D., and Karplus, W. (2001a) *Visualization in Human-Computer Interaction*, UCLA, Computer Science Department, Report CSD – 010010, Los Angeles, July, 2001, 108 p.

[36] Burgin, M. and Tandon A. (2003) Software Verification in Algebraic Setting, in Proceedings of the 7th *IASTED International Conference on Software Engineering and Applications*, Marina Del Rey, California, pp. 499-504

[37] Burton, D.M. *The History of Mathematics*, The McGrow Hill Co., New York, 1997

[38] Buss, S.L., Kechris, A.S., Pillay, A., and Shore, R.A. (2001) The prospects for Mathematical Logic in the Twenty First Century, *Bulletin of Symbolic Logic*, v. &, No. **2**, pp.169-196

[39] Church, A. (1957) Application of Recursive Arithmetic to the Problem of Circuit Synthesis, in "*Summaries of Talks presented at the Summer Institute of Symbolic Logic at Cornell University*," **1**, pp. 3-50

[40] Cleland, C.E. (2001) Recipes, Algorithms, and Programs, *Minds and Machines*, v. 11, pp. 219-237

[41] Cohn, P.M. *Universal algebra*, New York/ Evanston/London, Harper & Row, 1965

[42] Colburn, T.R., Fetzer, J.H., and Rankin, T.L. (Eds.) *Program Verification*, Kluwer Academic Publishers, Dordrecht, 1993

[43]Davis, M. *Computability and Unsolvability*, Dover, New York, 1982

[44]Ercegovac, M.D. and Lang, T. *Digital Arithmetic*, Academic Publishing Services, UCLA, Los Angeles, 2002

[45]Feferman, S. (1992) A new approach to abstract data types, II. Computability on ADTs as ordinary computation, in *Computer Science Logic,* Lecture Notes in Computer Science vol. 626, pp. 79-95

[46]Feferman, S. (1993) Working foundations - `91, in *Bridging the Gap: Philosophy, Mathematics and Physics,* Boston Studies in the Philos. of Science, Kluwer, Dordrecht, vol. 140, pp. 99-124

[47]Feferman, S. (1993a) What rests on what? The proof-theoretic analysis of mathematics, in *Philosophy of Mathematics*, Proceedings of the 15th International Wittgenstein Symposium, Verlag Hölder-Pichler-Tempsky, Vienna, Part I, pp. 147-171

[48]Feferman, S. (1996) Computation on abstract data types. The extensional approach, with an application to streams, *Annals of Pure and Applied Logic*, 81, pp. 75-113

[49]Fischer, P.C. (1965) Multi-tape and infinite-state automata, *Communications of the ACM*, v. 8, No. 12, pp. 799-805

[50] Floyd, R.W. (1967) Assigning meanings to programs, *Mathematical Aspects of Computer Science, 19th Symp. of Appl. Math., AMS*, Providence, Rhode Island, 19-32.

[51] Fraenkel, A.A. and Bar-Hillel, Y. *Foundations of Set Theory*, North Holland P.C., Amsterdam, 1958

[52] Friedman H., and Hirst, J. (1990) Weak comparability of well orderings and reverse mathematics, *Annals of Pure and Applied Logic*, v. 47, pp. 11-29.

[53] Giusto, M. and Simpson, S. G. (2000) Located Sets and Reverse Mathematics. *The Journal of Symbolic Logic*, v. 65, No. 3, pp. 1451-1480

[54] Glushkov, V.M., Zeitlin, G.E., and Yushchenko, E.L. *Algebra, Languages, Programming*, Kiev, Naukova Dumka, 1974 (in Russian)

[55] Gödel, K (1931) Über formal unentscheidbare Sätze der Principia Mathematics und verwandter System I, *Monatshefte für Mathematik und Physik*, **b. 38**, s.173-198

[56]Goldin, D. and Wegner, P. *Persistent Turing Machines*, Brown University Technical Report, 1988

[57]Gurevich, Y. (1994) Evolving Algebras, in "*IFIP 1994 World Computer Congress, Volume I: Technology and Foundations,*" Elsevier, Amsterdam, pp. 423-427.

[58]Halmos, P.R. *Algebraic Logic*, New York, 1962

[59] Hamkins, J.D., and Lewis, A. (2000) Infinite time Turing machines, *Journal of Symbolic Logic*, v. 65, No. 3, pp. 567-604

[60] Higgins, P.J. (1963) Algebras with a scheme of operators, *Math. Nachrichten*, v. 27, No. 1-2, pp. 115-132

[61] Higgins, P.J. *Grupoids and categories*, North-Holland, 1973

[62] Hoare, C.A.R. (1969) An Axiomatic Basis for Computer Programming, *Communications of ACM*, v. 12, pp. 576-580, 583

[63] Hoare, C.A.R. and Wirth, N. (1973) An Axiomatic Definition of the Programming Language PASCAL, *Acta Informatica*, v. 2, pp. 335-355

[64] Hopcroft, J.E., Motwani, R., and Ullman, J.D. *Introduction to Automata Theory, Languages, and Computation*, Addison Wesley, Boston/San Francisco/New York, 2001

[65] Humby, E. *Programs from Decision Tables*, MacDonald, London, 1973

[66] Hune, T.S. and Sandholm, A.B. (2000) *Using Automata in Control Synthesis - A Case Study*, in Fundamental Approaches to Software Engineering, LNCS 1783, pp. 349-362

[67] Karpunin, G. A. and Shaposhnikov, I. G. (2000) Crossed homomorphisms of finite multibase universal algebras with binary operations, Discrete Math. Appl. v. 10, no. 2, pp. 183-202

[68] Kleene, S. (1956) Representation of events in nerve nets, *Automata Studies*, Princeton University Press, Princeton, N.J. pp. 3-41

[69] Knuth, D. *The Art of Computer Programming*, v.2: *Seminumerical Algorithms*, Addison-Wesley, 1981

[70] Kogge, P. *The Architecture of Pipeline Computers*, McGraw Hill, 1981

[71] Kolmogorov, A.N. (1953) On the Concept of Algorithm, *Russian Mathematical Surveys*, v. 8, No. 4, pp. 175-176

[72]Krinitsky, N.A. *Algorithms around us*, Moscow, Nauka, 1977 (in Russian)

[73]Kurosh, A.G. General algebra, Moscow, Nauka Press, 1974 (in Russian)

[74]Landow, G. *Hypertext: The Convergence of Contemporary Critical Theory and Technology*, Baltimare: Johns Hopkins University Press, 1992

[75]Leblanc, L. (1962) Nonhomogeniuos Polyadic Algebras, *Proc. American Mathematical Society*, v. 13, No. 1, pp. 59-65

[76]Lewis, J.P. (2001) Limits to Software Estimation, *Software Engineering Notes*, v. 26, No. 4, pp.54-59

[77]Li, M., and Vitanyi, P. *An Introduction to Kolmogorov Complexity and its Applications*, Springer-Verlag, New York, 1997

[78]Loeckx, J., Sieber, K. and Stansifer, R.D. *The foundations of program verification*, John Wiley & Sons, Inc. New York, 1985

[79]Malcev, A.I. (1954) To a general theory of algebraic systems, *Mat. Sbornik*, v. 35, No. 1, pp. 3-20

[80]Malcev, A.I. (1959) Model correspondences, *Izvestiya of the Academy of Sciences of the USSR*, v. 23, No. 3, pp. 313-336

[81]Malcev, A.I. *Algebraic systems*, Moscow, Nauka, 1970 (in Russian)

[82]Manna, Z. and Pnueli, A. *Specification and Verification of Concurrent Programs by ∀-Automata*, Computer Science Department, Stanford University, Computer Science Department, Weizmann Institute of Science, 1986

[83]Mathienssen, G. (1978) A heterogeneous algebraic approach to some problems in automata theory, many-valued logics and other topics, *Contr. to General Algebra*, Proc. Klagenfurt Conf., pp. 193-211

[84]Mealy, G.H. (1953) A method for synthesizing sequential circuits, *Bell System Techn. J.*, v. 34, pp. 1045-1079

[85] Meyer, A. R. and Halpern, J.Y. (1980) Axiomatic definitions of programming languages: a theoretical assessment, Proceedings of the 7th ACM SIGPLAN-SIGACT symposium on Principles of programming languages, Las Vegas, Nevada, pp. 203 - 212

[86]Milner, M. *Communication and concurrency*, Prentice Hall, New York/London/Toronto, 1989

[87]Moore, E.F. (1956) Gedanken-experiments on sequential machines, in *Automata Studies*, Princeton University Press, Princeton, N.J. pp. 129-153

[88]Moore, C. (1996) Recursion Theory on the Reals and Continuous-time Computation: Real numbers and computers, *Theoretical Computer Science*, **162**, No. 1, pp. 23-44

[89]Moschovakis, Ya. (2001) What is an Algorithm?, in "*Mathematics Unlimited*: 2001 *and Beyond*", Springer, New York

[90]Ollongren, A. *Definition of programming languages by interpreting automata*, Academic Press, New York/London, 1974

[91]Naur, P. (1966) Proofs of algorithms by general snapshots, *BIT*, v. 6, pp. 310-316.

[92]von Neumann, J. (1951) The general and logical theory of automata. in "*Cerebral Mechanisms in Behavior*," The Hixon Symposium, Willey , New York, pp. 1-31

[93]Nielsen, J. *Hypertext and hypermedia*, New York: Academic Press, 1990

[94]Plotkin B.I. *Universal Algebra, Algebraic Logic, and Databases*, Moscow, Nauka, 1991 (in Russian)

[95]Prather, R.E. (1984) An axiomatic theory of software complexity research, *The Computer Journal*, v. 27, pp. 340-346

[96]Rabin, M.O. (1969) Decidability of Second-order Theories and Automata on Infinite Trees, *Transactions of the AMS*, v. 141, pp. 1-35

[97]Rabin, M.O., and Scott, D. (1959) Finite Automata and Their Decision Problems, *IBM Journal of Research and Development*, v. 3, pp. 114-125

[98]Rice, H.G. (1951) Recursive Real Numbers, *Proceedings of the AMS*, v. 5, pp. 784-791

[99]Rice, H. G. (1953) Classes of Recursively Enumerable Sets and Their Decision Problems, *Trans. Amer. Math. Soc.*, v. 74, pp. 358-366

[100] Rogers, H. *Theory of Recursive Functions and Effective Computability*, MIT Press, Cambridge, Massachusetts, 1987

[101] Russel, S.J. and Norvig, P. *Artificial Intelligence: A Modern Approach*, Prentice-Hall, Englewood Cliffs, N.J., 1995

[102] Schmidt, A. (1938) Über deductive Theorien mit mehreren Sorten von Grunddingen, *Math. Ann.*, b. 115, s. 485-506

[103] Schmidt, A. (1951) Die Zulässigkeit der Behandlung mehrsortigen Theorien mittels der üblichen einsortigen Prädikatenlogic, *Math. Ann.*, b. 123, s. 187-200

[104] Shannon, C. (1941) Mathematical Theory of the Differential Analyzer, *J. Math. Physics*, MIT, v. 20, pp. 337-354

[105] Shaposhnikov, I. G. (1999) Congruences of finite multibase universal algebras, *Discrete Math. Appl.* **9,** no. 4, pp. 403-418

[106] Sipser, M. *Introduction to the Theory of Computation*, PWS Publishing C., Boston, 1997

[107] Staiger, L. (1997) ω-Languages, in *Handbook of Formal Languages,* Vol. 3: *Beyond Words,* Chapter 6, Springer-Verlag, Berlin, pp. 339-387

[108] Suppes, P., and Han B. (2000) Brain-wave representation of words by superposition of a few sine waves. *Proceedings of the National Academy of Sciences*, v. 97, pp. 8738-8743

[109] Schwartz, R. *An axiomatic semantic definition of Algol 68*, UCLA-ENG-7838, LOS Angeles, California, 1978

[110] Thomas, W. (1990) Automata on infinite objects, in: J. van Leeuwen (Ed.), *Handbook of Theoretical Computer Science,* Vol. B: *Models and Semantics,* Elsevier Science Publishers, Amsterdam, pp. 135-191.

[111] Trahtenbrot, B.A. and Barzdin, J.M. *Finite Automata: Behavior and Synthesis*, Moscow, Nauka, 1970 (in Russian)

[112] Tucker, J.V. and Zukker, J.I. (1988) *Program Correctness over Abstract Data Types*, CWI Monographs, v. 6, North Holland

[113] Tucker, J.V. and Zukker, J.I. (1992) Deterministic and Nondeterministic Computation and Horn Programs on Abstract Data Types, *Journal Logic Prog.*, v. 13, pp. 23-55

[114] Tucker, J.V. and Zukker, J.I. (2002) Abstract Computability and Algebraic Specification, *ACM Transactions on Computational Logic*, v. 3, No.2, pp. 279-333

[115] Turing, A. (1936) On Computable Numbers with an Application to the Entscheidungs-problem, *Proc. Lond. Math. Soc.*, Ser.2, v. 42, pp. 230-265

[116] Van Leeuwen, J. and Wiedermann, J. (1985) Array Processing Machines, in Fundametals of Computation Theory, *Lecture Notes in Computer Science*, 199, Springer-Verlag, New York/Berlin, pp. 99-113

[117] Van Leeuwen, J. and Wiedermann J. *A computational model of interaction*, Techn. Rep. Dept. of Computer Science, Utrecht University, Utrecht, 2000

[118] Van Leeuwen, J. and Wiedermann, J. (2000b) On the Power of Interactive Computing, *Proceedings of the IFIP Theoretical Computer Science* 2000, pp. 619-623

[119] Vardi, M.Y. and Wolper P. (1986) An automata-theoretic approach to automatic program verification, in *Proceedings of the 1st Annual Symposium on Logic in Computer Science*, pp. 322-331

[120] Vardi, M.Y. and Wolper, P. (1994) Reasoning about Infinite Computations, *Information and Computation*, v. 115, No.1, pp. 1—37

[121] Voas, J.M. and Miller, K.W. (1995) Software Testability: The New Verification, *IEEE Software,* v. 12, No. 3, pp. 17-28

[122] Wakerly, J.F. *Digital Design Principles and Practices*, Prentice Hall, New Jersey, 2001

[123] Wegner, P. (1972) The Vienna Definition Language, *ACM Computing Surveys*, v. 4, No. 1, pp. 5-63.

[124] Wegner, P. (1998) Interactive Foundations of Computing. Theoretical aspects of coordination languages. *Theoretical Computer Science*, v. 192, no. 2, pp. 315-351

[125] Wikipedia, http://en.wikipedia.org/wiki/Turing-complete

In: Artificial Intelligence and Computer Science
Editor: Susan Shannon, pp. 63-86
ISBN 1-59454-411-5

Chapter 2

DISTRIBUTED, ASYNCHRONOUS ALGORITHMS FOR DATA NETWORKS CONTROL - A STATE OF THE ART REVIEW

*Andrzej Karbowski**
NASK (Research and Academic Computer Network)
and
Institute of Control and Computation Engineering,
Warsaw University of Technology,
Warsaw, Poland,

Abstract

The paper reviews current algorithms for distributed, asynchronous control of data networks. Different problem formulations are considered: from the simplest shortest-path approach, without Quality of Service (QoS) constraints, via total flow cost minimization for given traffic quality equations, until dynamic flow control with influencing users through transmission prices. These different formulations are presented in a unified way and compared from the possible application area point of view.

1 Introduction

The rapid expansion of the Internet changes not only the everyday life, but also the assessment of many scientific achievements. In the area of optimization and control one of the most important effects is the growing importance of decentralized optimization algorithms. Especially their asynchronous versions catch great attention of scientists dealing with efficient mechanisms of management and control of networks. It is due to the flexibility and scalability of asynchronous algorithms. In such algorithms, the computing nodes may use

*E-mail address: A.Karbowski@ia.pw.edu.pl

outdated information and communicate with each other at different, random times, but this does not destroy the convergence. Moreover, the situation in networks, for example traffic in data networks, changes dynamically. Asynchronous algorithms, using always the latest information, which is measured in the neighbourhood of the computing nodes, lead the network towards the current optimum. Nowadays, for such a big and nonhomogenous network as Internet, it is even difficult to imagine an effective optimization mechanism that would not be distributed and asynchronous!

The paper reviews current algorithms for distributed, asynchronous control of data networks. Different problem formulations are considered: from the simplest shortest-path approach, without Quality of Service (QoS) constraints, via total flow cost minimization for given traffic quality equations, until dynamic flow control with influencing users' transmission rates through internal prices.

These different formulations are presented in a unified way, both from the notation and the background mathematical theory point of view. Especially the unification of the notation was not a trivial task and in some cases to preserve it the author had to depart quite far from the notation in the original works.

At the end, the possibilities of application of these mechanisms by Internet providers to traffic control in different QoS networks are analyzed.

2 Simple Routing in Computer Networks

2.1 Classical Bellman-Ford Routing Algorithm

We consider a directed graph consisting of n nodes (routers). Let us denote by N the set of all these nodes, by A the set of all arcs (that is, the set of all links in the network) and by N_i the set of neighbours of the i-th node (that is, the set of all nodes from the set N, to which arcs starting from i go). Let us assume, that every arc $(i,j) \in A$ is characterized by a positive scalar value a_{ij}, which we will treat as the cost of passage from i to j, that is the distance measure (metric).

Let us choose a node $m \in N$ and assume, that it may be reached from all other nodes. It can be easily proved (e.g., by the contradiction), that the paths of the minimum costs $\hat{d}_{im}$ (so-called shortest paths) can be obtained through the solution of the following set of equations:

$$\hat{d}_{im} = \min_{j \in N_i} \left(a_{ij} + \hat{d}_{jm} \right) \quad i \neq m \tag{1}$$

Let us take now

$$h_{im}(d) = \begin{cases} \min\limits_{j \in N_i} (a_{ij} + d_{jm}) & i \neq m \\ 0 & i = m \end{cases} \tag{2}$$

and

$$d = [d_{11}, d_{12}, d_{13}, \ldots, d_{1n}, d_{21}, d_{22}, \ldots, d_{2n}, d_{n1}, d_{n2}, \ldots, d_{nn}] \tag{3}$$

$$h_i(d) = [h_{i1}(d), h_{i2}(d), \ldots, h_{in}(d)] \tag{4}$$

$$h = [h_1, h_2, \ldots, h_n] \tag{5}$$

To find the solution we may apply the Bellman-Ford algorithm

$$d := h(d) \tag{6}$$

starting from $d_{ii} = 0$; $d_{ij} = \infty, i \neq j$. This algorithm is based on the order preserving (monotone) mapping h, which may be implemented in a distributed, totally asynchronous version [9].

The optimization algorithm (1)-(6) may be applied repetitively - to adapt routing to the current situation in a network. In that case the cost a_{ij} should be a measure of the quality of transmission, dependent on the current flow (transmission rate) f_{ij} between nodes i and j. A very popular flow cost function $a_{ij}(.)$ is:

$$a_{ij}(f_{ij}) = \frac{f_{ij}}{(c_{ij} - f_{ij}) + \varepsilon_{ij}} + d_{ij} \cdot f_{ij} \tag{7}$$

where c_{ij} is the transmission capacity of arc (i, j) and d_{ij} is the processing and propagation delay (of course we assume $0 \leq f_{ij} \leq c_{ij}$; $\varepsilon_{ij} > 0$ is a small constant to avoid zero in the denominator). However, in this - adaptive - case one should remember, that the cost functions (7), dependent monotonically on flow, should be augmented with constant components δ_{ij} (so-called bias factors, interpreted as link costs/lengths at zero load), because otherwise oscillations (in subsequent optimal routings) may occur [7].

The presented adaptive routing approach is used in the Internet [10] in demons *routed*, *gated* and protocols RIP and Hello. In the first protocol so-called 'hop count metrics' is used, what means, that simply all elementary arcs are counted for; in the second 'network delay metrics', that is the time of transmission is taken into account. In the active state, all messages used to the optimization of the routing tables (i.e., the tables of the shortest path neighbours for different destinations) are sent by every computer to all direct neighbours every 30 seconds.

2.2 Generic Shortest Path Algorithm

The algorithm presented in the previous section may be treated as a special case from a more general class of algorithms.

We will present these algorithms to solve problems as formulated in the cited works. Hence, now we will be looking for the shortest paths from an origin to different destinations. These algorithms may be similarly applied to problems with multiple origins and a single destination, by reversing the roles of origins and destinations and the direction of each arc.

Let us take, that for each node $i \in N$ we want to find a path of minimum length (cost) that starts at node 1 and ends at i. We assume, that all arc lengths are positive and that there exists at least one path from node 1 to each other node.

The label correcting algorithms is a general class of algorithms to which belongs, among others, Bellman-Ford algorithm presented in Section 2.1. The name "label" refers to the

distance $d_i \triangleq d_{1i}$ from the origin node "1" to a node $i \neq 1$, the correction is its change in subsequent iterations of the algorithm leading towards the optimum. A notion of the candidate list of nodes is introduced. Let us denote it by V.
Assuming that V is nonempty, a typical iteration of a shortest path algorithm (not necessarily of label correcting type) is as follows [5]:

Initialization:

$$d_1 = 0, \;\; d_i = \infty \quad \text{for} \;\; i \neq 1$$

$$V = \{1\}$$

Typical Iteration of the Generic Shortest Path Algorithm:

Remove a node i from the candidate list V. For each outgoing arc $(i,j) \in A$, with $j \neq 1$, if $d_j > d_i + a_{ij}$, set:

$$d_j := d_i + a_{ij} \tag{8}$$

and add j to V if it does not already belong to V.

Different shortest path algorithms are distinguished by the method of selecting the node to exit the candidate list V at each iteration. For example, in Dijkstra method the node exiting V is the node which has the minimum label over V. This guarantees, that every node enters and exits V exactly once and its label is not changed in later iterations. Because of that, these methods are called label setting methods. Label correcting methods avoid the overhead associated with finding the minimum label node at the expense of multiple entrances of nodes into V. In these methods a queue Q is used to maintain the candidate list V. Bellman-Ford method is the simplest method from this family. In the terms of the above generic shortest path algorithm it maintains V in a FIFO queue Q: nodes are removed from the top of the queue and added at the bottom of Q. More sophisticated label correcting methods maintain V in one or in two queues (eg. in so-called threshold algorithms the candidate list is partitioned into two separate queues on the basis of some threshold parameter) and use more complex removal and insertion strategies. The objective is to reduce the number of node reentries in V. Some of these methods are significantly faster than Bellman-Ford method. The most effective proved to be SLF and SLF-LLL strategies.

2.3 SLF and LLL Strategies

In the SLF (Small Label First) method [8] the candidate list V is maintained as double ended queue Q. At each iteration, the node removed is the top node of Q. The rule for inserting new nodes is as follows:

Let i be the top node of Q, and j be a node that enters Q.
if $d_j \le d_i$, then enter j at the top of Q;
else, enter j at the bottom of Q.

The LLL (Large Label Last) method [8] defines a more complicated strategy of removal a node from Q, which aims to remove from Q nodes with small labels. At each iteration, when the node at the top of Q has a larger label than the average node label in Q (defined as the sum of the labels of the nodes in Q divided by the cardinality $\overline{\overline{Q}}$ of Q), this node is not removed from Q, but rather it is repositioned to the bottom of Q. It may be described as follows:

Let i be the top node of Q, and let $\theta = \sum_{j \in Q} d_j / \overline{\overline{Q}}$.
if $d_i > \theta$, then move i to the bottom of Q.
Repeat until a node i such that $d_i \le \theta$ is found and is removed from Q.

It is possible to combine the SLF queue insertion and the LLL node selection strategies. The resulting method is denoted by SLF-LLL. The proof of convergence of these two algorithms closely resembles the proof of the convergence of Bellman-Ford algorithm and is based on the monotonicity property of the label modification mapping [8],[13].

In the parallel implementation, each processor removes the top node from Q (perhaps after some shifts of the queue in the case of LLL strategy), updates the labels of its adjacent nodes and adds these nodes (if necessary) into Q according to SLF insertion strategy. This means, that several nodes can be simultaneously removed from the candidate list and the labels of the adjacent nodes can be updated in parallel. In the distributed version an additional processor responsible for maintaining the candidate queue Q is useful. When the algorithm is implemented in an asynchronous version a new node may be removed from the candidate list by some processor while other processors are still updating the labels of other nodes. Of course, only one processor at a time can modify a given label. Hence, it is very easy to implement this method on a parallel shared-memory or NUMA machines using locks to assure the consistency of data. A multiple queues version of this algorithm showed very good features [8]. In this version each processor uses a separate queue (a node can reside in at most one queue). It extracts nodes from the top of its queue, updates the labels for adjacent nodes and uses a heuristic procedure for choosing the queue to insert a node that enters V. For example, it may be the one with the minimum current value of the sum of the outgoing arcs of nodes in that list. This heuristics is easy to implement and ensures good load balancing among the processors. For checking whether a node is present in the candidate list (that is, in some queue) it is suggested [8], [13] to associate with every node a Boolean variable, which is updated each time a node enters or exits a candidate list. This algorithm is easily generalized to the problem of finding several distinct shortest paths [13] showing in many problems very high efficiency.

Other label correcting methods (not so efficient in parallel tests), e.g. with a threshold dividing queues are presented in [8].

2.4 Auction Algorithm

A more efficient alternative to the presented algorithms seem to be auction algorithms. In the basic version [4], [19] the algorithm maintains a path starting at the origin s and a price for each node. The terminal node of the path "bids" for neighboring nodes basing on their prices and the lengths of the connecting arcs. At each iteration the path is either extended by adding a new node or contracted by deleting its terminal node. When the destination becomes the terminal node of the path, the algorithm terminates.

To present the algorithm in a formal way, let us denote by P a path starting at the origin, that is: $P = (s, i_1, i_2, \ldots, i_k)$, where $(i_m, i_{m+1}) \in A$, $m = 1, \ldots, k-1$. We assume that $i_{j_1} \neq i_{j_2}$, $j_1 \neq j_2$, that is a path does not contain any cycle. The node i_k is called the terminal node of P. The degenerate path $P = (s)$ may be also obtained in the course of the algorithm. If i_{k+1} is a node that does not belong to a path $P = (s, i_1, i_2, \ldots, i_k)$ and (i_k, i_{k+1}) is an arc, extending P by i_{k+1} means replacing P by the path $(s, i_1, i_2, \ldots, i_k, i_{k+1})$. If P does not consist of just the origin node s, contracting P means replacing P with the path $(s, i_1, i_2, \ldots, i_{k-1})$.

In addition to the path the algorithm maintains a price p_i for each node $i \in N$ in the network. Let us denote by p the vector of prices p_i. We say that a path-price pair (P, p) satisfies complementary slackness (CS) if the following relations hold:

$$p_i \leq a_{ij} + p_j, \ \forall (i,j) \in A \tag{9}$$

$$p_i = a_{ij} + p_j, \ \text{for all pairs of successive nodes } i \text{ and } j \text{ of } P \tag{10}$$

An important property is that if a path-price pair (P, p) satisfies CS, then portion of P between node s and any node $i \in P$ is a shortest path from s to i and $d_{si} = p_s - p_i$ is the corresponding shortest distance.

The algorithm proceeds in iterations, transforming a pair (P, p) satisfying CS into another pair satisfying CS. At each iteration the path P is either extended by a new node or else is contracted by deleting its terminal node. In the latter case the price of the terminal node is increased strictly. In may be described in the following way:

Typical iteration

Let i be the terminal node of P.

- Step 0: (Scanning of successor nodes) If

$$p_i < \min_{\{j|(i,j) \in A\}} \{a_{ij} + p_j\} \tag{11}$$

  go to Step 1; else go to Step 2.

- Step 1: (Contract path) Set

$$p_i := \min_{\{j|(i,j) \in A\}} \{a_{ij} + p_j\} \tag{12}$$

  and if $i \neq s$ contract P. Go to the next iteration.

- Step 2: (Extend path) Extend P by node j_i where

$$j_i = arg \min_{\{j|(i,j)\in A\}} \{a_{ij} + p_j\} \tag{13}$$

If j_i is the destination d, stop; P is the desired shortest path. Otherwise, go to the next iteration.

The algorithm starts with the default pair:

$$P = (s), \quad p_i = 0, \; \forall i$$

and stops when the destination node d becomes the terminal node of the path. This iteration is called the "forward algorithm". It is possible to apply also the "reverse algorithm", where not the source s, but the destination node d is fixed (and forms the initial path) and the path extends by inserting and contracts by deleting the starting node.

Typical iteration of the Reverse Algorithm

Let j be the starting node of P.

- Step 0: (Scanning of predecessor nodes) If

$$p_j > \max_{\{i|(i,j)\in A\}} \{p_i - a_{ij}\} \tag{14}$$

go to Step 1; else go to Step 2.

- Step 1: (Contract path) Set

$$p_j := \max_{\{i|(i,j)\in A\}} \{p_i - a_{ij}\} \tag{15}$$

and if $j \neq d$, contract P, that is delete j from P. Go to the next iteration.

- Step 2: (Extend path) Extend P by node i_j where

$$i_j = arg \max_{\{i|(i,j)\in A\}} \{p_i - a_{ij}\} \tag{16}$$

that is add i_j as the starting node of P. If i_j is the origin s, stop; P is the desired shortest path. Otherwise, go to the next iteration.

It is also possible to use a combined algorithm, where there are two paths: P_f - starting at the origin s and P_r - ending at the destination d. In this algorithm alternately several forward and reverse iterations are performed at least one of which leads to, respectively, an increase of the origin price p_s or to a decrease of the destination price p_d. This two-sided algorithm terminates when the two paths have a common node. In many tests [4] this hybrid approach proved to be the most effective, much faster than the sided Dijkstra algorithm.

When there are several origin nodes, the shortest path auction algorithm may be implemented in a parallel way in a distributed environment [4]. In the basic (i.e. forward) version for each origin i there is a a separate processor that executes the forward algorithm and keeps in local memory a price vector p^i (build of the snapshots of prices p_l^j sent by other nodes) and a corresponding path P^i satisfying CS together with p^i. The price vectors are communicated at various times to other processors, perhaps irregularly. A processor operating on P^i upon reception of a price vector p^j from another processor j, adopts as the price of each node l the maximum of the prices of l according to the existing and the received (i.e. the snapshots) price vectors, that is:

$$p_l^i := \max(p_l^i, p_l^j), \ \forall l \in N \tag{17}$$

This guarantees keeping the CS property, monotonicity of the mapping:

$$p_i := \min_{\{j|(i,j)\in A\}} \{a_{ij} + p_j\} \tag{18}$$

and the asynchronous convergence of the algorithm.

The parallel, synchronous and asynchronous implementations of the two-sided different shortest path algorithms for different problems (including many origin - many destinations routing problem) are more complicated due to the possibility of losing CS and, in the consequence, the oscillation of prices. To avoid it, all nodes are equipped with counters for forward and reverse extensions without an intervening contractions. However, in most tests (on a shared-memory machine) much simpler, one sided, forward scheme showed superiority. The details are described in [19].

For a single connection it is also possible to formulate a shortest path problem as a linear minimum flow cost problem. It will be presented in Section 3.2.1.

3 The Optimization of Flows in Single Commodity Networks with Linear and Nonlinear Cost Functions

3.1 General Convex Functions

Now every arc $(i,j) \in A$ will be characterized by a continuous, convex function $a_{ij}(f_{ij})$ of the cost of the realization of the flow f_{ij} from the node i to j and box flow constraints:

$$f_{ij} \in F_{ij} = [b_{ij}, c_{ij}] \tag{19}$$

With every node $i \in N$ we connect a given supply $s_i > 0$ or demand $s_i < 0$. Our goal is the calculation of such a distribution of flows between nodes, that all demands are satisfied and the total cost of these flows is minimal, that is

$$\min_f \sum_{(i,j)\in A} a_{ij}(f_{ij}) \tag{20}$$

$$\sum_{\{j|(j,i)\in A\}} f_{ji} + s_i = \sum_{\{j|(i,j)\in A\}} f_{ij}, \ \forall i \in N \tag{21}$$

$$b_{ij} \le f_{ij} \le c_{ij}, \ \forall (i,j) \in A \tag{22}$$

where f is a vector of all flows. Equations (21) result from the balance of flows in the nodes (so-called 1st Kirchhoff rule).
We assume, that supplies and demands s_i are balanced over the network, that is:

$$\sum_{i\in N} s_i = 0 \tag{23}$$

and, of course, that the set of admissible solutions (i.e., the set of possible combinations of coordinates of the vector of flows f) is not empty.

In the Internet such problem may be important for wide area operators, who have several connection points with other operators.

To solve this problem we formulate a Lagrange function [2], but taking into account only balance constraints (21). If we denote the multiplier corresponding to the i-th node equation as p_i, it will be:

$$L(f,p) = \sum_{(i,j)\in A} a_{ij}(f_{ij}) + \sum_{i\in N} p_i \left(\sum_{\{j|(j,i)\in A\}} f_{ji} + s_i - \sum_{\{j|(i,j)\in A\}} f_{ij} \right) \tag{24}$$

Making some simple transformations we can present the Lagrange function in the following way:

$$L(f,p) = \sum_{(i,j)\in A} \left[a_{ij}(f_{ij}) - (p_i - p_j) f_{ij} \right] + \sum_{i\in N} p_i s_i \tag{25}$$

Hence, the dual function in problem (20)-(22) will have the form:

$$\begin{aligned} L_D(p) &= \min_{b\le f\le c} \left\{ \sum_{(i,j)\in A} \left[a_{ij}(f_{ij}) - (p_i - p_j) f_{ij} \right] + \sum_{i\in N} p_i s_i \right\} \\ &= \sum_{(i,j)\in A} \left\{ \min_{b_{ij}\le f_{ij}\le c_{ij}} \left[a_{ij}(f_{ij}) - (p_i - p_j) f_{ij} \right] \right\} + \sum_{i\in N} p_i s_i \\ &= \sum_{(i,j)\in A} L_{ij}(p_i - p_j) + \sum_{i\in N} p_i s_i \end{aligned} \tag{26}$$

where L_{ij} is a component of the dual function corresponding to the arc (i,j), that is:

$$L_{ij}(p_i - p_j) = \min_{b_{ij}\le f_{ij}\le c_{ij}} \left[a_{ij}(f_{ij}) - (p_i - p_j) f_{ij} \right] \tag{27}$$

According to the duality theory [12], [2], the solution of the problem (20)-(22) may be obtained by the solution of the dual problem:

$$\max_{p\in\mathbb{R}^n} L_D(p) \tag{28}$$

To find the optimal solution of the problem (28) one may use gradient of the dual function L_D, with coordinates:

$$\begin{aligned} \frac{\partial L_D}{\partial p_i} &= -\sum_{\{j|(j,i)\in A\}} L_{ji}^{'}(p_j - p_i) + \sum_{\{j|(i,j)\in A\}} L_{ij}^{'}(p_i - p_j) + s_i \\ &= \sum_{\{j|(j,i)\in A\}} f_{ji} - \sum_{\{j|(i,j)\in A\}} f_{ij} + s_i \end{aligned} \tag{29}$$

The equivalent statement of optimality conditions stemming from duality theory is, that a flow vector $\hat{f}$ is optimal if and only if it is primal feasible, that is $\hat{f}_{ij} \in F_{ij} \ \forall \ i,j$ and there exists a price vector $\hat{p}$ satisfying together with $\hat{f}$ the following conditions (called complementary slackness conditions - CS) [6]:

$$a_{ij}^{-}(\hat{f}_{ij}) \leq \hat{p}_i - \hat{p}_j \leq a_{ij}^{+}(\hat{f}_{ij}) \tag{30}$$

In this expression leftmost and rightmost are, respectively, the left and the right derivatives of the arc cost function. Usually we deal with smooth cost functions and we have:

$$a_{ij}^{-}(\hat{f}_{ij}) = a_{ij}^{+}(\hat{f}_{ij}) = a_{ij}^{'}(\hat{f}_{ij}) \tag{31}$$

In practical numerical calculations, while looking for a good approximation of the optimal solution, a relaxed version of the CS conditions proved to be very useful. For a given scalar $\varepsilon > 0$ inequalities (30) are replaced by the following:

$$a_{ij}^{-}(f_{ij}) - \varepsilon \leq p_i - p_j \leq a_{ij}^{+}(f_{ij}) + \varepsilon \tag{32}$$

These conditions are called ε-complementary slackness conditions, ε-CS for short. The optimization approach which applies ε-CS conditions is called ε-relaxation method [6]. It consists in adjusting flows ("flow push") and increasing prices ("price rise") at appropriate nodes in such a way, that ε-CS conditions are maintained. This algorithm may be implemented in a distributed, asynchronous version [3], where each node i is a processor that updates its own price and its arcs flows, and exchanges information with its forward

$$F_i = \{j|(i,j) \in A\} \tag{33}$$

and backward

$$B_i = \{j|(j,i) \in A\} \tag{34}$$

adjacent nodes.

The information available at node i for any time t is as follows:

- $p_i(t)$: the price of node i
- $p_j(i,t)$: the price of node $j \in F_i \cup B_i$ communicated by j to i at some earlier time
- $f_{ij}(i,t)$: the estimate of the flow on the arc $(i,j), j \in F_i$, available at node i at time t
- $f_{ji}(i,t)$: the estimate of the flow of arc $(j,i), j \in B_i$ available at node i at time t

At each time t, each node i may be in one of the following four phases:

1. *Idle Phase.* Node i does nothing

2. *Computational Phase.* Node i computes the surplus $g_i(t)$:

$$g_i(t) = \sum_{j \in B_i} f_{ji}(i,t) - \sum_{j \in F_i} f_{ij}(i,t) + s_i \quad (35)$$

If $g_i(t) < 0$, node i does further nothing, Otherwise the following values:

$$p_i(t), \; f_{ij}(i,t), \, j \in F_i, \; f_{ji}(i,t), \, j \in B_i \quad (36)$$

are updated. The updating is performed due to the following procedure:

Step 1: (Calculation of the push list and the flow margin)
Given a flow-price vector satisfying the ε-CS conditions, *the push list* L_i of node i, $\forall i \in N$, is defined as follows:

$$L_i = \{(i,j) | \, \varepsilon/2 < p_i(t) - p_j(i,t) - a^+_{ij}(f_{ij}(i,t)) \leq \varepsilon \}$$

$$\cup \{(j,i) | -\varepsilon \leq p_j(i,t) - p_i(t) - a^-_{ji}(f_{ji}(i,t)) < -\varepsilon/2 \} \quad (37)$$

For each arc (i,j) or (j,i) in the push list L_i, the supremum of σ for which

$$p_i(t) - p_j(i,t) \geq a^+_{ij}(f_{ij}(i,t) + \sigma) \quad (38)$$

or, respectively, $p_j(i,t) - p_i(t) \leq a^-_{ji}(f_{ij}(i,t) - \sigma)$, is called the *flow margin.*

Step 2: (Scan of the push list) If $L_i = \emptyset$ go to Step 4

Step 3: (δ-Flow push) Choose an arc from the push list L_i and let

$$\delta = \min(g_i(t), \text{flow margin of the chosen arc}) \quad (39)$$

Increase f_{ij} by δ if (i,j) is the arc, or decrease f_{ji} by δ if (j,i) is the arc. If as a result the surplus becomes zero, go to the next iteration; otherwise, go to Step 2

Step 4: (Price rise) Increase the price p_i by the maximum amount that maintains ε-CS conditions. Go to the next iteration.

3. *Output Phase.* The values of $p_i(t), f_{ij}(i,t), f_{ji}(i,t)$, computed during the computational phase, are communicated to the adjacent nodes $j \in F_i \cup B_i$.

4. *Input Phase.* Node i receives from one or more adjacent nodes $j \in F_i \cup B_i$ a message containing the price $p_j(t')$ and the arc flow $f_{ij}(j,t')$ (when $j \in F_i$) or $f_{ji}(j,t')$ (when $j \in B_i$), computed by node $j, j \in F_i \cup B_i$, at some earlier time $t' < t$.
On the basis of this information, the node i updates $p_j(i,t)$ and $f_{ij}(i,t)$ if $j \in F_i$, ($f_{ji}(i,t)$, if $j \in B_i$).
If $p_j(t') \geq p_j(i,t)$, then $p_j(i,t) = p_j(t')$.
In addition, if $j \in F_i$, the value of $f_{ij}(i,t)$ is replaced by $f_{ij}(j,t')$ if

$$p_i(t) < p_j(t') + a^+_{ij}(f_{ij}(j,t')) + \varepsilon \quad \text{and} \quad f_{ij}(j,t') < f_{ij}(i,t) \quad (40)$$

In the case of $j \in B_i$, the value of $f_{ji}(i,t)$ is replaced by $f_{ji}(j,t')$ if

$$p_j(t') \geq p_i(t) + a^-_{ji}(f_{ji}(j,t')) - \varepsilon \quad \text{and} \quad f_{ji}(j,t') > f_{ji}(i,t). \tag{41}$$

The algorithm terminates if there is a time t_k such that, for all $t \geq t_k$:

$$g_i(t) = 0 \;\; \forall i \in N$$

$$f_{ij}(i,t) = f_{ij}(j,t) \;\; \forall (i,j) \in A$$

$$p_j(t) = p_j(i,t) \;\; \forall j \in F_i \cup B_i$$

It may be shown, that the algorithm converges if the initial prices and flows satisfy ε-CS conditions, the nodes never stop executing iterations and communication and assuring that the old information is eventually purged from the system [3].

3.2 Linear Cost Functions

In this case the optimization problem has the following form:

$$\min_f \sum_{(i,j)\in A} a_{ij}(f_{ij}) = \alpha_{ij} f_{ij} \tag{42}$$

$$\sum_{\{j|(j,i)\in A\}} f_{ji} + s_i = \sum_{\{j|(i,j)\in A\}} f_{ij}, \;\; \forall i \in N \tag{43}$$

$$b_{ij} \leq f_{ij} \leq c_{ij}, \;\; \forall (i,j) \in A \tag{44}$$

We may apply the algorithm presented in Section 3.1 in a simplified version [9][1], taking as :

- arc cost derivatives:

$$a'_{ij}(f_{ij}) = \alpha_{ij} \tag{45}$$

- the ε-CS conditions:

$$f_{ij} < c_{ij} \Rightarrow p_i - p_j \leq \alpha_{ij} + \varepsilon, \;\; \forall (i,j) \in A \tag{46}$$

$$b_{ij} < f_{ij} \Rightarrow p_i - p_j \geq \alpha_{ij} - \varepsilon, \;\; \forall (i,j) \in A \tag{47}$$

- the push list

$$L_i = \{(i,j)|\; p_i(t) = p_j(i,t) + \alpha_{ij} + \varepsilon \;\text{ and }\; f_{ij}(i,t) < c_{ij}\,\}$$

$$\cup \{(j,i)|\; p_i(t) = p_j(i,t) - \alpha_{ji} + \varepsilon \;\text{ and }\; b_{ji} < f_{ji}(i,t)\,\} \tag{48}$$

[1]Chronologically the asynchronous version of the ε-relaxation algorithm for linear minimum cost flow problems was presented much earlier in [9]; the version for convex problems from [3] was its extension.

- the flow margin

$$\sigma = \begin{cases} c_{ij} - f_{ij}(i,t) & j \in F_i \\ f_{ji}(i,t) - b_{ji} & j \in B_i \end{cases} \tag{49}$$

- the replacement conditions for flow estimates ((40),(41)):
  In the case of $j \in F_i$, the value of $f_{ij}(i,t)$ is replaced by $f_{ij}(j,t')$ if

$$p_i(t) < p_j(t') + \alpha_{ij} \text{ and } f_{ij}(j,t') < f_{ij}(i,t) \tag{50}$$

  In the case of $j \in B_i$, the value of $f_{ji}(i,t)$ is replaced by $f_{ji}(j,t')$ if

$$p_j(t') \geq p_i(t) + \alpha_{ji} \text{ and } f_{ji}(j,t') > f_{ji}(i,t). \tag{51}$$

3.2.1 Application to the Shortest Path Problem

It is possible to cast the problem of finding a shortest path from node s to node d as the following minimum cost flow problem [6]:

$$\min_f \sum_{(i,j)\in A} \alpha_{ij} f_{ij} \tag{52}$$

$$\sum_{\{j|(j,i)\in A\}} f_{ji} - \sum_{\{j|(i,j)\in A\}} f_{ij} = \begin{cases} -1 & \text{if } i = s \\ 1 & \text{if } i = d \\ 0 & \text{otherwise} \end{cases} \quad \forall i \in N \tag{53}$$

$$0 \leq f_{ij},\ (i,j) \in A \tag{54}$$

It may be solved in a distributed, asynchronous way through the ε-relaxation algorithm. The optimal path will be made of those arcs (i,j) for which $\hat{f}_{ij} = 1$ (for the remaining $\hat{f}_{ij} = 0$).

3.3 Strictly Convex Arc Cost Functions

In this section we assume, that the functions $a_{ij}(f_{ij}), (i,j) \in A$ in problem (20)-(23) are strictly convex. This problem, both the formulation and the basic features were taken from the book [9].

First, let us notice from (25) and (23), that the optimal Lagrange multipliers are not unique, because one may add to all of them the same constant and the function value will not change. Hence, it is worthwhile to fix one of the coordinates of the vector p and take for example:

$$p_1 = r \tag{55}$$

where r is an arbitrary nonzero real constant.

To solve the dual optimization problem (28) it is necessary to solve the family of scalar optimization problems (27), separately for every arc. They are very easy to solve, often even analytically.

According to the duality theory [12] [2] the function L_D and all functions L_{ij} are concave. It can be proved [9], that the algorithm of the Lagrange multiplier iteration of the form:

$$p_i := \begin{cases} r & i = 1 \\ arg\max_{\xi} L_D(p_1, p_2, \ldots, p_{i-1}, \xi, p_{i+1}, \ldots, p_n) & i = 2, 3, \ldots, n \end{cases} \tag{56}$$

is also an order preserving mapping and it is convergent in a totally asynchronous version.

In fact, it is not necessary to perform optimization of L_D with the $i-$th coordinate. To explain it let us define for every $i \in N \setminus \{1\}$ a *point-to-set* mapping R_i, which assigns to every Lagrange multipliers vector p a set of all prices which maximize the dual function L_D with respect to the i-th price p_i, that is:

$$R_i(p) = Arg\max_{\xi} L_D(p_1, p_2, \ldots, p_{i-1}, \xi, p_{i+1}, \ldots, p_n) \tag{57}$$

It can be proved, that if the problem (20)-(22), (23) is feasible, that is:

$$\sum_{\{j|(i,j)\in A\}} b_{ij} - \sum_{\{j|(j,i)\in A\}} c_{ji} \le s_i \le \sum_{\{j|(i,j)\in A\}} c_{ij} - \sum_{\{j|(j,i)\in A\}} b_{ji} \tag{58}$$

then the set $R_i(p)$ is either a singleton or a closed interval. Due to the concavity and differentiability of L_D every point $\xi \in \mathbb{R}$ belonging to $R_i(p)$ is a root of the scalar equation:

$$\frac{\partial L_D(p_1, p_2, \ldots, p_{i-1}, \xi, p_{i+1}, \ldots, p_n)}{\partial p_i} = 0 \tag{59}$$

that is due to Eq. (29):

$$R_i(p) = \left\{ \xi : \sum_{\{j|(j,i)\in A\}} L'_{ji}(p_j - \xi) = \sum_{\{j|(i,j)\in A\}} L'_{ij}(\xi - p_j) + s_i \right\} \tag{60}$$

Let us denote now as $\underline{R}_i(p)$ and $\overline{R}_i(p)$, respectively, the left and the right end of this interval. It turns out, that both these functions preserve the order. In the consequence, the algorithm of the Lagrange multiplier iteration of the form:

$$p_i := \begin{cases} r & i = 1 \\ \gamma \underline{R}_i(p) + (1-\gamma)\overline{R}_i(p) & i = 2, 3, \ldots, n \end{cases} \tag{61}$$

is equivalent to (56) for every $\gamma \in [0, 1]$ and of course also convergent in a totally asynchronous version [9].

If it is not difficult to calculate the intervals $R_i(p)$, $i = 1, \ldots, n$, one may propose another algorithm, which is convergent under the partial asynchronism assumptions [20], [9]. In this algorithm the i-th coordinate is changed due to the iteration:

$$p_i := \gamma \cdot p_i + (1-\gamma) \arg \min_{\xi \in R_i(p)} |\xi - p_i| \quad i = 1, 2, 3, \ldots, n \tag{62}$$

with $0 < \gamma < 1$. The computational experiments [20] showed, that this algorithm is considerably faster than the algorithm (61).

4 The Optimization of Flows in Multicommodity Networks with Contracted Transmission Rates for Virtual Connections

Now we will consider a more complicated situation, where from the network we expect not only the transport of the total volume of traffic, from all sources to all destination nodes, but also the guarantees on the flow between given pairs of nodes. So we will deal with networks which actually provide virtual connections, in other words with virtual-circuit data networks.

We define a set W of origin-destination pairs and assume, that for every connection $w = (s,d),\ s,d \in N, s \neq d$ the total flow r_w may be split to several paths P_w. We also assume, that the sets P_w for different w are disjoint. We will denote by A_p the set of all arcs (links) belonging to (i.e. forming) the path p.

Let x_p be the flow through a particular path $p \in P_w$. According to our assumptions, the flow f_{ij} through an arc (i,j) equals:

$$f_{ij} = \sum_{p \in P_{ij}} x_p \tag{63}$$

where $P_{ij} = \{p : (i,j) \in A_p\}$ is the set of all paths traversing arc (i,j). Denoting, as before, by $a_{ij}(f_{ij})$ the cost of assuring the flow f_{ij} in the arc (i,j), we may formulate the optimization problem as:

$$\min_x \left[z(x) = \sum_{(i,j)\in A} a_{ij}(f_{ij}) = \sum_{(i,j)\in A} a_{ij}\left(\sum_{p\in P_{ij}} x_p\right)\right] \tag{64}$$

$$\sum_{p\in P_w} x_p = r_w, \quad \forall w \in W \tag{65}$$

$$x_p \geq 0, \quad \forall p \in P_w, \quad \forall w \in W \tag{66}$$

As a cost function one may apply for example the congestion-delay function (7) used as a metric in simple routing algorithms presented in Section 2.

It turns out [9], [21], that the optimal distribution of path flows may be obtained by distributed partially asynchronous iterations of path flows x_p, grouped with respect to the realized connections w. The so-called "minimum first-derivative length" (MFDL) principle is applied. It says, that we should allocate more traffic to this path from the set P_w, for which the partial derivative of the cost function $\sum_{(i,j)\in A_p} \frac{\partial a_{ij}}{\partial x_p}$ is minimal. Applying the Taylor expansion series, it can be easily proved, that it guarantees for small amounts of shifted flow the decrease of the total cost. The assessment of MFDL path may be performed locally for every connection, that is in a distributed way, and asynchronously.

Since the information on flows in different arcs $(i,j) \in A_p$ for $p \in P_w$ comes from different times (e.g. the data concerning closer nodes is more recent) the $w-$th processor, which calculates path flows of the $w-$th connection, actually uses an estimate $\tilde{f}_{ij}^{w}(t)$ of these flows in some time window before the time of calculations t:

$$\tilde{f}_{ij}^{w}(t) = \sum_{\tau=t-B}^{t} \eta_{ij}^{w}(t,\tau) f_{ij}(\tau) \tag{67}$$

where $f_{ij}(\tau)$ is the actual flow at time τ in the arc (i,j), B is the length of the time window, and $\eta_{ij}^{w}(t,\tau)$ are (usually unknown) nonnegative coefficients such that:

$$\sum_{\tau=t-B}^{t} \eta_{ij}^{w}(t,\tau) = 1 \tag{68}$$

Let us denote the estimate of the derivative of the cost of the flow along the path $p \in P_w$ calculated at time t by $\lambda_p(t)$, that is:

$$\lambda_p(t) = \sum_{(i,j)\in A_p} a_{ij}^{'}(\tilde{f}_{ij}^{w}(t)) \tag{69}$$

and the index of the MFDL path by p_m, that is:

$$\lambda_{p_m}(t) = \min_{p\in P_w} \lambda_p(t) \tag{70}$$

In the general model it is assumed, that flows are not changed immediately and two phases are distinguished: the calculation of desired flows $\bar{x}_p$ and their realization x_p. According to this model, the new (actual) routing $x_p(t+1)$, $p \in P_w$ is determined as a convex combination of the desired routing $\bar{x}_p(t)$ and the current one $x_p(t)$:

$$x_p(t+1) = \beta_p(t)\bar{x}_p(t) + (1-\beta_p(t))x_p(t), \ \ p \in P_w \tag{71}$$

where $0 < \beta < \beta_p(t) \leq 1$ are generally unknown coefficients reflecting a smooth (with geometric rate) movement from the current to the desired routing. Of course whichever they are, the transmission rate constraints (65) have to be satisfied.

The desired flows $\bar{x}_p$ for all paths in the connection w are calculated differently for the MFDL path and for the remaining ones. For paths $p \neq p_m$ the following formula is used:

$$\bar{x}_p(t) = \max\left\{0, x_p(t) - \frac{\gamma}{H_p(t)}\left(\lambda_p(t) - \lambda_{p_m}(t)\right)\right\} \tag{72}$$

where $\gamma > 0$ is a stepsize and $H_p(t)$ is an estimate of the second derivative length of path p

$$H_p(t) = \sum_{(i,j)\in A_p} a_{ij}^{''}(\tilde{f}_{ij}^{w})$$

Afterwards, for the MFDL path the desired flow is calculated from the expression:

$$\bar{x}_{p_m}(t) = r_w - \sum_{p\in P_w, p\neq p_m} \bar{x}_p(t) \tag{73}$$

It may be proved, that there exists some $\gamma_0(B)$ such that for $0 < \gamma < \gamma_0(B)$ the described algorithm implemented asynchronously converges, delivering the minimum total cost of transmission $z(x)$. Luo and Tseng [18] showed, that when the cost function a_{ij} (e.g. the expected delay) on each link is a strictly convex function on the link flow, the sequence generated by this algorithm converges in the space of path flows at a linear rate.

It is possible to apply instead of (72)-(73) another scaled gradient algorithm:

$$\bar{x}_w(t+1) = \left[\bar{x}_w(t) - \gamma M_w^{-1} \lambda_w(t)\right]^+_{M_w(t)} \tag{74}$$

where $\bar{x}_w$, λ_w are vectors formed of components $\bar{x}_p$, λ_p for $p \in P_w$, $M_w(t)$ is a symmetric positive definite matrix (usually it is an estimate of the Hessian matrix $\frac{\partial^2 z}{\partial x_w^2}$, and the algorithm (74) is an approximation of the projected Newton method), $[.]^+_{M_w(t)}$ denotes the projection on the simplex

$$\left\{ x_w \middle| \sum_{p \in P_w} x_p = r_w \text{ and } x_p \geq 0, \forall p \in P_w \right\} \tag{75}$$

with respect to the norm $||x_w||_{M_w(t)} = \left(x_w' M_w(t) x_w\right)^{1/2}$. However, since this algorithm takes into account the current value of the desired flows $\bar{x}_w(t)$ instead of the current value of the actual flows $x_w(t)$ one may expect that it will be slower in the adaptation to sudden changes in the problem data r_w. Surprisingly, the replacement in (74) $\bar{x}_w(t)$ with $x_w(t)$ destroys the descent property and the convergence of the algorithm [9].

Recently Elwalid et al. [11] noticed, that the above scheme may be successfully adapted to Internet traffic engineering in MPLS (multiprotocol label switching) networks. They introduced two changes:

- They do not distinguish between the actual $x_p(t)$ and the desired $\bar{x}_p(t)$ source rates, that is a new rate vector is calculated from the formula:

$$x_w(t+1) = [x_w(t) - \gamma \lambda_w(t)]^+ \tag{76}$$

  where $[.]^+$ denotes the projection on the feasible space (75) with respect to the Euclidean norm. The justification is, that if one is only dealing with IP datagrams it is reasonable to assume that each ingress node can shift its traffic among the label switched paths available to it immediately after each update.

- They relax the assumption that at time t each source has available the current first derivative lengths (69) and uses it in place of the gradient in the update algorithm. Instead, they assume, that at time t, the source may only have outdated first derivative lengths. Moreover, the source uses a weighted average over several past lengths in the update algorithm. That is, the price used in algorithm (76) is calculated in the following way:

$$\lambda_p(t) = \sum_{\tau=t-B}^{t} \sum_{(i,j) \in A_p} \rho_{ij}^w(t,\tau)\, a'_{ij}(\tilde{f}_{ij}^w(\tau)) \tag{77}$$

where $\tilde{f}_{ij}(\tau)$ is an estimate of flow in the arc (i,j) calculated at time τ (67), B is the length of the time window, and $\rho_{ij}^{w}(t,\tau)$ are (usually unknown) nonnegative coefficients such that:

$$\sum_{\tau=t-B}^{t} \rho_{ij}^{w}(t,\tau) = 1 \tag{78}$$

This is because, in the distributed and decentralized implementation of the algorithm, the source can only estimate the first derivative lengths through noisy measurement.

Despite these differences, stability of this algorithm (called MATE - from Multipath Adaptive Traffic Engineering) in [11] has been established using the same techniques as in [21], [9].

5 The Multicommodity Flow Networks with the Influence on Users through Internal Prices

In this section we consider the situation, where the capacities of links are too small to carry all demanded traffic and it is necessary to reduce the users' transmission rates $r_w, w \in W$ (w is a connection index and W is the set of all active connections) in Eq. (65), which were fixed there. So, the decision variables - distribution of path rates for a given connection x_w - will be more flexible.
For simplicity, we will assume, that for every connection w there is only one path between source and destination nodes, that is x_w is a scalar variable and it is simply the transmission rate.

The transmission rates should belong to some intervals:

$$\underline{x}_w \leq x_w \leq \overline{x}_w \tag{79}$$

Every customer, that is the user of the network, assesses the satisfaction from the use of the network through his utility function $U_w(x_w)$, defined on the interval $[\underline{x}_w, \overline{x}_w]$. In this problem, instead of minimization of the total cost of transmission, which is not so important for the operator of the network (because most links are fully used), we will strive to maximize the satisfaction of the customers, that is the sum of their utility functions.

Hence, our problem will be as follows:

$$\max_{x} \sum_{w \in W} U_w(x_w) \tag{80}$$

$$\underline{x}_w \leq x_w \leq \overline{x}_w, \quad w \in W \tag{81}$$

$$f_{ij} = \sum_{w \in W_{ij}} x_w \leq c_{ij}, \quad \forall (i,j) \in A \tag{82}$$

The last inequality expresses capacity constraints of the links; W_{ij} denotes the set of connections (virtual paths) traversing arc (i,j), that is:

$$W_{ij} = \{w | (i,j) \in A_w\} \tag{83}$$

where A_w is the set of arcs (links) used by the connection w; x is the vector of all transmission rates:

$$x = \left[x_w, w \in W\right] \tag{84}$$

The Lagrange function for problem (80)-(82) will be as follows:

$$L(x,p) = \sum_{w \in W} U_w(x_w) - \sum_{(i,j)\in A} p_{ij}\left(\sum_{w \in W_{ij}} x_w - c_{ij}\right) \tag{85}$$

Let us notice now that:

$$\begin{aligned}\sum_{(i,j)\in A} p_{ij}\left(\sum_{w \in W_{ij}} x_w - c_{ij}\right) &= \sum_{(i,j)\in A} p_{ij} \sum_{w \in W_{ij}} x_w - \sum_{(i,j)\in A} p_{ij} c_{ij} = \\ &= \sum_{w\in W} \sum_{(i,j)\in A_w} p_{ij} x_w - \sum_{(i,j)\in A} p_{ij} c_{ij} \\ &= \sum_{w\in W} x_w \sum_{(i,j)\in A_w} p_{ij} - \sum_{(i,j)\in A} p_{ij} c_{ij} \\ &= \sum_{w \in W} x_w p_w - \sum_{(i,j)\in A} p_{ij} c_{ij}\end{aligned} \tag{86}$$

where

$$p_w = \sum_{(i,j)\in A_w} p_{ij} \tag{87}$$

is the price for the connection w along its path formed of arcs $(i,j) \in A_w$.

Applying (86) to (85) we get:

$$L(x,p) = \sum_{w\in W}\left(U_w(x_w) - x_w p_w\right) + \sum_{(i,j)\in A} p_{ij} c_{ij} \tag{88}$$

According to the duality theory ([12], [2]) the optimal solutions, both the optimal distribution of flows $\left(\hat{x}_w, w \in W\right)$ and the vector of optimal prices $[\hat{p}_{ij}, (i,j) \in A]$ may be obtained via the two-phase procedure:

$$\min_{p \geq 0}\left[L_D(p) = \sum_{w\in W} \max_{\underline{x}_w \leq x_w \leq \overline{x}_w}\left(U_w(x_w) - x_w p_w\right) + \sum_{(i,j)\in A} p_{ij} c_{ij}\right] \tag{89}$$

In this way we obtained $\overline{\overline{W}}$ problems of optimization of connection transmission rates and a problem of optimization of prices of unit bandwidth of the dimension $\overline{\overline{A}}$ ($\overline{\overline{V}}$ denotes the number of elements of the set V). It can be proved [17], [14], that they may be solved in a distributed, partially asynchronous way.

More precisely, the w-th user solves the local optimization problem:

$$\max_{\underline{x}_w \leq x_w \leq \overline{x}_w}\left(U_w(x_w) - x_w \tilde{p}_w(t)\right) \tag{90}$$

where $\tilde{p}_w(t)$ is the current estimate of the price of transmission w, that is:

$$\tilde{p}_w(t) = \sum_{(i,j)\in A_w} \sum_{\tau=t-B}^{t} \eta_{ij}^{w}(t,\tau) p_{ij}(\tau) \tag{91}$$

In the last equation $\eta_{ij}^{w}(t,\tau)$ are (usually unknown) nonnegative coefficients such that:

$$\sum_{\tau=t-B}^{t} \eta_{ij}^{w}(t,\tau) = 1, \;\; \forall t, (i,j), w \in W_{ij} \tag{92}$$

and B is the length of the time window (i.e., the measure of asynchronism). The optimal solution of the local problem (90) may be determined analytically [17] from the expression:

$$\hat{x}_w = \left[U_w^{'-1}(\tilde{p}_w) \right]_{\underline{x}_w}^{\overline{x}_w} \tag{93}$$

where $[z]_a^b = \min\{\max\{z,a\},b\}$ and $U_w^{'-1}$ is the inverse of $U_w^{'}$.

The optimal link prices $\hat{p}_{ij}$ in problem (89) may be calculated in different ways. In the simplest case the steepest descent method is applied. According to Eq. (85) this is realized by the iteration:

$$p_{ij}(t+1) = \left[p_{ij}(t) - \gamma \Big(c_{ij} - \tilde{f}_{ij}(t) \Big) \right]^{+} \tag{94}$$

where

$$\tilde{f}_{ij}(t) = \sum_{w\in W_{ij}} \sum_{\tau=t-B}^{t} \rho_{ij}^{w}(t,\tau) x_w(\tau) \tag{95}$$

is the estimate of the total flow through the link (i,j). In the last equation $\rho_{ij}^{w}(t,\tau)$ are (usually unknown) nonnegative coefficients such that:

$$\sum_{\tau=t-B}^{t} \rho_{ij}^{w}(t,\tau) = 1, \;\; \forall t, (i,j), w \in W_{ij} \tag{96}$$

and B is the length of the time window. Due to the theory presented in [17], [14], for sufficiently small values of the stepsize γ and bounded time intervals between consecutive updates of the optimal link prices p_{ij} and transmission rates x_w, the algorithm converges partially asynchronously.

Since the algorithm was devoted to flow control in the Internet, where sending information on current internal prices of links (from the operator to users) and the calculation of current average transmission rates in all virtual paths would mean some additional equipment and the communication overheads, the following estimation mechanisms were proposed [15], [1]:

1. Instead of calculation of the aggregated flow rate $\tilde{f}_{ij}(t)$ in the link (i,j), the link operator measures the link buffer occupancy $v_{ij}(t)$. This occupancy evolves according to the equation:

$$v_{ij}(t+1) = \left[v_{ij}(t) + \sum_{w\in W_{ij}} x_w(t) - c_{ij} \right]^{+} \tag{97}$$

where $x_w(t)$ is the current flow rate of the transmission w. Then, the new link price $p_{ij}(t+1)$ is set as:

$$p_{ij}(t+1) = \gamma v_{ij}(t) \tag{98}$$

2. Instead of passing the users directly the information on the current price of the unit of the bandwidth, the link operator applies Random Exponential Marking (REM) algorithm. It allows for encoding this information in only one bit[2] of the stream of packets.

   Namely, it is assumed, that the link (i,j) marks each packet with a probability $m_{ij}(t)$ which is exponentially increasing in the price $p_{ij}(t)$ (or in the buffer occupancy $v_{ij}(t)$ - see (98)):

$$m_{ij}(t) = 1 - \phi^{-p_{ij}(t)} \tag{99}$$

   where $\phi > 1$ is a constant. Once a packet is marked, its mark is carried to the destination and then conveyed back to the source via acknowledgement (due to the TCP/IP protocol). The *end-to-end* probability that a packet of the connection w is marked after traversing the whole its way made of arcs from the set A_w is then:

$$m_w(t) = 1 - \prod_{(i,j)\in A_w} (1 - m_{ij}(t)) = 1 - \phi^{-p_w(t)} \tag{100}$$

   where $p_w(t) = \sum_{(i,j)\in A_w} p_{ij}(t)$ is the price for the transmission of the unit of bandwidth along the virtual path w. Then, the customer using this connection estimates the price of it $\tilde{p}_w(t)$ by the fraction $\tilde{m}_w(t)$ of his packets marked in some window before time t and inverting (100), that is:

$$\tilde{p}_w(t) = -\log_\phi(1 - \tilde{m}_w(t)) \tag{101}$$

Owing to this two improvements, there is no need for administrative communication between the operators of links and the end users of the network.

It should be noted, that the prices in this model are regarded rather as a control signal to guide sources' decisions, than a part of the charge a user pays [17]. In particular, these prices (i.e. Lagrange multipliers) equal zero when the traffic is below the capacity of the network. In other words: the user pays nothing for the highest desirable quality! On the contrary, he pays more and more for connections of lower quality, when there is a congestion in the network. Such pricing mechanism would be hardly acceptable for a human. So it is rather a tool for software agents.

In the latest article Low [16] presents few such agents and interprets their utility functions. It is shown, that for example in the Internet these agents are simply different implementations of TCP congestion control protocols. The basic idea is to regard the process of congestion control as carrying out a distributed computation by sources and links over a network in real time to solve an optimization problem. The objective is to maximize aggregate source utility subject to capacity constraints. The source rates are interpreted as primal

[2] We mean ECN - Explicit Congestion Notification bit in the IP header.

variables, congestion measures as dual variables, and TCP/AQM (Active Queue Management) protocols as distributed primal-dual algorithms to solve this optimization problem and its associated dual problem. Different protocols, such as Reno, Vegas, RED, and REM, all solve the same prototypical problem with different utility functions, Moreover, all these protocols generate congestion measures (Lagrange multipliers) that solve the dual problem in equilibrium.

The multipath version of this algorithm, being a combination of methods described in Sections 3 and 4 was presented in [15].

6 Conclusions

All presented distributed, asynchronous optimization methods for data networks management may be interesting to network operators. For mass client market simple routing algorithm (see sect. 2) or traffic balance routing (see sect. 3) may be sufficient. For more demanding users: state services, governmental institutions, big companies, banks, etc. the model with guaranteed connection rates (see sect. 4) should be applied. The group of customers who need higher quality of traffic only from time to time is between these two groups. Such users may probably postpone their connections if the network is congested. The best method of influencing them consists in presenting them the current price for the desired connection (see sect. 5). This price has an internal and provisional character (in fact, it is a sum of Lagrange multipliers), that is, it does not have the direct monetary sense (although it may influence somehow the charge for the connection - but it is beyond the subject of this paper). Since its dynamics is rather big and the user has to respond quite fast (otherwise, the algorithm may not converge), the only solution is ceding this task to a software agent.

There is also a possibility of using hybrid approaches - applying different methods in different hours (of the day) or in different time scales. For example: the simple routing algorithms calculate the sets of paths P_w for different origin-destination pairs and the virtual connection-based optimization algorithms allocate traffic to these already given paths.

References

[1] Athuraliya, S., and Low, S.H., Optimization Flow Control, II: Implementation, `http://netlab.caltech.edu`, 2000.

[2] Bazaraa, M.S., Sherali, H.D., and Shetty, C.M., *Nonlinear Programming: Theory and Algorithms*, John Wiley and Sons, New York - Chichester - Brisbane - Toronto - Singapore, 1993.

[3] Beraldi, P., Guerriero, F., and Musmanno, R., Parallel Algorithms for Solving the Convex Minimum Cost Flow Problem, *Computational Optimization and Applications*, vol. 18, pp. 175–190, 2001.

[4] Bertsekas, D. P., An Auction Algorithm for Shortest Paths, *SIAM J. on Optimization*, Vol. 1, pp. 425–447, 1991.

[5] Bertsekas, D. P., A Simple and Fast Label Correcting Algorithm for Shortest Paths, *Networks*, Vol. 23, pp. 703-709, 1993.

[6] Bertsekas, D. P., Network Optimization: Continuous and Discrete Models, *Athena Scientific*, Belmont, 1998.

[7] Bertsekas, D., and Gallager, R., *Data Networks*, Prentice-Hall, Englewood-Cliffs, 1992.

[8] Bertsekas, D. P., Guerriero, F., and Musmanno, R., Parallel Asynchronous Label-Correcting Methods for Shortest Paths,*Journal of Optimization Theory and Applications*, Vol. 88, pp. 297–321, 1996.

[9] Bertsekas, D.P., and Tsitsiklis, J.N., Parallel and Distributed Computation: Numerical Methods, *Athena Scientific*, Belmont, 1997.

[10] Comer, D.E., *Internetworking with TCP/IP, Vol. I : Principles, Protocols, and Architecture*, Prentice-Hall, Englewood Cliffs, 1991.

[11] Elwalid, A., Jin, C., Low, S., and Widjaja, I., MATE: multipath adaptive traffic engineering, *Computer Networks*, Vol. 40, Issue 6, pp. 695–709, 2002.

[12] Findeisen, W., Bailey, F.N., Brdy, M., Malinowski, K., and Woniak, A., *Control and Coordination in Hierarchical Systems*, John Wiley & Sons, Chichester - New York - Brisbane - Toronto, 1980.

[13] Guerriero, F., and Musmanno, R., Parallel Asynchronous Algorithms for the K Shortest Paths Problem, *Journal of Optimization Theory and Applications*, **104**(1), pp. 91-108, 2000.

[14] Karbowski, A., Correction to Low and Lapsley's article "Optimization Flow Control, I: Basic Algorithm and Convergence", *IEEE/ACM Transactions on Networking* vol. 11, Issue: 2 , pp. 338-339, 2003.

[15] Low, S., Optimization Flow Control with On-line Measurement or Multiple Paths, *Proc. of 16th International Teletraffic Congress*, Edinburgh, UK, June 1999.

[16] Low, S.H., A Duality Model of TCP and Queue Management Algorithms, *IEEE/ACM Transactions on Networking*, vol. 11, no. **4**, pp. 525-536, 2003

[17] Low, S., and Lapsley, D.E., Optimization Flow Control, I: Basic Algorithm and Convergence, *IEEE/ACM Transactions on Networking*, Vol. 7, Issue: 6, pp. 861–874, 1999.

[18] Luo, Z.-Q., and Tseng, P., On the Rate of Convergence of a Distributed Asynchronous Routing Algorithm, *IEEE Transactions on Automatic Control*, Vol. 39, Issue 5, pp. 1123–1129, 1994.

[19] Polymenakos, L., and Bertsekas, D. P., Parallel Shortest Path Auction Algorithms, *Parallel Computing*, Vol. 20, pp. 1221-1247, 1994.

[20] Tseng, P., Bertsekas, D. P., and Tsitsiklis, J. N., Partially Asynchronous Algorithms for Network Flow and Other Problems, *SIAM Journal on Control and Optimization*, Vol. 28, pp. 678-710, 1990.

[21] Tsitsiklis, J., and Bertsekas, D., Distributed Asynchronous Optimal Routing in Data Networks, *IEEE Trans. Automatic Control*, vol AC-31, No. **4**, pp. 325-332, 1986.

In: Artificial Intelligence and Computer Science
Editor: Susan Shannon, pp. 87-125
ISBN: 1-59454-411-5

Chapter 3

REINFORCEMENT LEARNING AND FORGETTING FOR KNOWLEDGE BASED CONFIGURATION

Ingo Kreuz
DaimlerChrysler AG, Stuttgart, Germany
Dieter Roller
University of Stuttgart, Germany

Abstract

In order to solve complex configuration tasks in technical domains, various knowledge based methods have been developed. However, their applicability is often unsuccessful due to their low efficiency. One of the reasons for this is that (parts of the) problems have to be solved again and again, instead of being "learnt" from preceding processes. However, learning processes bring with them the problem of conservatism, for in technical domains *innovation* is a deciding factor. On the other hand, a certain amount of conservatism is often desired since uncontrolled innovation as a rule is also detrimental.

This paper proposes the heuristic RKF (Relevant Knowledge First) for making decisions in configuration processes, based on the so-called *relevance* of objects in a knowledge base. The underlying relevance-function has two components, one based on reinforcement learning and the other based on forgetting (fading). The relevance of an object increases with its successful use and decreases with age, when it is not used. RKF has been developed to speed up the configuration process and to improve the quality of the solutions in relation to the user's rating of the solutions.

1 Motivation

We will begin with a brief introduction to *knowledge based configuration*, the field for which *Relevant Knowledge First* (RKF) has been developed. After that we propose possible improvements and report on effects of cognitive psychology, which will lead us into the introduction of RKF.

1.1 Knowledge-Based Configuration

Several definitions of configuration have been proposed (e.g. **[21]**, **[23]**). It's interesting that configuration is sometimes more generally called "design" (e.g. **[22]**, **[29]**). A definition that goes with our understanding of configuration in this article has been presented by Günter. In **[8]** he defines configuration as *a task of synthesis of domain objects* and in **[9]** the characteristics of configuration are described as follows: *„Configuration tasks have the following characteristics:*

- *A set of objects in the application domain and their properties (parameters),*
- *A set of relations between the domain objects where the taxonomical and compositional relations are of particular importance for configuration,*
- *A task specification (configuration objectives) that specifies the demands a created configuration has to accomplish and*
- *Control knowledge about the configuration process."*

The configuration or domain knowledge in configuration systems is usually structured in one of the following ways (see **[9]**):

- *Object or frame-based approach* (e.g. in KONWERK **[8]**, SCE **[10]**)
- *Resource oriented approach* (e.g. in COSMOS **[11]**
- *Rule oriented approach* (e.g. in XCON **[21]**)
- *Mixed forms.*

In this article we will introduce our heuristic RKF in the context of the first approach (object/frame based) because our application uses this form of representation. However, RKF can always be used to make decisions, regardless of the form of representation. Whenever we speak of objects in this article, it can be generalized to any piece of information or knowledge. In section 2.5 we give an overview of the types of objects for which we intend to use RKF.

1.2 Possible Improvements for Knowledge Based Configuration

The performance and quality of knowledge-based methods are essentially determined by the search methods used, e.g. the methods to draw back decisions (revision, e.g. backtracking) and the heuristics employed. In the following, characteristics of knowledge-based methods will be considered, which offer the potential for improvements. This list, which is probably incomplete, gave us a starting point for developing RKF.

- *Making "correct" decisions:* All heuristics aim to make the best possible decisions. In other words, revision should be avoided in order to accelerate the knowledge-based process. At the same time the best possible solutions concerning one or several optimization criterions are to be found without investigating the whole search space.
- *Learning from successful preceding processes:* Feedback from a solution on the knowledge base is desirable: The knowledge-based system "learns" similarly to the way

human experts do from preceding solutions. This "experience" can be applied to new solutions.

- *Avoid conservatism despite learning:* One danger of self-learning methods is conservatism. If the main reason for making a decision is because "it has always been done in this way", then a system is not in a position to adequately take new factors into consideration. Innovation is an important economic factor, especially in technical areas (e.g. engineering domains or sales of systems consisting of electronic or other engineered components).
- *Version control of knowledge bases:* Version control is not typical for objects in knowledge bases. Obviously they can be modeled in general systems for knowledge representation[1]. This modeling is mostly not trivial if old versions of knowledge should be left in the knowledge base. For example if old versions are already in use in the original system which has to be *re*configured, they must also be accessible. In general it is often better to give *preference* to new knowledge, without deleting the old.
- *Maintenance of the Knowledge Base:* Knowledge bases can become extremely large after a period of time. The larger the knowledge base, the larger (exponentially!) the search space and the slower the average running time of a knowledge-based search algorithm. The need for knowledge base maintenance is also mentioned in chapter 4.4 of **[3]**. It should be pointed out that on principle it is risky, to completely erase knowledge, simply because it has not been needed for some time.

1.3 Effects of Cognitive Psychology

Although incomplete, the list of possible improvements in section 1.1 leads us to the question of how humans handle knowledge. An enormous number of NP-complete problems are "solved" every second by humans who are able to fall back on an enormous knowledge base. In this context David Waltz (see **[30]**) sees the human brain as an important means of survival, e.g. to work out the answer to significant questions such as *"can I eat it or can it eat me?"*. He comes to the conclusion that the "importance" of information is crucial to determine how the world model changes and whether information should generally be stored.

In his book **[2]** Anderson reports of a model where the human brain is able to handle enormous amounts of information and therefore large search spaces. From this model we shall firstly consider the so-called ***activation*** *of a memory trace*. It indicates how accessible information is for a given problem, i.e. how fast and with what probability information can be accessed. Anderson puts forward analyses which show that along with the accessed information, related information is also activated. Every time we use a memory trace, its activation increases a little. In this model the gradual effect of training is recorded for each piece of information by the so-called ***strength*** *of the according* ***memory trace***. This leads to the effect that during problem solving information is *in principle varyingly easy to access*, that is to say access is slower or faster. If a piece of information is needed frequently, the *strength* of its memory trace increases. We will call this "training" or "learning". The relationship between the quantity of exercise and the access efficiency (e.g. measured as reaction time) results in a power function which is known in cognitive psychology terms as

---

[1] in chapter 2 of [Karbach et al. 1990] a definition of "knowledge representation systems" can be found

the *power law of learning*. Figure 1 has been taken from **[2]** and shows some results from J. M. Blackburn: In 1936 he investigated the effect of training when subjects added numbers in 10,000 exercises.

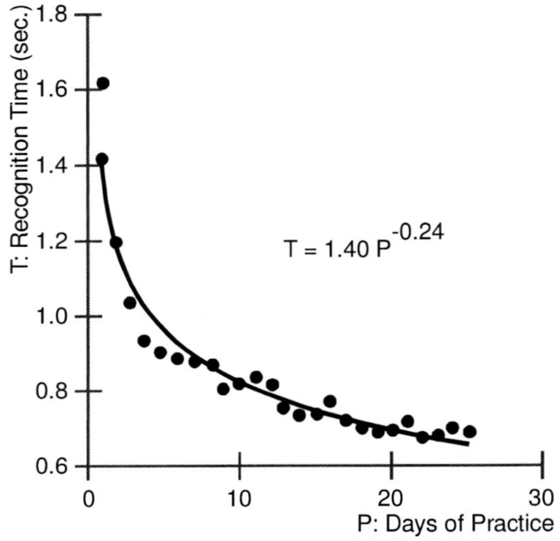

Figure 1: Blackburn's results concerning the **power law of learning**

Forgetting counteracts learning: If a piece of information is not used over a period of time, the strength of its memory trace fades. Experiments show that forgetting can also be described as a power function, which amongst other things could be explained by the decaying processes of the neural connections.

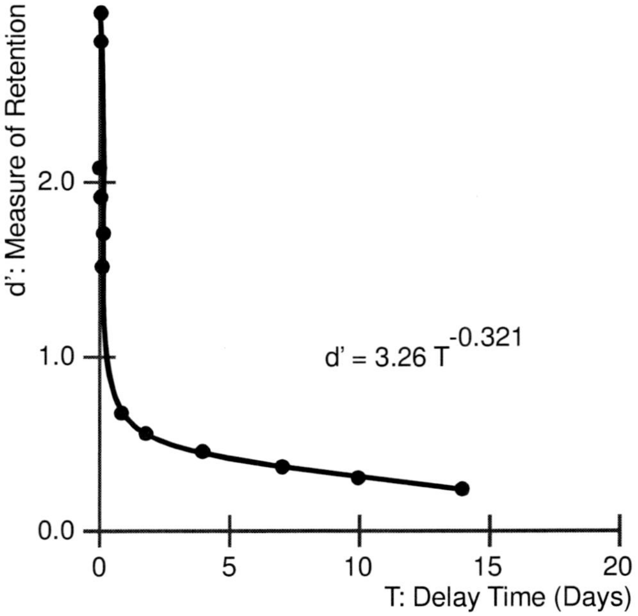

Figure 2: Wickelgren's results concerning the **power law of forgetting**

Anderson refers to the experiments carried out by W.A. Wickelgren, who asked subjects to learn lists of words. He investigated the probability of the words being recalled after various time spans (one minute to 14 days). This probability served as a measure for the memory's performance *d'* and is represented in figure 2 as a function of the time taken to recall the list of words.

The effects described above show that people can *concentrate* on *relevant* information (high activation level of a certain memory trace) to solve given problems and they make relevant information more or less accessible through the processes of "learning" and "forgetting". The assessment of the relevance of information could be a deciding factor in managing the vast amount of information stored in the human brain.

This idea encouraged us to develop a heuristic in the area of knowledge based configuration which can identify relevant information for a given problem and thereby drastically accelerate the solution process. In order to find a solution not only quickly, but one also of "good" quality, the principle suggested by Anderson had to be adapted.

2 Relevant Knowledge First (RKF)

2.1 Principle of RKF

For the assessment of the relevance of objects there are two deciding factors which correspond to the antagonism between conservatism and innovation: On the one hand objects are very likely to be *relevant* again if they have already been useful for similar tasks (see *training* in section 2.4.1) and objects that did not help to find solutions will probably not help in the future (see *forgetting* in section 2.4.2). On the other hand *new* objects should be taken into consideration in order to avoid conservatism: Because objects can be forgotten, it is possible that new objects which "prove their worth" can replace objects which have been relevant so far. To assess objects, we calculate their so-called *relevance* from the time since they were last used (during a so-called forgetting phase) and the rewards obtained by users (during learning phases).

With RKF, the search for solutions is supported by *preferring relevant* objects: Every time a decision has to be made, the relevance of all objects *in question* $o_i \in \boldsymbol{O}$ at the point in time t is calculated. One object $o \in \boldsymbol{O}$ is selected by a random generator, where the probability of choosing an object o is proportional to its relevance.

$$P(o, t, c) := \frac{\text{rel}(o, t, c)^{\nu}}{\sum_{i=1}^{|\boldsymbol{O}|} \text{rel}(o_i, t, c)^{\nu}} \qquad o, o_i \in \boldsymbol{O} \tag{1}$$

o	An object "in question"
$\boldsymbol{O}$	Set of all objects in question
o_i	i^{th} object of $\boldsymbol{O}$
t	Current time (number of configuration run)
c	Context ("task class") for relevance (see 2.3)
rel(o_i, t, c)	The calculated relevance of o_i at time t in context c (see 2.4)

v Parameter to control the conservatism for selections ("variance")

After a solution has been found, the user of the configuration system assesses the solution by giving a *reward* for all objects of the solution. For subsequent search processes the relevance increases for successfully used objects proportional to their reward (train) and decreases for all other objects (forget).

2.2 Relevance

The term "relevance" is also known in the field of information retrieval. In this context "relevance" is used as a measure of how well a list of documents found by an information retrieval system answers a user's query (**[28]**, **[5]**, **[1]**). Schamber remarks *"relevance is currently recognized as a multidimensional and dynamic concept extending beyond the traditional definition so closely associated with topic-matching and an identification of relevance as the relation between a document and a search question"*. We also think that the relevance of knowledge is dynamic in configuration tasks in technical domains because facts change, e.g. as a result of innovations. A more common definition of relevance is given by Pearl **[25]**: *"Relevance is a relationship indicating a potential change of belief due to a specified change in knowledge. Two propositions A and B are said to be relevant to each other in context C if adding B to C would change the likelihood of A"*. When we use relevance, we will derive a probability value from it and we will also define a context for the relevance-values that we call *task class*. The system described by Crestani **[5]** learns relevance-values using feedback mechanisms. As described above, RKF includes a learning part that uses ideas from reinforcement learning. In the context of forgetting, Lin and Reiter give a definition of relevance **[19]**: *"Let T be a theory, q a query and p a ground atom. We say that p in T is irrelevant for answering q, iff T and forget(T, p) are equivalent"*, where forget(T, p) means the deletion of p from T. We have a different interpretation of forgetting (see 2.4.1), which for our purposes describes a continuous process that is similar to "fading" in the system "aHUGIN" **[24]**; but we will also suggest a mechanism for deleting knowledge, dependent upon its relevance (see "Maintenance of Knowledge Bases" in section 2.5).

Very similar to our understanding of relevance is the *utility* of control rules (which can also be seen as objects) that is discussed in **[26]**: *"As we add more and more control knowledge to a system, the system is able to search more judiciously. [...] However deliberating about which step to take next in the search space, the system must consider all the control rules. If there are many control rules, simply matching them all can be very time-consuming [...] PRODIGY maintains a utility measure for each control rule. This measure takes into account the average savings provided by the rule, the frequency of its application, and the cost of matching it."* The *value* of information, introduced by Markovitch and Scott **[20]**, is also similar to our relevance. In their L*F heuristic, the *"length of a macro and the number of times information was used in the evaluation phase"* serves to select knowledge from a vast amount of automatically generated rules. In all these considerations, the value of information is used to estimate to what extent it will probably help to solve tasks in the future.

We will now put forward our definition of relevance in the form of a piecewise representation: The relevance at the time t of an object o in the context of a task class c is calculated as a function of time since the last access (forget, if o is **not** part of the solution) and the assessment (so-called *rewards* in the field of reinforcement-learning) given by a user (train, if o **is** part of the solution).

$$\text{rel}(o, t, c) := \begin{cases} \text{train}(o, t, c) & \text{if } o \text{ is part of the solution} \\ \text{forget}(o, t, c) & \text{if } o \text{ is } \textbf{not} \text{ part of the solution} \end{cases} \quad (2)$$

The power functions in section 1.3 show desirable characteristics for train(o, t, c) and forget(o, t, c) in technical domains. They were therefore a starting point for the "train" and "forget" functions, which we will introduce in section 2.4.

2.3 Task Classes

As described in 2.2, we always understand the relevance of an object in relation to a context c which we call *task class*. The selection of a task class corresponds to the activation of a memory trace for a given problem in the model of Cognitive Psychology (see section 1.3).

For task classes the following axioms are postulated:

Axiom 1: Task classes are the "contexts" for the relevance of objects, i.e. every object has one relevance value per task class

Axiom 2: Task classes form a partitioning of the set of all possible configuration tasks of a domain, i.e. every task can be unambiguously assigned to one task class

Axiom 3: The rewards given for an object as part of a solution are (nearly) constant or change slowly in the context of one single task class as long as the domain is not changed (objects or dependencies are added or removed)

Axiom 4: Changes of the domain are seldom

Axiom 5: Task Classes imply optimization goals

One target of our heuristic RKF is to learn which objects get the highest rewards, i.e. each task class implies the task specification which will be learnt by RKF. The highest relevance corresponds to the highest rewards that an object has yielded recently. It is necessary to have multiple task classes (axiom 1) because conflicting goals can exist in a domain which we take into consideration by multiple relevance values. Before a current configuration task is started, a task class has to be selected as the context for the task. The second axiom ensures that this selection is unambiguous. Axiom 3 and 4 ensure that there is enough time to *learn* which objects have the highest rewards per task class. The permanent learning enables RKF to follow changes. The forgetting part ensures that an abrupt change of rewards, which is allowed as a consequence of domain changes, can result in a new "most relevant" object. These abrupt changes should seldom occur, because RKF needs time to learn the altered rewards. What "slowly" and "seldom" mean is determined by the parameters of the relevance function (which will be introduced in section 2.4). These parameters control how fast or how conservative the learning and forgetting behavior of RKF is and how much time is needed to *learn* the objects with the best rewards.

The above statements lead to the problem of finding suitable task classes for a domain. Interestingly, task classes already exist in many configuration domains: User or target groups of a product.

For example, the set of task classes $\boldsymbol{C}$ of a personal computer domain can be derived from the fields of use and target groups for PCs:

$$\boldsymbol{C} = \{\text{Home-PC, Server-PC, CAD-PC, ...}\}.$$

If no such groups exist for a domain, a second indicator for task classes emerges from axiom 5: The task classes can result from the combinations of various global optimization goals. For example, if the optimization goals "price" and "performance" are decisive in a domain, the set of task classes can be generated by combining the objectives for price and performance, such as "high", "low" and "don't care". The result would be $3 \cdot 3 = 9$ task classes: "low price / high performance", "don't care the price / high performance", "high price / high performance", "low price / don't care performance" etc.

It is also possible to start with a course partitioning of the set of tasks and to refine the task classes later. Therefore, the task classes can be further partitioned with the following algorithm:

Divide *c* into *c1* and *c2*:

Rename *c* into *c1*.
Create a new task class *c2*.
Copy all relevance information for all objects from *c1* to *c2*.
Modify the partitioning function to classify tasks from *c* from now on as *c1* or *c2* (exclusively).

The following example shows that the refinement of task classes is very natural: The above mentioned task class "Home-PC", which was probably a typical target group some years ago, can nowadays be refined to "Game-PC", "Internet-PC", "Private-Office-PC", "Video-PC" etc.

2.4 Relevance Function for Technical Domains

Equation (2 shows that training and forgetting are effects that alternate over time. For the following considerations we have used the number of configuration runs as time. This discrete time measure especially simplifies the description of learning phases because a user reward is only available in the context of a configuration run. With this method, time has to be determined separately for each task class because every configuration run is in the context of exactly one task class, so the time continues only for this task class. In this paper we will write t for time as a substitution for t_c (time t in context of task class c) to make the equations clearer.

Initially we will consider the processes of training and forgetting separately.

2.4.1 Function for Training

The learning portion of RKF is very similar to reinforcement learning (see **[12]**). This learning model uses the following standard model:

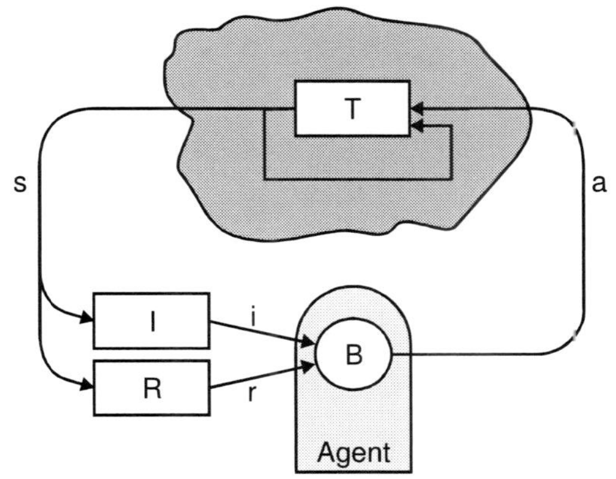

Figure 3: The standard reinforcement-learning model

The model consists of a discrete set of environment states ***S***, a discrete set of agent actions ***A***, a set of scalar reinforcement signals, typically {0, 1} or the real numbers, a state transition probability function T: s' = T(s, a), an input function I, which determines how the agent views the environment state I: I = I(s) (usually the identity function), a reward function R: r = R(s) and a behavior function B to choose actions B: a = B(I, r). *"The agent's behavior, B, should choose actions that tend to increase the long-run sum of values of the reinforcement signal.[...] The simplest possible reinforcement-learning problem is known as the k-armed bandit problem, which has been the subject of a great deal of study in the statistics and applied mathematics. The agent is in a room with a collection of k gambling machines (each called a "one-armed bandit" in colloquial English). The agent is permitted a fixed number of pulls, h. Any arm may be pulled on each turn. The machines do not require a deposit to play; the only cost is wasting a pull playing a suboptimal machine. When arm i is pulled, machine i pays off 1 or 0 according to some underlying probability parameter p_i, where payoffs are independent events and the p_is are unknown."* Kaelbling, Littman and Moore use the term "action" to indicate the agent's choice of arm to pull. It is very important to note that bandit problems fit the definition of a reinforcement-learning environment with a single state, with only self transitions.

A decision between *all pieces of information in question* during a configuration process using RKF can be compared to the k-armed bandit problem: pulling arm i means selecting the object *o* in question. The reward or payoff is given by the user's rating *reward(o, t, c)*. The usage of task classes assures that the rating for an object selection remains approximately constant (axiom 3 in section 2.3).

In contrast to the reinforcement learning model described in **[12]**, we do not linearly sum up the rewards but instead use an exponential function to calculate the relevance from the rewards given by users. We are motivated to do so by looking at results of Cognitive Psychology (see 1.3). The Power Function of Learning shows characteristics which also seem to be adequate for technical domains:

- An object seems to be important if it is used frequently. The "access time" should be reduced, i.e. it should be preferentially selected. In other words, its relevance should be increased
- Learning increases relevance starting from the last relevance value resulting from the preceding forgetting phase lastForgetRel(*o, t, c*) and approaches 1 (=100%)
- The first accesses make information relevant more quickly than later accesses. If, for example, the same object is used in 10,000 configuration processes of a particular task class, ten further accesses no longer have particular importance. Experts have thus learnt that this object is suitable in the context of the task class
- Relevance approaches a maximum value

We reduce the range of values to the interval [0, 1]. Since we calculate the 'relevance' in contrast to the 'access time' of Figure 1, the function has been horizontally reflected. This is based on the fact that a high relevance corresponds to a small access time.

Our exponential function for training is modeled by the following recursive formula: The difference between a last relevance value rel(*o, t*-1, *c*) and the maximum possible relevance (100%) is divided by a "basis" b_t. Then the last relevance value is increased by the resulting value. The user's rating reward(*o, t, c*) ∈ [0,1] is considered by multiplying it with the increasing amount, i.e. the user's reward is the percentage value for which the increment of the last relevance value is to be performed. We have used this recursive version of the train function in our implementation because it is efficient to implement and easy to understand.

Definition 1:
The effect of "training" for an object *o* in technical domains can be described by the following function:

$$\text{train: } \mathrm{rel}(o,t,c) = \mathrm{rel}(o,t-1,c) + \frac{1-\mathrm{rel}(o,t-1,c)}{b_t} \cdot \mathrm{reward}(o,t,c) \tag{3}$$

starting with lastForgetRel(*o, t, c*)

with

$t \in \{0, 1, \ldots\}$	"Time": number of solution processes in context c	(4)
rel(*o, t, c*) ∈ [0,1]	Relevance for an object *o* at time *t* in the context of task class *c*	(5)
reward(*o, t, c*) ∈ [0,1]	The reward during the current learning phase (at time t)	(6)
$b_t \in (1,\infty)$	"Basis" for the train function determining the "speed" of training. The larger b_t, the slower the training. Typical values lie between one and three.	(7)
lastForgetRel(*o, t, c*) ∈ [0, 1]	last relevance value of *o* before *t* when the last forgetting phase ended in the context of the task class *c*	(8)

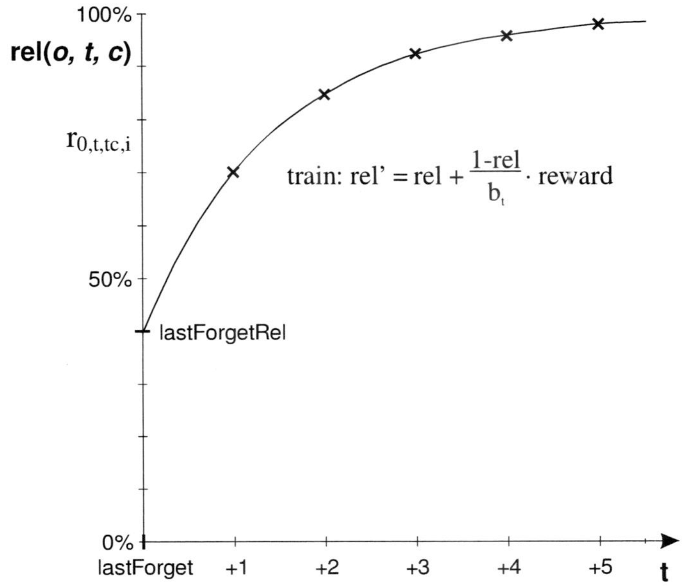

Figure 4: Recursive train function with lastForgetRel(o, t, c)=0.4, reward=100% and b_t=2.0

The following considerations show that this recursive function is equivalent to a power function: The rewards during a single training phase are constant for an object *o* in the context of a single task class *c*, according to axiom 3 (section 2.3):

$$\text{reward}(o, t, c) = r_{o\,c}.$$

Additionally, we use the following substitutions:

rel' := rel(*o*, *t*, *c*)	new relevance value
rel := rel(*o*, *t*-1, *c*)	last relevance value

This results in

$$\text{rel}' = \text{rel} + \frac{1-\text{rel}}{b_t} \cdot r_{o,c} \text{ starting with lastForgetRel}(o, t, c) \tag{9}$$

$$\text{rel}' = \left(1 - \frac{r_{o,c}}{b_t}\right) \cdot \text{rel} + \frac{r_{o,c}}{b_t} \tag{10}$$

with help of a z-transformation we get a non-recursive representation

$$r = \left(1-\frac{r_{o,c}}{b_t}\right)^t \cdot \text{lastForgetRel}(o, t, c) + 1 - \left(1-\frac{r_{o,c}}{b_t}\right)^t \tag{11}$$

and finally

$$\text{train: rel}(o, t, c) = 1 + (\text{lastForgetRel}(o, t, c) - 1) \cdot \left(1 - \frac{r_{o,c}}{b_t}\right)^t \tag{12}$$

2.4.2 Function for Forgetting

The importance of *forgetting* for the performance of knowledge base search has been shown by several authors (e.g. **[20]**, **[4]**, **[24]**, **[19]**). Most of them use forgetting synonymously with the deletion of knowledge. Anderson has put forward that forgetting is a continuous process for humans (see section 1.3) and we are of the opinion that it should also be a continuous process in configuration domains, since the deletion of knowledge is in this case mostly inadequate. For example, the deletion of an old concept in a passenger car configuration domain would not only make the configuration of old timer cars impossible but also the reconfiguration of existing cars (which lies in our focus, see **[15]**). The continuous process of ignoring old knowledge has also been used in aHUGIN **[24]** and is therein called *fading*: *"Variables in adaptation mode have an extra feature, fading, which makes them tend to ignore things they have learnt a long time ago, considering them as less relevant."* As a starting point for our forget-function we considered the power law of forgetting (see Section 1.3). The reason for this is that in technical domains similar characteristics to those in the human brain are desirable for the development of relevance:

- New objects have an initial value of relevance which is much higher than old and unused objects. The information concerning the objects ages continuously
- Initially objects lose their relevance faster. For example, after 10 years, one week either way will no longer have a great effect on the relevance of objects in technical configuration domains
- The relevance approaches zero, whereas objects are never really irrelevant. The access just lasts longer

Real forgetting, i.e. the irreversible erasure of objects, is not desirable at first. However, in section 2.5 the issue is addressed as to how maintenance of a knowledge base can be supported with the help of relevance.

To simplify matters, the following assumptions were made, compared with the function for the "power law of forgetting":

- Reduction in the range of values to [0, 1]
- The relevance value during a forgetting phase should start at the last value of a preceding training phase lastUseRel(o, t, c) $\in$ [0,1] and approach zero

The aforementioned "desired" characteristics remain. The first assumption is for the reason that we want to model relevance as percentage values. The second is because it is presumed that forgetting is a decay-process, starting with the "*activation level*" after the last access.

If we try to determine the start relevance lastUseRel(o, t_0, c) at the moment t_0 when an object o is stored, we recognize that many parameters of the original function in the model of Cognitive Psychology are not available at first. For example, in **[30]** it is described how the start relevance depends on the estimation of the importance of the information. In the best case, the start relevance can be provided by the knowledge engineer who adds the object. If such an assessment is not available, we must assume that all objects that are added to a knowledge base are of the same importance because a computer cannot make "emotional" assessments. In this case we define a start relevance lastUseRel(o, t_0, c) := 50% because with this relevance, o has the same chance to become relevant (to prove its worth) or to become irrelevant (to be forgotten).

Definition 2:
The start relevance for an object o at the time t_0 when it is stored in context c is set to 50%:

$$\text{start relevance: rel}(o, t_0, c) := 0.5 \tag{13}$$

The basis b_f of the power function is a parameter that is domain dependent, analog to the fact that some things are forgotten faster than others. The larger b_f, the faster the decay process is. The following definition describes the forget-function which we have applied:

Definition 3:
The process of gradually forgetting an object o in technical domains can be described by the following function:

$$\text{forget: rel}(o, t, c) = \text{lastUseRel}(o, t, c) \cdot b_f^{-\text{age}} \tag{14}$$

with

$\text{rel}(o, t, c) \in [0,1]$	The relevance of an object o at time t during a forgetting phase in the context of task class c	(15)
$\text{age} \in \{0,1,...\}$	$= t - \text{lastUse}(o, t, c)$, time since the last use of o before t in the context of c = time since the last training phase	(16)
$\text{lastUseRel}(o, t, c) \in [0, 1]$	$= \text{rel}(o, \text{lastUse}(o, t, c), c)$, the relevance value after the last use of o	(17)
$\text{lastUse}(o, t, c) \in \{0,1,...\}$	The last time when o has been used before t in context of c	(18)
$b_f \in (1,\infty)$	"Basis" for the forget function determining the "speed" of forgetting. The larger b_f, the faster objects are forgotten	(19)

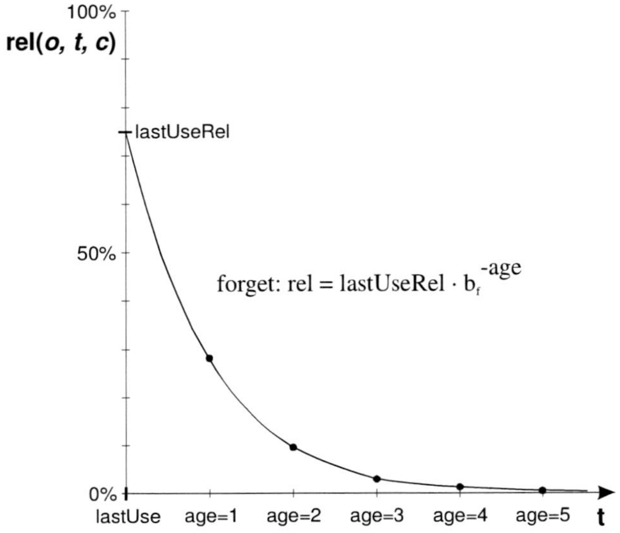

Figure 5: The forget function for lastUseRel=75%, $b_f = \boldsymbol{e}$

2.4.3 Relevance of Objects

In equation (2, the relevance function for an object *o* results from combining the forget and the train functions, dependent on whether object *o* is part of the solution or not. With equations (3) and (14, the following definition results from (2:

Definition 4:

The relevance of objects in a knowledge base is described by the following function:

$$\text{rel}(o, t, c) := \begin{cases} \text{rel}(o, t\text{-}1, c) + \dfrac{(1 - \text{rel}(o, t\text{-}1, c))}{b_t} \cdot \text{reward}(o, t, c) & \text{if } ① \\ \text{lastUseRel}(o, t, c) \cdot b_f^{-\text{age}(o, t, c)} & \text{if } ② \end{cases} \tag{20}$$

① **train**, if *o* **is** part of the solution, start with lastForgetRel(*o*, *t*, *c*)

② **forget**, if *o* is **not** part of the solution

with

age ∈ {0,1,...}	= t – lastUse(*o, t, c*) , time since the last use of *o* before *t* in the context of *c* = time since the last training phase (see (16))
$b_f \in (1,\infty)$	"Basis" for the forget function determining the "speed" of forgetting. The larger b_f, the faster objects are forgotten (see (19))
$b_t \in (1,\infty)$	"Basis" for the train function determining the "speed" of training. The larger b_t, the slower the training. Typical values lie between one and three (see (7))

c	Task class (context), e.g. a target group.
lastForgetRel(o, t, c) $\in$ [0, 1]	Last relevance value of o before t, when the last forgetting phase ended in the context of the task class c (see (8))
lastUse(o, t, c) $\in$ {0,1,...}	The last time when o has been used before t in the context of c (see (18))
lastUseRel(o, t, c) $\in$ [0, 1]	= rel(o, lastUse(o, t, c), c), the relevance value after the last use of o (see(17))
lastUseRel(o, t_0, c) := 0.5	The start relevance is set 50% when o is stored (see (13))
rel(o, t, c) $\in$ [0,1]	Relevance for an object o at time t in the context of task class c
reward(o, t, c) $\in$ [0,1]	The user reward for object o at time t in context of c (see (6))

The following diagram shows an example of the relevance function from equation (20):

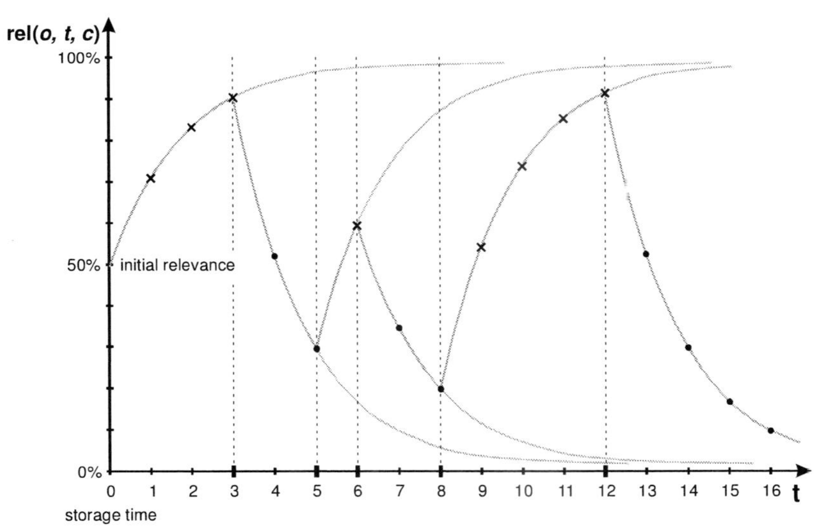

Figure 6: Train and forget phases alternate in the relevance function, dependent on whether object o is part of a solution or not

In this example, an object o has been stored at t=0 and has been part of the solution at $t \in \{1, 2, 3, 6, 9, 10, 11, 12\}$ with a constant user reward ("crosses" in Figure 6). According to this, the intervals (0, 3], (5, 6] and (8, 12] are training phases. During the remaining intervals, the object is continuously forgotten and from t=13 onwards it ages infinitely ("dots" in Figure 6).

2.5 Determination of Parameters

2.5.1 Effect of Parameters

The parameters[2] b_t, b_f and v can be used to adapt the relevance and selection functions to a given configuration domain. They control how fast something is forgotten or learnt and how conservatively a selection by RKF should be performed.

The effects of changing the parameters are listed in tables 1, 2 and 3. These effects were directly expected from the relevance formula (equation (20)) and the selection formula (equation (1)). They have been proved by the experiments that we have performed in different domains. Some of these experiments are discussed in section 4.3

Table 1: Effects arising from different values for $\mathbf{b_t}$

t1	The speed of training determines how fast the relevance of an object that is repeatedly part of the solution approaches **100%**
t2	Larger b_t → slower training Smaller b_t → faster training
t3	Since the user rewards are multiplied with $1/b_t$ a large value also has the effect that the rewards are not considered so strongly in addition to slower training
t4	The **smallest** possible value of 1.0, together with a user reward of 100% would cause the relevance of an object to become 100% in just one step!
t5	The **largest** value we have used was 10.0 which made the influence of the rewards already so little, that we could not observe any learning which would reflect the rewards given (see equation (3))

Table 2: Effects arising from different values for $\mathbf{b_f}$

f1	The speed of forgetting determines how fast the relevance of the objects, which were not part of the solution approach **0%**
f2	Larger b_f → faster forgetting Smaller b_f → slower forgetting
f3	The **smallest** possible value of 1.0 makes forgetting infinitely slow and switches off forgetting!
f4	The **largest** value we have used was 10.0 which made forgetting so fast, that all objects that were not chosen in the first experiment immediately had a relevance of near zero and have not been chosen anymore. Since all objects in the first experiment have their start relevance, they are chosen randomly and consequently it is also random which object wins

[2] b_t stands for "**b**asis of **t**rain function", b_f for "**b**asis of **f**orget function" and v stands for "**v**ariance".

Table 3: Effects arising from different values for **v**

v1	Being "more conservative" during a selection means that an object that has been selected before is more likely to be selected again , due to its slightly higher relevance value
v2	If an object is selected repeatedly it gets rewards more often and consequently its relevance reaches 100% more quickly
v3	Larger → more conservative → faster training smaller → less conservative → slower training
v4	The **smallest** possible value of 1.0 causes a probability that is linear to the relative relevance of an object
v5	Values **larger** than 2.5 make the selection so conservative that it becomes impossible to replace an object with a new one

Parameter v changes the relative probability of the objects in question. Relevant objects are more strongly preferred if v is large. This can be illustrated by the following example:

One object is to be chosen from the set $\boldsymbol{O} = \{o_1, o_2, o_3, o_4, o_5\}$. The object's current relevance values for this example are listed in table 4.

Table 4: Relevance values of the example

O_1	$r_1 = 0.25$
O_2	$r_2 = 0.5$
O_3	$r_3 = 0.8$
o_4	$r_4 = 0.2$
o_5	$r_5 = 0.25$

From these values the probability distribution can be calculated, using equation (1). The left-hand pie chart diagram in Figure 6 shows the probability distribution resulting from $v = 1$. If each of the relevance values are raised to the power of three ($v = 3$), then a probability distribution results which is illustrated in the right-hand pie chart of Figure 6.

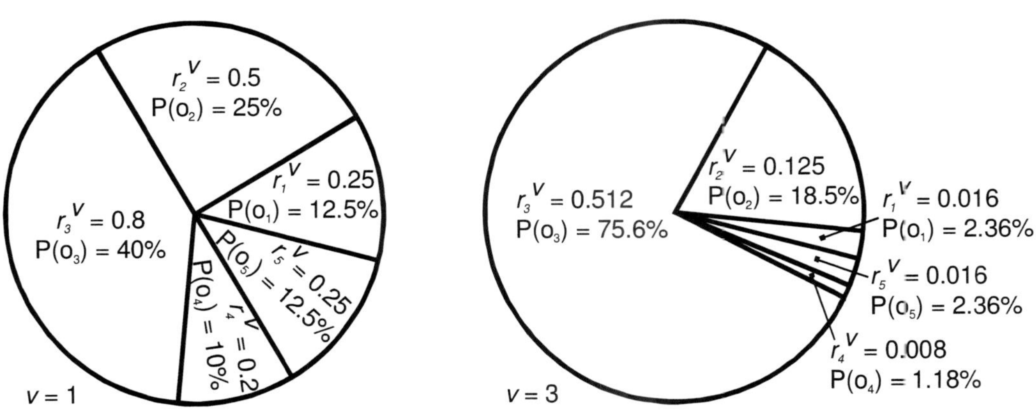

Figure 7: Probability distribution with v = 1 and v = 3

A selection with $v \geq 1$ is more conservative, in so far as an object which is slightly more relevant than the others in question is more likely to be selected again and again.

The effects of the parameters b_t, b_f and v influence each other. For example, if v is enlarged to make a selection more conservative, then learning becomes faster at the same time without changing b_t: The same object is very frequently chosen with a higher probability and as a consequence it very frequently gets a reward from the users which results in an increasing relevance (see v2 and v3 in table 3). To compensate faster learning, b_t should also be enlarged. However, this is not reasonable for all values of b_t (see 2.5.2). Fast learning can also be compensated by giving the heuristic more time for learning, by slowing down the forgetting of the objects which have not been chosen. For this, b_f can be reduced (see f2 in table 2).

The influence of the three parameters on each other makes it impossible to calculate the parameters exactly. In section 2.5.2 we will derive relations between the three parameters which help to find sensible values for the other parameters, as soon as one parameter has been determined. These relations only provide intervals of sensible values. As a consequence, we assume that a triple of exact parameter values, which is suitable for a task class of a given domain, can only be determined empirically. For this, automated configuration runs can be performed, where the expected user rewards are provided from tables. The parameters can be adjusted for the simulations, until the desired learning behavior is achieved. A "desired learning behavior" can be described by the following considerations:

After some time one single object with high rewards asserts itself. If the three parameters are set correctly, this is the object which receives the highest rewards. The reason for this is that an object receiving the highest rewards becomes relevant most quickly. In subsequent choices it is more likely to be chosen and receives rewards again which in turn makes it more probable again. Our experiments have shown that an object is very likely to *always* be chosen as soon as it has reached a probability of 90%. At this point all other objects in question have a joint probability of 10%. We call this a steady state. The time after objects have been added to a set of alternative objects of a domain, before one object has reached 90%, is called "*transient oscillating phase*". This steady state will end only as soon as the relevance of another object in question becomes so large that the most probable object falls short of 90%. This can occur as a consequence of the following events:

Table 5: events which can end a steady state

r1	A new object is added and starts with a relevance value of 50% (see equation (13)).
r2	An irrelevant object recovers (at least) the start relevance value because it has been chosen by another heuristic (e.g. by a manual user selection) and from that point on receives high user rewards.
r3	It is also possible to adjust the relevance values manually, for example, based on expert knowledge.
r4	The relevance values of a set of alternative objects are initialized with 50% which is necessary after the structure of a domain has been changed. This initialization is important because RKF only learns the structure of a domain implicitly. After an initialization, all relevance values have to be learnt again and the new structure can be taken into account.

The following statements about transient oscillating phases are based on mathematical considerations concerning the selection and relevance functions (equation (1) and (20)) and have been confirmed by our experiments (see section 4.3):

Table 6: Oscillating phases

e1	Slow learning prolongs transient oscillating phases (small v, large b_l) and an oscillating phase is shortened by fast learning.
e2	Slow forgetting prolongs transient oscillating phases (small b_f) and an oscillating phase is shortened by fast forgetting.
e3	Oscillating phases last longer if the user rewards for the best two objects in question get rewards which are only slightly different
e4	Oscillating phases last longer if not the complete interval of possible reward values between 0% and 100% is used because then the rewards will only be slightly different
e5	An oscillating phase for a set of objects in question $\boldsymbol{O}$ should at least last long enough that every object $o \in \boldsymbol{O}$ is chosen at least once and gets at least one user reward. As a consequence, the more objects in $\boldsymbol{O}$, the longer the oscillating phases should last.
e6	If an oscillating phase is too short, it might happen that an object which doesn't get the highest user rewards becomes most relevant. If no oscillating phase is allowed (e.g. by setting $b_l = 1.0$), then any object $o \in \boldsymbol{O}$ can become most relevant at random.
e7	Oscillating phases should be as short as possible because during these phases objects which don't receive the highest user rewards can be chosen

According to the statements e5 through e7, the oscillating phases depend on the set $\boldsymbol{O}$. Additionally the expected user rewards have an influence on the oscillating phases (see e3 and e4). Therefore, the question arose concerning whether it would be possible at all to use the *same* parameters for *all* sets of objects. Our experiments could however corroborate the following considerations:

- If the user rewards for the best objects of a set $\boldsymbol{O}$ are very similar, it is adequate that the oscillating phase lasts long: In fact it is possible that more than one object is suitable for a task class. Such sets should not be used to adjust the parameters for oscillating phases (see e3).
- It can be assumed that the behavior of the users when they give rewards is the same for all sets of objects in the context of one task class. This means that the interval of values which are used for rewards is the same for all sets of objects and that this interval can be scaled to the complete interval [0, 1]. Both the interval used by the users and the scaling can be influenced by the user interface (see e4).

- The optimal result is not provided by RKF until the oscillating phase has ended for all sets of objects in a domain. This means that the largest set of objects can be used to adjust the parameters b_t, b_f and v (see e5).

Following these considerations, it can be assumed that the same parameters can be used for all sets of objects of a domain – at least per task class.

2.5.2 Replacement Condition

Further clues for determining the parameters b_t, b_f and v are provided by the so-called replacement condition: One fundamental demand on RKF is to enable *re*learning. This means that according to the first three situations (r1-r3), stated in table 5, an object o_{new} can replace an object o_{old} which has been the most relevant of a set of objects $\boldsymbol{O}$ so far, if it receives at least the same (or higher) rewards as o_{old}.

According to r2 (table 5), it should be possible for an object to recover at least the start relevance after receiving a user reward:

- At least after receiving a maximum user reward of reward(o, t, c) = 100%, the start relevance rel(o, t, c) = 50% should be recovered.
- In the worst case, the relevance value before was near zero (rel(o, t-1, c) ≈ 0%).

Together with the learning portion of equation (20), this results in

$$0 + \frac{(1 - 0)}{b_t} \cdot 1 > 0.5 \tag{21}$$

$$\frac{1}{b_t} > 0.5 \tag{22}$$

$$b_t < 2 \tag{23}$$

Theorem 1:

Parameter b_t should have values smaller than 2, to enable relearning.

The replacement condition requires the length of an oscillating phase e to be adjusted, to enable an new object o_{new}, with a relevance value of rel(o_{new}, t_r, c) = 50% to replace an object o_{old}, which has a relevance of rel(o_{old}, t_r, c)=100% in the worst case, where t_r is the moment when the replacement takes place. All other objects of $\boldsymbol{O}$ can be ignored at that moment, because if the relevance of o_{old} is assumed to be rel(o_{old}, t_r, c) = 100%, then all the other "old" objects will have a relevance value near zero.

The probabilities to be chosen can be calculated according to equation (1)

$$P(o_{old}, t_r, c) = \frac{1^v}{1^v + \text{rel}(o_{new}, t_r, c)^v} = \frac{1^v}{1^v + 0.5^v} = \frac{1}{1 + 0.5^v} < 90\% \tag{24}$$

$$P(o_{new}, t_r, c) = \frac{0.5^v}{1^v + 0.5^v} = \frac{0.5^v}{1 + 0.5^v} \quad (25)$$

The probability for o_{old} to be chosen should fall under 90% (see"<90%" in equation (24)) in order to end the stable state just by adding the new object with rel(o_{new}, t_r, c) = 0.5. However, if o_{old} is chosen instead of o_{new} after it has been added, then o_{new} will age and its relevance will fall under the start relevance value (0.5). The relevance of o_{old}, however, cannot rise because the maximum relevance value of 100% has already been assumed.

If o_{new} is never chosen (at random), in the worst case, its relevance fades and the probability of o_{old} will rise over 90% after some time which will end the oscillating phase. The maximum length of the oscillating phase e can then be calculated with the following considerations:

The fading of the relevance of o_{new} starts with rel(o_{new}, t_r, c) = 0.5 and from then on can be calculated according to the forgetting part of the relevance formula (equation (20)):

$$\text{rel}(o_{new}, t_r + e, c) = 0.5 \cdot b_f^{-e} \qquad \text{with } e \in \{0, 1, \ldots\} \quad (26)$$

With this relevance value for o_{new} and a relevance value of 100% for o_{old}, the oscillating phase continues for as long as the probability that o_{old} will be chosen remains under 90%. From equation (1) follows:

$$P(o_{old}, t_r + e, c) = \frac{1}{1 + 0.5 \cdot b_f^{-e \cdot v}} < 0.9 \quad (27)$$

We are looking for the length of the oscillating phase e, i.e. the time after o_{new} becomes so irrelevant that the probability that o_{old} will be chosen rises just over 90%. From equation (27) follows

$$1 + 0.5 \cdot b_f^{-e \cdot v} > \frac{10}{9} \quad (28)$$

$$b_f^{e \cdot v} < 4.5 \quad (29)$$

$$e \cdot v < \log_{b_f} 4.5 \quad (30)$$

$$e < \frac{\ln 4.5}{v \cdot \ln b_f} \quad (31)$$

Theorem 2:

The length of the oscillating phase depends on the parameters v and b_f, as described in inequality (31).

During this time span e, the object o_{new} has to be chosen at least once to recover its initial relevance. In addition, o_{new} only gets a chance to be chosen again if e is at least 1.

$$e \geq 1 \tag{32}$$

With equation (31):

$$1 \leq e < \frac{\ln 4.5}{v \cdot \ln b_f} \tag{33}$$

$$v < \frac{\ln 4.5}{\ln b_f} \qquad \text{where } v \geq 0 \tag{34}$$

If more than one object is added to a domain at once, e has to be at least long enough that all new objects could be chosen at least once. Let n_O be the maximum number of objects that are added to a set of objects $\boldsymbol{O}$ at once, where $\boldsymbol{O}$ is in a stable state before the addition. This results in

$$e \geq n_o \tag{35}$$

Together with equation (31)

$$n_o \leq e < \frac{\ln 4.5}{v \cdot \ln b_f} \tag{36}$$

$$v < \frac{\ln 4.5}{n_o \cdot \ln b_f} \qquad \text{where } v \geq 0,\ n_o > 0 \tag{37}$$

Theorem 3:

Equation (37) describes the interdependence of the parameters v and b_f, when the maximum number of new objects which are added to a set of objects at one time can be estimated.

To ensure that an object o_{old} can be replaced by an object o_{new}, we demand that the probability for the choice of the new object o_{new} will be higher than for o_{old}

- if o_{new} has been chosen with a relevance of 0.5 (start relevance) at time t_r (time of replacement)
- and if the best user reward (100%) has been received for o_{new}:

$$P(o_{new}, t_r{+}1, c) > P(o_{alt}, t_r{+}1, c) \tag{38}$$

For the relevance calculation at the moment t_r+1, the forgetting part of (20) is used for o_{old} (not chosen) and the learning part is used for o_{new} (which has been chosen).

The worst case is assumed again with rel(o_{old}, t_r, c) = 1. From the relevance formula (20) follows

$$\text{rel}(o_{old}, t_r{+}1, c) = 1 \cdot b_f^{-1} = b_f^{-1} \qquad (age = 1) \tag{39}$$

$$\text{rel}(o_{new}, t_r{+}1, c) = 0.5 + \frac{1 - 0.5}{b_r} \cdot 1 = 0.5 + \frac{1}{2\,b_r} \qquad (reward = 100\%) \tag{40}$$

With equation (1) and inequality (38) this results in:

$$\frac{\left(0.5 + \frac{1}{2\,b_r}\right)^{v}}{b_f^{-v} + \left(0.5 + \frac{1}{2\,b_r}\right)^{v}} > \frac{b_f^{-v}}{b_f^{-v} + \left(0.5 + \frac{1}{2\,b_r}\right)^{v}} \tag{41}$$

$$b_f^{-v} < \left(0.5 + \frac{1}{2\,b_r}\right)^{v} \tag{42}$$

$$\frac{1}{bf} < \frac{1}{2} + \frac{1}{2\,b_r} \tag{43}$$

$$b_f > \frac{2\,b_r}{b_r + 1} \tag{44}$$

Theorem 4:

Equation (44) describes the interdependence of the parameters b_f and b_r:

The interdependencies derived in this section help to restrict the intervals of possible values for the parameters b_f, b_t and v. Our experiments (see 4.3) have confirmed, however, that the *exact* values in the context of a given domain can only be empirically determined, dependent on

- the expected user rewards and
- the expected number of objects which are added at one time.

3 Application of RKF in Configuration Domains

With equation (1), RKF will always help if one object has to be selected from a discrete and finite set of possible objects. During a configuration process in a domain that has been modeled with objects or frames, selections of that kind occur during the following configuration steps (we have oriented ourselves with *possible configuration steps* at PLAKON (see chapter 4.5 in **[6]**):

- Specialization

During a specialization step, the "type" of a solution's instance has to be specialized from an abstract concept to one of its children, according to the taxonomical hierarchy. In this case, the set of objects in question $\boldsymbol{O}$ is formed by the child concepts and o is one specialization to be selected.

- Decomposition

A decomposition step determines the number of components a concept consists of. In many technical domains the set of possible numbers is discrete and each number can be understood as an object. Unfortunately, in many examples no upper boundary for the number of components can be given at first and consequently "infinite" (∞) is often used as an "upper boundary" in the compositional hierarchies. Since RKF can only be applied to finite sets, the determination of the number of components cannot generally be supported by RKF. Nevertheless, we were able to find an upper boundary in all investigated domains, by adding information from experts to the domain analogues to the following example: It's true that a PC can contain any number of hard disks in principle. But if we would ask an expert on PCs he or she would know that the maximum number of hard disks is probably given in a server PC, which "had never more than about 20 hard disks as far as he or she can remember". If we double this value we will probably not exclude any solution in that domain. The set of numbers [0..40] can be understood as a discrete and finite set of 41 objects and RKF can be used to select one number.

- Parameterization of instances

With the use of RKF for parameters of instances, it is very much the same as with the use for decompositions, as before: As long as the sets are discrete and finite, RKF can be used. For example, the set of colors of cars satisfies the presumption. However, the value ranges of parameters like the size or position of an instance are not even discrete. So again we can say that RKF cannot help in principle to determine the parameters of instances. Nevertheless, methods exist to reduce such sets to discrete finite sets, for example by dividing the value range into a discrete and finite set of intervals. RKF can help to select the right interval.

- Integration

An integration step determines how many existing instances of an incomplete solution can be used to satisfy a relation between instances and how many concepts have to be instantiated additionally. With the same limitations as with decomposition, these values can have a discrete and finite value range. How many concepts should be instantiated or integrated usually depends on the control knowledge and not on task classes. However, RKF only uses a task class c as the context for learning and forgetting and will usually not help in this case.

- Agenda

Configuration systems that use a structure-based or object-orientated representation typically use a so-called agenda to collect the configuration steps which have to be performed before the configuration is complete. Before each configuration step, the configuration system has to determine which entry of the agenda should be processed next. The set of entries in the agenda is discrete and finite but no user assessments are available, since the user is shielded against the control of a configurator.

- Selection of a heuristic

The above list of possible applications shows that RKF, like almost all heuristics, cannot be optimally used in all situations. In his doctoral thesis, Günter **[7]** has proposed the use of a flexible control that uses multiple heuristics, dependent on so-called control knowledge. The set of heuristics is discrete and finite but again which heuristic to use is usually not typical for a task class and RKF will probably not help with this. However, if the heuristics to be used are typical for the task classes in a domain, RKF can be used as a meta heuristic which learns which heuristic helped most often to find a solution in the context of a task class. In any case, RKF is an additional heuristic that can be selected using the flexible control of a configuration system.

- Maintenance of Knowledge Bases

One important disadvantage of long-existing databases and therefore also of knowledge bases is that objects which are no longer relevant cannot be automatically deleted. It is a conventional approach to delete *old* objects. With RKF, this approach can be considerably improved by deleting not *old* but *no longer relevant* objects, thereby taking into consideration how often an object has been used "during the last time". For this, the relevance of all objects in the knowledge base could be determined and as soon as it falls short of a certain level of relevance, the object can be deleted. For each object, the highest relevance of all task classes is used, i.e. an object should only be deleted if it is no longer relevant in the context of all task classes.

4 Realization and Experiments

4.1 RKF-Configurator

RKF should be used together with other heuristics when used in a professional configuration system as already mentioned under "Selection of a heuristic" in section 2.5. To be able to demonstrate the effects arising solely from RKF, we have built up a configuration prototype ("RKF-Configurator") in JAVA. We have already presented a first version of it on PUK2000 (see **[17]**). It supports an object-oriented representation of the configuration knowledge with concept hierarchies (taxonomical and compositional), n:m-relations and parameter relations (JAVA methods that return true or false), which we call "parameter constraints". With the RKF-Configurator we have implemented a depth-first search with chronological backtracking. RKF is the only heuristic used and we have compared the results with "no heuristic used", which is equal to a random selection of objects during the depth-first search. RKF is used during all specialization and decomposition steps. The use of RKF for decomposition steps is always possible because we do not allow infinite (∞) as a number in the compositional hierarchies. The use of RKF for the parameterization of instances has been planned but we do not expect effects different to those arising from the use in selecting numbers during decomposition steps. Consequently, we have not implemented full support for parameterization and parameters are instead only collected along the taxonomical hierarchy. The configuration is built up using specialization, decomposition and "parameterization". Subsequently, the n:m-relations and parameter constraints are tested at the end of such configuration steps, when the configuration is possibly complete and might cause backtracking (build and test). In our simple implementation, we presume that *all* n:m-relations can be realized by integrating the existent instances. Therefore, we do not need to support instantiation with RKF during integration steps. Since we use depth-first search and chronological backtracking as the only strategies, no selection from the agenda can be supported by RKF and because RKF is the only heuristic, it is also not used as a meta-heuristic.

To start a configuration, a user can select a concept from the compositional hierarchy as the root of the system to be configured and the task class as the context for the current configuration task. RKF needs no further user input during the configuration process and the configurator will then present a solution, if possible. In this case, the user is prompted to give an assessment (reward) for every single component of the solution. In the case that the configuration found is still not "good" enough (according to the above assessment) the configuration can be restarted. Due to the probabilistic selection method in RKF, the same task specification can lead to different (but similar) solutions. In our project, at this point we export the solution as a XML-file, the so-called *Exact Configuration Onboard* which is a documentation of a vehicle that is stored onboard this vehicle (see **[14]**, **[16]**, **[18]**).

4.2 Implementation Considerations

The most important extension for a configuration system that should use RKF is the storing of the relevance information for each object that should be selectable by the heuristic RKF. Relevance information consists of two elements:

1. lastUse(o, t, c) The point in time when o has been last used
2. lastUseRel(o, t, c) The relevance value which o had at that point in time

With this information, the current relevance of an object can always be calculated during a configuration process, by using the "forget" part of the relevance formula (20): If o was **not** part of the solution in the configuration run before, this is obviously the correct part to be used. If o **was** part of the solution, age(o, t, c) will return 1, which results in the proper value in that case, because one time unit lies between the current time and the last use.

As soon as a configuration run has finished, only the relevance information of those objects that were part of the solution (which are typically few relative to the total number of objects stored in a knowledge base) has to be updated. The relevance information of all other objects does not need to be updated: The "forget"-part of the relevance formula will provide the current relevance value *if required*, as just described.

To update the relevance information of objects that were part of the solution, the current relevance value is calculated and used as rel(o, t-1, c) in the "train" part of (20). The result of this calculation is stored as lastUseRel(o, t, c) and t as lastUse(o, t, c). Time t of the current task class is always updated (increased) after all necessary relevance information has been updated.

With this method only two additional elements are needed per object of the knowledge base for every task class. If $n=|\boldsymbol{O}|$ is the number of objects stored in a knowledge base and $k=|\boldsymbol{C}|$ is the number of task classes of a domain, then a linear amount of $2k \cdot n$ of additional memory is needed.

4.3 Experiments

4.3.1 Example Domains and Conditions for the Experiments

We have successfully tested RKF in five very different technical domains. Although none of them consist of more than 127 concepts, the number of possible combinations of these concepts (search space) is already enormous (see "possible combinations" in table 7). Without the help of heuristics the whole search space had to be scanned in the worst case scenario, to find any or even a "good" solution. Dependent on the nesting of a domain, our implementation is able to compute ("build and test") about 3,000 combinations per second on an 850 MHz PC. As an example about $323 \cdot 10^{12}$ years (10^{12} = trillion = million · million) would be necessary to scan the complete PC Domain (2.) with 125 concepts. To come to the point, RKF has helped in all domains to find a good solution quickly, by learning which objects can be used (only these get rewards as a part of the solution) and what are "good" solutions in respect to the user rewards.

Table 7: Complexity of the domains in which we have applied RKF

Domain	Number of concepts	Possible combinations	Remarks
1. Simple ABC Domain	26	s1: 1,872 s2: 18,162,144 s3: 9,702 s4: 91,327,950	We have used this very simple domain with 4 possible system roots to study the complexity of configuration problems
2. PC Domain	123 125	$4.65 \cdot 10^{24}$ $21.22 \cdot 10^{24}$	A typical domain for RKF use with short innovation cycles
3. Simple PC Domain	20 22	192,024 801,864	We have used this simplified version of the PC Domain for extended experiments since all combinations can be completely calculated in 80 seconds, even with wrong parameters for the RKF function
4. Backrest Drive	46 48	36,400,428 44,489,412	Prototypical example domain for a current project at the University of Stuttgart, see **[27]**
5. COSIMA	127	$2.95 \cdot 10^{298}$	Prototypical example domain for a current project at DaimlerChrysler R&T

Most of the domains have been investigated with a basic number of concepts and with "two additional" concepts. The change of a domain should cause RKF to "retrain".

We will now introduce some of our experiments which we have performed with the "Simple PC Domain". The goals of the experiments were to prove that it is possible with RKF to *learn* which concepts should be used to get high rewards and that RKF can react to changes in a domain ("*re*training"). We have also investigated the effects arising from different values for the parameters of RKF (b_t, b_f and v).

We will first briefly introduce the domain:

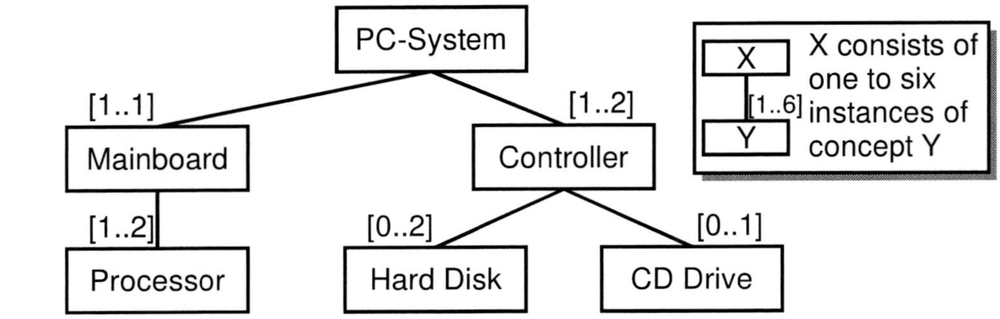

Figure 8: Compositions of the "Simple PC Domain" example

In this simplified version of the PC-Domain, a PC-System consists of exactly one main board, which again consists of one or two processors, and one or two controllers, which again consist of up to two hard disks and one optional CD-Drive. The following specializations can be used for the concepts:

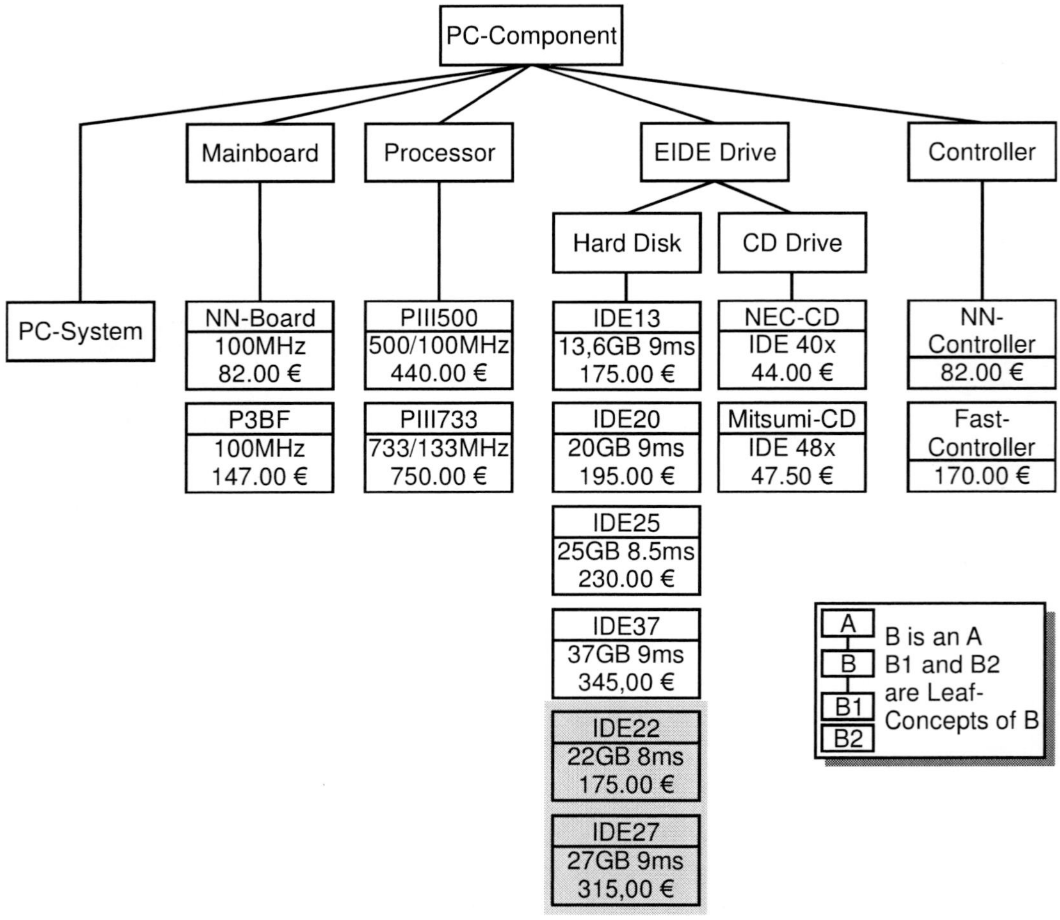

Figure 9: Taxonomy "Simple PC Domain"

The concepts "IDE22" and "IDE27" are used to change the domain and they are added during the experiments. Two n:m relations exist in the domain (see Figure 10) which have the effect that a cheap NN-Board must only be used together with cheap NN-Controllers and the more expensive P3BF main board must only be used together with the faster processor.

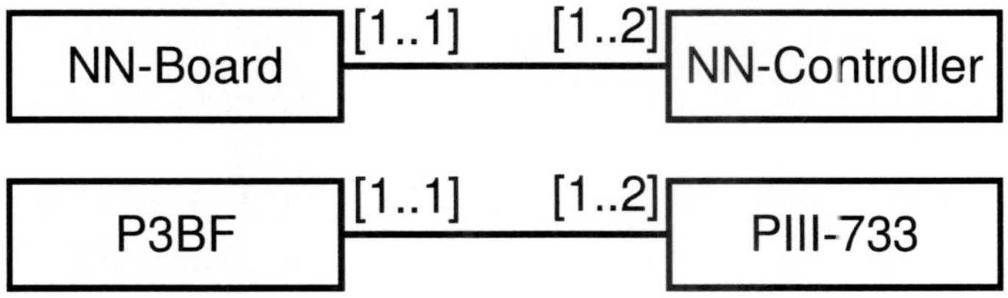

Figure 10: Two n:m relations exist in "Simple PC Domain"

Our configurator tries to fulfill the relations by integration only ("test"), after a combination has been built on the basis of the composition and taxonomy ("build"). Consequently 40,068 of the 192,024 possible combinations (four hard disks) and 167,184 of the 801,864 possible combinations (six hard disks) become invalid and will cause backtracking. RKF should learn how to choose concepts to avoid backtracking.

All experiments have been performed in the context of the same task class "Home-PC". To make an unattended batch operation possible, the rewards ically are provided automatically according to table 8 and table 9.

Table 8: Rewards for concepts in context of the task class "Home PC"

Concept	**Reward** $t < 100$	**Reward** $t \geq 100$	**Implicit specification to be learnt in context of class "Home-PC"**
NN-Board	100%		Cheapest main board
P3BF	30%		
PIII-500	100%		Cheapest processor
PIII-733	30%		
IDE13	100%	1%	Cheapest or maybe largest hard disk. After addition of the two new hard disks, IDE22 should dissolve the most relevant so far
IDE20	10%	10%	
IDE25	10%	10%	
IDE37	50%	10%	
IDE22		100%	
IDE27		5%	
NEC-CD	20%		Cheapest CD drive
Mitsumi-CD	100%		
NN-Controller	100%		Cheapest controller
Fast-Controller	20%		

All experiments consisted of 200 configuration runs. Halfway through each experiment (t=100) the two hard disks IDE22 and IDE27 have been added and the table of rewards has been altered. Each experiment with 200 runs has been repeated at least 10 times, to minimize the possibility of "by chance" results.

Table 9: Rewards for the number of contents in context of "Home PC"

content relation	reward	implicit specification to be learnt
PC-System - - - [1..1] Mainboard	1: 100%	
PC-System - - - [1..2] Controller	1: 100% 2: 100%	Whatever is allowed is ok
Mainboard - - - [1..2] Processor	1: 100% 2: 10%	A Home PC consists of one processor
Controller - - - [0..2] Hard disk	0: 0% 1: 100% 2: 10%	Normally one hard disk, two are not really wanted and a diskless PC is definitely not preferred
Controller - - - [0..1] CD-Drive	0: 10% 1: 100%	One CD-ROM is recommended for Home PCs

4.3.2 Results

First we have investigated the effect of the constants b_t, b_f and v, i.e. the effect from faster or slower forgetting and training as well as the control of conservatism in selections. The curve of the relevance values of the six hard disks were of special interest to us because here we applied the change to the domain and we can observe how training and retraining works.

In our first experiment we have used the parameter values $b_f = b_t = 2.0$ like we have used them in section 2.4, deriving the relevance formula. With $v = 1.0$, we have selected a linear interpretation of relevance during selections. Figure 11 shows a typical result for these values. The diagram shows the probability with which a hard disk concept is chosen, according to its relevance (see equation (1)).

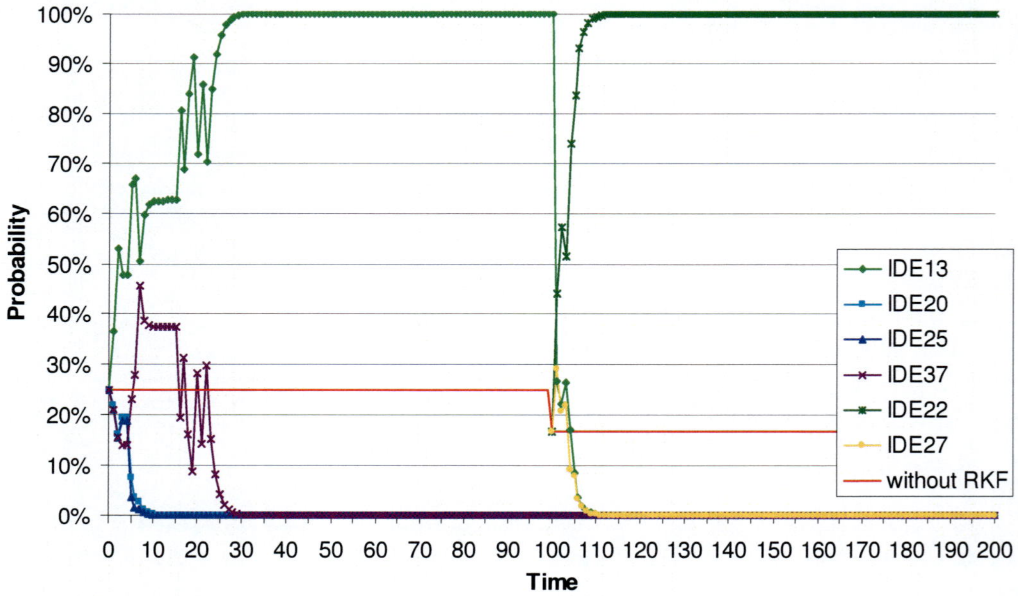

Figure 11: IDE13 has been correctly learnt as the concept with highest rewards ($b_f = b_t = 2.0$ and $v = 1.0$)

At first the probability of being selected is 25% for all of the four hard-disk-concepts, because initially their relevance is the start relevance value of 50%. After a short transient oscillation IDE13 "wins" because of a permanent high rating of 100%. The values of b_f and b_t make learning and forgetting so quick that other concepts are no longer chosen after 30 configuration runs. As soon as the two new hard disks are added (t = 100), the relevance (and with it the probability) of IDE13 decreases as a consequence of fast forgetting and slower learning, due to low rewards. The new concept IDE22 can replace IDE13 after less than 10 runs. With their start relevance of 0.5, the new hard disks are the only concepts that can compete with IDE13 and although IDE13 is selected once more (t=103), it is outdone by IDE22 quickly, due to its low reward and the high reward of IDE22. IDE27 had only been chosen twice during the experiment (t=101 and t=103) because of bad rewards following these choices.

These results appear to show the exact behavior which we had desired: The concept with the best rewards is chosen with highest probability after a short learning phase and "forgotten" as soon as a better concept exists. Unfortunately, not all of the experiments we have performed with these constants show the same results. Since we use a probabilistic method, it is possible that IDE37 is chosen at the beginning, when all concepts have the same relevance and since it gets a fairly good reward, it becomes quite a bit more relevant and therefore more probable for the next run. All the others, including IDE13, are becoming less relevant because they were not part of the solution. If training and forgetting is too fast, RKF will trust such an "early starter": In five out of ten experiments with these parameters, IDE37 has become most relevant instead of IDE13, one of them is shown in Figure 12.

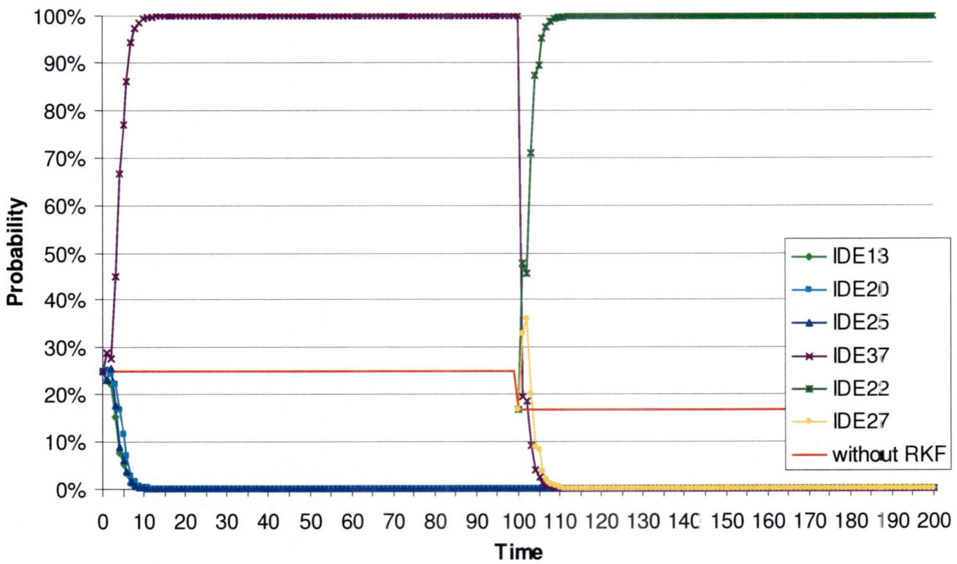

Figure 12: Sometimes IDE37 "wins" erroneously using $b_f = b_t = 2.0$ and v = 1.0

This result is not surprising because the value b_t = 2.0 already violates theorem 1 (see equation (23)).

We can solve the above problem with "wrong" objects becoming the most relevant by slowing down the speed of training and forgetting by adjusting the three parameters (large b_t, small b_f and small v). By doing this, the transient oscillation lasts longer and it becomes more probable that the concept that really gets the best rewards will be chosen during that time and will consequently win. The price we pay is a longer period with possibly sub-optimal results.

With this in mind, we have performed a series of experiments with different parameter sets. We wanted to find a combination that allows the configurator to learn which objects do not get good rewards (≤ 10%) within the first few runs (<10). The probability of IDE37 with a reward of 50% and IDE13 with the highest reward of 100% should oscillate but IDE13 should ultimately "win" (have a higher probability than 90%) before t=100.

To consider the rewards more particularly, we have chosen a smaller value of 1.4 for b_t according to statement *t3* (see table 1). This value is consistent with equation (23).

From (44) $b_t = 1.4$ follows:

$$b_f > \frac{2 \cdot 1.4}{1.4 + 1} \tag{45}$$

$$b_f > 1{,}167 \tag{46}$$

Therefore, we could also use a smaller value for b_f, which causes slower forgetting and a longer oscillating phase. We started with b_f=1.95, gradually decreased the value and finally used b_f=1.3.

The maximum value that can be used for parameter v calculates as follows: In the beginning n0 = 4 new objects are added to the set of hard disks. With inequality (37)

$$v < \frac{\ln 4.5}{4 \cdot \ln 1.3} \tag{47}$$

$$v < 1{,}433 \tag{48}$$

We received very good results with v = 1.3.

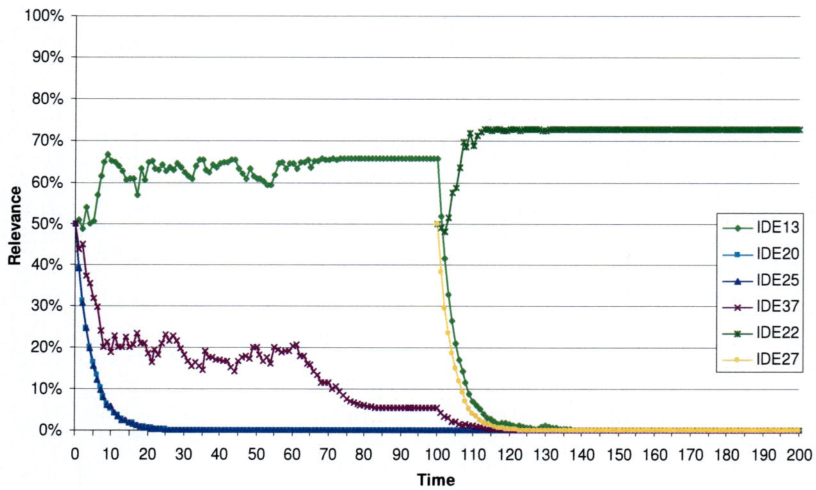

Figure 13: Relevance values (average of 10 subsequent experiments) with parameters b_t = 1.4, b_f = 1.3, v = 1.3

Figure 14 and Figure 13 show the results of the experiments with these parameters. The curves show the average values of 10 subsequent experiments; but all the single experiments also showed the desired characteristics.

The red line in figure 14 shows the probability for the drives if they were chosen at random, i.e. without RKF.

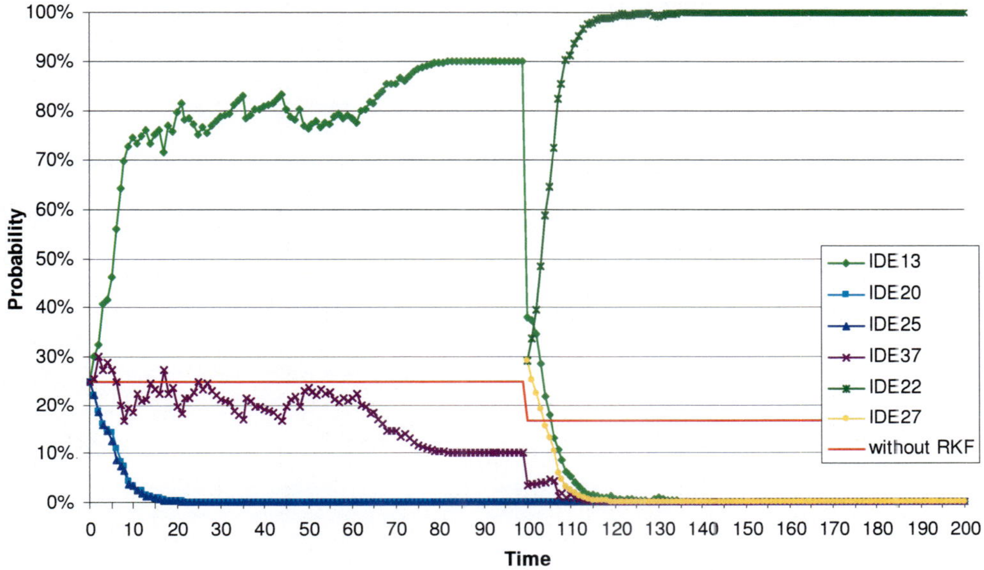

Figure 14: Average probability values from 10 subsequent experiments with parameters b_t = 1.4, b_f = 1.3, v = 1.3

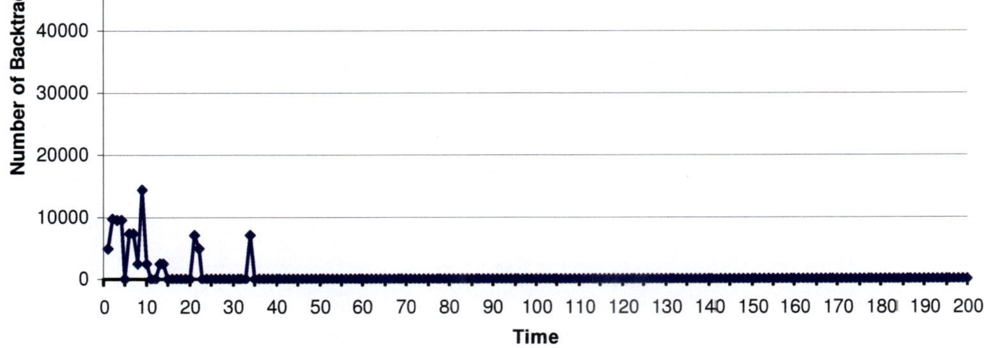

Figure 15: Number of backtracking steps needed in "Simple PC Domain" (average of 10 subsequent experiments) with b_t:=1.4; b_f:=1.3; v:=1.3

RKF should not only learn which concepts receive high user reward but also which combinations are allowed (see relations shown in figure 10). Only the concepts that are part of an (allowed) solution will get rewards and finally only these concepts will be chosen by RKF. Figure 15 shows how many backtracking steps have been needed. The long oscillation phase is also reflected here and after about 65 runs RKF only selects concepts of an allowed combination: In the following configuration runs, backtracking is not needed anymore which also means that in a well trained system a solution can be found in a fraction of a second.

One question we had was *"what happens without forgetting?"*. To switch off forgetting we can simply set $b_f := 1.0$. The results are shown in figure 16.

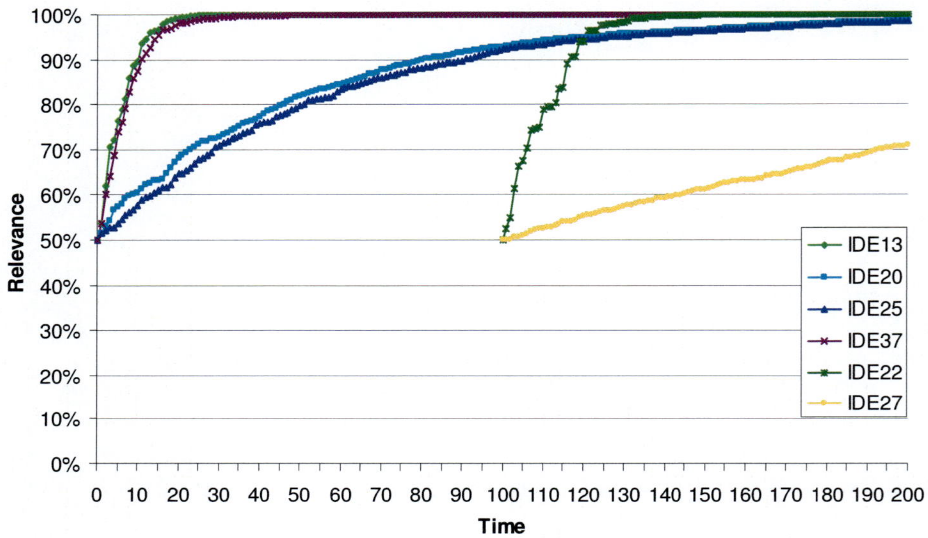

Figure 16: Average relevance values without forgetting (b_t:=2.0; $\mathbf{b_f}$**:=1.0**; v:=1.0)

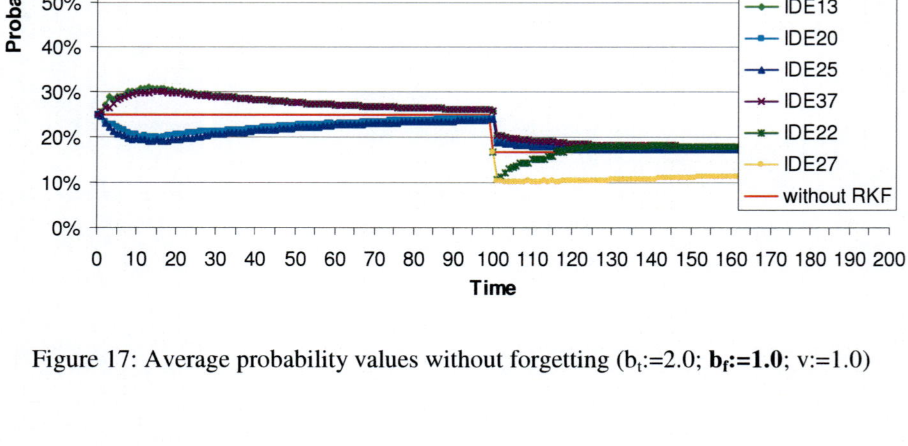

Figure 17: Average probability values without forgetting (b_t:=2.0; $\mathbf{b_f}$**:=1.0**; v:=1.0)

The relevance of *all* hard disks approach 100% because without forgetting the relevance function is monotonously growing. As a consequence the probability that a concept will be chosen only differs at the beginning, when high rewards make the "good" hard disks relevant more quickly. After a short time, the probability of all concepts approaches the value "without RKF" (see Figure 17).

Other methods that use reinforcement learning without forgetting can do so because they do not use an exponential function that approaches any value. They learn infinitely instead (for example see **[12]**), mostly using a linear learning function. With this they will have the problem that they cannot react to changes in the knowledge base.

4.4 Effects Arising from RKF

With our experiments we could confirm the following effects:

- *Increase in Efficiency:*

RKF supports the search for solutions by helping to make correct decisions and thereby avoiding backtracking. Through the application of RKF, a knowledge-based system "learns" from previous successes.

The search space is not really restricted with RKF. However, the paths in the search tree which have often led to a solution are favored. Figure 18 shows part of the taxonomy of the PC Domain.

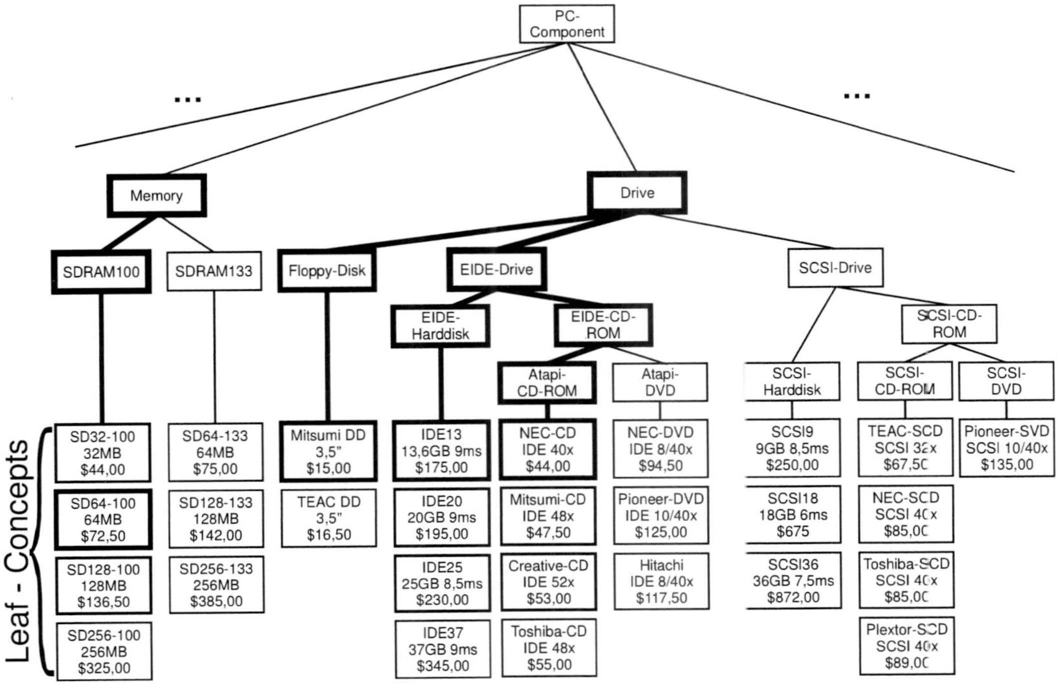

Figure 18: Part of the taxonomy of the PC Domain. The thickness of the lines indicates the relevance for the task class "Home-PC"

The thickness of the lines indicates the relevance learnt for the task class "Home PC", i.e. this form of PC most often contains a SD64-100 memory module, a Mitsumi DD disc drive, an IDE13- hard drive and a NEC-CD drive. The figure also shows how RKF supports the depth-first search in this hierarchy: Paths of high relevance develop because whenever a daughter concept was useful, the respective father concept was also useful. This is the main reason why configuration with RKF is so fast: If a specialization of a concept has to be chosen during the configuration process, the RKF heuristic will search first along the relevant paths with high probability.

- *"Soft" versioning management*

Newer objects and therefore also objects of newer versions are preferred by RKF and so these are more predominantly used. The old versions can remain in the knowledge base. What is particularly pleasing about this procedure is that newer versions are automatically no longer used, if they do not prove to be good and older versions are simply fallen back on. On the other hand, if a new version works well, an old version is used less. The old version however still remains available for "exotic" cases or other task classes.

- *Task Classes do not age*

Task classes have some similarities to *cases* which are used in case-based methods (CBR). An important advantage of task classes over cases is that they do not age. For example a "Home-PC" was completely different 10 years ago to today. A "representative" case from that time is completely useless today. The task class "Home-PC Class", however, is unchanged because the task, optimization objectives, the expected cost etc. stay the same.

- *Not Conservative*

Through preference to *new* objects, RKF is a heuristic which is not conservative, despite learning from preceding solutions: New objects have the opportunity to "prove their worth" and they become irrelevant if they cannot receive good rewards. This characteristic is certainly one of the most important advantages of RKF over methods which likewise include preceding solutions, e.g. pure reinforcement learning methods, as these are conservative as a rule.

4.5 Limitations

As well as the positive results already described, our experiments also confirmed the weak points we had expected with the use of RKF.

- *At least n non-optimal runs*

RKF shares this problem with all reinforcement learning methods: If an object has to be chosen from a set of n objects, at least n runs are necessary to get rewards for all of the objects. In RKF, the parameters b_t, b_f and v have to be adjusted in a way that the oscillation phase lasts at least n runs. During these runs non optimal results are gained. Domains probably exist where the largest n cannot be estimated in advance. Another possibility is not to begin with a start relevance of 0.5, but with a relevance equal to a first representative user reward for each object (if such values are available). In a trained system the value of n is not so important: Only one object per selection set can ultimately stay relevant. The oscillation phase then only needs to be long enough to get rewards for *m* new objects, which is considerably less according to our experience.

- *The set of task classes is decisive*

RKF can only be used in domains where a limited set of task classes can be found. If this set does not exist naturally for a domain (e.g. user groups), it might be a problem to find a set that is not too small (contradictory rewards would make learning impossible) and not too large (it becomes more difficult to classify a single task). In the worst case, each task class consists of only a single task, which would also make learning impossible.

- *Dependencies are not learnt explicitly*

With RKF we only learn which objects to use in context of a task class *c*. Dependencies are only learnt in such a way that only the *objects* which fulfill these dependencies become relevant. The learning processes of the objects involved in a dependency are more or less isolated. Particularly those dependencies that will affect the rewards of dependent objects are not allowed in RKF, since RKF presumes constant or slow changing rewards for objects in the context of a task class. For example, dependencies such as the following cannot be learnt: If A (90% reward) is selected then C will get a reward of 10% and if B (also 90% reward) is selected then C will get a reward of 70%. Both combinations could be learnt by RKF to be best, while a choice of B would result in a better sum of rewards.

- *User rewards*

RKF will only learn optimally if rewards for each component of the solutions are available. This might be a problem in complex systems, where solutions consist of hundreds of components. Therefore, we have made experiments with simplified assessment schemes. One is to rate the complete solution and use this value as the reward of all components of the solution. The simplest assessment scheme in this context can simply consist of the values 0%= "system could **not** be sold" and 100%="system **has** been sold". With this simplified reward scheme, the allowed combinations could be learnt but the training of a "good" solution is very slow and not possible in large domains (if RKF is the only heuristic used).

5 Summary and Outlook

Our heuristic Relevant Knowledge First (RKF) has been developed based on a general study of potential improvements for knowledge-based search methods and was influenced by effects of cognitive psychology. First, the method of selecting objects with RKF has been introduced, i.e. a choice based on random sampling, where the probability to choose an object is proportional to its *relevance*. After that, a function has been specified which calculates the relevance of objects. This function consists of two parts, which describe the training and forgetting phases separately, assuming that these phases occur alternately. Subsequently, the application of RKF in structure based configuration domains has been described and some results of our extensive experiments have been demonstrated. The specific characteristic of this heuristic is that objects cannot only be *learnt*, but can also be *forgotten* without being deleted. This can always be an advantage if a domain is subjected to changes, which again is typical for most technical domains. Finally, the effects arising from the use of RKF and limitations which have been observed during our experiments have been named. In summary, it may be said that RKF could successfully be applied to all of our five different technical domains.

An interesting continuation of our examinations could be an adaptation of RKF to domains other than configuration. For example, we expect that relevance calculations are also adequate for diagnosis tasks. We presume this because an error will very likely always occur on the same part of a mass product. With the statistic learning method of RKF, such weak points could be learnt. The ability to *re*learn could also be significant because these weak points could change during the life cycle of a mass product.

References

[1] T. Anderson: *Mapping the development of user constructs of relevance assessment as informed by topicality* in Tom D. Wilson: *Information Research, an international electronic journal*, Volume 4 No. 2, Sheffield, October 1998

[2] J. R. Anderson: *Cognitive Psychology and Its Implications,* Fifth Edition, Worth Publishers, New York, 2000, chapter 6 and 7

[3] H. Bense, W. Bodrow (ed.): *Objektorientierte und regelbasierte Wissensverarbeitung* (Angewandte Informatik), Spektrum Akademischer Verlag GmbH Heidelberg, Berlin, Oxford, 1995

[4] M. T. Cox, A. Ram: *An Explicit Representation of Forgetting* in J. W. Brahan and G. E. Lasker (eds.) *Proceedings of the Sixth International Conference on Systems Research, Informatics and Cybernetics,* Baden Baden, Germany, August 1992, pp. 115-120

[5] F. Crestani: *Implementation and evaluation of a relevance feedback device based on neural networks* in J. Mira and J. Cabestany (ed): *From Natural to Artificial neural Computation*, International Workshop on Artificial Neural Networks, Spain, Springer-Verlag GmbH Heidelberg, Berlin, Oxford, 1995

[6] R.. Cunis, A. Günter, H. Strecker*: Das Plakon-Buch. Ein Expertensystemkern für Planungs- und Konfigurierungsaufgaben in technischen Domänen*, Springer-Verlag, Berlin Heidelberg, 1991

[7] A. Günter: *Flexible Kontrolle in Expertensystemen für Planungs- und Konfigurierungsaufgaben in technischen Domänen,* Doctoral Thesis, University of Hamburg, Germany, 1991

[8]A. Günter (ed.): *Wissensbasiertes Konfigurieren. Ergebnisse aus dem Projekt PROKON*, Infix-Verlag, Sankt Augustin, 1995

[9] A. Günter, C. Kühn*: Knowledge-Based Configuration – Survey and Future Directions –* in *Knowledge based systems: survey and future directions*; proceedings of XPS 99, Würzburg, Springer Verlag Berlin, Heidelberg 1999, pp. 47-66

[10] A. Haag: *Sales Configuration in Business Processes* in *IEEE Intelligent Systems* Jul/Aug 98, 1998, pp. 78-85

[11] M. Heinrich, E.-W. Jüngst: *The Resource-Based Paradigm: Configuring Technical Systems from Modular Components* in *AAAI-96 Fall Sympos. Series: Configuration*, MIT, Cambridge, MA, November 9 - 11, 1996, pp. 19-27

[12] L. P. Kaelbling, M. L. Littman, A. W. Moore: *Reinforcement Learning: A Survey*, in *Journal of Artificial Intelligence Research 4 (1996)*, AI Access Foundation and Morgan Kaufmann Publishers, 1996, pp. 237-285

[13] W. Karbach, M. Linster: *Wissensakquisition für Expertensysteme: Techniken, Modelle und Softwarewerkzeuge*, Carl Hanser Verlag München; Wien, 1990.

[14] I. Kreuz, U. Bremer: *Exact Configuration Onboard. Onboard Documentation of Electrical and Electronical Systems consisting of ECUs, Data Buses and Software*, ERA conference 1999, Coventry, UK, 1999, pp. 5.2.1-5.2.8

[15] I. Kreuz, D. Roller: *Knowledge Growing Old in Reconfiguration Context*, in Boi Faltings, Eugen C. Freuder, Gerhard Friedrich, Alexander Felfernig: *Configuration, Papers from the AAAI Workshop*, Technical Report WS-99-05, Orlando, 1999, pp. 54-59

[16] I. Kreuz, U. Bremer, Z. Zhang: *Generierung und Erfassung der exakten Fahrzeugkonfiguration*, patent no. DE19926206 A1 (Germany), 1999

[17] I. Kreuz: *Considering the Dynamic in Knowledge Based Configuration* in Jürgen Sauer, Jana Köhler: *Proceedings of the ECAI 2000 Workshop on New Results in Planning, Scheduling and Design*, PUK2000, Berlin, 21.-22.08.2000, pp. 83-89

[18] I. Kreuz, U. Bremer, Z. Zhang: *Generating the Exact Configuration Onboard*, international patent no. WO00/77692 A2, 2000

[19] F. Lin, R. Reiter: *Forget It!*, AAAI Fall Symposium on Relevance, New Orleans, http://www.cs.toronto.edu/cogrobo/forgetting.ps.z, 1994

[20] S. Markovitch, P. D. Scott: *The role of Fogetting in Learning* in *Proceedings of The Fifth International Conference on Machine Learning, Ann Arbor*, MI, Morgan Kaufmann, 1988, pp. 459-465

[21]J. McDermott: *R1:* A Rule-based Configurer of Computer Systems in *Artificial Intelligence* **19**(1), 1982, pp. 39-88

[22] S. Mittal, A. Araya: *A Knowledge-Based Framework for Design* in Tom Kehler and Stan Rosenschein *Proceedings of the Fifth National Conference on Artificial Intelligence*, The AAAI Press, Menlo Park, California 1986, pp. 856-865

[23] S. Mittal: *Towards a Generic Model of Configuration Tasks* in Tom Dean: *IJCAI: Proceedings of the 1989 International Joint Conference of Artificial Intelligence*, Morgan Kaufmann Publishers, 1989

[24]K. G. Olesen, S. L. Lauritzen, F. V. Jensen: *aHUGIN: A System Creating Adaptive Causal Probabilistic Networks* in Didier Dubois, Michael P. Wellman, Bruce D'Ambrosio, Phillipe Smets: *Uncertainty in Artificial Intelligence*, Proceedings of the Eighth Conference Stanford University, Morgan Kaufmann Publishers, San Mateo, California, 1992, pp. 223-229

[25] J. Pearl: *Probabilistic Reasoning in Intelligent Systems: Networks of Plausible Inference*, revised second printing, Morgan Kaufmann Publishers Inc., San Francisco CA 94104, 1988

[26] E. Rich, K. Knight: *Artificial Intelligence,* Second Edition, McGraw-Hill Book Co, Singapore, 1991

[27] D. Roller, I. Kreuz: *Selecting and Parameterising Components using Knowledge Based Configuration and a Heuristic that Learns and Forgets,* Accepted Paper (10/2002) in *Computer-Aided Design*, Elsevier Science Ltd., 2002, to appear

[28] L. Schamber, M. B. Eisenberg, M. S. Nilan: *Re-examination of relevance: toward a dynamic, situational definition* in *Information Processing and Management 26 (no. 6, 1990)*, Elsevier Science 1990, pp. 775-776

[29] C. Tong, D. Sriram (ed.): *Design Representation and Models of Routine Design*, Academic Press, 1992

[30] D. Waltz: The Importance of Importance in AImagazine, Volume 20, No. 3, Fall 1999, *American Association for Artificial Intelligence* (AAAI), Menlo Park, CA, USA, 1999, pp. 18-35

In: Artificial Intelligence and Computer Science
Editor: Susan Shannon, pp. 127-138
ISBN: 1-59454-411-5

Chapter 4

AN ACTIVE AGENT PORTFOLIO MANAGEMENT ALGORITHM

Wah-Sui Almberg [1]

Department of Computer and Systems Sciences,
Stockholm Univ and the Royal Inst of Technology,
Forum 100, SE-164 40 Kista, Sweden

Magnus Boman [2]

Swedish Institute of Computer Science,
Box 1263, SE-164 29 Kista, Sweden

Abstract

An algorithm for managing a portfolio of stocks using a trading agent is presented. A simulation game inspired by history-based Parrondo games is described. A performance measure is defined, with which various strategy mixes can be judged. Even when transaction costs are taken into account, active portfolio management (as opposed to Buy and Hold) is shown to be profitable.

Keywords: Trading agent, volatility, history-based Parrondo, portfolio management

1 Introduction

There are good reasons for investigating trading agents and the modeling of financial markets using computer agents [6] [11] [12]. While the main objective is to investigate the feasibility of introducing agents as new services on real markets [15], we limit ourselves here to portfolio management on receding markets. Of particular interest are so-called Parrondo strategies [9] [19], which combine two losing strategies into a winning strategy, subject to certain conditions (recently described by Harmer and Abbott in an excellent survey [10]).

[1] E-mail address: w-s-almb@dsv.su.se
[2] E-mail address: mab@sics.se

Parrondo-inspired strategies have been used for stock market applications before (see [7]), demonstrating that under certain conditions, such strategies could outperform value and trend investor strategies for day trading. As a benchmark, \Buy and Hold" (i.e., leave the portfolio untouched) is often used, and we will continue to do so here.

Parrondo and other strategies imported from statistical physics are especially applicable to equity fund management or other forms of portfolio maintenance in which stocks are not replacable. The entire portfolio can be seen as sold and repurchased periodically, for instance utilising the sawtooth decline of the value function often present in stocks on receding markets [16] [17]. Many equity funds also have adamant regulations that force them to hold out during a fall. Trading agents could ideally make it possible to cut losses, increase the liquidity of the market, and ultimately contribute to the stability of a globalized market. More specifically, agents could mitigate the leverage effect [8] (i.e. the negative correlation between past returns and future volatility [3]), support fair dissemination [4], and avoid the kind of herd behavior [13] evidenced by the power law distribution of the price return [14].

In Section 3, we describe the design of a trading agent for active portfolio management on a receding market. The design is inspired by history-based Par-rondo games, and the role of Parrondo game A is here a coinipping function affecting history but not capital, while Parrondo game B is here active management of a portfolio that decreases in value over time. In Section 4, we present the results of our tests on real stock market data (described in Section 2). Section 5 describes algorithmic aspects, and we conclude by giving some directions for future research.

2 Data

The data samples used were selected from the Trust database (historical quotes from the Nordic stock markets adjusted for splits, new issues of shares, etc.). The samples encompass the Stockholm stock market closing rates and span the period between 26th February 1999 and 30th October 2001. The stocks used were picked from the A-list and the Attract40-list, as these stocks are the most frequently traded, and therefore most representative of the stock market as a whole. Even so, there were stocks that did not register a single trade for whole days during the period in question. These stocks were left out. The full data set is available upon request.

To obtain a comparative measure of the performance of a trading agent or a subagent on a specific sample, we compared it to the performance of a benchmark strategy on the same sample. This benchmark strategy, Buy and Hold, divides the same amount of money as the trading agent is allotted at the beginning of a run into as many equally sized shares as there are stocks in the sample. Using these equal amounts of money, stocks of the sample are each bought in the same proportions. Then these stocks are held on to until the end of the period of the sample in question. The total value of these stocks is then taken as a measure of performance for that particular sample. By dividing the final sum, achieved by a trading agent on a particular sample with that of Buy and Hold on the same sample, the agent's performance on different samples could be measured.

3 The Trading Agent Design

Four subagents together with a random function constitute the trading agent. The random function lets two trading agents with the same settings obtain different results on the same sample, thus avoiding a known volatility driver. Second, it makes it possible to run several agents at the same time, resulting in a mean performance more stable than the performance of a single agent.

The subagent uses the three most recent stock quotes of each stock of the chosen sample. If t is a time-variable and if $f(t)$ denotes the most recent quote of a specific equity line, $f(t-1)$ the one before that, and $f(t-2)$ the first quote in this series of consecutive quotes, the function used is:

$$F(t) = (f(t) + f(t-2) - 2 * f(t-1)) \,/\, (f(t) + f(t-2)) \qquad (1)$$

The time elapsed between two quotes is 1, in our case 1 day. The numerator of the function can be seen as an incremental form of the second derivative of the graph of a stock's price over time. We deemed it plausible that stockbrokers and traders would react to changes of the speed with which share prices went up or down. We furthermore divided by $(f(t) + f(t-2))$ to compensate for the varying absolute values of the different stocks, making it possible to direct the subagent's efforts towards the cheaper shares, while each share would give possibly the same absolute return rate as the more expensive shares. As the distribution of function values over a sample spanning one year is Gaussian [1], the denominator is the mean value of $f(t)$ and $f(t-2)$. At the beginning of each run the subagent was given a set amount of money. Then, at the first checkpoint in time (i.e., the third day), it checked all the stocks in a given sample (8 or 10 stocks) for the stock with the highest value of (1). If that value exceeded a preset threshold value, it would buy that particular stock using all the money allotted. Otherwise the algorithm continued to the next checkpoint in time (the following day), with its new set of stock quotes pertaining to that particular time. When a share had been thus purchased, the agent held on to that share until the share's function value fell below another threshold value, also set in advance. After having sold the share, the procedure was repeated until the end of the period of the sample in question.

4 Test Results

The outcome of the tests can be seen in Figure 1 and Figure 2. In each case the subagent was given an initial amount of 10,000 Swedish crowns (SEK). An assumption was made that the total cost of transaction would be 0.05 per cent of the absolute worth of the stock traded, for both purchase and sale. The Internet based broker Avanza (www.avanza.se) offers a brokerage of 0.12 per cent, which should be close to an upper boundary for the transaction fee. Moreover, as a trading agent initiates all transactions on its own, starting or stopping a full run of these agents could be looked upon as a single separate type of order, just like an ordinary limit order, for example. There would not be any need for any communication with outer sources except at the very start and at the very end of a run. Apart from the transaction fee, there is also the implicit transaction cost of the spread (the difference between the highest bid and the lowest ask price in a double auction). It is impossible to simulate a real stock market, and thereby the cost of the spread, in a realistic way. Since we give priority to real data and realistic agent interaction with the matching service (cf. [15]), we decided against an artificial stock market approach (see, e.g., [2]). Instead we made the idealistic assumption that the rates would not be affected by the agents' orders and that the stock market would be extremely liquid.

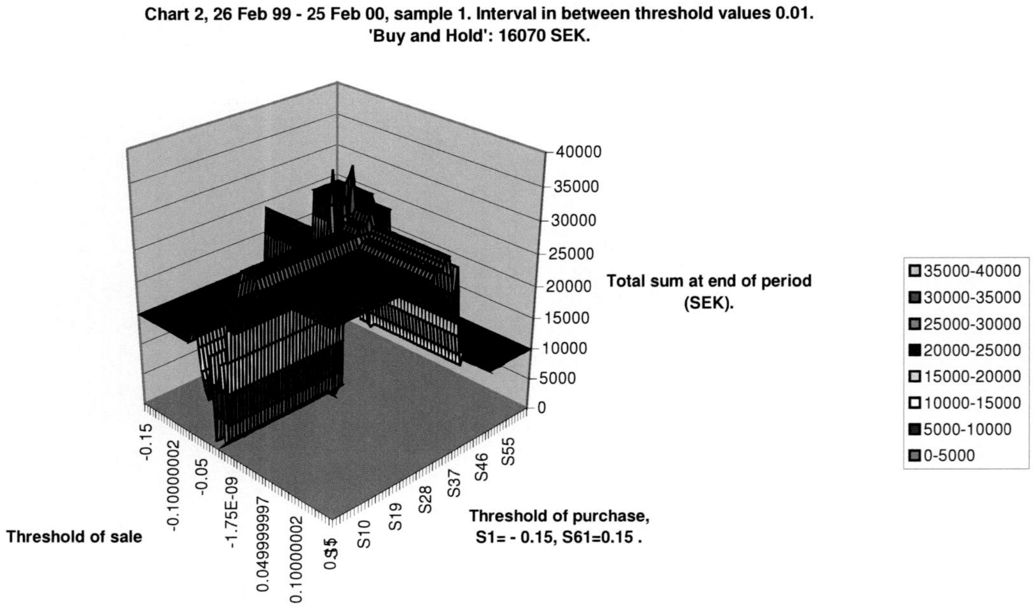

Figure. 1

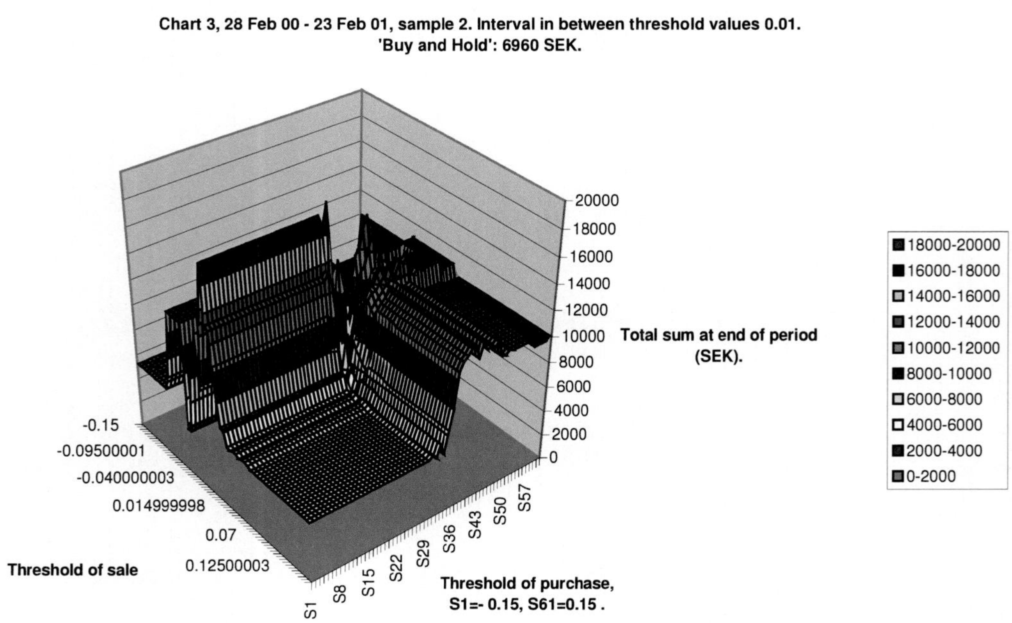

Figure. 2

In the charts (Figure 1 and Figure 2) every crossing of two lines represents a pair of parameters (threshold values). The performance of the corresponding Buy and Hold strategy is also given in the headings of the individual charts. Searching for patterns in these landscapes, one easily spots the plateaux and valleys in the lower and right quarters of the charts. In Figure 2, corresponding to a fall of the exchange, there is a plateau in the right quarter and a valley in the lower quarter. This corresponds to high values for both the threshold of sale and the threshold of purchase, and to high values for the threshold of sale and low values for the threshold of purchase, respectively. At the very edge of the right corner, just a few or no transactions have taken place. The threshold of purchase is set at a level too high for any transaction to be initiated, except for possibly a few stray transactions. If bought, a stock would immediately be sold owing to the very high-set threshold of sale. In the chart pertaining to a rise of the exchange (Figure 1), the reverse scenario arises. In this chart there is a plateau in the lower quarter and a lowland plain in the right quarter. The plateau corresponds to a high value for the threshold of sale and a low value for the threshold of purchase, and the valley corresponds to high values for both the threshold of sale and the threshold of purchase.

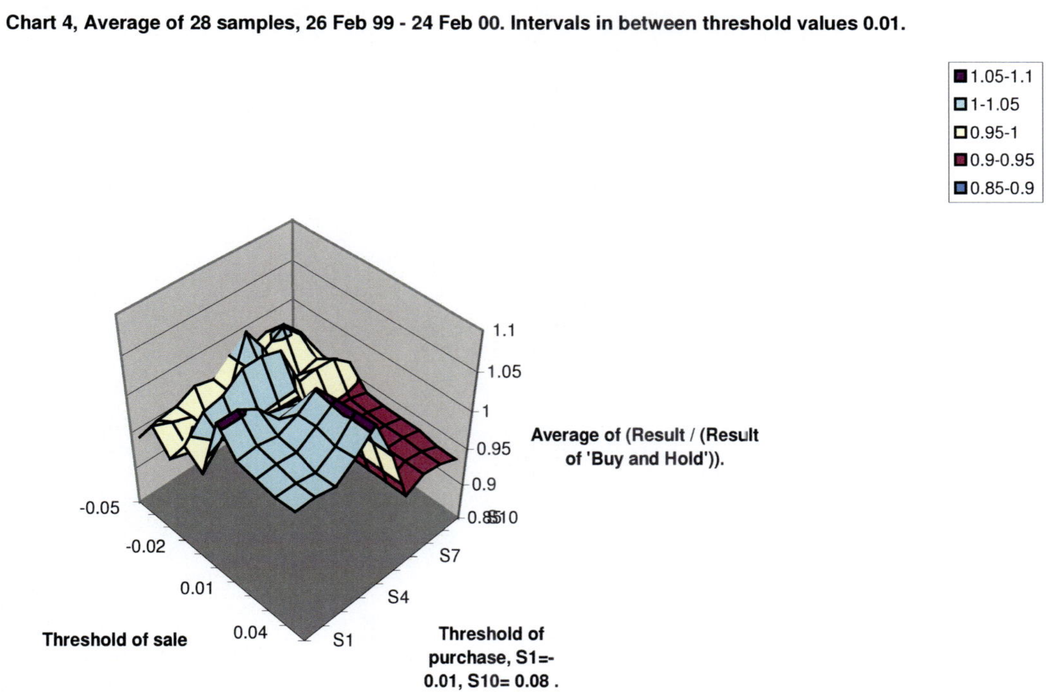

Figure. 3

The results are not too astonishing: It is always good to sell early so that you can switch to the best performing stocks. In bad times you should only invest in stocks with really good prospects, and in good times one should aim at always remaining invested in stocks. Focusing on the area where most values of (1) were centred, we investigated its generality. For this purpose, 56 samples were used; 28 samples covered the period between 26 February 1999 and 24 February 2000 (an overall rise of the exchange), and the remaining 28 samples the period between 25 February 2000 and 23 February 2001 (an overall fall of the exchange). A few of the samples of the period starting 26 February 1999 had overall falling rates, and similarly, a few samples of the period starting 25 February 2000 had rising rates. Figure 3 and Figure 4 show the average outcome of the respective 28 samples. Each sample contains eight stocks and covers about three months (63 days of trading). As can be seen, the pattern seems to persist. Figure 3 depicts a landscape of an overall rise of the exchange and Figure 4 an overall fall of the exchange. To get a more precise understanding of this pattern we also tested for the standard deviation and other measures of accuracy of eight pairs of parameters for both sets of samples (see [1]).

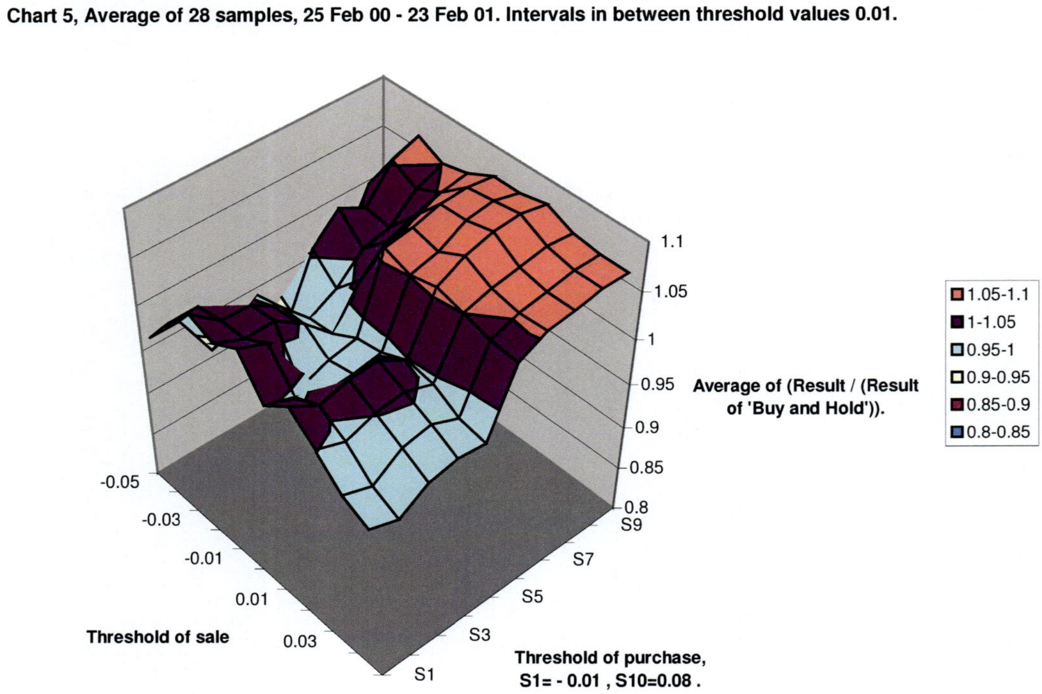

Figure. 4

5 The Trading Algorithm

The four subagents and the random function come into play according to the following scheme. At every juncture, after having run the random function, or one of the subagents has sold its stock, or at the very start of a run of the trading agent, there is a fifty per cent chance of turning to the random function, and a fifty per cent chance of running one of the four subagents. An overview of the algorithm can be seen in the owchart in Figure 5. The random function has equal probability of resulting in either a win or a loss. This function incurs no real loss or gain of capital to the trading agent. We note that in order to match the conditions for a Parrondo game, the random function should really have a slight negative bias, but given the large movements of value of the stocks in our portfolio, this adjustment has very little bearing on the end result, and we thus ignore it here.

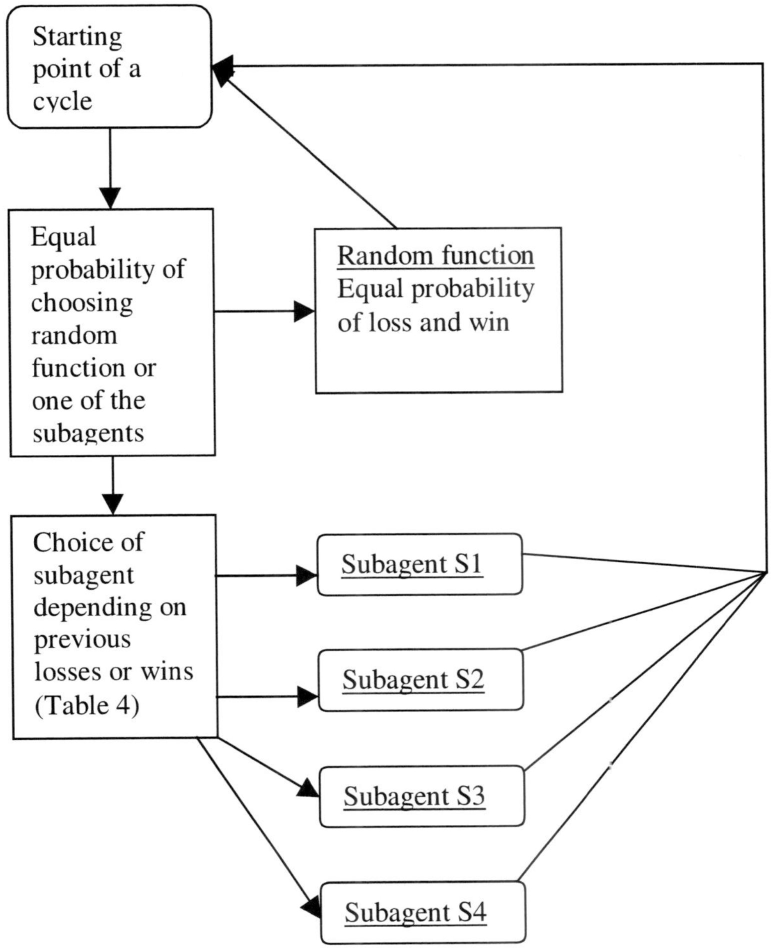

Figure 5.

If the overall game is set to run one of the four subagents, the subagent is chosen according to the scheme of Table 1. This means, for example, that $S1$ is chosen if both the previous run and the one before that have been losses, incurred by either one of the four subagents or the random function of the computer. In order to test for behavior similar to those of Parrondo games, we gave the subagents $S1$ and $S4$ threshold values of winning subagents, and $S2$ and $S3$ threshold values of losing subagents. We then compared the performance of this trading agent with the average performance of the four subagents. We placed subagents $S1$ and $S4$ on the plateau of the falling market and the other two in the valley. The real test was whether the combined agent would do better than the average of its constituent subagents would, given that these subagents performed according to a certain scheme. If the plateaux and the valleys could be anticipated, then (and only then) the results could be useful. In Table 2, the resulting values are shown.

Table 1. The choice of subagent.

The run before last	Last run	Subagent chosen for the coming run, each with its own pair of limit values
Loss	Loss	S1
Loss	Win	S2
Win	Loss	S3
Win	Win	S4

Table 2. Performance of four variations of the trading agent compared to the average of their four constituent subagents. The results are given in bold type. All values are relative to the 'Buy and Hold' strategy. The trading agents, corresponding to the four columns, were run 10,000 times on every sample to obtain a mean. Transaction fee was set at 0.05 per cent. The resulting improvements of the trading agents compared to their constituent subagents are highlighted with a shaded background.

	Column 1	**Column 2**	**Column 3**	**Column 4**
Rates	**Rising**	**Falling**	**Rising**	**Falling**
Period, Samples 3 to 58	26 Feb 99 – 24 Feb 00	25 Feb 00 – 23 Feb 01	26 Feb 99 – 24 Feb 00	25 Feb 00 – 23 Feb 01
Subagent S1	In the valley	On the plateau	On the plateau	In the valley
Threshold of sale	0.01	0.01	0.02	0.02
Threshold of purchase	0.06	0.06	0.03	0.03
Subagent S2	On the plateau	In the valley	In the valley	On the plateau
Threshold of sale	0.0	0.0	0.0	0.0
Threshold of purchase	0.0	0.0	0.07	0.07
Subagent S3	On the plateau	In the valley	In the valley	On the plateau
Threshold of sale	0.02	0.02	0.01	0.01
Threshold of purchase	0.03	0.03	0.06	0.06
Subagent S4	In the valley	On the plateau	On the plateau	In the valley
Threshold of sale	0.0	0.0	0.0	0.0
Threshold of purchase	0.07	0.07	0.0	0.0
Average of agent	***0.955***	***1.082***	***0.970***	***1.073***
Average of constituent subagents	***0.998***	***1.037***	***0.998***	***1.037***
Mean value of improvement	**- 0.043**	**0.045**	**- 0.028**	**0.036**
Standard deviation of mean value of improvement	**0.021**	**0.019**	**0.017**	**0.018**

As can be seen in this table, the trading agent does on average 4.5 per cent better over a three-month period than the average of its constituent subagents do, on a market of falling rates (column 2). The result seems quite remarkable as the performance of the combined agent reaches the same level as those of the two winning subagents do separately. Letting the subagents S2 and S3 be the winning type of subagent, with rates falling, and with S1 and S4 going below Buy and Hold, the good results persist (column 4). Looking at the period of rising rates (column 1), it seems the good performance during the period of falling rates has been traded for bad performance during the period of rising rates. The pattern is the same as in the analytical results of Parrondo et al [18].

To give an idea of how volatile the performance of a single trading agent could be, we tested for two separate periods: one period of rising rates and one period of falling rates. The results are shown in Table 3. For the sample of the falling exchange the corrected standard deviation is 275 SEK. If the distribution of the results of the 1000 runs would be Gaussian, it would mean that the confidence of a value to lie within the range 9685 275 SEK to 9685 + 275 SEK would be 68 per cent. This means that an agent, on a single run, might very well get results below the level of Buy and Hold. It should also be noted that the standard deviation of the mean value is as low as 8.70 SEK. This margin of error is independent of the type of distribution at hand. Thus, the mean value should be quite accurate. This should not be too surprising. As the volatility of the results is due to the random function of the agent, the combined results of several agents should be less volatile. Table 3 also shows that the margins of error of the period of rising rates reach the same magnitudes as those of the period of the falling rates.

Table 3. Standard deviation of a 1000 runs over 63 days of trading in 2 samples with the trading agent. Initial amount 10,000 (SEK). Transaction fees set at 0.05 per cent. Results in bold type.

Rates	**Rising**	**Falling**
	30 Aug 99 – 24 Nov 99	**29 May 00 – 28 Aug 00**
Subagent S1	In the valley	On the plateau
Threshold of sale	0.01	0.01
Threshold of purchase	0.06	0.06
Subagent S2	On the plateau	In the valley
Threshold of sale	0.0	0.0
Threshold of purchase	0.0	0.0
Subagent S3	On the plateau	In the valley
Threshold of sale	0.02	0.02
Threshold of purchase	0.03	0.03
Subagent S4	In the valley	On the plateau
Threshold of sale	0.0	0.0
Threshold of purchase	0.07	0.07
Mean value (SEK)	**9895**	**9685**
Mean value of 'Buy and Hold' strategy (SEK)	**11135**	**9414**
Corrected Standard Deviation (SEK)	**156**	**275**
Standard deviation of mean value (SEK)	**4.9**	**8.7**

Finally, we tested the trading agent on previously unseen financial data, except for the observation that it was data taken from a period of falling rates. The result is shown in Table 4. We had to resort to over-sampling in these tests. As the closing rates of the period in question were obtained at a later hour, the movements of the rates might have been slightly different. Institutional investors might not have been active to the same degree, for example; liquidity might at times have dropped drastically resulting in erratic rates, etc. From the viewpoint of testing this was good, as testing on material different in character tests in a better way the generality of the model or theory tested, or in our case, the trading agent.

Table 4. Performance of the trading agent 26 Feb 01 – 26 Sept 01, a period of fall of the exchange. Calculations based on closing rates of evening exchange (20:00). Initial amount 10,000 (SEK). Results in bold type. Values for standard deviation pertaining to performance divided by 'Buy and Hold' (shaded background).

Number of runs on each sample	**100**				**1000**	
Brokerage (per cent)	0.05	0.12	0.12	0.12	0.05	0.12
Number of samples	21	21	*10*	*5*	21	21
Mean value of performance (SEK)	**9975**	**9887**	**10391**	**10299**	**9965**	**9888**
Mean value of 'Buy and Hold' strategy (SEK)	**9289**	**9276**	**9376**	**9510**	**9289**	**9276**
Mean value of performance divided by 'Buy and Hold'	**1.095**	**1.086**	**1.127**	**1.083**	**1.094**	**1.087**
Standard deviation of mean	**0.042**	**0.041**	**0.060**	**0.065**	**0.042**	**0.042**
Corrected standard deviation	**0.195**	**0.190**	**0.189**	**0.146**	**0.191**	**0.190**

In Table 4 it can be seen that even with just a hundred runs on 21 samples the standard deviation of the mean is about the same as that of a thousand runs. We also conducted tests with the cost of transaction set at 0.12 per cent, the same percentage as the brokerage of the Internet broker Avanza. With a cost of transaction set at 0.05 per cent, and still running the trading agent 100 times, the agent achieved an average final sum 9.5 per cent higher than that of the corresponding Buy and Hold strategy. Translated to a yearly basis that would be 44 per cent. Similarly, with a transaction fee of 0.12 per cent and 100 runs, it would amount to 39 per cent. We have not accounted for the margins of error here.

6 Conclusions and Further Research

We have demonstrated that active stock portfolio management on a receding market using a day trading agent can cut losses. Providing the opportunity to stock traders to use such agents, or indeed only vaguely similar agents, thus constitutes important added value to market operators and to suppliers of stock market software. More specifically, we have supplied an easily modifiable algorithm for exploiting sawtooth declining patterns in the stocks in the portfolio, in a manner inspired by recent developments in physics, notably Parrondo strategies. All data is available upon request and alignment studies are encouraged.

A point for future research is time and the possibility for a third parameter. Instead of being fixed, the increments of time could be adjustable, or even dynamic. Moreover, the agent does not have the money invested in shares all the time. Probably its good performance is, to some extent, due to this fact. It would be interesting to see how much time the agent keeps its capital invested relative to the length of the period it is active.

As it turned out, the cost of transaction was of paramount importance. Our agent engaged in about 100 transactions a year. Our estimate is that the total cost of transaction cannot exceed a figure of somewhere in between 0.15 and 0.5 per cent for the agent to remain profitable. One way to circumvent this problem could be to for the market owner or broker to introduce transaction fees based on a different set of criteria for agent-initiated transactions.

Investors would like stock prices to be as close to the equilibrium price as possible. A volatile market carries with it a greater risk for not trading at this price. The agent we have constructed probably trades stocks a little earlier than the herd, thereby facilitating a turn of a trend earlier than it would otherwise. This is another area for further research.

Acknowledgment

We thank David Lybäack, Stefan Johansson, Jan Odelstad, and Lars Rasmusson for their comments. Magnus Boman carried out this work within the VINNOVA-funded project TAP, on accessible autonomous software.

References

[1] Wah-Sui Almberg, Improved Pricing on the Stock Market with Trading Agents, Dept of Computer and Systems Sciences, *Technical report* 02-25-DSV-SU, Stockholm Univ, 2002.

[2] W. Brian Arthur, John Holland, Blake LeBaron, Richard Palmer, and Paul Tayler, Asset Pricing under Endogenous Expectations in an Artificial Stock Market, in *The Economy as an Evolving Complex System II*, Arthur, W. B.; Durlauf, S.; Lane, D., eds., pp. 15-44, Addison-Wesley, Reading, MA, 1997.

[3] Fischer Black, Studies of Stock Price Volatility Changes, *Proceedings of the 1976 American Statistical Association, Business and Economical Statistics Section*, 177 – 181, 1976.

[4] Robert Bloomfield, Robert Libby, and Mark W. Nelson, Underreactions, Overreactions and Moderated Confidence, *Financial Markets* **3**:113 – 137, 2000.

[5] Magnus Boman, Norms in Artificial Decision Making, *Artificial Intelligence and Law* **7**:17 – 35, 1999.

[6] Magnus Boman, Lisa Brouwers, Karin Hansson, Carl-Gustaf Jansson, Jo-han Kummeneje and Harko Verhagen, Artificial Agent Action in Markets, *Electronic Commerce Research* **1**:159 – 169, 2001.

[7] Magnus Boman, Stefan Johansson and David Lybäack, Parrondo Strategies for Artificial Traders, in Zhong, N.; Liu, J.; Ohsuga, S. and Bradshaw, J., eds., *Intelligent Agent Technology*, 150 – 159. World Scientific, Singapore, 2001.

[8] Jean-Philippe Bouchaud, Andrew Matacz and Marc Potters, *The Leverage Effect in Financial Markets: Retarded Volatility and Market Panic*, arxiv. org/abs/cond-mat/0101120, 2000.

[9] Gregory P. Harmer and Derek Abbott, Losing Strategies can Win by Par-rondo's Paradox, *Nature* **402**(6764):864, 1999.

[10] Gregory P. Harmer and Derek Abbott, A Review of Parrondo's Paradox, *Fluctuation and Noise Letters* **2**(2):R71 – R107, 2002.

[11] Jeffrey O. Kephart, Software Agents and the Route to the Information Economy, *PNAS* **99**(suppl.3):7207 – 7213, 2000.

[12] Blake LeBaron, Agent Based Computational Finance: Suggested Readings and Early Research, *Economic Dynamics and Control* **24**:679 – 702, 2000.

[13] T. Lux, Herd Behaviour, Bubbles and Crashes, *The Economic Journal* **105**:881 – , 1995.

[14] T. Lux and M. Marchesi, Volatility Clustering in Financial Markets: A Microsimulation of Interacting Agents, *Theoretical and Applied Finance* **3**(4):675 – 702, 2000.

[15] David Lybäack and Magnus Boman, Agent Trade Servers in Financial Exchange Systems, *ACM Transactions on Internet Technology*, in press, 2003.

[16] Matteo Marsili, Sergei Maslov and Yi-Cheng Zhang, Dynamical Optimization Theory of a Diversified Portfolio, *Physica A* **253**:403 – 418, 1988.

[17] Sergei Maslov and Yi-Cheng Zhang, Optimal Investment Strategy for Risky Assets, *Theoretical and Applied Finance* **1**(3):377 – 387, 1998.

[18] J. M. R. Parrondo, J. M. Blanco, F. J. Cao, and R. Brito, Efficiency of Brownian Motors, *Europhys. Lett.* **43**(3):248 – 254, 1998.

[19] Lars Rasmusson and Magnus Boman, Analytical expressions for Parrondo games, *Fluctuation and Noise Letters* **2**(4):L343 – L348, 2002.

In: Artificial Intelligence and Computer Science
Editor: Susan Shannon, pp. 139-154
ISBN 1-59454-411-5

Chapter 5

SVM That Maximizes the Margin in the Input Space

Shotaro Akaho
AIST Neuroscience Research Institute,
1-1-1 Central 2, Umezono, Tsukuba,
Ibaraki 305-8568 Japan

Abstract

We propose a novel criterion for support vector machine (SVM) learning: maximizing the margin in the input space, not in the feature space like the original SVM. This criterion is appropriate in particular when some prior knowledge is given by a metric in the input space. We derive an algorithm that consists of two alternating steps to estimate the dual sets of parameters, where those parameters are first initialized by the original SVM. The first step is to update one set of parameters by a Newton-like procedure, and the second step is to update the dual set by solving a quadratic programming (QP) problem. The algorithm converges to a local optimum in a few steps under mild conditions, and it preserves the sparsity of support vectors. Although the complexity for calculating temporal variables becomes large, the complexity for the QP problem does not change. It is also shown that the original SVM can be seen as a special case of this framework. We further derive a simplified algorithm which enables us to use existing codes for the original SVM.

1 Introduction

The support vector machine (SVM) is known as a state-of-the-art method especially for pattern recognition[4, 8, 14]. The original SVM maximizes the margin which is defined by the minimum distance between samples and a separating hyperplane in a Hilbert space $\mathcal{H}$ (feature space). Even when the dimensionality of $\mathcal{H}$ is very large, it has been proved that the original SVM has a generalization error bound which is independent of the dimensionality, hence the SVM is considered to be free from a curse of dimensionality. In practice, however, the original SVM sometimes gives a very small margin in the input space, because the metric of the feature space is usually quite different from that of the input space. Therefore, the margin in the feature space is not an appropriate criterion, in particular when the input space is already a well-designed feature space by some prior knowledge[2, 5, 7, 11, 12].

In this article, we derive a learning algorithm to maximize the margin in the input space. A major difficulty is that we cannot get an explicit form of the margin in the input space in general, because the classification boundary is curved in a complicated way and the vertical projection from a sample point to the boundary is not always unique. We solve this problem by linear approximation techniques. This approximation leads to the algorithm that consists of iterations of alternating two stages as follows: one is to estimate the projection points and the other is to solve a quadratic programming problem to find optimal parameter values.

Such a dual structure appears in other frameworks, such as the EM algorithm and the variational Bayes framework. Much more related work is the principal curve proposed by Hastie et al[6]. The principal curve algorithm minimizes the sum of squared distance to sample points measured vertically in the input space. In this article, we consider the classification problem rather than regression and the margin rather than the quadratic loss.

The algorithm is not gradient-descent type but Newton-like, which means the step size is not necessarily small; hence we have to investigate its convergence property carefully. It will be shown that the algorithm converges to a local optimum under mild conditions, though it does not always converges to the global optimum. We also show some interesting relations to the original SVM: the original SVM can be seen as a special case of the algorithm, and the number of support vectors does not increase so much from the original SVM. The algorithm is verified through simple simulations.

2 Generalized Margin in the Input Space

We consider a binary classification problem. The purpose of learning is to construct a map from an m-dimensional input $x \in \Re^m$ to a corresponding output $y \in \{\pm 1\}$ by using a finite number of samples $(x_1, y_1), \ldots, (x_n, y_n)$.

Let us consider a linear classifier, $y = \text{sgn}[f(x)]$, where $f(x) \equiv \omega \cdot \phi(x) + f_0$; $\phi(x)$ is a feature of an input x in a Hilbert space $\mathcal{H}$, $\omega \in \mathcal{H}$ is a weight parameter and $f_0 \in \Re$ is a bias parameter. Those parameters ω and f_0 define a separating hyperplane in the feature space. As a feature function $\phi(x)$, we only consider a differentiable nonlinear map.

A margin in the input space is defined by the minimum distance from the sample points $\{(x_i, y_i), i = 1, \ldots, n\}$ to the classification boundary $f(x) = 0$ in the input space. Since the classification boundary forms a complicated curved surface, the distance cannot be obtained in an explicit form, and more significantly, the vertical projection from a point to the boundary is not unique.

Here, the metric in the input space is not necessary to be Euclidean. Some Riemannian metric $G(x)$ may be defined, which enables us to represent many kinds of prior knowledge. For example, the invariance of patterns[8, 11] can be implemented in this form. In the invariance of patterns, we apply the knowledge of invariant transformations, e.g. scaling and rotation in the character recognition problem. The distance between patterns transformed by such invariant transformations is preferable to be small. For that purpose, one can take small metric values corresponding to the invariant directions. Another example is a Fisher information matrix that is a natural metric when the input space is a parameter space of probability distributions[2, 7]. In such a Riemannian space, although the distance is theoretically preferable to be measured by the length of a geodesic, it causes computational difficulty. Since we only need a distance from a sample point to another point, we use a computationally feasible (nonsymmetric) distance from a sample point x_i to another point x in the quadratic norm,

$$\|x - x_i\|_{G_i}^2 = (x - x_i)^{\mathsf{T}} G_i (x - x_i),$$

where $G_i \equiv G(x_i)$.

For simplicity, we mainly consider the hard margin case in which sample points are separable by a hyperplane in the Hilbert space. The soft margin case is discussed in section 6.

Let x_i^* be the closest point on the boundary surface from a sample point x_i, and $d_i \equiv x_i^* - x_i$ (fig.1). Since d_i is invariant under a scalar transformation of (ω, f_0), we assume all points are separated with satisfying

$$\|d_i\|_{G_i}^2 \geq 1/\omega \cdot \omega, \quad i = 1, \cdots, n, \tag{1}$$

Further, let us assume at least one of them fulfills an equality, then the margin is given by $1/\sqrt{\omega \cdot \omega}$. As a result, our problem is to find the optimal parameter by minimizing a quadratic objective function $\omega \cdot \omega$ with the constraints (1) and $y_i f(x_i) > 0$.

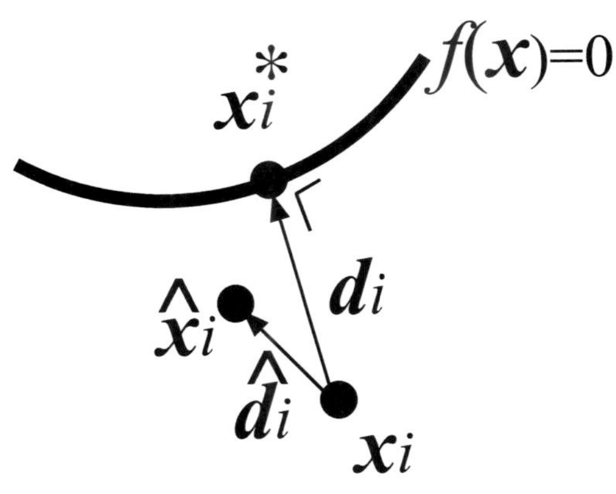

Figure 1: Distance from a point to a separating hyperplane

In order to solve the optimization problem, we start from solving the original SVM and update the solution iteratively. By linearization technique and a kernel trick described in the next section, we obtain a discriminant function at the k-th iteration step in the form,

$$f(x) = \sum_{i \in \mathrm{S.V.}} \{a_i^{(k)} \mathrm{k}(\hat{x}_i^{(k)}, x) + b_i^{(k)\mathsf{T}} \mathbf{k}_x(\hat{x}_i^{(k)}, x)\} + f_0^{(k)}, \tag{2}$$

where S.V. is a set of indices of support vectors, $\mathrm{k}(x,y)$ is a kernel function and $\mathbf{k}_x(x,y)$ is its derivative defined by $\mathbf{k}_x(x,y) \equiv \partial \mathrm{k}(x,y)/\partial x$. We have two groups of parameters here: One is of a_i, b_i and f_0 which are parameters of linear coefficients of kernels, and the other is of $\hat{x}_i$ which is an estimate of the projection point x_i^* and forms base functions. a_i and f_0 are initialized by the corresponding parameters in the original SVM and the other parameters are initialized by $b_i = \mathbf{0}$, $\hat{x}_i = x_i$.

3 Iterative QP by Linear Approximations

In this section, we overview the derivation of update rules of the parameters. The overall algorithm is summarized in sec.3.6.

3.1 Linear Approximation of the Distance to the Boundary

Suppose an estimated projection point $\hat{x}_i$ is given, we can get an approximate distance $\|d_i\|_{G_i}$ by a linear approximation[1]. Taking the Taylor expansion of $f(x_i^*) = 0$ around $\hat{x}_i$ up to the first order, we obtain a constraint on d_i,

$$f(\hat{x}_i) + \nabla f(\hat{x}_i)^{\mathsf{T}} (d_i - \hat{d}_i) = 0,$$

where $\hat{d}_i = \hat{x}_i - x_i$. Minimizing $\|d_i\|_{G_i}^2$ under this constraint, we have

$$\|d_i\|_{G_i}^2 = \frac{(\omega \cdot \{\phi(\hat{x}_i) - \psi(\hat{x}_i)^{\mathsf{T}} \hat{d}_i\} + f_0)^2}{\|\omega \cdot \psi(\hat{x}_i)\|_{G_i^{-1}}^2}, \tag{3}$$

where $\psi(\hat{x}_i) \equiv \nabla \phi(\hat{x}_i) \in \mathcal{H}^m$. Note that this approximate value is unique, and it is invariant under a scalar transformation of (ω, f_0). Moreover, the approximation is strictly correct when $\hat{x}_i = x_i^*$ and $\omega \cdot \psi(\hat{x}_i) \neq 0$.

3.2 Linearization of the Constraint

Using the approximate value of the distance, we have a nonlinear constraint,

$$y_i \left[\omega \cdot \{\phi(\hat{x}_i) - \psi(\hat{x}_i)^{\mathsf{T}} \hat{d}_i\} + f_0 \right] \geq \frac{\|\omega \cdot \psi(\hat{x}_i)\|_{G_i^{-1}}}{\sqrt{\omega \cdot \omega}}. \tag{4}$$

Since it is a nonlinear constraint of ω, we linearize it around an approximate solution $\omega = \hat{\omega}$ that is the current estimate. This linearization not only simplifies the problem, but also enables us to derive the dual problem.

Let $g_i(\omega)$ be the right hand side of (4), the first order expansion is written as

$$g_i(\omega) = g_i(\hat{\omega}) + (\partial g_i(\hat{\omega})/\partial\omega)\cdot(\omega-\hat{\omega}).$$

Let us define $\hat{g}_i \equiv g_i(\hat{\omega}), \hat{\eta}_i \equiv \partial g_i(\hat{\omega})/\partial\omega$, then we can prove the equality

$$\hat{\omega}\cdot\hat{\eta}_i = 0, \qquad \forall i = 1,\ldots,n, \tag{5}$$

and using the equality, we obtain a linear form of the constraint for ω,

$$\omega\cdot[y_i\left\{\phi(\hat{x}_i) - \psi(\hat{x}_i)^{\mathsf{T}}\hat{d}_i\right\} - \hat{\eta}_i] \geq \hat{g}_i - f_0 y_i. \tag{6}$$

Suppose $\hat{q}_i \equiv \hat{\omega}\cdot\psi(\hat{x}_i)$ and $\hat{r} \equiv \hat{\omega}\cdot\hat{\omega}$, then $\hat{g}_i$ and $\hat{\eta}_i$ are written as

$$\begin{aligned} \hat{g}_i &= \frac{1}{\sqrt{\hat{r}}}\|\hat{q}_i\|_{G_i^{-1}}, \\ \hat{\eta}_i &= \frac{1}{\hat{g}_i\hat{r}}\left\{\hat{q}_i^{\mathsf{T}}G_i^{-1}\psi(\hat{x}_i) - \frac{1}{\hat{r}}\|\hat{q}_i\|^2_{G_i^{-1}}\hat{\omega}\right\}. \end{aligned} \tag{7}$$

By the linearization above, we obtain the dual problem in a similar way to the original SVM,

$$\begin{aligned} W(\alpha) = \sum_i \hat{g}_i\alpha_i - \frac{1}{2}\sum_{i,j}\alpha_i\alpha_j \\ [y_i\{\phi(\hat{x}_i) - \psi(\hat{x}_i)^{\mathsf{T}}\hat{d}_i\} - \hat{\eta}_i]\cdot[y_j\{\phi(\hat{x}_j) - \psi(\hat{x}_j)^{\mathsf{T}}\hat{d}_j\} - \hat{\eta}_j], \end{aligned}$$

which is maximized under the constraints[1],

$$\alpha_i \geq 0, \qquad \sum_i y_i\alpha_i = 0. \tag{8}$$

The solution ω is given by

$$\omega = \sum_i \alpha_i[y_i\{\phi(\hat{x}_i) - \psi(\hat{x}_i)^{\mathsf{T}}\hat{d}_i\} - \hat{\eta}_i]. \tag{9}$$

Here we see an apparent relation to the original SVM, i.e., by letting $\hat{x}_i = x_i$, $\hat{\eta}_i = 0$, and $\hat{g}_i = 1$, we have exactly the same optimization problem as the original SVM.

3.3 Kernel Trick

In order to avoid the calculation of mapping into high dimensional Hilbert space, SVM applies a kernel trick, by which an inner product is replaced by a symmetric positive definite kernel function (Mercer kernel) that is easy to calculate[10, 4, 8, 14]. In our formulation, $\phi(x)\cdot\phi(y)$ is replaced by a Mercer kernel $\mathrm{k}(x,y)$. We also have to calculate the inner product

[1] If the bias f_0 is fixed to zero, the constraint $\sum_i y_i\alpha_i = 0$ is not necessary.

related to ψ (the derivative of ϕ). Let us assume that the kernel function k is differentiable. Then, $\psi(x)\cdot\phi(y)$ is replaced by a vector $\mathbf{k}_x(x,y) \equiv \partial \mathrm{k}(x,y)/\partial x$, and $\psi(x)\cdot\psi(y)^\mathsf{T}$ is replaced by a matrix $\mathrm{K}_{xy}(x,y) \equiv \partial^2 \mathrm{k}(x,y)/\partial x \partial y^\mathsf{T}$.

Now let us derive the kernel version of the optimization problem. In (9), $\hat{\eta}_i \in \mathcal{H}$ has bases related to $\psi(\hat{x}_i)$ and $\hat{\omega}$, and the solution ω has bases $\phi(\hat{x}_i)$ additionally. Although $\hat{\omega}$ can have any kinds of bases, we restrict it in the following form to avoid increasing number of bases.

$$\hat{\omega} = \sum_i \{\hat{a}_i \phi(\hat{x}_i) + \hat{b}_i^\mathsf{T} \psi(\hat{x}_i)\}.$$

Then we have $\hat{q}_i = \sum_j \{\hat{a}_j \mathbf{k}_x(\hat{x}_i,\hat{x}_j) + \mathrm{K}_{xy}(\hat{x}_i,\hat{x}_j)\hat{b}_j\}$. Now let

$$\hat{p}_i \equiv \hat{\omega}\cdot\phi(\hat{x}_i) = \sum_j \{\hat{a}_j \mathrm{k}(\hat{x}_j,\hat{x}_i) + \hat{b}_j^\mathsf{T} \mathbf{k}_x(\hat{x}_j,\hat{x}_i)\},$$

then $\hat{r}$ is given by $\hat{r} = \sum_i (\hat{a}_i \hat{p}_i + \hat{b}_i^\mathsf{T} \hat{q}_i)$, and $\hat{g}_i$ by (7). Further, let us define additional temporal variables that represent several terms in the objective function,

$$\begin{aligned}
\hat{s}_{ij} &\equiv \{\phi(\hat{x}_i) - \psi(\hat{x}_i)^\mathsf{T}\hat{d}_i\}\cdot\{\phi(\hat{x}_j) - \psi(\hat{x}_j)^\mathsf{T}\hat{d}_j\} \\
&= \mathrm{k}(\hat{x}_i,\hat{x}_j) + \hat{d}_i^\mathsf{T} \mathrm{K}_{xy}(\hat{x}_i,\hat{x}_j)\hat{d}_j - \hat{d}_i^\mathsf{T} \mathbf{k}_x(\hat{x}_i,\hat{x}_j) - \hat{d}_j^\mathsf{T} \mathbf{k}_x(\hat{x}_j,\hat{x}_i), \\
\hat{t}_{ij} &\equiv \hat{\eta}_i\cdot\{\phi(\hat{x}_j) - \psi(\hat{x}_j)^\mathsf{T}\hat{d}_j\} \\
&= \frac{1}{\hat{g}_i \hat{r}}\left\{\hat{q}_i^\mathsf{T} G_i^{-1}\left(\mathbf{k}_x(\hat{x}_i,\hat{x}_j) - \mathrm{K}_{xy}(\hat{x}_i,\hat{x}_j)\hat{d}_j\right) - \frac{\|\hat{q}_i\|^2_{G_i^{-1}}}{\hat{r}}(\hat{p}_j - \hat{d}_j^\mathsf{T}\hat{q}_j)\right\}, \\
\hat{u}_{ij} &= \hat{\eta}_i\cdot\hat{\eta}_j = \frac{1}{\hat{g}_i \hat{g}_j \hat{r}^2}(\hat{q}_i^\mathsf{T} G_i^{-1} \mathrm{K}_{xy}(\hat{x}_i,\hat{x}_j) G_j^{-1} \hat{q}_j - \frac{\|\hat{q}_i\|^2_{G_i^{-1}}\|\hat{q}_j\|^2_{G_j^{-1}}}{\hat{r}}),
\end{aligned}$$

then we have the objective function in the kernel form,

$$W(\alpha) = \sum_i \hat{g}_i \alpha_i - \frac{1}{2}\sum_{i,j} \alpha_i \alpha_j (y_i y_j \hat{s}_{ij} - y_j \hat{t}_{ij} - y_i \hat{t}_{ji} + \hat{u}_{ij}), \tag{10}$$

which is maximized under constraints $\alpha_i \geq 0$ and $\sum_i y_i \alpha_i = 0$.

The new parameters can be determined from (9) by

$$a_i^{(k+1)} = \alpha_i y_i + \beta \hat{a}_i, \tag{11}$$

$$b_i^{(k+1)} = -\alpha_i \left(y_i \hat{d}_i + \frac{G_i^{-1}\hat{q}_i}{\hat{g}_i \hat{r}} \right) + \beta \hat{b}_i, \tag{12}$$

$$\beta = \sum_j \frac{\alpha_j \|\hat{q}_j\|^2_{G_i^{-1}}}{\hat{g}_j \hat{r}^2}.$$

As for the bias term f_0, since the constraint (6) should be satisfied in equality for $J = \{i \mid \alpha_i \neq 0\}$ from the Kuhn-Tucker condition, we have for any $i \in J$,

$$f_0^{(k+1)} = y_i \hat{g}_i - \sum_j \alpha_j (y_j \hat{s}_{ji} - \hat{t}_{ji} - y_i y_j \hat{t}_{ij} + y_i \hat{u}_{ij}) \tag{13}$$

From (11) and (12), we can estimate the number of support vectors. Let J_k be the indices of nonzero α_i's at the k-th step, then the number of support vectors is bounded from upper by $|J_0 \cup J_1 \cup \cdots \cup J_k|$. Since J_k does not change much as long as the structure of classification boundary is similar, the number of support vectors is expected to be not so larger than the original SVM.

3.4 Update of the Approximate Projection of the Points

To complete the algorithm, we have to consider the update of the approximate value of the projection point $\hat{x}_i$ which is initialized by x_i, otherwise the convergent solution is not precisely what we want. If good approximation of $\hat{\omega}$ and $\hat{f}_0$ is given, we can refine $\hat{x}_i$ iteratively in the same way as in sec. 3.1: Suppose $\hat{\omega} = \sum_j \{\hat{a}_j \phi(\hat{x}_j^{\text{old}}) + \hat{b}_j^{\mathsf{T}} \psi(\hat{x}_j^{\text{old}})\}$, the projection point $\hat{x}_i$ can be estimated by iterating the following steps for $l = 0, 1, 2, 3, \cdots$,

$$\hat{x}_i^{[l+1]} = x_i - \frac{\hat{q}_i^{[l]}}{\|\hat{q}_i^{[l]}\|^2_{G_i^{-1}}} \left[\hat{p}_i^{[l]} - (\hat{x}_i^{[l]} - x_i)^{\mathsf{T}} \hat{q}_i^{[l]} + \hat{f}_0\right] \tag{14}$$

where $\hat{x}_i^{[0]}$ is initialized by $\hat{x}_i^{\text{old}}$; $\hat{p}_i^{[l]}$ and $\hat{q}_i^{[l]}$ are defined in a similar way as $\hat{p}_i$ and $\hat{q}_i$,

$$\begin{aligned}
\hat{p}_i^{[l]} &\equiv \hat{\omega} \cdot \phi(\hat{x}_i^{[l]}) \\
&= \sum_j \{\hat{a}_j \mathrm{k}(\hat{x}_j^{\text{old}}, \hat{x}_i^{[l]}) + \hat{b}_j^{\mathsf{T}} \mathbf{k}_x(\hat{x}_j^{\text{old}}, \hat{x}_i^{[l]})\}, \\
\hat{q}_i^{[l]} &\equiv \hat{\omega} \cdot \psi(\hat{x}_i^{[l]}) \\
&= \sum_j \{\hat{a}_j \mathbf{k}_x(\hat{x}_i^{[l]}, \hat{x}_j^{\text{old}}) + \mathrm{K}_{xy}(\hat{x}_i^{[l]}, \hat{x}_j^{\text{old}}) \hat{b}_j\}.
\end{aligned}$$

Note that locally maximum points and saddle points of the distance are also equilibrium states of (14). The following proposition guarantees such a point is not stable.

Proposition 1 *A point $\hat{x}_i \in \Re^m$ is an equilibrium state of the iteration step (14), when and only when the point is a critical point of the distance from x_i to the separating boundary, i.e., a local minimum, a local maximum or a saddle point. The equilibrium state is not stable when the point is a local maximum or a saddle point.*

Proof: It is straightforward to show that a point is an equilibrium state of the iteration step (14), only when the point is a critical point of the projection point $\|d_i\|^2_{G_i}$. Without loss of generality, we assume the uniform metric case $G_i = I$, because update rule (14) is invariant of a metric transformation. We consider the behavior around a critical point x_i^*. Let $\hat{x}_i^{[l]} = x_i^* + \varepsilon$, for a sufficiently small vector ε. One can show that $\hat{x}_i^{[l]}$ is mapped into the separating hypersurface $f(x) = \hat{\omega} \cdot \phi(x) + \hat{f}_0 = 0$ for a small ε after one step iteration. Therefore, we only consider the case $\hat{x}_i^{[l]}$ is on the hypersurface.

Since x_i^* is a critical point of the distance, the tangent vector $\nabla f(x_i^*)$ is collinear to the distant vector $d_i = x_i^* - x_i$, i.e., for some constant λ, it holds

$$\nabla f(x_i^*) = \lambda d_i. \tag{15}$$

Furthermore, if $\hat{x}_i^{[l]}$ is in a point of $f(x) = 0$, $\nabla f(x_i^*)$ is nearly orthogonal to ε, i.e.,

$$\nabla f(x_i^*)^{\mathsf{T}} \varepsilon \simeq 0. \tag{16}$$

By expanding (14) around x_i^*, we have a new estimation $\hat{x}_i^{[l+1]}$ by

$$\hat{x}_i^{[l+1]} \simeq x_i^* + \frac{1}{\lambda} \nabla^2 f(x_i^*) \varepsilon - \frac{d_i^{\mathsf{T}} \nabla^2 f(x_i^*) \varepsilon}{\lambda \|d_i\|} d_i, \tag{17}$$

where $\nabla^2 f$ is a hessian matrix of $f(x)$. Without loss of generality, we can take the coordinate of x as follows: the first coordinate is the direction of d_i, and the second to the m-th coordinates are taken orthogonally such that an $(m-1) \times (m-1)$ submatrix of $\nabla^2 f(x_i^*)$ for those coordinates is diagonalized, i.e., $\nabla^2 f(x_i^*)$ is in the form,

$$\nabla^2 f(x_i^*) = \begin{pmatrix} c_1 & & b^{\mathsf{T}} & \\ & c_2 & & 0 \\ b & & \ddots & \\ & 0 & & c_m \end{pmatrix}. \tag{18}$$

Under this coordinate system, since ε_1 is of small order value, the first element calculated from the second and third term in (17) vanishes and we have

$$\hat{x}_i^{[l+1]} - x_i^* \simeq \frac{1}{\lambda} (0, c_2 \varepsilon_2, \ldots, c_m \varepsilon_m)^{\mathsf{T}}. \tag{19}$$

The iteration step is stable at x_i^* only when $\|\hat{x}_i^{[l+1]} - x_i^*\| \leq \|\forall \varepsilon\|$, i.e., $|c_j| < |\lambda|$ for all $j = 2, \ldots, m$. □

The condition for 1-j plane is shown in figure 2.

When the point is a local maximum or saddle, the hypersurface is in the unstable region. However, even in the case of local minimum, there exist an unstable region, intuitively when the hypersurface is strongly curved. We can avoid the undesired behavior by slowing down. For example, first $c_2, \ldots, c_m$ and λ are estimated from ∇f and $\nabla^2 f$ values at the current estimate, and then if $c_j < |\lambda|$ for all $j = 2, \ldots, m$, the point must be local minima, then the movement $\hat{x}_i^{[l+1]} - \hat{x}_i^{[l]}$ to the axes in which $c_j < -|\lambda|$ should be shortened by multiplying some factor $0 < e_j < |\lambda|/|c_j|$.

This computationally intensive treatment would be usually necessary only after the several steps, because it is considered that the unstablity for local minima occurs a small region relatively to the size of d_i.

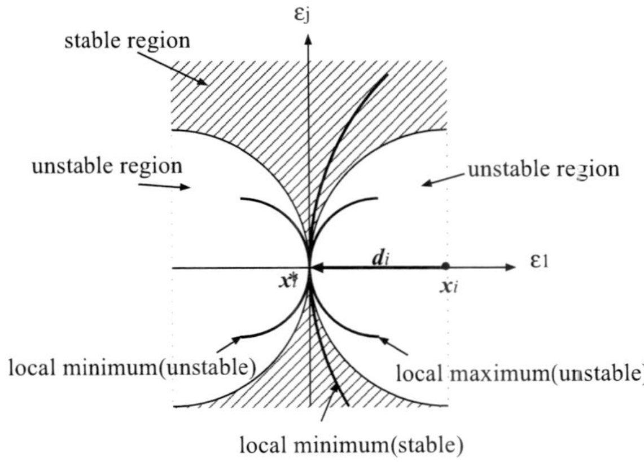

Figure 2: Stability of the update of projection points. The update rule is stable when the separating curve is in the hatched region

3.5 Projection of the Hyperplane

The update of $\hat{x}_i$ causes another problem: We assumed in section 3.2 that ω and $\hat{\omega}$ have the same bases. However, $\hat{\omega}$ has bases based on the old $\hat{x}_i$, while we need the new ω based on the new $\hat{x}_i$. To solve that problem, we project $\hat{\omega}$ onto the space spanned by new bases, i.e., from the old one $\hat{\omega}^{\text{old}} = \sum_{i \in \text{S.V.}} \{\hat{a}_i^{\text{old}} \phi(\hat{x}_i^{\text{old}}) + \hat{b}_i^{\text{old}\mathsf{T}} \psi(\hat{x}_i^{\text{old}})\}$ to a new one, $\hat{\omega}^{\text{new}} = \sum_{i \in \text{S.V.}} \{\hat{a}_i^{\text{new}} \phi(\hat{x}_i^{\text{new}}) + \hat{b}_i^{\text{new}\mathsf{T}} \psi(\hat{x}_i^{\text{new}})\}$. Although $\hat{\omega}^{\text{new}}$ can have more bases other than S.V., we restrict the bases to support vectors to preserve the sparsity of bases.

There are several possibilities of the projection. In this article, we use the one which minimizes the cost function

$$\frac{1}{2} \sum_{x \in T} \{\hat{\omega}^{\text{new}} \cdot \phi(x) + \hat{f}_0^{\text{new}} - (\hat{\omega}^{\text{old}} \cdot \phi(x) + \hat{f}_0^{\text{old}})\}^2, \tag{20}$$

where T is a certain set of x, and we use $T = \{x_i, \hat{x}_i^{\text{old}}, \hat{x}_i^{\text{new}}; i = 1, \cdots, n\}$.

Minimizing (20) leads to a simple least square problem, which can be solved by linear equations. Another possibility of the cost function is $\|\hat{\omega}^{\text{new}} - \hat{\omega}^{\text{old}}\|^2$, which leads to another set of linear equations.

3.6 Overall Algorithm and the Convergence Property

Now let us summarize the algorithm below.

Algorithm 1: Maximizing the margin in the input space

Initialization step: Let the solution of the original SVM be $a_i^{(0)}$ and $f_0^{(0)}$; let $b_i^{(0)} = \mathbf{0}$ and $\hat{x}_i^{(0)} = x_i$.

For $k = 0, 1, 2, \ldots$, repeat the following steps until convergence:

1. Update of $\hat{x}_i$: Calculate $\hat{x}_i^{(k+1)}$ by applying (14) iteratively to $\hat{x}_i^{(k)}$.

2. Projection of hyperplane: Calculate $\hat{a}_i$, $\hat{b}_i$ and $\hat{f}_0$ based on $\hat{x}_i^{(k+1)}$ by a certain projection method from $a_i^{(k)}$, $b_i^{(k)}$ and $f_0^{(k)}$ based on $\hat{x}_i^{(k)}$ (sec.3.5).

3. QP step: Solve the QP problem (10) with respect to α_i.

4. Parameter update: Calculate $a_i^{(k+1)}$, $b_i^{(k+1)}$ and $f_0^{(k+1)}$ by (11), (12) and (13).

The discriminant function at the k-th step is given by (2).

Although the Algorithm 1 does not always converge to the global minimum, we can prove the following proposition concerning about the convergence of the algorithm.

Proposition 2 *Equilibrium points of the Algorithm 1 are critical points of the margin in the input space. The algorithm is stable, when the update rule of $\hat{x}_i$ (14) is stable for all i (see also Proposition 1).*

This proposition can be proved basically by proposition 1 and the fact that the linearization of QP is almost exact by a small perturbation of ω. As in the case of (14), we can modify the algorithm by slowing down in (3) and (14) so that the equilibrium state is stable when and only when the margin is locally optimal. However, we don't use it in the simulation because the case that the local minimum is unstable is expected to be rare.

Another problem of the algorithm is that each iteration step does not always increase the margin monotonically. Although it is usually faster than gradient type algorithms, the algorithm sometimes does not improve the solution of the original SVM at all. Because the original SVM can be seen as a special case of the algorithm, we can use some annealing technique, for example, updating temporal variables and parameters more gradually from their initial values. However, for simplicity, we use a crude method in the simulation as follows: Repeat several steps of the algorithm (5 steps in the simulation) and then choose the best solution which gives the largest estimated value of the margin.

As for the complexity of the algorithm, we need $O(m^2n^2)$ space and $O(m^3n^2)$ time complexity to calculate temporal variables if the computation of a kernel function is $O(m)$, while the original SVM requires $O(n^2)$ space and $O(mn^2)$ time. Those calculation can be pararellized easily. This complexity is not so different when m is comparatively small. Once the variables are calculated, the complexity for QP is just the same. Therefore, as far as the calculation for temporal variables is comparative to the QP time, the proposed algorithm is comparative to the original SVM. If the Algorithm 1 is heavy because of the large m, we can use a simplified algorithm as shown in section 4.

As for the iteration of QP which is carried out usually for a few steps, since a current solution is an estimate of the solution, it may be able to reduce the complexity of the QP at the next iteration step.

4 Simplified Algorithm for a High Dimensional Case

Although the Algorithm 1 achieves the precise solution, the computation costs is high for large dimensionality of inputs. In this section, we give a simplified algorithm.

If we don't update $\hat{x}_i$, the first and the second steps of the Algorithm 1 is not necessary any more. This simplification makes the algorithm simpler because all $\hat{d}_i$ terms vanish. However, let us consider further simplification.

We have shown the relation to the original SVM: the original SVM can be derived $\hat{g}_i = 1$ and $\hat{\eta}_i = 0$. Since $\hat{\eta}_i$ causes many temporal variables, we only maintain $\hat{g}_i$. Then all the terms related to $\hat{b}_i$'s vanish.

Consequently, the above simplifications lead to the algorithm much like the original SVM.

Algorithm 2: Maximizing the margin in the input space (simplified)

Initialization: Let the solution of the original SVM be $a_i^{(0)}$ and $f_0^{(0)}$;
For $k = 0, 1, 2, \ldots$, repeat the following steps until convergence:

1. Calculate $\hat{g}_i$: $\hat{g}_i = \dfrac{\|\sum_j a_i^{(k)} \mathbf{k}_x(x_i, x_j)\|_{G_i^{-1}}}{\sqrt{\sum_{j,l} a_j^{(k)} a_l^{(k)} \mathrm{k}(x_j, x_l)}}$.
2. QP step: maximize
   $\sum_i \hat{g}_i \alpha_i - \frac{1}{2} \sum_{i,j} \alpha_i \alpha_j y_i y_j \mathrm{k}(x_i, x_j)$ with respect to α_i under $\alpha_i \geq 0$, $\sum_i y_i \alpha_i = 0$
3. Update parameters: $a_i^{(k+1)} = \alpha_i y_i$, $f_0^{(k+1)} = \hat{g}_l y_l - \sum_j \alpha_j y_j \mathrm{k}(x_j, x_l)$, where l is any support vector.

The discriminant function at the k-th step is given by $f(x) = \sum_{i \in \mathrm{S.V.}} a_i^{(k)} \mathrm{k}(x_i, x) + f_0^{(k)}$.

Although the Algorithm 2 is an approximate algorithm, the time complexity is dominant for the QP step and the space complexity is dominant to store $\mathbf{k}_x$. Furthermore, the number of basis functions is same as the original SVM. Therefore, if the dimensionality of input space is large, the Algorithm 2 is suitable to improve the performance of the original SVM. In the following section, we investigate the performance of the Algorithm 2 for real dataset.

5 Simulation Results

5.1 Synthetic Data

In this section, we give a simulation result for synthetic data sets in order to verify the Algorithm 1 and to examine the basic performance. 20 training samples and 1000 test samples were randomly drawn from positive and negative distribution, each of which is a Gaussian mixture of 3 components with uniformly distributed centers $[0, 1)^2$ and fixed spherical variance $\sigma^2 = 0.2^2$. The kernel function used here is a spherical Gaussian kernel with $\sigma^2 = 1^2$. We took the Euclidean metric (i.e., G_i is the unit matrix). Figure 3 and 4 show an example of results by the original SVM (initial condition) and the proposed algorithm (after 5 steps). In this case, the margin value increased from 0.040 to 0.096. Such a simulation was repeated for 100 sets of samples with different random numbers

The estimated margins in the input space for the original and proposed algorithm is shown in figure 5 (log-log scale). By the crude algorithm described in the previous section, there are 4 cases among 100 runs that were not able to improve the margin of the original SVM. The ratios of the margin are distributed from 1.00 (no improvement) to 27.9.

The misclassification errors for test samples is shown in figure 6. The ratios of error are distributed between [0.40(best),1.37(worst)].

This results indicates that the margin in the input space is efficient to improve the generalization performance in average, but there are cases that cannot reduce the generalization error even when the margin in the input space increases.

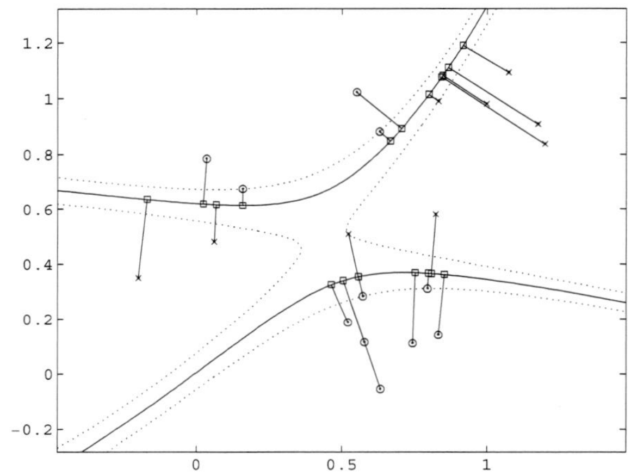

the original SVM (margin .040)

Figure 3: Result of the original SVM (margin .040). Circles (○) and crosses (×) are positive and negative samples. Squares (□) represent estimates of the projection of the points by applying (14) for 10 steps.

5.2 Real Data

We applied the simplified algorithm (Algorithm 2) to real data, WDBC (Wisconsin diagnostic breast cancer) dataset[13] in the UCI machine learning repository. This database consists of binary classification for lung cancer diagnosis by 30 real explanatory variables. The total number of data is 569.

Here we extracted 30 training samples randomly, and applied the Algorithm 2 for 3 steps, and then evaluated the test error using the rest of data. We repeated this procedure

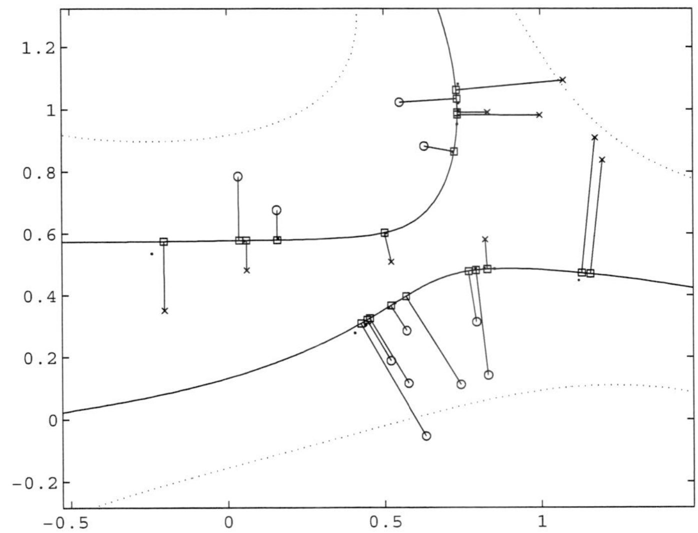

(b) Algorithm 1 (after 5 steps, margin .096)

Figure 4: Result of the Algorithm 1 (after 5 steps, margin .096) for the same data set as fig.3

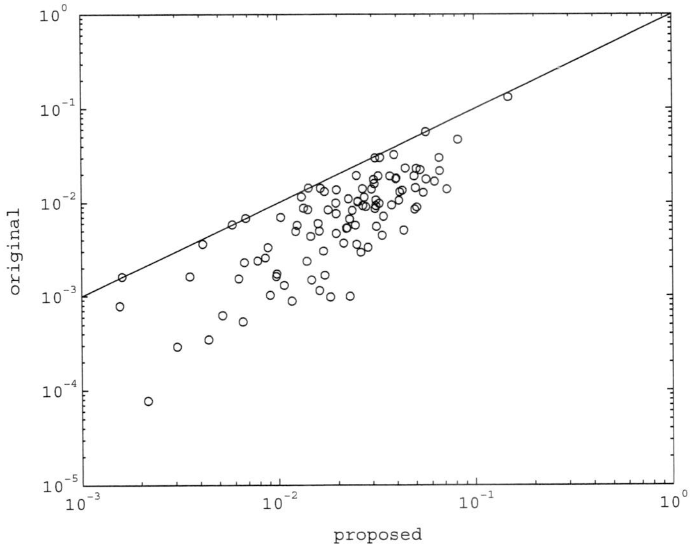

Figure 5: Margin comparison with the original SVM for synthetic data for 100 runs (log-log scale)

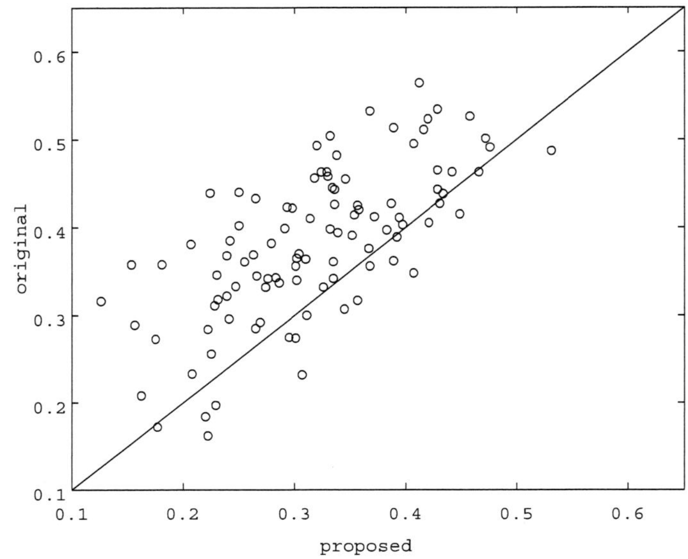

Figure 6: Test error comparison with the original SVM for synthetic data for 100 runs

for 30 different random seeds.

We used spherical Gaussian kernel whose variance is determined by the variance of the principal direction of data.

Fig.7 shows the plot of test error, where the ratio of test error is distributed $[0.58(\text{best}), 1.18(\text{worst})]$ and the average is 0.96.

6 Soft Margin

For noisy situation, we may need soft margin. Soft margin is derived by introducing slack variables z_i. If we use a soft constraint in the form

$$\omega \cdot [y_i \{\phi(\hat{x}_i) - \psi(\hat{x}_i)^{\mathsf{T}} \hat{d}_i\} - \hat{\eta}_i] \geq \hat{g}_i - f_0 y_i - z_i, \tag{21}$$

and adding penalty for the slack variables,

$$\frac{1}{2}\omega \cdot \omega + C \sum_i z_i, \tag{22}$$

By this modification, only the constraint (8) for α_i is changed to

$$0 \leq \alpha_i \leq C, \tag{23}$$

which is the same constraint as the soft margin of the original SVM. However, the geometrical meaning of (21) is not clear, and it is left as a future work.

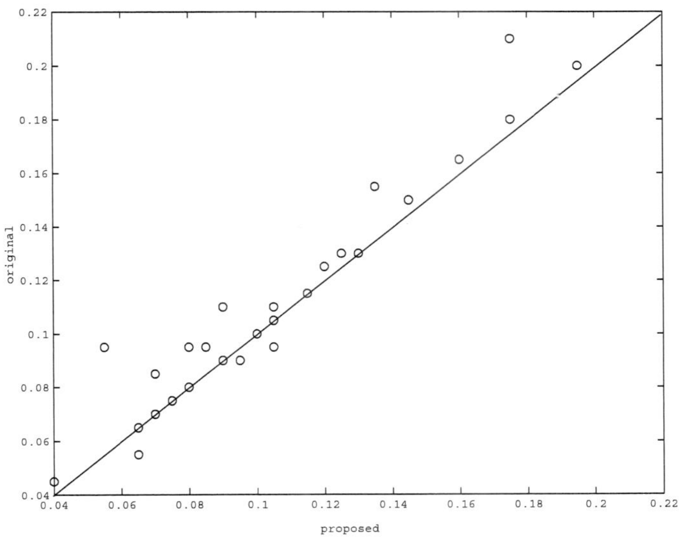

Figure 7: Test error for WDBC data for 30 runs (horizontal axis: Algorithm 2; vertical axis: Original SVM)

7 Conclusion

We have proposed a new learning algorithm to find a kernel-based classifier that maximizes the margin in the input space. The derived algorithm consists of an alternating optimization between the foot of perpendicular and the linear coefficient parameters. Such a dual structure appears in other frameworks, such as EM algorithm, variational Bayes, and principal curve.

There are many issues to be studied about the algorithm. It is theoretically important to clarify the relation between the margin in the input space and the generalization performance.

From the practical viewpoint, it is an interesting issue to find an efficient algorithm that reduces the complexity and converges more stably. In our case, the Algorithm 1 sometimes behaves unstably in particular for real dataset. It is also an interesting issue to extend our framework to other problems than classification, such as regression[1, 9, 8].

In this article, we have assumed that the kernel function is given and fixed. Recently, several techniques and criteria to choose a kernel function have been proposed extensively. Amari et al defined the metric in the input space that is naturally determined by the kernel function, and then proposed the method to apply a conformal transform to the kernel function in order to magnify the resolution around support vectors[3]. This approach is conceptually similar to our framework, and in fact, the Algorithm 2 does a kind of conformal transform. However, in our framework, the metric in the input space can be defined independently of the kernel function. Anyway, we expect that those techniques and much other knowledge for the original SVM can be incorporated in our framework.

Applying the algorithm to real world data is also important, in particular, the case some specific metric is given by a prior knowledge.

References

[1] S. Akaho, Curve fitting that minimizes the mean square of perpendicular distances from sample points, *SPIE Vision Geometry II* (also found in *Selected SPIE Papers on CD-ROM*, **8**, 1999), 237–244 (1993)

[2] S. Amari, *Differential Geometrical Methods in Statistics*, Springer-Verlag (1984)

[3] S. Amari and S. Wu, Improving support vector machine classifiers by modifying kernel functions, *Neural Networks*, **12**(6), pp. 783–789 (1999)

[4] C. Cortes and V.N. Vapnik, Support vector machines, *Machine Learning*, **20**, pp. 273–297 (1995)

[5] D. DeCoste and B. Schölkopf, Training invariant support vector machines, *Machine Learning*, **46**(1), pp. 161–190 (2002)

[6] T. Hastie and W. Stuetzle, Principal curves, *Journal of the American Statistical Association*, **84**(406), pp. 502–516 (1989)

[7] T.S. Jaakkola and D. Haussler, Exploiting generative models in discriminative classifiers, *NIPS 11*, pp. 487–493 (1998)

[8] K.R. Müller, S. Mika, G. Rätch, K. Tsuda, B.Schölkopf, An Introduction to Kernel-Based Learning Algorithms, *IEEE Trans. on Neural Networks*, **12**, pp. 181–201 (2001)

[9] N. Otsu, Karhunen-Loeve line fitting and a linearly measure. In *IEEE Proc. of ICPR'84*, pp. 486–489 (1984)

[10] J.O. Ramsey, B.W. Silverman, *Functional Data Analysis*, Springer-Verlag (1997)

[11] P.Y. Simard, Y.A. Le Cun, J.S. Denker, B. Victorri, Transformation Invariance in Pattern Recognition – Tangent Distance and Tangent Propagation, in *Neural Networks: Tricks of the Trade*, G. Orr and K.-R. Müller, eds., Springer-Verlag, vol.1524, pp.239–274 (1998)

[12] K. Tsuda, M. Kawanabe, G. Rätsch, S. Sonnenburg, K.R. Müller, A New Discriminative Kernel from Probabilistic Models, *NIPS 14* (2001)

[13] W.H.Wolbert, W.N.Street, O.L.Mangasarian, Wisconsin diagnostic breast cancer database (1995) In UCI machine learning repository http://www.ics.uci.edu/~mlearn/MLRepository.html

[14] V.N. Vapnik, *The Nature of Statistical Learning Theory*, Springer-Verlag (1995)

In: Artificial Intelligence and Computer Science
Editor: Susan Shannon, pp. 155-180
ISBN 1-59454-411-5

Chapter 6

DESYNCHRONIZATION AND SPEEDUP IN AN ASYNCHRONOUS CONSERVATIVE PARALLEL UPDATE PROTOCOL

A. Kolakowskaand M. A. Novotny*[†]
Department of Physics and Astronomy,
and ERC Center for Computational Sciences,
P.O. Box 5167, Mississippi State, MS 39762-5167

Abstract

In a state-update protocol for a system of L asynchronous parallel processes that communicate only with nearest neighbors, global desynchronization in operation times can be deduced from kinetic roughening of the corresponding virtual-time horizon (VTH). The utilization of the parallel processing environment can be deduced by analyzing the microscopic structure of the VTH. In this chapter we give an overview of how the methods of non-equilibrium surface growth (physics of complex systems) can be applied to uncover some properties of state update algorithms used in distributed parallel discrete-event simulations (PDES). In particular, we focus on the asynchronous conservative PDES algorithm in a ring communication topology. The time evolution of its VTH is simulated numerically as asynchronous cellular automaton whose update rule corresponds to the update rule followed by this algorithm. There are two cases of a balanced load considered: (1) the case of the minimal load per processor, which is expected to produce the lowest utilization (the so-called worst-case performance scenario); and, (2) the case of a general finite load per processor. In both cases, we give theoretical estimates of the performance as a function of L and the load per processor, i.e., approximate formulas for the utilization (thus, the mean speedup) and for the desynchronization (thus, the mean memory request per processor). It is established that the memory request per processor, required for state savings, does not

*E-mail address: alicjak@bellsouth.net
[†]E-mail address: man40@ra.msstate.edu

grow without limit for a finite number of processors and a finite load per processor but varies as the conservative PDES evolve. For a given simulation size, there is a theoretical upper bound for the desynchronization and a theoretical non-zero lower bound for the utilization. We show that the conservative PDES are generally scalable in the ring communication topology. The new approach to performance studies, outlined in this chapter, is particularly useful in the search for the design of a new-generation of algorithms that would efficiently carry out an autonomous or tunable synchronization.

Keywords: distributed parallel discrete-event simulations, virtual time, desynchronization, asynchronous cellular automata

1 Introduction

Parallel discrete-event simulations (PDES) are a technical tool to uncover the dynamics of information-driven complex systems. Their wide range of applications in contemporary sciences and technology [1] has made them an active area of research in recent years. Parallel and distributed simulation systems constitute a complex system of their own, whose properties can be uncovered with the well-established tools of statistical physics.

In PDES physical processes are mapped to logical processes (assigned to processors). Each logical process manages the state of the assigned physical subsystem and progresses in its *local virtual time* (LVT). The main challenge arises because logical processes are not synchronized by a global clock. Consequently, to preserve causality in PDES the algorithms should incorporate the so-called local causality constraint [2, 3] whereby each logical process processes the received messages from other processes in non-decreasing time-stamp order. Depending on the way the local causality constraint is implemented, there are two broadly defined classes of update protocols [1]: conservative algorithms [2, 4, 5, 6] and optimistic algorithms [7, 8, 9, 10, 11]. In conservative PDES, an algorithm does not allow a logical process to advance its LVT until it is certain that no causality violation can occur. In the conservative update protocol a logical process may have to wait to ensure that no message with a lower time stamp is received later. In optimistic PDES, an algorithm allows a logical process to advance its LVT regardless of the possibility of a causality error. The optimistic update protocol detects causality errors and provides a recovery procedure from the violation of the local causality constraint by rolling back the events that have been processed prematurely.

There are several aspects of PDES algorithms that should be considered in systematic efficiency studies. Some important aspects are: the synchronization procedures, the utilization of the parallel environment as measured by the fraction of working processors, memory requirements which may be assessed by measuring the statistical spread in LVTs (i.e., the desynchronization), inter-processor communication handling, scalability as measured by evaluating the performance when the number of computing processors becomes large, and the speedup as measured by comparing the performance with sequential simulations. In routinely performed studies to date, the efficiency is investigated in a heuristic fashion by testing the performance of a selected application in a chosen PDES environment, i.e., in a parallel simulator.

Only recently a new approach in performance studies has been introduced [12, 13, 14, 15, 16, 17, 18, 19, 20] in which the properties of the algorithm are examined in an abstract way, without a reference to a particular application platform. In this approach the main concept is the simulated *virtual time horizon* (VTH) defined as the collection of LVTs of all logical processes. The evolution rule of this VTH is defined by the communication topology among processors and by the way in which the algorithm handles the advances in LVTs. The key assumption here is that the properties of the algorithm are encoded in its representative VTH in analogy with the way in which the properties of a complex system are encoded in some representative non-equilibrium interface. In this way, fundamental properties of the algorithm can be deduced by analyzing its corresponding simulated VTH.

In this chapter we give an overview of how the methods of non-equilibrium surface growth (physics of complex systems) can be applied to uncover some properties of state update algorithms used in PDES. In particular, we focus on the asynchronous conservative PDES algorithm in a ring communication topology, where each processor communicates only with its immediate neighbors. The time evolution of its VTH is simulated numerically as an asynchronous cellular automaton whose update rule corresponds to the update rule followed by this algorithm. The purpose of this study is to uncover generic properties of this class of algorithms.

In modeling of the conservative update mode in PDES, we represent sequential events on processors in terms of their corresponding LVTs. A system of processors or *processing elements* (PE) is represented as a one-dimensional grid. The column height that rises above the k-th grid point is a building block of the simulated VTH and represents the total time of operations performed by the k-th processor. These operations can be seen as a sequence of update cycles, where each cycle has two phases. The first phase is the processing of the assigned set of discrete events (e.g., spin flipping on the assigned sublattice for dynamic Monte Carlo simulation of lattice systems). This phase is followed by a messaging phase that closes the cycle, when a processor broadcasts its findings to other processors. But the messages broadcasted by other processors may arrive any time during the cycle. Processing related to these messages (e.g., memory allocations/deallocations, sorting and/or other related operations) are handled by other algorithms that carry their own virtual times. In fact, in actual simulations, this messaging phase may take an enormous amount of time, depending on the hardware configuration and the message processing algorithms. In our modeling the time extent of the messaging phase is ignored as though communications among processors were taking place instantaneously. In this sense we model an ideal system of processors. The LVT of a cycle represents only the time that logical processes require to complete the first phase of a cycle. Therefore, the spread in LVTs represents only the desynchronisation that arises due to the asynchronous conservative algorithm alone. By the same token, all other performance indicators such as, e.g., the overall efficiency or the utilization of the parallel processing environment, that are read out of the simulated VTH are the intrinsic properties of this algorithm.

This chapter is organized as follows. The simulation model of asynchronous conservative updates and the mapping between the logical processes and the physical processes considered in this study are explained in Sec. 2. Section 3 outlines the selected ideas taken from non-equilibrium surface science that are used in the interpretation of simulation results; in particular, the concepts of universality and a non-universal microscopic structure that are relevant in deducing algorithmic properties from the simulated VTH. One group of these properties includes the utilization and the speedup, which is provided in Sec. 4. Another group includes the desynchronization and the memory request per processor, required for past state savings, which is presented in Sec. 5. Performance of the conservative and the optimistic PDES algorithms is discussed in Sec. 6. The new approach to performance studies, outlined in this chapter, can be a very convenient design tool in the engineering of algorithms. This issue and directions for future research are discussed in Sec. 7.

2 Simulated Virtual Time Horizon

In simulations a system of L processors is represented as a set of equally spaced lattice points k, $k = 1, 2, ..., L$. Each processor performs a number of operations and enters a communication phase to exchange information with its immediate neighbors. This communication phase, called an update attempt, takes no time in our simulations. In this sense we simulate an ideal system of processors, as explained in Sec. 1. An update attempt is assigned an integer index t that has the meaning of a wall-clock time (in arbitrary units, which may be thought of as a fixed number of ticks of the CPU clock). The local virtual time $h_k(t)$ at the k-th processor site represents the cumulative local time of all operations on the k-th processor from the beginning at $t = 0$ to time t. These local processor times are not synchronized by a global clock.

There is a two-way correspondence between the physical system being simulated in PDES and the system of PEs that are to perform these PDES in a manner *consistent with and faithful to* the underlying stochastic dynamics of the physical system, as depicted in Fig.1. On the one hand, by spatially distributing a physical lattice with the nearest-neighbor interactions and periodic boundaries among L processors, the asynchronous nature of physical dynamics is carried over to the asynchronous nature of logical processes in the ring communication topology of the computing system. On the other hand, the ring communication topology among processors is mapped onto a lattice arrangement with periodic boundary conditions, $h_{L+k}(t) = h_k(t)$, and asynchronous update events in the system of PEs can be modeled as an asynchronous cellular automaton on this lattice.

The set of local virtual times $h_k(t)$ forms the VTH at t (see Fig. 2). The time-evolution of the VTH is simulated by an update rule, where local height increments $\eta_k(t)$ are sampled from the Poisson distribution of unit mean $\mu_P = 1$. The form of the deposition rule depends on the processor load N, as explained later in this section.

A general principle that governs the conservative update protocol requires a processor to idle if at update attempt t the local causality constraint may be violated. This happens when at t the k-th processor does not receive the information from its neighboring processor (or processors) if such information is required to proceed in its computation. This corresponds

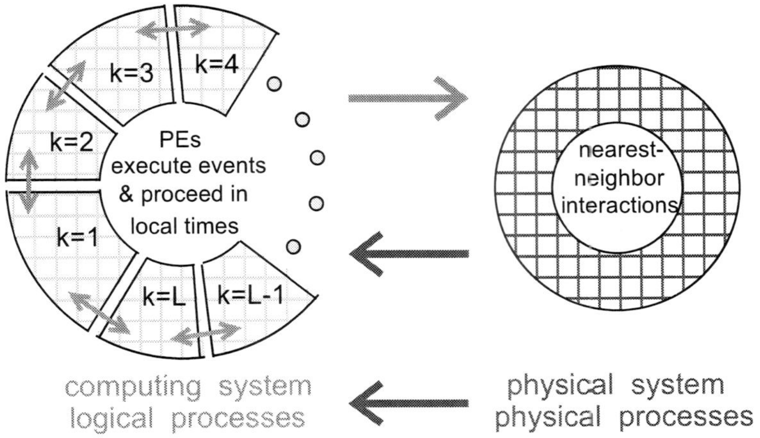

Figure 1: The mapping between physical processes and logical processes. The nearest-neighbor physical interactions on a lattice with periodic boundary conditions (the right part) are mapped to the ring communication topology of logical processes (two-sided arrows in the left part). Each PE carries a sublattice of N sites. Communications take place only at border sites. Each PE has at most two effective border sites, i.e., neighboring PEs that it communicates with.

to a situation when the local virtual time $h_k(t)$ of the k-th processor is ahead of either one of the local virtual times $h_{k-1}(t)$ or $h_{k+1}(t)$ of its left and right neighbors, respectively. In this unsuccessful update attempt the local virtual time $h_k(t)$ is not incremented, i.e., the kth processor waits: $h_k(t+1) = h_k(t)$. In another case, for example, when at t the kth processor does not need information from its neighbors it performs an update regardless of the relation between its local virtual time and the local virtual times on neighboring processors. At every successful update attempt, the simulated local virtual time at the k-th PE-site is incremented for the next update attempt: $h_k(t+1) = h_k(t) + \eta_k(t)$, where $\eta_k(t) = -\ln(r_{kt})$, and $r_{kt} \in (0;1]$ is a uniform random deviate. The simulations start from the *flat-substrate condition* at $t = 0$: $h_k(0) = 0$.

One example of computations that follow the above model is a *dynamic Monte Carlo* simulation for Ising spins [6, 21, 22, 23]. In a parallel environment, a spin lattice is spatially distributed among L processors in such a way that each processor carries an equal load of one contiguous sublattice that consists of N spin sites (i.e., each processor has a load of N volumes). Some of these N spin-lattice sites belong to border slices, i.e., at least one of their immediate neighbors resides on the sublattice of a neighboring processor. Processors perform concurrent spin-flip operations (i.e., increment their LVTs) as long as a randomly selected spin-site is not a border site. If a border spin-site is selected, to perform a state update a processor needs to know the current spin-state of the corresponding border slice of its neighbor. If this information is not available at the t update attempt (because the neighbor's local time is behind), by the conservative update rule the processor waits until this information becomes available, i.e., until the neighbor's local virtual time catches up with or passes its own local virtual time.

The least favorable parallelization is when each processor carries the minimal load of $N = 1$. Computationally, this system can be identified with a closed spin chain where each processor carries one spin-site. At each update attempt each processor must compare its LVT with the local times on both of its neighbors. The second least favorable arrangement is when $N = 2$. As before, at each update attempt every processor must compare its local time with the local time of one of its neighbors. When $N \geq 3$, at update attempt t, the comparison of the local virtual times between neighbors is required only if the randomly selected volume site is from a border slice.

The above three cases are realized in simulations by the following three update rules. When $N = 1$, the update attempt at t is successful iff

$$h_k(t) \leq \min\{h_{k-1}(t), h_{k+1}(t)\}\,. \tag{1}$$

When $N = 2$, at any site k where the update attempt was successful at $(t-1)$, at t we first randomly select a neighbor (left or right). This is equivalent to selecting either the left or the right border slice on the kth processor. The update attempt is successful iff

$$h_k(t) \leq h_n(t), \tag{2}$$

where n is the randomly selected neighbor ($n = k-1$ for the left, $n = k+1$ for the right). At any site k where the update attempt was not successful at $(t-1)$, at t we keep the last n value. When $N \geq 3$, at any site k where the update attempt was successful at $(t-1)$, at t we first randomly select any of the N volume sites (indexed by n_k) assigned to a processor. The selected site can be either from the border sites (either $n_k = 1$ or $n_k = N$) or from the interior. The attempt is successful if the selected site is the interior site. When the border site is selected, the attempt is successful if condition (2) is satisfied. As for $N = 2$, at any site k where the update attempt was not successful at $(t-1)$, at t we keep the last n_k value.

In this way the simulated VTH, corresponding to the conservative update rule followed by the PDES algorithm, emerges as a one-dimensional non-equilibrium surface grown by depositions of Poisson-random time increments that model waiting times. Two sample VTH surfaces are presented in Fig. 2. Major properties of the corresponding algorithm are encoded in these interfaces. In principle, with the help of statistical physics, one should be able to obtain from VTH such properties as the utilization, the ideal speedup, the desynchronization, the memory request per processor, the overall efficiency and the scalability. One basic property is the *mean utilization* $\langle u(t)\rangle$, which can be assessed as the fraction of sites in the VTH interface that performed an update at t, averaged over many independent simulations. For the minimal load per processor $N = 1$, $\langle u(t)\rangle$ is simply the mean density of local minima of the interface (Fig. 2). Another basic property is the *mean desynchronization* $\langle w(t)\rangle$ in operation times, which can be estimated from simulations as the mean statistical spread (roughness) of the VTH interface. In the following section we review some useful concepts from surface physics relevant to our study.

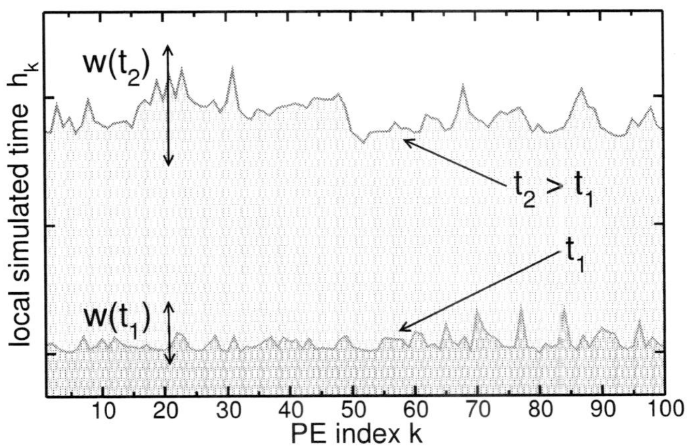

Figure 2: The growth and roughening of the simulated VTH interface: snapshots at t_1 and at a later time t_2. Local heights h_k are in arbitrary units. Here, $L = 100$ and $N = 1$.

3 The $(1+1)$ Dimensional Nonequilibrium Interfaces

The roughness of a surface that grows on a one dimensional substrate of L sites can be expressed by its interface width $w(t)$ at time t

$$\langle w^2(t)\rangle = \left\langle \frac{1}{L}\sum_{k=1}^{L}\left(h_k(t) - \bar{h}(t)\right)^2 \right\rangle, \tag{3}$$

where $h_k(t)$ is the height of the column at site k and $\bar{h}(t)$ is the average height over L sites, $\bar{h}(t) = (1/L)\sum_{k=1}^{L} h_k(t)$. The angular brackets denote the average over many interface configurations that are obtained in many independent simulations. In our study these configurational averages were computed over 800 simulations, unless noted otherwise.

Based on the time-evolution of $w(t)$, interfaces can be classified in various *universality classes* (for an overview see Ref. [24]). The idea behind the concept of universality is that, in a statistical description, the growth of the surface depends only on the underlying mechanism that generates correlations among time-evolving columns $h_k(t)$ and *not* on the physical particulars of physical (or other) interactions that cause the growth. For instance, two completely different physical interactions among deposited constituents (e.g., one of a magnetic nature and the other of a social nature) may generate two equivalent surfaces of one universality class, depending on the observed evolution of $w(t)$. The simplest case of surface growth is *random deposition* (RD), when the column heights $h_k(t)$ grow independently of each other. The RD interface is totally uncorrelated. The time-evolution of its width is characterized by a never-ending growth in accordance to the power law $w(t) \sim t^{\beta}$, with the *growth exponent* $\beta = 1/2$. Such growth defines the RD universality class.

The self-affined roughness of the interface manifests itself by the existence of Family-

Vicsek scaling [25]:

$$w^2(t) = L^{2\alpha} f\left(\frac{t}{L^z}\right), \tag{4}$$

where the scaling function $f(y)$ describes two regimes of the width evolution:

$$f(y) \sim \begin{cases} y^{2\alpha/z} & , \quad y \ll 1 \\ \text{const.} & , \quad y \gg 1. \end{cases} \tag{5}$$

The *dynamic exponent* z gives the time-evolution of the lateral correlation length $\xi(t) \sim t^{1/z}$, i.e., at a given t the largest distance along the substrate between two correlated columns. When $\xi(t)$ exceeds the system size L the width saturates and does not grow any more. At saturation, for $t \gg t_\times$, for a given L the width remains constant and obeys the power law $w \sim L^\alpha$, where α is the *roughness exponent*. The growth phase is the initial phase for $t \ll t_\times$ before the *cross-over time* $t_\times \sim L^z$ at which saturation sets in. The growth phase is characterized by the single growth exponent $\beta = \alpha/z$. The roughness, growth and dynamic exponents are universal, i.e., their values depend only on the underlying mechanism that generates correlations.

A simple continuum model of non-equilibrium growth that leads to scaling is provided by the Kardar-Parisi-Zhang (KPZ) equation [26]:

$$h_t = v(t) + \nu\, h_{xx} + \frac{\lambda}{2} h_x^2 + \zeta\,, \tag{6}$$

where $h = h(x,t)$ is the height field (subscripts denote partial derivatives), $v(t)$ is the mean interface velocity, $v(t) = \langle d\bar{h}(t)/dt \rangle$, and $\zeta(x,t)$ is the uncorrelated Gaussian noise. The coefficients ν and λ give the strength of the linear damping and the coupling with the nonlinear growth, respectively. A renormalization group analysis [24, 26] can provide a connection between the stochastic growth equation and scaling exponents.

The *KPZ universality class*, governed by the dynamics of Eq.(6), is characterized by $\alpha = 1/2$ and $\beta = 1/3$, and the exponent identity $\alpha + z = 2$. When $\lambda = 0$ in Eq.(6), the growth is governed by the linear Edwards-Wilkinson (EW) equation [27]. The *EW universality class* is characterized by $\alpha = 1/2$ and $\beta = 1/4$, and the EW exponent identity is $2\alpha + 1 = z$. When $\lambda = 0$ and $\nu = 0$ in Eq.(6), the growth belongs to the RD universality class. Unlike the KPZ and EW interfaces, the RD interface is not self-affined.

The origins of scale invariance, as in Eq.(4), and the universal properties of time-evolving surfaces are well understood [24]. In this study, we use the universal properties of the simulated VTH to investigate the scalability of the corresponding PDES algorithm. However, there are many instances where non-universal properties, i.e., those pertaining to the *microscopic structure* of the interface, are of importance. In this study, one example is the density of local minima or the density of update sites of the VTH interface. It is safe to say that there is no general silver-bullet-type of approach to these problems. For the case study of VTH interfaces, we were able to develop a discrete-event analytic technique that provides a means for calculating a probability distribution for events that take place on the surface [17, 28]. For the closed linear chain of L processors carrying minimal load,

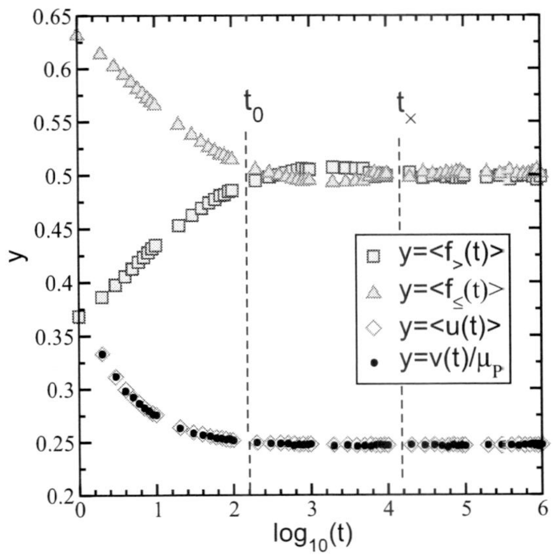

Figure 3: Simulated time evolutions of characteristic densities and the scaled VTH interface velocity during simulations with the minimal load $N = 1$ per processor ($L = 1000$). Time t_0 marks the transition to steady-state simulations and $t_\times$ is the saturation time, as explained in the text. For times later than t_0, both the utilization $\langle u \rangle$ (diamonds) and the velocity v (filled circles) are constant.

when the VTH is simulated by Poisson-random depositions at local interface minima, the probability distribution $P(p; L)$ of the update events on the corresponding VTH surface is [17]:

$$P(p; L) = \frac{1}{2^{L-2}} \binom{L-1}{2p-1}, \tag{7}$$

where p is the number of updates at the t-th update attempt after the simulations reach a steady state. This distribution can be used to derive approximate closed formulas for mean quantities measured in simulations, e.g., for $\langle u(t) \rangle$. Also, it is a starting point in the derivation of analogous distributions $P(p; L; N)$ for the cases when each processor carries a larger load of $N = 2$ or $N \geq 3$ [28]. The advantage of knowing $P(p; L; N)$ is that it enables one to compute analytically quantities that otherwise can be only estimated qualitatively in simulations.

4 Utilization of the Parallel Processing Environment

For a real system, the mean utilization $\langle u(t) \rangle$ is defined either as the number or as the fraction of processors that on average work simultaneously at a time. In our model, $\langle u(t) \rangle$ is the mean fraction (i.e., the density) of update sites in the simulated VTH. The simulated time evolution of $\langle u(t) \rangle$ is presented in Fig. 3 (for $N = 1$) and in Fig. 4 (for $N = 100$) that illustrate the following observations. First, $\langle u(t) \rangle$ is not constant as the simulations

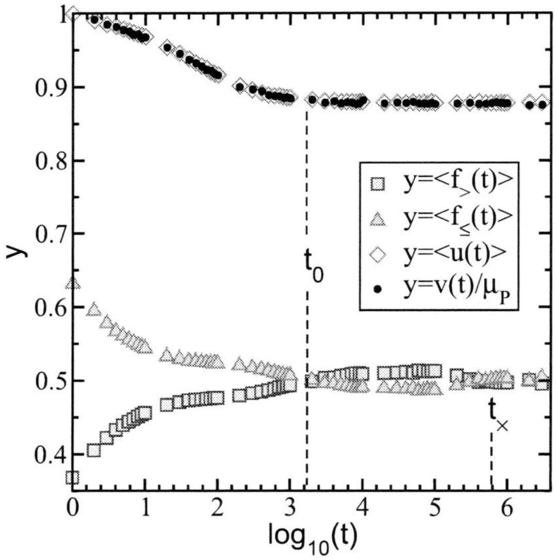

Figure 4: Simulated time evolutions of characteristic densities and the scaled VTH interface velocity during simulations with the load $N = 100$ per processor ($L = 1000$). As in Fig. 3, for times later than t_0 both the utilization $\langle u \rangle$ (diamonds) and the velocity v (filled circles) are constant, but their values are significantly higher than in the worst-case performance scenario presented in Fig. 3.

evolve but abruptly decreases from its initial value at $t = 0$ and very quickly, after a few hundred steps, settles down at its steady value when it no longer depends on time. Both the utilization and the transition period t_0 to the *steady state* depend strongly on the processor load N. Second, the VTH velocity $v(t)$ must be related to $\langle u(t) \rangle$ by a simple linear scaling relation. Third, the transition time t_0 to the steady state can be estimated from simple statistics of the interface. Let us elaborate on these issues.

The characteristic densities $\langle f_>(t) \rangle$ and $\langle f_\leq(t) \rangle$, plotted in Figs. 3–4, are the fractions of the interface sites (processors) that have their LVT larger and equal-or-smaller, respectively, than the mean virtual time $\bar{h}(t)$. Their relation to each other is a simple indicator of the skewness of the distribution of the LVTs about the mean virtual time. For the times when they approximately coincide this distribution is approximately symmetric. The reason for a non-zero skewness for the early times $t < t_0$ is the flat-substrate initial condition, i.e., the initial null LVT on all processors (the detailed analysis of this issue can be found in [29]). In the worst-case performance scenario, when each processor has the minimal load of $N = 1$ (Fig. 3), the duration of this initial transition time t_0 to the steady state is a non-universal property of the VTH interface. This means that in real applications the time t_0 will depend on the application platform, i.e., the hardware configuration and parameters. But, for a real application t_0 can be determined in a non-expensive way by monitoring $\langle f_>(t) \rangle$ and $\langle f_\leq(t) \rangle$ in a trial simulation with a fixed $N = N_0$. Then, the results can be scaled either up or down for an arbitrary load N. The existence of such scaling is the universal property of the VTH interface, which is discussed in Sec.5 where the explicit scaling relations are given.

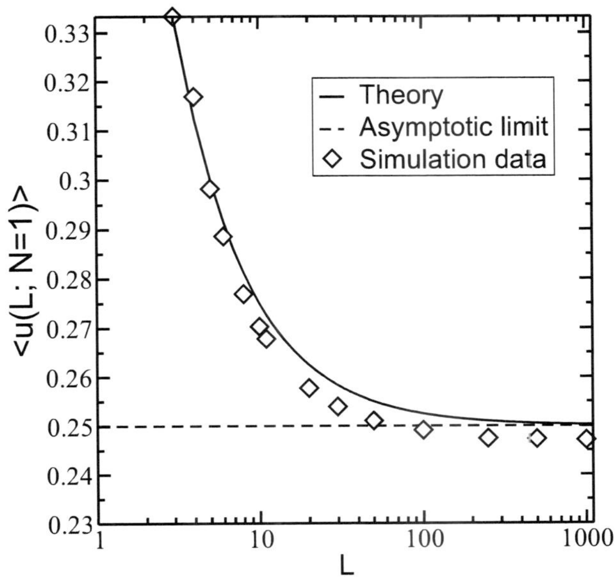

Figure 5: The steady-state mean utilization vs the number of processors L for the minimal load per processor: the analytical result (continuous curve), its asymptotic limit $\lim_{L\to\infty}\langle u(L;1)\rangle = 1/4$ (horizontal line) and simulation results (symbols). The error bars are smaller than the symbol size.

The overall progress of PDES can be estimated from the time rate of the *global virtual time* (GVT) that is the smallest LVT from all processors at t. The GVT determines the fossil collection, i.e., the memory that can be re/de-allocated from past-saved events. In our model, the mean GVT is the mean global minimum $\langle h_{GVT}(t)\rangle$ of the simulated VTH: $h_{GVT}(t) = \min\{h_k(t) : 1 \le k \le L\}$. On the average, the time rate of $\langle h_{GVT}(t)\rangle$ is not larger than the VTH interface velocity $v(t)$ and after cross-over time $t_\times$ to saturation (indicated in Figs. 3–4 and Figs. 8–10) these two rates are equal. Thus, $v(t)$ is the measure of progress. It is shown analytically [29] that $v(t) = \langle u(t)\rangle\mu$, where μ is a constant. For the simulated VTH $\mu = \mu_P = 1$, as can be seen in Figs. 3–4. In a real application μ is a hardware dependent parameter.

Since the overall progress in PDES connects linearly to $\langle u(t)\rangle$, the mean utilization is the most important property of this algorithm. The steady-state utilization $\langle u(L; N = 1)\rangle$ for the worst-case performance as a function of the number L of processors is presented in Fig. 5. For brevity of notation, from now on we omit the index t because for $t > t_0$ the utilization is constant. Considering the simulation data alone (symbols in Fig. 5) it is easily seen that even at the infinite limit of L the mean utilization has a non-zero value. In fact, this asymptotic value is approached very closely with less than a thousand processors. The existence of this limit guarantees a non-zero progress of PDES for any value of L and for any processor load N, since the curve $\langle u(L; N = 1)\rangle$ is the lower bound for the steady-state utilization $\langle u(L; N)\rangle$ (compare with Fig. 6).

The presence of this non-zero limit for $\langle u(L;1)\rangle$ as $L \to \infty$ and the global behavior

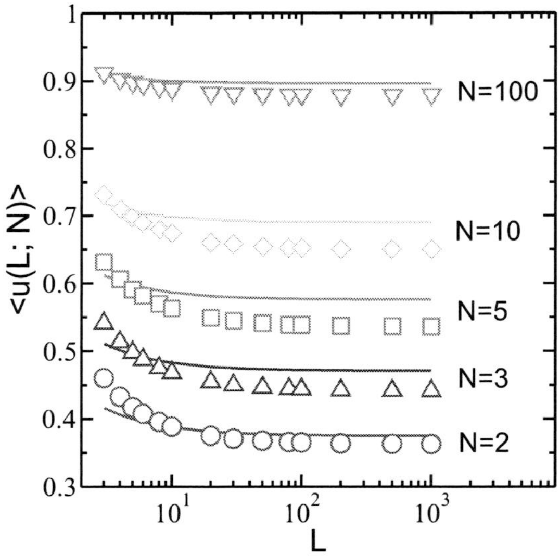

Figure 6: The steady-state mean utilization vs the number of processors L for loads $N \geq 2$ per processor: analytical results (continuous curves) and simulation results (symbols). The error bars are smaller than the symbol size.

of the simulation data, observed in Fig. 5, suggest the existence of some underlying scaling law for $\langle u(L;1)\rangle$. It appears that, indeed, the underlying scaling law can be obtained analytically from the first moment of the probability distribution $P(p;L)$ given by Eq.(7) and the result is [17]

$$\langle u(L \geq 3;1)\rangle = \frac{L+1}{4L}, \tag{8}$$

and $\langle u(L=2;1)\rangle = 1/2$. This function is plotted in Fig. 5 for $L \geq 3$. Similarly for any $N \geq 2$, starting with $P(p;L)$, one can construct the probability distribution $P(p;L;N)$ of updates in the system of L processors, each having a load of N (i.e., the distribution of updates on the corresponding VTH interface). The mean utilization $\langle u(L;N)\rangle$ can then be obtained from the first moment of $P(p;L;N)$ [28]:

$$\langle u(L \geq 3; N \geq 2)\rangle = \left(1 - \frac{q(N)}{2}\right)\left(1 - \frac{q(N)}{4}\frac{L-1}{L}\right), \tag{9}$$

where $q(N) = \sqrt{2/N}$, and

$$\langle u(L=2; N \geq 3)\rangle = 1 - \frac{1}{\sqrt{2N}}, \tag{10}$$

and $\langle u(L=2;N=2)\rangle = 1/2$. Relation (10) is exact. Relation (9) is presented in Fig. 6. As $L \to \infty$ the asymptotic limit is $\langle u(\infty; N \geq 3)\rangle = (2-q)(4-q)/8 > \langle u(\infty; N = 1)\rangle = 1/4$.

The computational speedup s of a parallel algorithm is defined as the ratio of the time required to perform a computation in serial processing to the time the same computation takes in concurrent processing on L processors. It is easy to derive from the above definition that for an *ideal system of processors*, that is for the particular update *algorithm* considered in this work, the mean speedup is

$$\langle s \rangle = L\langle u(L;N) \rangle. \tag{11}$$

In other words, $\langle s \rangle$ is measured by the average number of PEs that work concurrently between two successive update attempts.

We observe that for ideal PEs the speedup as a function $F(L)$ must be such that the equation $F(L) = s$ has a unique solution, where s is a fixed positive number. This requirement follows naturally from the logical argument that distributing the computations over L ideal PEs gives a unique speedup, i.e., two ideal systems having sizes L_1 and L_2, respectively, may not give the same s. This means that $F(L)$ must be a monotonically increasing function of L.

Combining Eq.(11) and Eq.(8), in the worst-case performance when the load per processor is minimal, the mean speedup is $\langle s(L;N=1) \rangle = (L+1)/4$ and $\langle s(L=2,3;N=1) \rangle = 1$. The latter relation says that this algorithm produces no speedup when the computations are distributed over 2 or 3 processors. In this case, although the utilization is $1/2$, the processors do not work concurrently but *alternately*, i.e., one is working while the other is idling. For a real system of PEs performing PDES, in such a situation the communication overhead will produce an actual slowdown, i.e., the parallel execution time will be longer than the sequential execution time on one processor. When $L \geq 4$, to take an advantage of concurrent processing the average number of PEs working in parallel between two successive update attempts must satisfy $(L+1)/4 > 2$, which gives $L > 7$. Still, depending on the implementation platform, the actual speedup of PDES may be negligible or not present at all for small L.

For a general load per processor, combining Eq.(11) and Eq.(9) gives a linear relation with respect to L:

$$\langle s(L \geq 3; N \geq 2) \rangle = \left[L\left(1 - \frac{q(N)}{4}\right) + \frac{q(N)}{4} \right] \left(1 - \frac{q(N)}{2}\right). \tag{12}$$

Equation (12) can be rearranged to

$$\langle s(L \geq 3; N \geq 2) \rangle = \frac{L-1}{8} \left(\bar{q}(N) + \frac{2L}{L-1} \right)^2 - \frac{(L+1)^2}{8(L-1)}, \tag{13}$$

where $\bar{q}(N) = 1 - q(N)$ is the probability that a processor performs an update without the need of communicating with other processors [28, 29]. This probability sharply increases with the processor load. Since the mean speedup increases quadratically with $\bar{q}(N)$ and only linearly with L, for some PDES that perform the updates in accordance to this algorithm it may be more advantageous to assign more load per processor than to distribute the computations over a large number of processors. In any case, either of the above relations, Eq.(12) or (13), can be used to assess the upper bound for the speedup in actual applications.

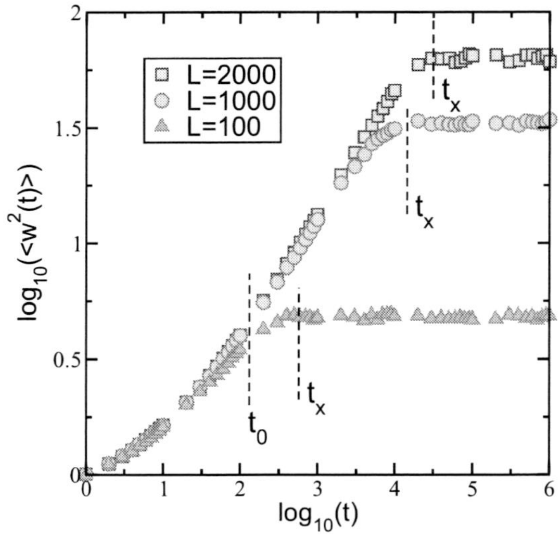

Figure 7: Simulated time evolution of the VTH width in the worst-case performance scenario $N = 1$. Time t_0, common for all L, marks the transition to the steady-state simulations of Fig. 3.

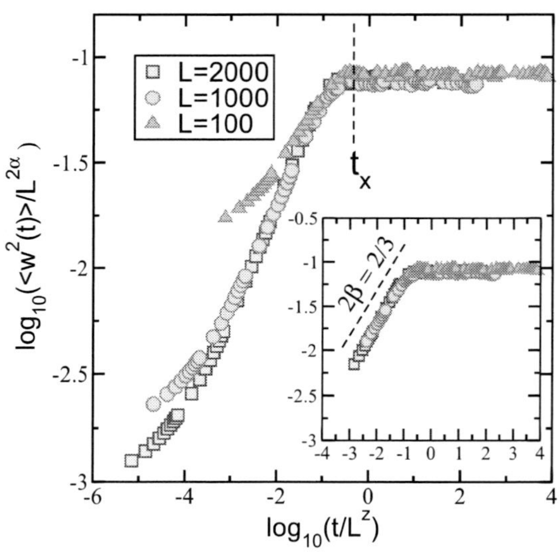

Figure 8: The scaled time evolution of the simulated VTH widths of Fig. 7 for all times $t > 0$. The insert shows the full data collapse for $t > t_0$, with the growth exponent $\beta = 1/3$.

5 Dynamics of Desynchronization

In PDES the memory request per processor, required for past-state savings, depends on the extent to which processors get desynchronized during simulations. In our model, the statistical spread $w(t)$ of the simulated VTH, as illustrated in Fig. 2, provides the measure of this desynchronization. In simulations the width of the VTH interface is computed using Eq. (3). The representative results of simulations for the case of the minimal load per processor are presented in Fig. 7. For any number L of processors the time evolution of the VTH width has two phases. The first phase, for $t \ll t_\times$, is the growth regime, where for $t > t_0$ the width $w(t)$ follows a power law in t with the growth exponent $\beta = 1/3$. The second phase, after the cross-over time $t_\times$, is the saturation regime, where $w(t)$ has a constant value that depends only on the system size and follows a power law in L with the roughness exponent $\alpha = 1/2$. The values of these exponents are characteristic of the KPZ universality class. Explicitly, the evolution can be written as

$$\langle w^2(t)\rangle \sim \begin{cases} t^{2\beta} & , \quad t_0 \ll t \ll t_\times \\ L^{2\alpha} & , \quad t \gg t_\times , \end{cases} \tag{14}$$

where t_0 is the initial regime where the Family-Vicsek scaling law, Eqs.(4–5), does not hold. This can be seen directly when the scaling is performed for all $t > 0$, as illustrated in Fig. 8. The whisker-like structures that appear after data collapse in the growth phase, clearly observed in Fig. 8, indicate that in the initial start-up time $t < t_0$ the curves in Fig. 7 before scaling follow one evolution for all L. The insert shows the universal Family-Vicsek scaling function, Eq.(5), for $t > t_0$. Here, the cross-over time scales as $t_\times \sim L^z$, where $z = \alpha/\beta = 3/2$. The presence of the initial non-scaling growth regime is an artifact of the flat-substrate initial condition. Its duration t_0 is a non-universal parameter that can be determined in PDES by monitoring characteristic densities and the utilization, as discussed in Sec. 4.

When the simulations are performed for the case when each processor carries a load N, the evolution of the VTH width changes. Now, as illustrated in Fig. 9 for $L = 1000$, there are two distinct phases in the initial growth regime. The early phase evolves in the RD fashion, having the growth exponent $\beta_0 = 1/2$, and the later phase has signatures of the KPZ scaling:

$$\langle w^2(t)\rangle \sim \begin{cases} t^{2\beta_0} & , \quad t < t_0(N) \\ t^{2\beta} & , \quad t_0(N) \ll t \ll t_\times(N) \\ L^{2\alpha} & , \quad t \gg t_\times(N), \end{cases} \tag{15}$$

where both t_0 and $t_\times$ depend on the processor load. The initial RD-like growth does not scale with L. This lack of scaling extends to approximately $t_0(N) \propto t_0 N/2$, where t_0 marks the end of the initial relaxation period when $N = 1$ or $N = 2$. The physical justification for the presence of the RD growth is that when $N \geq 3$ there is a non-zero probability of having some processors performing state updates without the need of communicating with other processors. This probability of "uncorrelated" updates increases when the processor load increases. However, even for a large but finite N there are some processors that may not complete an update without communication with another processor, thus, correlations are build among the processors and propagate throughout the system. Eventually these "correlated" updates cause the VTH interface to saturate. The net effect of having a large load per processor is the noticeable elongation of the time scale over which the correlations are build, but the dynamics of building these correlations belongs to the same universality

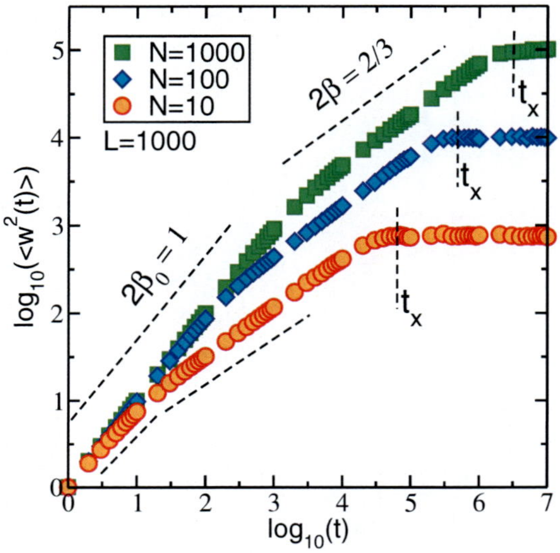

Figure 9: Simulated time evolution of the VTH width for loads $N > 1$. There are two growth regimes, characterized by two exponents β_1 and β_2. The duration of the early phase depends on N. In this early phase, simulations are not in the steady-state: the squared width increases linearly with time.

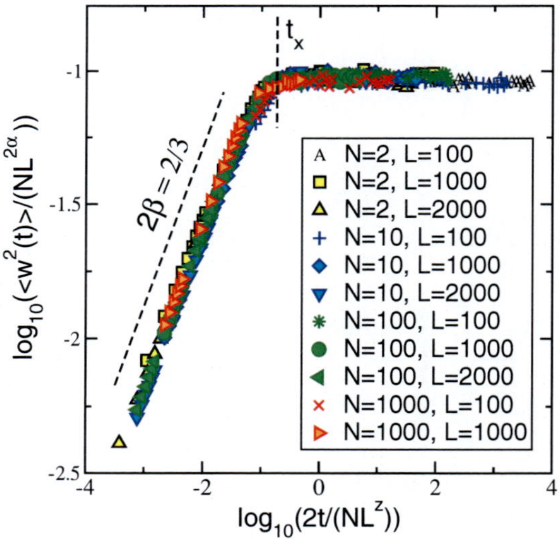

Figure 10: The scaled time evolution of the simulated VTH widths for general values of N and L. This scaling function is valid only for steady-state simulations. In the scaling regime the growth exponent is $\beta = 1/3$, as in Fig. 8. The time to saturation, when the width is constant, depends on both N and L.

class as in the case of the minimal load per processor. Therefore, it is expected that the simulated VTH should exhibit KPZ universality in this case as well, as soon as the correlations become apparent. Indeed, after the initial transition time $t_0(N)$ the VTH widths can be collapsed onto the following scaling function [29]:

$$\langle w^2(t)\rangle = \frac{N}{2}L^{2\alpha} f\left(\frac{2}{N}\frac{t}{L^z}\right), \tag{16}$$

where $f(y)$ satisfies Eq.(5), and $z = 2-\alpha$ with $\alpha \approx 1/2$. This scaling function is presented in Fig. 10. Accordingly, the VTH interfaces belong to the KPZ universality class. In the scaling regime, the evolution can be written explicitly as

$$\langle w(t)\rangle \sim \begin{cases} \left(\sqrt{N/2}\right)^{1-2\beta} t^{\beta} & , \quad t_0(N) \ll t \ll t_\times(N) \\ \sqrt{N/2}\, L^{\alpha} & , \quad t \gg t_\times(N), \end{cases} \tag{17}$$

where $t_\times(N) \sim (N/2)L^z$, $\beta = 1/3$, $\alpha = 1/2$ and $z = 3/2$. For $0 \le t < t_0(N) \sim t_0 N/2$, for all L the width follows the power low $\langle w(t)\rangle \sim t^{\beta_0}$, where $\beta_0 = 1/2$.

The consequence of Eq.(17) is that the memory request per processor does not grow without limit but varies as the computations evolve. The fastest growth characterizes the initial start-up phase. The length of the start-up phase depends on the load per processor. The start-up phase is characterized by decreasing values of the utilization. In the steady-state simulations, when the utilization has already stabilized at a mean constant value the memory request grows slower, at a decreasing rate $\sim 1/t^{2/3}$. In this phase, the mean request can be estimated globally from Eq.(17). The important consequence of scaling, expressed by Eq.(16), is the existence of the upper bound for the memory request for any finite number of processors and for any load per processor. On the average, this upper bound increases proportionally to $\sqrt{NL}$ with the size of conservative PDES.

The characteristic time scale $t_0(N)$ from the first step to the steady-state simulations can be estimated by monitoring the utilization for the minimal processor load (to determine t_0) and, subsequently, scaling this time with N. Similarly, the characteristic time scale to $t_\times(N)$, when the desynchronization reaches its steady state, can be scaled with the processor load to determine an approximate number of simulation steps to the point when the mean memory request does not grow anymore.

6 Conservative vs Optimistic

While the conservative algorithm strictly avoids the violation of the local causality constraint, the optimistic algorithm may process the events that are out of the time-stamp order which might violate this constraint. At times when the conservative algorithm forces the processors to idle the optimistic algorithm enforces the computations and state-updates, thus, according to our adopted definition, the theoretical utilization of the optimistic update scheme is always at its maximum value of one because the processors never idle. However, some of the events in the thus processed stream of events on a processor must be processed prematurely, judging by the random nature of the optimistic scheme that takes a risk of guessing whenever the next event is not certain. When in the course of an update cycle a processor receives a *straggler message*, i.e., a message "from the past" that has its time-stamp smaller than the clock value, all the later events that have been processed incorrectly must be cancelled. The processor must then send out cancellation messages (called *anti-messages*) to other processors to *roll back* all the events that have been processed prematurely. Thus, in the optimistic update scheme, although the processors never idle, the computation time of the update cycle is not utilized fully efficiently because some part of this time is used for the meaningless operations (i.e., creation and processing of the rollbacks) and only part of a cycle represents the computations that assure the progress of PDES.

There are many variations of optimistic update schemes, e.g., Refs. [7, 8, 9, 10, 11] and references in [1], oriented to building implementations with better efficiencies and memory management. The key feature of the update mechanism, as described above, and main concepts such as rollback and GVT, first introduced in Jefferson's Time Warp [7], can be treated as the generic properties of the optimistic algorithm. In its generic form, the algorithm keeps the already processed events in the memory in case of the necessary re-processing required by the rollbacks.

For the ring communication topology, we simulate the growth of the VTH corresponding to the optimistic update procedure as Poison-random depositions to the lattice sites in analogy to the model described in Sec. 2. However, in the optimistic model the deposition rule is modified to mimic key features of the optimistic algorithm. We assume that each update cycle on each processor consists of processing N_c events, only some of which can be eventually committed. With each of these events there is the associated random time increment η. Now the integer index t represents the update cycle. The main difference between the optimistic and the conservative simulation models is that any time the conservative would wait the optimistic is allowed to perform a random guess. In the simplest case of totally unbiased guesses, in each cycle the number of correctly guessed events is obtained from a uniform distribution. The cumulative simulated LVTs that correspond to processing all events form the simulated *optimistic* VTH. The cumulative simulated LVTs that correspond to processing only the correctly guessed events form the simulated *progress* VTH, which is embedded in the optimistic VTH. The difference between the optimistic VTH and the progress VTH represents the cumulative time that has been wasted by generating and processing erroneously guessed events and their associated rollback operations. We define the overall efficiency of the optimistic algorithm as the ratio of *the total progress time* to *the total computation time*. At t, the total progress time and the total computation time are obtained by integrating the progress VTH and the optimistic VTH, respectively, and are represented by the areas under these VTH interfaces. In analogy with the above definition, we define the overall efficiency of the conservative algorithm as the ratio of the total computation time (i.e., the area under the conservative VTH) to the total time that the processors spend on computations and idling. These efficiencies are presented in Fig. 11 for the worst-case scenario of the minimal load per processor and $N_c = 1$.

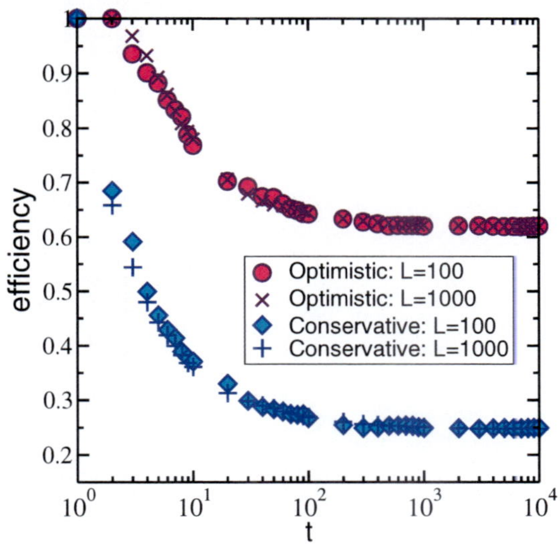

Figure 11: Simulated time-evolution of overall efficiencies in an optimistic (upper curve) and a conservative (lower curve) PDES when processors carry minimal loads ($L = 10,000$).

Our simulations (Fig. 11) confirm the common conception that, in the ideal setting, the optimistic algorithm should outperform the conservative algorithm [1]. As Fig. 11 shows, the lower bound for the steady-state conservative efficiency is about 25% and coincides with the lower bound obtained for the utilization (Fig. 3). For the same case, the steady-state optimistic efficiency is about 62%; accordingly, the optimistic algorithm has a better utilization of the parallelism. In actual applications the conservative efficiency can be improved by exploiting in programming a concept of lookahead, based on actual properties of the distributed PDES physical model under consideration.

The statistical spread of the simulated optimistic VTH is presented in Fig. 12 (note, this figure presents the results obtained in only one simulation). The simulated optimistic VTH belongs to the RD universality class and the spread in local virtual times grows without limit in accordance to the power law $w(t) \sim \sqrt{t}$. Intuitively, this result should be expected because, by analyzing the operation mode of optimistic updates, one notices that the processors work totally independently, progressing their LVTs in an uncorrelated fashion. Thus, it should be expected that the memory request per processor required to execute generic optimistic PDES grows without bounds as $\sqrt{t}$ when the simulations are progressing in t.

The unboundedness of the memory request in a generic optimistic scheme can be also justified using quite different arguments [1], however, the power-law growth for this request, illustrated in Fig. 12, has been never reported before. The adverse ways in which such an unbounded desynchronization affects the performance and standard remedies that can be taken to improve on the use of computing resources by optimizing the optimistic memory management, are well-known issues (a comprehensive discussion can be found in Ref. [1]). In general, the generic optimistic update scheme requires some kind of explicit synchronization procedure that would limit the lengths of rollbacks.

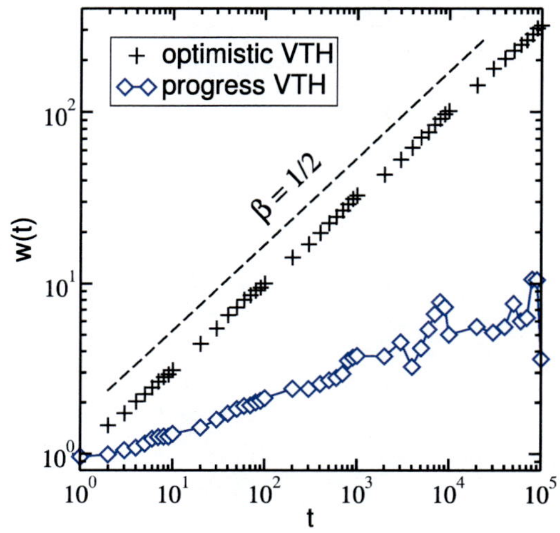

Figure 12: Simulated time-evolution of desynchronizations in an optimistic PDES when processors carry minimal loads ($L = 10,000$): the widths of the optimistic VTH (upper curve, "plus" symbol) and of the progress VTH (lower curve, diamonds).

The actual performance of the PDES application may depend on the particulars of the underlying physical dynamics of the physical system being simulated and the best choice of the algorithm may be uncertain in advance without some heuristic trial studies. For example, recently, Overeinder *et al.* [30, 31] reported the first observation of self-organized critical behavior in the performance of the optimistic Time Warp algorithm when applied to dynamic Monte Carlo simulations for Ising spins on a regular two-dimensional lattice. They found that when this PDES approaches a point when the physical Ising-spin phase transition is being simulated (i.e., the critical point of the physical dynamics), the average rollback length increases dramatically and simulation runtimes increase nonlinearly. In Ising-spins simulations, increases in rollback lengths are to be expected since around the Ising critical temperature the physical system is characterized by the presence of long-range spin-spin correlations and collective behavior, where large-scale spin-domains may be overturned simultaneously. Consequently, approaching the critical point of physical dynamics should produce a decreased number of committed events. However, the simultaneous nonlinear increase of the simulation runtime when PDES approaches this critical point seems to be a property of the optimistic algorithm since a similar problem is not observed when the same physical system is being simulated using the conservative algorithm [22]. One possible explanation for this nonlinear deterioration in runtime may be a nonlinear cache behavior when rollback lengths increase beyond a certain critical value and memory requests increase. The role of the cache behavior, in particular, the nonlinear performance degradation with the number of cache misses, has been recently discussed in regard with the efficient implementation of an asynchronous conservative protocol for a different physical system [32]. Another possible explanation, as conjectured in Ref. [30], may be the onset of self-organized criticality in the Time Warp simulation systems, unrelated to the physical critical state. Further studies are required to extract universal properties of optimistic protocols to identify a class of simulation problems that would show in computations a similar behavior to that encountered in PDES for Ising spins.

7 Conclusion

The performance of the distributed PDES algorithms depends in general on three main factors: the partitioning of the simulated system among processors, the communication topology among the processors, and the update protocol being adopted. In a heuristic approach to performance studies (e.g., as in Ref. [22, 30]) the application algorithm often utilizes physical properties of the model to be simulated; thus, the conclusions of such studies, as being application specific, may have a limited scope of generalization. In this chapter, we presented a new way to study the performance of PDES algorithms, which makes no explicit reference to any particular application. In this new approach, the system of processors that perform concurrent update operations in a chosen communication topology is seen as a complex system of statistical physics. First, based on the update and the communication patterns of the algorithm, we construct a simulation model for its representative virtual time horizon. The statistical properties of this virtual time interface correspond to the properties of the algorithm, that is, to the properties of the pattern in which the correlations are formed and propagate in the computing system. Second, we extract the properties of the algorithm from the statistical properties of its simulated virtual time horizon.

In this chapter, we demonstrated how this approach can be used to elucidate the key generic properties of the asynchronous conservative parallel update protocol in the ring communication topology among processors. For a finite PDES size, i.e., a finite load N per processor and a finite number L of processors, our findings can be summarized as follows. Both the utilization of the parallel processing environment and its desynchronization can be derived explicitly as theoretical functions of L and N (these are Eqs.(8-10) and Eqs.(15-17), respectively). These functions express the existence of the underlying scaling laws for the corresponding virtual time horizon and are understood as approximate relations in the sense of statistical averages. The existence of these scaling laws presents one aspect of scalability of this type of PDES algorithm. The other aspect of algorithmic scalability is the behavior of these functions when N and L increase. In the limit of large L there is a theoretical non-zero lower bound for the utilization, for any N, and the value of this bound increases with N. On the other hand, for any N and L there is a finite upper bound for the desynchronization, thus, for the mean memory request per processor during steady-state simulations. Therefore, this kind of conservative PDES algorithm is generally scalable.

The model simulation of the virtual time horizon for the generic optimistic update protocol in the ring communication topology (Sec. 6) showed that the optimistic algorithm lacks the algorithmic scalability. As the optimistic simulations evolve in the steady state, the width of the optimistic virtual time horizon grows without limit for any finite PDES system. In other words, even for the minimal load per processor, the memory request per processor ever increases as the square root of the performed number of time-stamped update cycles, as the simulations evolve in time. Therefore, the generic version of this algorithm demands some form of explicit periodic synchronization.

One advantage of studying the PDES algorithms in terms of their corresponding virtual time interfaces is the possibility of deriving explicit diagnostic formulas for the performance evaluation, such as, e.g., the evaluation of the speedup given by Eqs.(12-13) or the estimate of the memory request given by Eq.(17) for the conservative algorithm considered in this study. These theoretical estimates should be treated as the ideal upper bounds for the performance when PDES are implemented on the real computing systems. A real implementation will produce a deviation from the theoretical prediction, depending on the computing platform and on other components of simulation algorithms. The extend to which the performance of the implementation scales down from the ideal performance should provide important information about possible bottlenecks of the real implementation and should be a guide to improving the efficiencies.

The other benefit that comes from the modeling of virtual-time interfaces is a relatively inexpensive design tool for new-generation algorithms, without a prior need for heuristic studies. For example, knowing that in the ring communication topology the maximal conservative memory request per processor for past state savings gets larger as the simulation model gets larger, it is easy to predict the maximum model size that would fit the available memory in the system. However, the available memory resources vary across implementation platforms, so it may happen that one size simulation model may fit on one platform and may be too large for the other, having the same number of available processors. The question then is: how to modify the update algorithm to allow for the tunable memory request? Obviously, the question concerns the control of the extent to which the processors get desynchronized in the course of simulations, i.e., the control of the VTH width. One can think about a suitable update pattern that would model the virtual-time interface of the desired properties and then translate this pattern to a new update procedure of the modified algorithm. This approach has been used to design a constrained conservative update algorithm [16], where the desynchronization is controlled by the width of a moving virtual update window and the ring communication topology is modified to accommodate multiple connections between a processor that carries GVT at given update attempt and other processors. In another group of conservative algorithms an implicit autonomous synchronization may be achieved by modifying the ring communication pattern to accommodate connections with the build-in small-world type of communication network [18, 19]. In both of these modifications, the additional communication network imposed on the original ring communication topology serves the sole purpose of reducing the desynchronization. Further studies are required in this matter to identify best efficient ways of tuning the desynchronization and the memory request.

In summary, the new approach to performance studies, outlined in this chapter, that utilizes simulation modeling of virtual-time interfaces as a tool in algorithm design, opens new interdisciplinary research methodologies in the physics of complex systems in application to computer science. Promising avenues where this kind of approach to complex systems of computer science should lead to useful practical solutions may include the criticality issues in distributed PDES algorithms, their scalability, prognostication, the design of efficient communication networks as well as the development of new diagnostic tools for the evaluation of hardware performance.

Acknowledgments

This work is supported by the ERC Center for Computational Sciences at MSU. This research used resources of the National Energy Research Scientific Computing Center, which is supported by the Office of Science of the US Department of Energy under contract No. DE-AC03-76SF00098. Partially supported by NSF grants DMR-0113049 and DMR-0426488.

References

[1] Fujimoto R.M., *Parallel and Distributed Simulation Systems* (John Wiley and Sons, Inc., New York, 2000).

[2] Chandy K.M. and Misra J., Distributed Simulation: A case Study in Design and Verification of Distributed Programs, *IEEE Transactions on Software Engineering*, **5** (1979), pp.440–452.

[3] Fujimoto R., Parallel Discrete Event Simulation, *Communications of the ACM*, **33** (1990), pp.30–53.

[4] Misra J., Distributed Discrete-Event Simulation, *ACM Computing Surveys*, **18** (1986), 39–65.

[5] Lubachevsky B.D., Efficient Parallel Simulations of Asynchronous Cellular Arrays, *Complex Systems*, **1** (1987), pp.1099–1123.

[6] Lubachevsky B., Efficient parallel simulation of dynamic Ising spin systems, *Journal of Computational Physics*, **75** (1988), pp. 103–122.

[7] Jefferson D.A., Virtual time, *ACM Transactions on Programming Languages and Systems*, **7** (1985), pp.404–425.

[8] Dickens P.M. and Reynolds P.F., SRADS with local rollback, in *Proceedings of the SCS Multiconference on Distributed Simulation, San Diego*, edited by Nicol D. and Fujimoto R., *Simulation Series*, **22** (1990), pp.161–164.

[9] Prakash A. and Subramanian R., An efficient optimistic distributed scheme based on conditional knowledge, in *Proceedings of the Sixth Parallel and Distributed Simulation Workshop, 1992 SCS Western Multiconference* (IEEE Press, New York, 1992), pp.85–96.

[10] Steinman J.S., Breathing Time Warp, in *Proceedings of the Seventh workshop on Parallel and Distributed Simulation*, edited by Bagrodia R. and Jefferson D. (IEEE Computer Society Press, Los Alamitos, CA, 1993), pp.109–118.

[11] Ferscha, A. and Chiola G., Self Adaptive Logical Processes: The Probabilistic Distributed Simulation Protocol, in *Proceedings of the 27th Annual Simulation Symposium, LaJolla*, 1994 (IEEE Computer Society Press, Los Alamitos, CA, 1994), pp.78–88.

[12] Korniss G., Toroczkai Z., Novotny M.A., and Rikvold P.A., From Massively Parallel Algorithms and Fluctuating Time Horizons to Non-equilibrium Surface Growth, *Physical Review Letters*, **84** (2000), pp.1351–1354.

[13] Korniss G., Novotny M.A., Toroczkai Z., and Rikvold P.A., Non-equilibrium surface growth and scalability of parallel algorithms for large asynchronous systems, in *Computer Simulation Studies in Condensed Matter Physics XIII* ed. by Landau D.P., Lewis S.P., and Schuettler H.-B., *Springer Proceedings in Physics*, **86** (Springer-Verlag, 2001), pp.183–188.

[14] Korniss G., Novotny M.A., Rikvold P.A., Guclu H., and Toroczkai Z., Going through rough times: from non-equilibrium surface growth to algorithmic scalability, *Materials Research Society Symposium Proceedings Series*, **700** (2001), pp.297–308.

[15] Korniss G., Novotny M.A., Kolakowska A., and Guclu H., Statistical properties of the simulated time horizon in conservative parallel discrete-event simulations, in *Proceedings of the 2002 ACM Symposium on Applied Computing, SAC 2002*, (2002), pp.132–138.

[16] Kolakowska A., Novotny M.A., and Korniss G., Algorithmic scalability in globally constrained conservative parallel discrete-event simulations of asynchronous systems, *Physical Review E*, **67** (2003), article No 046703, 13 pages.

[17] Kolakowska A., Novotny M.A., and Rikvold P.A., Update statistics in conservative parallel-discrete-event simulations of asynchronous systems, *Physical Review A*, **68** (2003), article No 046705, 14 pages.

[18] Korniss G., Novotny M.A., Guclu H., Toroczkai Z., and Rikvold P.A., Suppressing Roughness of Virtual Times in Parallel Discrete-Event Simulations, *Science*, **299** (2003), pp.677–679.

[19] Toroczkai Z., Korniss G., Novotny M.A., and Guclu H., Virtual Time Horizon Control via Communication Network Design, in *Computational Complexity and Statistical Physics* ed. by Percus A., Istrate G., and Moore C., Santa Fe Institute Studies in the Sciences of Complexity Series (Oxford University Press, 2003), in press, ArXiv: cond-mat/0304617.

[20] Guclu H., Korniss G., Toroczkai Z., and Novotny M.A., Small-World Synchronized Computing Networks for Scalable Parallel Discrete-Event Simulations, in *Complex Networks* ed. by Ben-Naim E., Frauenfelder H., and Toroczkai Z., *Lecture Notes in Physics*, Vol.650 (Springer-Verlag, Berlin, 2004) pp.255–275.

[21] Landau D.P. and Binder K., A Guide to Monte Carlo Simulations in Statistical Physics (Cambridge University Press, Cambridge, 1995).

[22] Korniss G., Novotny M.A., and Rikvold P.A., Parallelization of a Dynamic Monte Carlo Algorithm: a Partially Rejection-Free Conservative Approach, *Journal of Computational Physics*, **153** (1999), pp.488–508.

[23] Novotny M.A., Kolakowska A., and Korniss G., Algorithms for Faster and Larger Dynamic Metropolis Simulations, in *The Monte Carlo Method in the Physical Sciences*, ed. by Gubernatis J.E, AIP Conference Proceedings, Vol. 690 (American Institute of Physics, New York, 2003), pp. 240–247.

[24] Barabasi A.-L. and Stanley H.E., Fractal Concepts in Surface Growth (Cambridge University Press, Cambridge, 1995).

[25] Family F. and Vicsek T., Scaling of the active zone in the Eden process on percolation networks and the ballistic deposition model, *Journal of Physics A*, **18**, (1985), pp.L75–L81.

[26] Kardar M., Parisi G., and Zhang Y.-C., Dynamic scaling of growing interfaces, *Physical Review Letters*, **56** (1986), pp.889–892.

[27] Edwards S.F. and Wilkinson D.R., The Surface Statistics of a Granular Aggregate, *Proceedings of the Royal Society London A*, **381** (1982), pp.17–31.

[28] Kolakowska A. and Novotny M.A., Discrete-event analytic technique for surface growth problems, *Physical Review B*, **69** (2004), article No 075407, 5 pages.

[29] Kolakowska A., Novotny M.A., and Verma P.S., Roughening of the interfaces in $(1+1)$ dimansional two-component surface growth with an admixture of random deposition, *Physical Review E*, **70** (2004), article No 051602, 16 pages, ArXiv: cond-mat/0403341.

[30] Overeinder B. J., Schoneveld A., and Sloot P. M. A., Self-Organized Criticality in Optimistic Simulations of Correlated Systems, in *Parallel and Distributed Discrete Event Simulation*, edited by Tropper C. (Nova Science Publishers, New York, 2002), pp.79-98.

[31] Sloot P. M. A., Overeinder B. J., and Schoneveld A., Self-Organized Criticality in Simulated Correlated Systems, *Computer Physics Communications*, **142** (2001), pp.76-81.

[32] Gan B.-P. and Turner, S. J., An Asynchronous Protocol for Virtual Factory Simulation on Shared Memory Multiprocessor Systems, *Journal of Operational Research Society, Special Issue on Progress in Simulation Research*, Vol. 51, No. 4 (2000), pp.413-422.

In: Artificial Intelligence and Computer Science
Editor: Susan Shannon, pp. 181-200
ISBN 1-59454-411-5

Chapter 7

A ROBUST SEMANTIC PARSING APPROACH

Jordi Atserias[*†]
TALP Research Center, Universitat Politècnica de Catalunya
Jordi Girona Salgado, 1-3. E-08034 Barcelona, Catalonia

Abstract

This work explores a new robust approach for Semantic Parsing of unrestricted texts. Our approach formalizes Semantic Parsing as a Consistent Labelling Problem (CLP), allowing the integration of several knowledge types (syntactic and semantic) obtained from different sources (linguistic and statistical). The current implementation obtains 95% accuracy in model identification and 72% in case-role filling.

1 Introduction

A central issue in Semantic Parsing is the production of a case-role analysis in which the semantic roles –such as *agent* or *instrument*– played by each entity are identified [Brill & Mooney 97]. This is a crucial task in any application which involves some level of Natural Language Understanding.

This paper presents a new approach to Semantic Parsing (SP). The aim of this research is to develop a robust (able to work on unrestricted text) and flexible (portable and extensible) approach to Semantic Parsing. We will try to do so by formalizing Semantic Parsing as a Consistent Labelling Problem (CLP), specially focusing on the interaction between syntax and semantics, as well as on verbs, as the head sentence components.

Mahesh [Mahesh 93] proposes a classification of Natural Language Understanding models in: *sequential*, *integrated* and *interactive*, depending on the interaction between syntax and semantics. In *Sequential* models, each level receives the output of the previous one,

---

*E-mail address: batalla@talp.upc.es

†I would like to thank Victoria Arranz for her useful comments and suggestions.

and sends its output to the next. Thus, syntax is solved before any semantic analysis is carried out. On the other hand, in *Integrated* and *Interactive* models, syntactic and semantic processing are performed simultaneously and share a common knowledge representation.

Another relevant issue related to the interaction of syntax and semantics is the required level of syntactic analysis. Chunk parsing [Abney 91] has been widely used in several fields (e.g. Information Extraction) as an alternative to deal with the lack of robustness presented by traditional full parsing approaches. Chunk parsing softens problems with close world assumption (full coverage grammar and lexicon), local errors produced by global parsing considerations [Grishman 95] and the selection of the best parse tree among a forest of possible candidates.

Given that the verb is the core sentence component, there is no doubt that subcategorization information may not only improve parsing —e.g. taking into account probabilistic subcategorization on a statistical parser [Carroll *et al.* 98]— but also provide the basic information to assemble those chunks into larger structures.

Despite full parsing's lack of robustness (specially for a free word-order language), it could provide useful information for the identification of roles that a simple chunk analysis is unable to capture [Gildea & Palmer 02]. However, our approach allows to integrate the subcategorization information used by statistical full parsers and combine it with the information used to identify roles, thus, using this knowledge simultaneoulsy in a collaborative and integrated manner.

Following this brief introduction, sections 2, 3 and 4 explain, respectively, the basic ideas behind our system, its architecture, as well as the different sources of knowledge and the way in which they are integrated. Section 5 describes the experiments carried out and reports the results obtained. Finally, section 6 draws some conclusions and outlines further research lines.

2 PARDON's Approach

Our view of semantic parsing is based on compositional semantics and lexicalized models (i.e. the meaning of a sentence is the result of combining the meaning of its words and the possible combinations are determined by models associated to these words). Bearing that in mind, PARDON's approach combines the *Interactive Model* and chunk parsing. Roughly speaking, PARDON combines Semantic Objects associated to chunks in order to build a case-role representation of the sentence. This combination is carried out using syntactic and semantic knowledge obtained from a linguistic approach (subcategorization frames) and complemented with a statistical model of lexical attraction.

For instance, starting with the chunks in the sentence "Este año en el congreso del partido se habló de las pensiones"[1] shown in Figure 1, we will obtain the case-role representation shown in Figure 2 by combining:

- The initial semantic objects associated to those chunks.

[1] *Literal Translation: This year in the meeting of the political party one talked about the pensions*

- The impersonal model of the verb "hablar" (to talk) shown in Table 2.
- The noun modifier model shown in Table 3.

Este año	en el congreso	del partido	se	habló	de las pensiones
head:año hdle: pos:NP num:sg gen:m sem:Time	head:congreso hdle:en pos:PP num:sg gen:m sem:Top	head:partido hdle:de pos:PP num:sg gen:m sem:Group	head:se hdle: pos:se num: per: sem:Top	head:hablar hdle:hablar pos:VP num:sg per:3 sem:Commun.	head:pensión hdle:de pos:PP num:pl per:3 sem:Top

Figure 1: Chunks for "Este año en el congreso del partido se habló de las pensiones"

Este año	model:impersonal event:habló se:se entity:de las pensiones	model:N_{de} head:en el congreso modif:del partido

Figure 2: Case-role structures obtained for the sentence in Figure 1

PARDON's approach proposes a novel architecture where decisions on high level syntax and semantics are fully integrated. As shown in figure 3, there are two main steps in PARDON: The first step is the *Sentence Analyzer*, which performs PoS-tagging, chunking and semantic annotation. It also has access to the subcategorization (hand built) and lexical attraction (statistical) knowledge bases to complete the sentence model with those kinds of knowledge.

The second step is *Selection*, which selects the most appropriate verbal model for the sentence and role filling for each chunk as a Consistent Labelling Problem.

Before describing the formalization of the Semantic Parsing as a CLP, the next section introduces the lexical model needed to identify the thematic roles.

3 Lexical Models

There has been a number of initiatives to build real-world lexicons for semantic processing, most of them somehow related to Levin's Verb Classes [Levin 93] and WordNet [Miller *et al.* 98]. Below follow some examples:

- **Univ. of Maryland's Lexical Conceptual Structures (LCS) Database**[2] [Dorr 93b] and related works (such as **LEXPIR** [Fernández & Martí 96] and [Vázquez *et al.* 00]). LCS [Jackendoff 72] is a compositional abstraction with language independent properties. It has being used, for example, as the *interlingua* representation in several Machine Translation Systems (such as in UNITRAN [Dorr 93a] and MILT [Dorr. 97]).

[2] http://www.umiacs.umd.edu/~bonnie/LCS_Database_Documentation.html

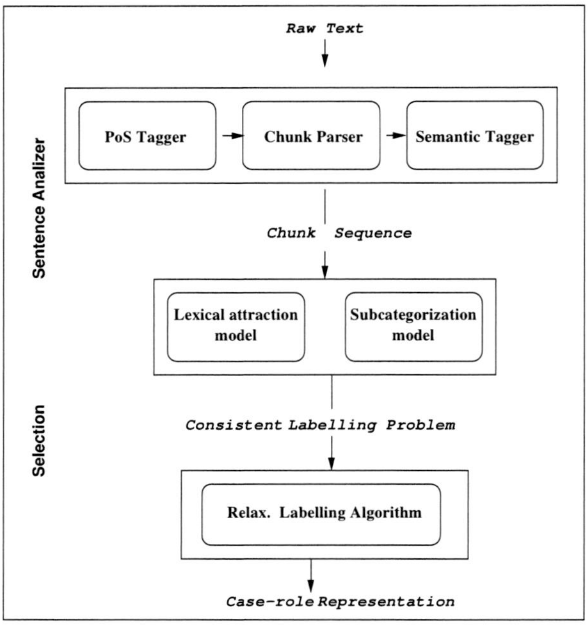

Figure 3: PARDON's Architecture

- **VerbNet**[3] [Kipper *et al.* 00], which is an enrichment of verb entries in WordNet that includes more specific syntactic information and verb class membership. It also draws heavily on the English Tree-Adjoining Grammar. Currently, the **PropBank** corpus[4] ([Kingsbury & Palmer 02], [Kingsbury *et al.* 02] and [Palmer *et al.* 02]) is being extended with VerbNet semantic predicate [Kipper *et al.* 02].

- The work of **Fernando Gomez**[5] to enhace WordNet with verbal predicates [Gomez 98] and to dessign and implement an algorithm that uses these predicates definitions to solve verb meaning, thematic roles and prepositional attachments [Gomez 01].

- **FrameNet**[6] [Baker *et al.* 98] which is based on frame semantics [Fillmore 68, Petruck 96][7]. Currently, FrameNet's lexicon contains more than 4,000 lexical units (word senses) but their aim is to annotate 10,000 or more by the end of the FrameNet II project. FrameNet also provides a corpus of annotated examples (about 100,000).

[3] http://www.cis.upenn.edu/verbnet/

[4] http://www.cis.upenn.edu/~mpalmer/project_pages/ACE.htm

[5] http://www.cs.ucf.edu/~gomez

[6] http://www.icsi.berkeley.edu/~framenet

[7] See [Baker *et al.* 02] for a comparison between FrameNet's Frames and Levin's Verb Classes.

These resources differ in their semantic representations (LCS vs Semantic Frames, arguments vs thematic roles) or semantic decomposition principles. However, some of these resources (e.g VerbNet, Framenet, ProBank and WordNet glosses) can be related through the **Unified index**[8].

One of our main goals is to explore and exploit the relations between syntax and semantics. Therefore, we need a model that makes this mapping explicit and free-word order languages are our big challenge.

At present, the availability of this type of resources for languages other than English is poor. Dorr's LCS has just become recently available for Spanish and Chinese. Also, a Spanish version of FrameNet is currently under early development, although, FrameNet is not directly suitable for our purposes because there is no explicit modelling of the syntactic realization of the frame elements. This relation is being made explicit in the annotation of the FrameNet corpus. Thus, they allow the automatic learning of these mapping/models by the application of Machine Learning/Statistical techniques (See [Gildea & Jurafsky 00, Gildea & Jurafsky 02]).

As a consequence of all this, we chose LEXPIR ([Fernández & Martí 96], [Fernández *et al.* 99] and [Morante *et al.* 98]) for our experiments, because it provides an explicit mapping between syntax and semantics and it focusses on a free-word order language (Spanish). But our approximation to semantic parsing could be applied to other lexicons by modelling the constraints associated with their models.

Below follows a description of the LEXPIR lexicon and its components.

3.1 LEXPIR

PIRAPIDES [Vázquez *et al.* 00] is a project centered on the study of the English, Spanish and Catalan verbal predicates. PIRAPIDES has several goals: On the one hand, from a theoretical point of view, a deep study is being carried out of the units that the model of a verbal entry has produced. This syntactic component focuses on the representation of the interaction between the syntactic and semantic components. On the other hand, from an application-oriented point of view, a lexicon (LEXPIR) based on this theoretical model is being developed, in order to perform corpus analysis.

Capturing the argumental structure or even the syntactic functions of a Spanish sentence may be a hard task, given the optionality of some constituents (such as the subject) and the free–order syntax structure of Spanish.

The classification is based on verb meaning components as well as their diathetic alternations [Vázquez *et al.* 00, Fernández *et al.* 99, Morante *et al.* 98]. The diathetic information allows to infer the number of semantic components which can be explicitly realized or implicitly understood. For the work presented here, information about the prepositional value of arguments is also included[9].

---

[8]See the Verb Frame Search Tool at http://www.cis.upenn.edu/~dgildea/Verbs/

[9]The information of LEXPIR has been augmented with prepositions for 61 trajectory verbs.

Verb classes are organized in a hierarchy which enables the use of default monotonic inheritance to describe verb properties. That is, each verb inherits the elements from its group and each group from its class. However, the inherited information can be overwritten by the information already associated to the specific verb entry.

basic model for Trajectory verbs					
Synt.	Prep.	Comp.	Seman.	Agree.	Opt.
NP	p_inic	starter	Human	yes	yes
x	x	entity	Top	no	yes
PP	p_ruta	route	Top	no	yes
PP	p_orig	source	Top	no	yes
PP	x	destination	Top	no	yes

Table 1: Basic Model for trajectory verbs

Table 1 presents the different elements that appear on the *basic* model for any *Trajectory* class verb:

- *Syntax*: Syntactic realization of the semantic component. For the second component this information is unspecified (x) as the syntactic realization depends on the subclass. Moreover, this element, which is usually the Direct Object, has other restrictions: if its semantics indicates that it is [+human/animate] it should be a PP, while if it is [-human/animate] it has to be realized as an NP.
- *Preposition*: List of prepositions that may introduce the component according to their meanings and occurrences.
- *Component*: Describes the meaning component, determined by the class.
- *Semantics*: Describes the semantics of the component. This is an argument–specific feature.
- *Agreement*: States whether person and number agreement with the verb is required.
- *Optionality*: States whether the component is optional.

Dealing with the optionality of the meaning components within the model itself allows us to reduce the number of possible alternations which have been established at a theoretical level (PIRAPIDES takes the underspecification of a component as an alternation). Only information which is different to the one associated to the class is actually marked. For instance, in the **periphrastic passive** model associated to the communication class, the entity element (defined as {entity;**NP**;x;Top:**yes**;no}), has to be realized as an NP and also has to agree with the verb.

Table 2 shows the resulting expansion of the *basic* and *impersonal* models for a concrete verb: "hablar" (*to talk*) which is an intance of a *Trajectory* class. Unspecified entries are inherited from the class model definition. The upper part of the table presents the basic model inherited from the *Trajectory* in Table 1 but using the specific preposition of the verb "hablar". The lower part shows an alternative model for impersonal uses (i.e 'se habla' – people talk –) which is not present either in the general class.

basic model for "hablar"					
Synt.	Prep.	Comp.	Seman.	Agree.	Opt.
NP	x	starter	Human	yes	yes
PP	de, sobre	entity	Top	no	yes
PP	con	destination	Top	no	yes

impersonal model for "hablar"					
Synt.	Prep.	Comp.	Seman.	Agree.	Opt.
SE	x	se	Top	no	no
PP	de, sobre	entity	Top	no	yes
PP	con	destination	Top	no	yes

Table 2: Models for the verb "hablar"

4 PARDON's Formalization

This work formalizes the PARDON's approach to semantic parsing by setting the case-role interpretation problem as a *Consistent Labelling Problem* (CLP), where the different kinds of knowledge are applied as weighted constraints.

A CLP basically consists in finding the most consistent label assignment for a set of variables, given a set of constraints. Once the sentence and its knowledge is represented in terms of a CLP, a relaxation labelling algorithm is used to obtain the most consistent interpretation[10].

This formulation allows us to naturally integrate different kinds of knowledge coming from different sources (linguistic and statistical), which may be partial, partially incorrect or even inconsistent.

PARDON represents the meaning of a sentence in terms of relationships between semantic objects, using two variables for each semantic object: the *model* ($object_{\text{model}}$) and *role* ($object_{\text{role}}$) variables. For instance, the semantic object associated to a chunk headed by "hablar" (to talk) can use a *basic* model (someone talks about something with someone: [$hablar_{\text{model}} = basic$]) or an *impersonal* model (*one* talks about something [$hablar_{\text{model}} = impersonal$]).

[10]See [Pelillo 91, Padró 98] for details on the use of this algorithm for other NLP tasks.

Variable Name	*Possible Labels*
$año_{\text{model}}$	N_{de} NONE
$año_{\text{role}}$	*(starter, basic, hablar)* TOP
$congreso_{\text{model}}$	N_{de} NONE
$congreso_{\text{role}}$	TOP
$partido_{\text{model}}$	N_{de} NONE
$partido_{\text{role}}$	*(entity, basic, hablar)* *(entity, impersonal, hablar)* *(modif,* N_{de}*, año)* *(modif,* N_{de}*, congreso)* *(modif,* N_{de}*, pension)* TOP
se_{model}	NONE
se_{role}	*(se, impersonal, hablar)* TOP
$hablar_{\text{model}}$	basic impersonal NONE
$hablar_{\text{role}}$	TOP
$pensión_{\text{model}}$	N_{de} NONE
$pensión_{\text{role}}$	*(entity, basic, hablar)* *(entity, impersonal, hablar)* *(modif,* N_{de}*, año)* *(modif,* N_{de}*, congreso)* *(modif,* N_{de}*, partido)* TOP

Figure 4: CLP associated to the objects in Figure 1

The *role* variable represents the role that a semantic object plays inside the model of another semantic object. For instance, the semantic object "pensiones" (the pensions) can play the role *entity* for both models of "hablar" (to talk) (e.g. [$pensiones_{\text{role}}$ = *(entity, basic, hablar)*]).

In order to identify a role from a model label we need a triplet *(role, model, semantic object)*. For instance, the role *starter* of the *basic* model for "hablar" is represented as *(starter, basic, hablar)*.

Since a CLP always assigns a label to all the variables, two null labels have to be added: the label NONE for the model variables (semantic objects which do not have/use a model, usually leaf semantic objects with no sub-constituents) and the label TOP for the role variables (semantic objects not playing a role in the model of a higher constituent, usually the sentence head). Figure 4 shows the variables and labels associated to the semantic objects in Figure 1.

The next step in the formalization of the Semantic Parsing as a CLP is to establish the possible assignments, that is, to determine which the possible models are, and which roles of these models can be played by the Semantic Objects associated to the initial chunks. Thus, we have to determine which of the restrictions expressed by the lexicalized model must hold (*Hard Constraints*) and which constraints can be softened in order to find a solution (*Soft Constraints*), (i.e. Selectional Preferences, heuristics or knowledge that we know could be inconsistent or incomplete).

When formalizing the problem, the models that can not fill any of their compulsory roles should not be taken into account and neither should all their associated roles (and their possible assignments). The *hard-constraints* involved in the identification of roles are applied in the function **match**[11]. Using this function, we would determine whether a Semantic Object could play a role (represented as a possible assignment) or not.The following general algorithm in pseudo-code describes the procedure for building the CLP:

```
foreach chunk C in the sentence do
   create the Semantic Object A for the chunk C
   foreach model M associated to the head of chunk C do
        add <M,A> to the activeModels list
   end foreach
end foreach

foreach <M,A> in the activeModels do
   if(all the compulsory roles of M have at least one match) then
     foreach role R of model M do
             foreach Semantic Object SO do
               if(match Role SO) then
                  add SO as possible player of role R
               end if
             end foreach
     end foreach
     add M as possible model for A
   end if
end foreach
```

[11]In our experiments **match** only takes into account the syntactic category of the chunk and the preposition restrictions.

In our current model, the features of the initial Sematic Object associated to the chunks do not change[12]. Therefore, the constraints that establish how likely it is that a Semantic Object plays a role can be calculated only once, at the beginning of the process.

The function **sim** measures the similarity between the Semantic Object and a Role, comparing both feature structures. The value returned is normalized in $[-1, 1]$ and it is inversely proportional to the number of relabelling operations needed to transform one feature structure into the other[13]. We use this measure to set the initial state (e.g. the starting point) of the Relaxation Labelling Algorithm.

After formalizing Semantic Parsing as a Consistent Labelling Problem, a set of constraints stating valid/invalid assignments is required to find a possible solution. PARDON uses three kinds of constraints: The first group contains the constraints that encode the linguistic information obtained from verb subcategorization models. The second group are additional constraints added to force a tree-like structure for the solution. Finally, a third set of constraints encoding statistical information about word co-occurrences was added in order to complement the subcategorization information available.

Constraints are noted as follows:

$[A = x] \approx^w [B = y]$ denotes a constraint stating a compatibility degree w when variable A has label x and variable B has label y. The compatibility degree w may be positive (stating compatibility) or negative (stating incompatibility).

4.1 Subcategorization Constraints

Two different kinds of subcategorization models have been used: one about verbal subcategorization and another one about noun modifiers.

For each chunk labelled as VP, all possible subcategorization models for the verb heading the chunk are retrieved from LEXPIR. For PP and NP we use the simple nominal modifier model N_{de} presented in table 3.

N_{de} model for nouns					
Synt.	Prep.	Comp.	Seman.	Agree.	Opt.
PP	de	modifier	Top	no	no

Table 3: Model for noun modifiers

Due to the richness and complexity of natural language, the prototypical subcategorization patterns defined in LEXPIR do not reflect exactly the complex patterns to be found in real data. Thus, a measure of the "goodness" of the possible model instantiation is defined in a similar way to the tree-edit based pattern matching used in [Atserias *et al.* 99, Atserias *et al.* 00].

In order to ensure the global applicability (minimal disorder, agreement, maximum similarity between the role and semantic object and maximal number of roles) and the

[12] Except role and model

[13] Currently, only semantics, person and number are considered.

consistence of the model (a unique instantiation per role and the instantiation of compulsory roles) the following constraints are automatically instantiated from the models:

- **Role Uniqueness**: The same role cannot be assigned to different chunks, e.g.:

  $[pension_{\text{role}} = (entity, basic, hablar)] \approx^{-1} [partido_{\text{role}} = (entity, basic, hablar)]$

  This constraint penalizes the current weight of the assignment [$pension_{\text{role}} = (entity, basic, hablar)$] according to the current weight of the assignment [$partido_{\text{role}} = (entity, basic, hablar)$]. Thus, the higher the weight for the latter assignment is, the faster the weight of the former will decrease.
- **Model Support**: A model assignment is compatible with its optional roles, e.g.: $[hablar_{\text{model}} = basic] \approx^{+1} [pension_{\text{role}} = (entity, basic, hablar)]$
- **Model Inconsistence**: A model assignment is incompatible with the inexistence of any of its compulsory roles, e.g.:

  $[hablar_{\text{model}} = impersonal] \approx^{-1} \neg [se_{\text{role}} = (se, impersonal, hablar)]$
- **Role Support**: A role assignment is compatible with the assignment of its model, e.g.:

  $[pension_{\text{role}} = (entity, basic, hablar)] \approx^{+sim(\ldots)} [hablar_{\text{model}} = basic]$

  The weight for this constraint is the *sim*ilarity[14] between the feature structures of both the Semantic Object and the Role (e.g in the constraint example, the similarity between the Semantic Object associated to *"pension"* and the Role *entity* of the *basic* model of the verb *"hablar"*).
- **Role Inconsistence**: A role assignment is incompatible with the *non existence* of the assignment of its own model, e.g.:

  $[pension_{\text{role}} = (entity, basic, hablar)] \approx^{-1} \neg [hablar_{\text{model}} = basic]$

Additionally, a special set of constraints has been introduced to deal with PP-attachment:

- **Local PP attachment**: A prepositional phrase tends to be attached to its nearest head. The weight assigned to each constraint will decrease along with the distance (in words) between the semantic objects involved, e.g.:

  $[pension_{\text{role}} = (entity, impersonal, hablar)] \approx^{-distance(pension,hablar)} [\,].$

4.2 Structural Constraints

Some further constraints must be included to force the solution to have a tree-like structure. These constraints are not derived from the subcategorization models:

- **TOP Uniqueness**: Different assignments of the label TOP are incompatible, e.g.:

  $[partido_{\text{role}} = TOP] \approx^{-1} [hablar_{\text{role}} = TOP].$

[14]The function *sim* has being defined earlier in this section.

- **TOP Existence**: There is at least one TOP. Note that there is no right-hand side on the constraint as it is valid for any context, e.g.:

  [hablar$_{\text{role}}$ *= TOP]* $\approx^{+1}$ *[ ]*
- **No Cycles**: Two assignments forming a direct cycle are incompatible[15], e.g.:

  [pension$_{\text{role}}$ *= (modif, N*$_{de}$*, partido)]* $\approx^{-1}$ *[partido*$_{\text{role}}$ *= (modif, N*$_{de}$*, pension)]*
- **NONE Support**: The NONE model is compatible with the inexistence of any role assignment of the semantic object models, e.g.:

  [congreso$_{\text{model}}$ *= NONE]* $\approx^{+1}$ $\neg$ *[pension*$_{\text{role}}$ *= (modif, N*$_{de}$*, congreso)]* $\wedge$
  $\neg$ *[partido*$_{\text{role}}$ *= (modif, N*$_{de}$*, congreso)]*

  If these constraints were not included, the NONE model would never be selected, since there would always be some other model with a very small non-zero support.

4.3 Statistical Constraints

In a similar way to [Yuret 98] we also define a language model based on lexical attraction. In our case, we estimate the likelihood of a syntactic relation not between two words but between two semantic objects.

Our hypothesis is that the relations between two semantic objects can be determined taking into account two special elements of their associated chunks, the *handle* and the *head.* The *handle* of a chunk is usually the preposition that specifies the type of relation that chunk has with another chunk, while the *head* of a chunk is supposed to capture the meaning of the chunk [Basili *et al.* 98]. For instance, the chunk “de las pensiones” (*about the pensions*) has handle “de” (*about*) and *head* “pensión” (*pension*).

Since related words are expected to occur together more likely than unrelated words, the lexical attraction (the likelihood of a syntactic relation) between two words can be estimated/modeled through co-occurrence. Co-occurrence data can also indicate negative relatedness, when the probability of co-occurrence is lower than by chance. Thus, we will measure lexical attraction between two sematic objects with the co-occurrence of both heads and the co-occurrence of the head and the handle (which gives an implicit direction of the dependence).

Since the co-occurrences were taken from the definitions of a Spanish dictionary, lemma co-occurrences were used instead of word co-occurrences in order to minimize the problems caused by unseen words [Dagan *et al.* 99]. 175,333 head-handle co-occurrences and 961,470 head-head co-occurrences were obtained out of 40,591 different head-lemmas and 160 different handle-prepositions. The co-occurrences were used to compute Mutual Information for each lemma–preposition pair.

$$MI(head_i, handle_j) = log\frac{P(head_i \cap handle_j)}{P(head_i) \times P(handle_j)}$$

[15] In this first prototype of PARDON indirect cycles are not taken into account.

In the case of lemma-lemma pairs, sparseness is much higher. Thus, an indirect measure was applied, namely context vector cosine (also used in IR and WSD [Schütze 92]) in order to calculate the lexical attraction between heads:

$$cos(head_i, head_j) = \frac{\sum_k a_{ki} a_{kj}}{\sqrt{\sum_k a_{ki}^2 \sum_k a_{kj}^2}}$$

where a_{pq} is the co-occurrence frequency of lemma p and lemma q, and k ranges over all the lemmas co-occurring with any of both heads.

Thus, for any two semantic objects the following constraints are added:

- A_i-H_j constraint, which supports any assignment of a role from $object_j$ to $object_i$, e.g.:

  [partido$_{\text{role}}$ = *(modif, N*$_{de}$*, congreso)]* $\approx^{MI(congreso,de)}$ *[ ]*
- H_i-H_j constraint, which supports any assignment of a role from $object_i$ to $object_j$, or viceversa, e.g.:

  [pensión$_{\text{role}}$ = *(entity, impersonal, hablar)]* $\approx^{cos(hablar,pension)}$ *[ ]*

H_i-H_j and A_i-H_j constraints can be used to identify adjuncts or relations for which we have no models. For instance, in the result obtained for the sentence shown in Figure 1, the sematic object "en el congreso" (*in the meeting*) will be identified as depending on the verb "hablar", even when its role can not be determined.

5 Experiments

170 real sentences were taken from a Spanish newspaper and were labelled by hand with their verbal models and meaning components. The sentence average length is 8.1 words, ranging from 3 to 23. Only one-verb sentences were selected, since our knowledge base does not include models for subordination or coordination. However, our approach to semantic parsing has been designed to manage multiple models simultaneously competing for their arguments.

Each sentence in the corpus was tagged and parsed with a wide-coverage grammar of Spanish [Castellón *et al.* 98] to obtain a chunk parse tree. Spanish Wordnet [Atserias *et al.* 97] was used to semantically annotate the corpus with the 79 semantic labels defined in the preliminary version of the EuroWordNet Top Concept Ontology [Rodríguez *et al.* 98].

As mention in section 4, in order to reduce the complexity of the relaxation process, the possible role labels (which indicate the roles an object can play in any of the models retrieved) are filtered considering the unary constraints about POS and prepositions, while constraints about semantics and agreement are taken as a measure of how similar (*sim*) the semantic object and the role are. Models which can not match compulsory roles are not considered.

For instance, the semantic object *año* (*year*) in the example sentence will be allowed to match the role *starter* of the impersonal model of the verb *hablar* even though its semantics is not Human, but the semantic object *congreso* will not be considered as a candidate to fill the *entity* role of *hablar*, since the preposition *en* in the semantic object does not match the model requirements for that role (preposition *de, sobre*). All these filters produce the candidate labels shown in Figure 4, which are the input to PARDON *Selection* step.

5.1 Results

The results reported have been calculated using Message Understanding Conferences [MUC95] evaluation metrics applied to our particular case of verbal model identification and case-role filling.

Model identification metrics evaluate how well our system identifies the right model for a semantic object. Our corpus has 2.7 models per verbal semantic object as average ambiguity.

Since it is assumed that there is only one right model per chunk in each sentence, the answer can only be correct (*COR*) or incorrect (*INC*), thus, the used metrics are precision and recall. Table 4 shows the results obtained in the verbal model identification task: 95% precision and 91% recall.

COR	*INC*	*PRE*	*REC*
155	8	95%	91%

Table 4: Verbal Model identification results

Case-role filling consists in assigning each semantic object to the right role it plays in the models for other semantic objects. In this case, the casuistry is more complex, since in addition to the correct/incorrect distinctions, other cases must be considered, such as the roles that are (correctly/incorrectly) left unassigned (because they were optional, or because there was no semantic object that fitted them, etc.). The MUC evaluation metrics establish the following cases:

- **Correct** (*COR*): Roles correctly assigned by the system.
- **Incorrect** (*INC*): Roles incorrectly assigned by the system.
- **Missing** (*MIS*): Roles unassigned by the system when they should have been assigned.
- **Spurious** (*SPU*): Roles assigned by the system when they should have been unassigned.

These cases lead to the definition of the following measures, where **Possible** (POS) are the roles that should be assigned (COR+INC+MIS) and **Actual** (ACT) are the roles actually assigned by the system under evaluation (COR+INC+SPU):

- **Undergeneration** $UND = 100 \times \frac{MIS}{POS}$
- **Overgeneration** $OVR = 100 \times \frac{SPU}{ACT}$

- **Substitution** $SUB = 100 \times \frac{INC}{COR+INC}$
- **Error** $ERR = 100 \times \frac{INC+SPU+MIS}{COR+INC+SPU+MIS}$
- **Precision** $PRE = 100 \times \frac{COR}{ACT}$
- **Recall** $REC = 100 \times \frac{COR}{POS}$

In addition, precision and recall may be combined in different F-measures (*P&R*, *2P&R* and *P&2R*). Table 5 shows the results in the case-role filling for verbal arguments.

COR	*INC*	*MIS*	*SPU*	*POS*	*ACT*
203	27	60	51	290	281

UND	*OVR*	*SUB*	*ERR*	*PRE*	*REC*	*P&R*	*2P&R*	*P&2R*
20%	18%	12%	40%	72%	70%	71%	70%	72%

Table 5: Verbal case-role filling results

To our knowledge there is neither a similar general approach nor case-role filling experiments to which our results can be compared. In any case, our preliminary results (72% *PRE* - 70% *REC*) are very encouraging.

It is also remarkable that our system produces low values for *UND*, *OVR* and *SUB* measures, pointing that it properly uses the different kinds of knowledge, and that it does not take uninformed or gratuitous decisions.

Errors in the preprocessing steps caused most of the mis-identified models (table 4, *INC*). The *missing* and *spurious* roles (table 5, *MIS* and *SPU*) were due either to the lack of semantic information or to the lack of a verbal model for adjuncts, which caused mis-identification of adjuncts as arguments, as in "(Juan) (esquía) (este fin) (de año)"[16], where the chunk "este fin de año" (*on New Year's Eve*) is wrongly identified to fill the *route* role even though its semantics is *Time*. This is due to the lack of a selectional restriction that forces the *route* to be a *Place*, and to the lack of a model that identifies the chunk as time adjunct.

6 Conclusions & Further Work

This paper has presented a new approach to Semantic Parsing for non domain-specific texts based on the *Interactive Model*. The robustness and flexibility of PARDON are achieved combining a chunk parsing approach with the framing of the semantic parsing problem in a CLP. The flexibility of our approach enables the integration of different types of knowledge (linguistically motivated subcategorization models plus statistical information obtained from corpora).

[16] *John is going skying on New Year's Eve.*

Currently, PARDON obtains a 95% precision on model identification and 72% precision on role filling. Although the experiments have been carried out on a limited corpus and lexicon, they have proven the feasibility of the method.

Further work should include a more realistic evaluation of the system, using a larger corpus with sentences having multiple verbs (maybe using the models and corpus related to other lexical resources available for English such as FrameNet or PropBank). In this case, verbal models would compete for their arguments in a sentence.

We also plan to include more statistical knowlege (measures/language models) and to extend the coverage and expressiveness of the subcategorization models. Exploting the integration of other semantic resources related to Wordnet (e.g the Multilingual Central Repository [Atserias *et al.* 03], developed inside the MEANING Project[17] [Rigau *et al.* 02] which contains selectional preferences automatically adquired from corpus). Furthermore, the output of the current system could also be used as feedback to improve the existing verbal models.

The problem of the recognition and classification of Name Entities (such as people's and companies' proper nouns, amounts of money, dates, etc.) should be adressed, studing how to extend the current lexical attraction model to cover Name Entities. Name Entities do not appear in the trainning data of the lexical attraction model but are quite frequent in our test corpus. Thus, the set of constraints generated using this model tends to support assignments which do not involve Name Entities.

Finally, the exploration of linguistic and statistical models for the identification/distinction of verbal adjuncts should also be investigated, since it seems to be one of the main causes of verbal argument mis-identification.

References

[Abney 91] (Abney 91) Steven Abney. *Parsing by chunks*. Kluwer Academic Publishers, 1991.

[Atserias *et al.* 97] (Atserias *et al.* 97) Jordi Atserias, Salvador Climent, Xavier Farreres, German Rigau, and Horacio Rodríguez. Combining Multiple Methods for the Automatic Construction of Multilingual WordNets. In *Procceeding of RANLP'97*, pages 143–149, Bulgaria, 1997.

[Atserias *et al.* 99] (Atserias *et al.* 99) Jordi Atserias, Irene Castellón, Montserrat Civit, and German Rigau. Using diathesis for semantic parsing. In *Proceedings of Venecia per il Trattamento automatico delle lingue (VEXTAL)*, pages 385–392, Venecia, Italy, 1999.

[Atserias *et al.* 00] (Atserias *et al.* 00) Jordi Atserias, Irene Castellón, Montserrat Civit, and German Rigau. Semantic analysis based on verbal sub-

[17] http://www.lsi.upc.es/~nlp/meaning/meaning.html

categorization. In *Proceedings of the Conference on Intelligent Text Processing and Computational Linguistics (CICLing)*, pages 330–340, Mexico City, Mexico, 2000.

[Atserias *et al.* 03] (Atserias *et al.* 03) Jordi Atserias, Luís Villarejo, and German Rigau. Starting up the Multilingual Central Repository. In *Proceedings of the SEPLN'03*, 2003.

[Baker *et al.* 98] (Baker *et al.* 98) C. Baker, C. Fillmore, and J. Lowe. The Berkeley FrameNet project. In *COLING/ACL'98*, Montreal, Canada, 1998.

[Baker *et al.* 02] (Baker *et al.* 02) Baker, Collin F., and Josef Ruppenhofer. FrameNet's Frames vs. Levin's Verb Classes. In *Proceedings of the 28th Annual Meeting of the Berkeley Linguistics Society*, February 15-18 2002.

[Basili *et al.* 98] (Basili *et al.* 98) R. Basili, M. T. Pazienza, and F. Zanzotto. Efficient parsing for information extraction. In Henri Prade, editor, *Proceedings of the 13th European Conference on Artificial Intelligence (ECAI-98)*, pages 135–139, Chichester, August 23-28 1998. John Wiley & Sons Ltd.

[Brill & Mooney 97] (Brill & Mooney 97) Eric Brill and Raymond J. Mooney. An Overview of Empirical Natural Language Processing. *Artificial Intelligence Magazine*, 18(14):13–24, Winter 1997. Special Issue on Empirical Natural Language Processing.

[Carroll *et al.* 98] (Carroll *et al.* 98) John Carroll, G. Minnen, and E. Briscoe. Can subcategorisation probabilities help a statistical parser? In *Proceedings of the 6th ACL/SIGDAT Workshop on Very Large Corpora*, pages 118–126, Montreal, Canada, 1998.

[Castellón *et al.* 98] (Castellón *et al.* 98) Irene Castellón, Montse Civit, and Jordi Atserias. Syntactic Parsing of Spanish Unrestricted Text. In *Proceedings of the 1st Conference on Language Resources and Evaluation (LREC'98)*, Granada. Spain, 1998.

[Dagan *et al.* 99] (Dagan *et al.* 99) Ido Dagan, Lillian Lee, and Fernando C. N. Pereira. Similarity-based models of word coocurrence probabilities. *Machine Learning*, (34):43–69, 1999.

[Dorr 93a] (Dorr 93a) B. J. Dorr. Interlingual machine translation: a parameterized approach. *Artificial Intelligence*, 63(1&2):429–492, 1993.

[Dorr 93b] (Dorr 93b) B.J. Dorr. A view from the lexicon. *Machine Translation*, 1993. MIT Press.

[Dorr. 97] (Dorr. 97) B. J. Dorr. Large- Scale Acquisition of LCS- Based Lexicons for Foreign Language Tutoring. In *Proceedings of the ACL Fifth Conference on Applied Natural Language Processing (ANLP)*, pages 139–146, 1997.

[Fernández & Martí 96] (Fernández & Martí 96) A. Fernández and M. A. Martí. Classification of psychological verbs. *SEPLN*, (20), 1996.

[Fernández *et al.* 99] (Fernández *et al.* 99) A. Fernández, M. A. Martí, G. Vázquez, and I. Castellón. Establishing semantic oppositions for typification of predicates. *Language Design*, (2), 1999.

[Fillmore 68] (Fillmore 68) Charles J. Fillmore. The case for case. *Bach and Harms (Ed.): Universals in Linguistic Theory*, pages 1–88, 1968. Holt, Rinehart, and Winston, New York.

[Gildea & Jurafsky 00] (Gildea & Jurafsky 00) Daniel Gildea and Daniel Jurafsky. Automatic labeling of semantic roles. In *Proceedings of the 38th Annual Conference of the Association for Computational Linguistics (ACL-00)*, pages 512–520, Hong Kong, October 2000.

[Gildea & Jurafsky 02] (Gildea & Jurafsky 02) Daniel Gildea and Daniel Jurafsky. Automatic labeling of semantic roles. *Computational Linguistics*, 28(3):245–288, 2002.

[Gildea & Palmer 02] (Gildea & Palmer 02) Daniel Gildea and Martha Palmer. The necessity of syntactic parsing for predicate argument recognition. In *Proceedings of the 40th Annual Conference of the Association for Computational Linguistics (ACL-02)*, Philadelphia, PA, 2002.

[Gomez 98] (Gomez 98) F. Gomez. Linking wordnet verb classes to semantic interpretation. In *Proceedings of the COLING-ACL Workshop on the Usage of WordNet on NLP Systems*, Universite de Montreal, Quebec, Canada, August 1998.

[Gomez 01] (Gomez 01) F. Gomez. An algorithm for aspects of semantic interpretation using an enhanced wordnet. In *Proceedings of the 2nd Meeting of the North American Chapter of the Association for Computational Linguistics, NAACL-2001,*, CMU, Pittsburgh, 2001.

[Grishman 95] (Grishman 95) Ralph Grishman. Nyu system or where's the syntax? In *MUC-6*, pages 167–175, 1995.

[Jackendoff 72] (Jackendoff 72) R Jackendoff. *Semantic Interpretation in Generative Grammar*. Cambridge, Massachusetts, The MIT Press, 1972.

[Kingsbury & Palmer 02] (Kingsbury & Palmer 02) Paul Kingsbury and Martha Palmer. From treebank to propbank. In *Proceedings of the 3rd International Conference on Language Resources and Evaluation (LREC-2002)*, Las Palmas, Spain, 2002.

[Kingsbury *et al.* 02] (Kingsbury *et al.* 02) Paul Kingsbury, Martha Palmer, and Mitch Marcus. Adding semantic annotation to the penn treebank. In *Proceedings of the Human Language Technology Conference*, 2002.

[Kipper *et al.* 00] (Kipper *et al.* 00) Karin Kipper, Hoa Trang Dang, and Martha Palmer. Class-based construction of a verb lexicon. In *Proceedings of the Seventeenth National Conference on Artificial Intelligence, AAAI'00*, 2000.

[Kipper *et al.* 02] (Kipper *et al.* 02) Karin Kipper, Martha Palmer, and Owen Rambow. Extending propbank with verbnet semantic predicates. In *Proceedings of AMTA'02*, 2002.

[Levin 93] (Levin 93) Beth Levin. *English Verb Classes and Alterations: A preliminar Investigation.* The University of Chicago Press, 1993.

[Mahesh 93] (Mahesh 93) Kavi Mahesh. A theory of interaction and independence in sentence understanding. Unpublished M.Sc. thesis, Georgia Institute of Technology, 1993.

[Miller *et al.* 98] (Miller *et al.* 98) George Miller, Katherine Miller, Christiane Fellbaum, Randee Tengi, Marti Hearst, Karen Kohl, Douglas Jones, Robert Bernick, Naoyuki Nommura, Uta Priss, Shari Landes, Claudia Leacock, Joachim Grabowski, Shari Landes, Philip Resnik, Martin Chodorow, Elen Voorhees, Graeme Hirst, David St-Onge, Reem Al-Halimi, Rick Kazman, J.F.M. Burg, R.P. Riet, Sanda Harabagiu, and Dan Moldovan. *Wordnet: An Electronic Lexical Database.* MIT Press, 1998. ISBN 0-262-06197-X.

[Morante *et al.* 98] (Morante *et al.* 98) R. Morante, Irene Castellón, and Gloria Vázquez. Los verbos de trayectoria. In *Proceedings of the conference of the SEPLN*, 1998.

[MUC95] (MUC95) *Sixth Message Undestanding Conference (MUC-6)*, 1995. ISBN 1-55860-402-2.

[Padró 98] (Padró 98) Lluís Padró. *A Hybrid Environment for Syntax-Semantic Tagging.* Unpublished PhD thesis, Departament de Llenguatges i Sistemes Informàtics. Universitat Politècnica de Catalunya. Barcelona, 1998.

[Palmer *et al.* 02] (Palmer *et al.* 02) Martha Palmer, Daniel Gildea, and Paul Kingsbury. Phase I of the Proposition Bank. Submitted to *Computational Linguistics*, 2002.

[Pelillo 91] (Pelillo 91) M. Pelillo. Syntactic category disambiguation through relaxation processes. In *Proc. EuroSpeech'91-2nd Europ. Conf. on Speech Commun. and Technologies, Genova, Italy*, 1991.

[Petruck 96] (Petruck 96) Miriam R.L. Petruck. Frame semantics. *Jef Verschueren, Jan-Ola Östman, Jan Blommaert, and Chris Bulcaen (eds.). Handbook of Pragmatics*, 1996. Philadelphia. John Benjamins.

[Rigau *et al.* 02] (Rigau *et al.* 02) G. Rigau, B. Magnini, E. Agirre, P. Vossen, and J. Carroll. Meaning: A roadmap to knowledge technologies. In *Proceedings of COLING Workshop "A Roadmap for Computational Linguistics"*, Taipei, Taiwan, 2002.

[Rodríguez *et al.* 98] (Rodríguez *et al.* 98) Horacio Rodríguez, Salvador Climent, Peek Vossen, L. Blocsma, Wim Peters, A. Alonge, F. Bertagna, and A. Rovertini. The top-down strategy for building euwn: Vocabulary coverage, base concepts and top ontology. *Computers and the Humanities*, 32(2-3), 1998.

[Schütze 92] (Schütze 92) Hinrich Schütze. Context space. In *Proceedings of the AAAI*, pages 113–120, 1992.

[Vázquez *et al.* 00] (Vázquez *et al.* 00) Glória Vázquez, Ana Fernández, and M. Antonia Martí. *Clasificación Verbal, Alternancias de Diátesis*. Number 3 in Cuaderns de Sintagma. Sintagma, 2000.

[Yuret 98] (Yuret 98) Deniz Yuret. *Discovery of Linguistic Relations Using Lexical Attraction*. Unpublished PhD thesis, Massachusetts Institute of Technology, 1998. Also available as cmp-lg/9805009.

In: Artificial Intelligence and Computer Science
Editor: Susan Shannon, pp. 201-216
ISBN: 1-59454-411-5

Chapter 8

LANGUAGE MODEL OF DATA AND SOME FEATURES OF ITS IMPLEMENTATION

Viacheslav Novikov*
VDO RSC Energia, Samara, Russian

Abstract

In the paper the description of the language model of data, offered by the author, responding the purposes of storage and retrieval of complicatedly structured data and initiation of control operations, according to recursive rules, having the same structure, as the data, is given. In the model, as it is accepted, the structural, manipulation and integrity parts are allocated, the features of implementation are considered. The possibilities of formulation and realization of the tasks of teaching and semantic search of information on natural language within the framework of the model are discussed also.

1 Introduction

More than 30 years have passed from the time of writing by Codd the key papers, given a push to development of the relational approach in databases [2,3]. For this time such characteristics of resources of computer facilities as processor productivity, size of operating and peripheral memories have increased on degrees both quantitatively and qualitatively. As well ways of usage of these resources have varied - the individual use of powerful processors, the work occurring everywhere with the RAM through the mechanism of the virtual memory, which size for 32-bit processors in case of a Unix-similar operating system reaches 4 Gbytes on a process. Therefore it is possible with the defined reliance to speak, that the quantitative limitations, with which the developers of systems of storage and information retrieval collided earlier, are removed or are, at least, moved away considerably.

Taking into account stated above, the ways of a data organizing on the first sight prodigal from the point of view of economy of resources (first of all of memories both core, and long-

* E-mail address: hbm@mail.radiant.ru

time) become realizable. The attempt of usage of the structural organization of the information storage medium, similar to the structure of natural language, is represented now as logical; that can remove many inconsistencies between the form of a data representation in the computer and needs of the subject, which uses them. The similar attempt was undertaken by the author on the basis of operating system Unix V.3 on workstations with processors Motorola and then of Windows NT (2000) on Intel compatible computers.

Before to give more exact definitions we shall specify, what is meaning in this case by the structure of the natural language. Not pressing in linguistic delicacies we shall consider, that in the language they distinguish: *characters*, *words* (including punctuation marks), *sentences* and *rules*. The word is some sequence of characters, the sentence - accordingly sequence of words, and the rule - a sequence of sentences. Now we shall remark, that the word in the RAM of the computer can be presented as the array (in the terms of programming on C) of characters or less compactly - as the array of pointer on storage locations containing same characters. The last representation, if by analogy to build other constructions of the language, reduces to the 4-level structure, on 0-th level of which the characters and their combinations represented, on 1-st level - words and sequences of words, on 2-nd level - sentences and their sequences, on 3-rd level - rules and aggregates of rules. At once it is necessary to be stipulated, that in base there can be data, which are not represented as similar structure, for example, graphics pictures or executive codes of programs. But in these cases always it is possible to speak about a name or complete name of file containing a picture, or about a pointer on appropriate area of the virtual storage.

Further I shall present, as it is accepted concerning relational model, main concepts and definitions of the structural part, ways of manipulations with the data, including main constructions of the language for record of rules, and also description of the integrity par of the model and the features of its implementation.

2 Structural Part of Model, Main Concepts and Definitions

In spite of the fact that at the description of algorithms of DBMS operations, such concepts as "relation", "the scheme of storage of the relation" etc. are widely used, they essentially differ from the concepts of the generally accepted relational data model (see, for example, [5]).

Relation is an n-ary relation given on some subset of the relations, or an elementary, 0-ary relation. To each relation the pointer on the sequence (which can be empty) of direct references is put in correspondence. Each non-elementary relation is being characterized by the inverse references and code. The relations, depending on the level, are distinguished according to the type.

References. The direct and inverse references are distinguished. The direct references define a set of relations, definition areas of which contain the given relation. The inverse references define a set of relations, which fix a definition area of the given relation.

Level of the relation. Four levels of relations are identified.

0-th level is characters, elementary numbers, combinations of characters and their relations, combinations of elementary numbers. The elementary relation of 0-th level defines the character code or elementary number. Elementary numbers are hexadecimal numbers from 0x00 up to 0xFF. In the database the numbers described on C as *short*, *integer*, *float* and *double* can be used. All numbers, except for elementary, are represented with sequences of elementary numbers. The order of creation of number sequences is reverse - at first rightmost digits, then left. The non-significant zero in the sequences of elementary numbers and trailing blanks in the sequences of characters, as a rule, are not mapped in the database.

1-st level is words, elementary relations of the 1-st level, combinations of words, elementary relations of the 1-st level and their relations. *The word* is a relation having the inverse reference to the relation of the 0-th level. The elementary relation of the 1-st level is a relation defining an arbitrary sequence of characters (for non-descriptors or arbitrary bit maps), or relation defining the address of subroutine/function (method of some class), or empty relation of the 1-st level.

2-nd level is sentences, aggregates of sentences. *The sentence* is a relation having the inverse reference to the relation of the1-st level.

3-rd level is rules, sequences (or *files*) of rules. *The rule* is a relation having the inverse reference to the relation of the 2-nd level.

Code of the relation is the code of predicate defining the relation. Except for the elementary relations the codes can be the following ones:

0 - the ordered sequence of the relations (or simply "sequence ');
1 - the conjunction of the relations;
2 - the disjunction of the relations;
3 - the disjunction of sequences of the relations (the term "list" is also applied).

If at recording sentences the relations with the code 0 are distinguished with help of parentheses ( ), the relations with the code 1 - with help of angular brackets < >, the relations with the code 2 - with help of square brackets [ ] and the relations with the code 3 - with help of braces { } respectively, then:

(a b) is predicate defining set, containing unique chain* **a b;**
<a b> is predicate defining set, containing chains **a b, b a;**
[a b] is predicate defining set, consisting of two elementary chains **a, b**;
{a b c} is predicate defining set, consisting of chains **a, b, c, a b, b c,**
a b c.

Type of the relation

On the 0-th level all relations except for special have the type 0. A relation defining the special combination of characters has type 1, and the combination of characters, including this special relation, has type 3.

On the1-st level names of variables and constants are distinguished. The name of variable (or current variable) is a special relation representing by the word with type 1. The name of global variable is a special relation representing by the word with type 2. The current and global variables are distinguished by visibility at recursive interpretation of rules. The

* Hereinafter concept "chain" is used according to the generally accepted definitions given, for example, in [1].

constants and constant expressions are referred to type 0. And the relations including the names of variables, current and/or global, have type 3.

The sentences on the 2-nd level can be *executable* (type 2), i.e., calling the control transfer to some subroutine/function, or *non-executable* (type 1).

On the 3-rd level *direct* and *inverse* rules are distinguished. The inverse rules are referred to type 1, the direct rules - to type 2. The rules in which the right part is absent are used for the definition of input data. Such rules are referred to type 1. The rules, in which there is no left part, are intended for control transfer immediately from the main program and are referred to type 2.

The types of the relations are stated by the system and are not analyzed by the programmer directly.

Paradigm is the relation with code 2, containing the special relation unambiguously defining paradigm - name of variable, and the collection of relations representing a set of possible values of variable, if those are generated during saving the data.

Variable. The concept of variable is external in relation to data structure of the model. If is spoken, that some variable or expression containing a variables, **v** accepts value **x**, it means, that in the given moment the substitution defined outside of 4-level structures, containing a pair **v/x**, where **v** is a relation with type 1, 2 or 3, and **x** is a relation with type 0, takes place.

Scheme (scheme of storage). This concept, applicable only to the relations of the 2-nd level, means a sentence containing paradigms and/or their derivatives.

File is the relation of 2-nd level containing as a scheme, and saved data, appropriate to it, i.e. relations of 2-nd level with type 0, structurally similar to the scheme of storage. The units of these relations, respective to paradigms of the scheme, are units of sets, on which these paradigms are defined.

File of rules is the relation of the 3-rd level, containing a set of rules mapping input data of the rules representation program and a special relation defining the time of the last modification of these data and their location.

From the point of view of the description of structural part it is necessary to underline, that any relation of any level is unique and represented only by one unit of structure.

3 Manipulation Part, the Language for Record of Inference Rules

Manipulation part of the model is constructed on the basis of the language for record of rules and the concept of interpretation of the relations.

Before to describe the language for record of inference rules it is necessary to be clarified itself with actions in relation to units of 4-level structure of data or, taking into account, that each unit of structure we have defined above as relation, to define actions with the relations, which are allowed in the model. I intentionally do not speak 'operation' to not fool the reader concerning parallels in nomenclature between relational databases or logic programming and offered data model. It fails to avoid such parallels nevertheless completely, therefore, as well as in case of the description of a structural part, it is necessary to notice, that entered here concepts and constructions resemble, as a rule, only outwardly constructions of relational DBMS or logic programming (see, for example, [6]).

So, the actions with the relations, which are allowed in considered data model, if not to take into consideration service utilities realizing, for example, operations, similar 'garbage-collect', are *creation* or *writing*, *deleting* and *interpretation* of the relations. If the sense of first two actions is obvious, 'interpretation' requires additional definitions.

Interpretation of the relations. During interpretation each of the relations, except for elementary, is unroll, i.e. it is represented by a collection of sequences of the making relations, with simultaneous substitution of values of variables.

The further operations depend on a level of the relation:

- The rules recursively define a sequence of interpretations of the relations of 2-nd level, i.e. sentences. Any of sentences, depending on a system return code, initiate recursive search of derivative rules, in which this sentence represents itself as a head of a rule.
- The executable sentences initiate execution of some controlling operation with the control transfer to program unit (method of some class), given by the first sequent of the making relations, then the appropriation of values of variables defined in sentence is made. At interpretation of non-executable sentences the appropriation of values of variables is carried out only. Besides setting a system return code, which is parsed during interpretation of rules, completes the interpretation of any sentence.
- The words are unrolling to sequences of characters or elementary numbers, which are divided, as a rule, by blanks.

Now about the language for record of rules. I shall once again be repeated, that the described here language does not claim to a rank of the language of logic programming. It is the language partially procedural. It allows the programmer to work with objects through their properties and methods, giving possibility to set algorithms of events processing. The language has arisen as a means of compact representation of the relations of 4-level dynamic structure; its syntax is being non-separable from the main concepts of the data model and in many respects is defined by them. Certainly, some features of the language described are a special case of concrete realization, but give representation about principles of its construction.

The following agreements are accepted for the record of rules.

Here the word is a sequence of letters, digits and symbols limited by separators. As separators, the codes of the beginning and extremity of a line, blanks, single characters **!"(),/:;=<>?\[]|{}** are used (point and sign _ are not separators). The sequences of characters taken in unary quotes ' ' are also considered as words. In double quotes the sequences of words are specified taking into account the separators. All words enclosed in quotes are considered as constants.

The sign # has a special assignment. This sign always precedes the names of subroutines/ functions. If the first character of the name is large - subroutine/ function is considered as a standard one.

The sign $ in first position specifies, that a name of 'non-executable function' further follows. This construction is entered with the purpose of obvious identification of non-executable sentences.

Any word not enclosed in quotes or which is not special, is interpreted as the name of a variable, being global if the word starts with a large character, otherwise current.

Special sequences **/* */** identify the comments, and **== != := += -= >= <=** set the relations causing calls to standard subroutines/functions.

For any word in quotes, double or unary, the attempt is made to present it as a number (format is defined by external representation by rules accepted in C), at failure the word is considered a character one.

The separators, as well as relations, are grouped as follows:

; is a separator of the 3-rd level, i.e. any rule should be terminated in a semicolon.
->, | are the separators of the 2-nd level, they select sentences and groups of sentences, besides **->** separates the left part of the rule from the right, and the sign **|** separates the conditions.

The level of the relations selected with brackets **( ) < > [ ] { }**, depends on the context. The remaining separators are considered as separators of the 1-st level.

The brackets always should be paired. The parentheses **( )** define the relations having the code 0, the angular brackets **< >** - code 1, the square brackets **[ ]** - code 2 and the braces **{ }** - code 3 respectively.

The executable relations of level 2 always look like:

#xxx (z1 z2 ... zN),

where **xxx** is the name of the subroutine/function, and **(z1 z2 ... zN)** is the relation with code 0 of the arbitrary number of the 1-st level relations (parameters of the subroutine/ function).

The non-executable relations of the 2-nd level look like:

$xxx (z1 z2 ... zN).

As compared to the executable relations, they do not call control transfer to any subroutine/ function, but initiate recursive search of derivative rules as the executable relations do.

The rule in a general view is written as:

***A* -> *B* | *C*;**

Here ***A*** is the left part of the rule, ***B*** is the right part, ***C*** is the conditions of transition from ***A*** to ***B***. Sometimes some parts can be absent. The expression:

***A* ->;**

sets the data defined immediately in the file of rules. And the expression:

$$\rightarrow B \mid C;$$

means the transition to ***B*** at execution of conditions ***C*** immediately from the main program. The unconditional transition from ***A*** to ***B*** and unconditional control transfer from the main program respectively is possible also:

$$A \text{ -> } B;$$
$$\text{ -> } B;$$

A in a general view can be represented as the sequence

$$A1, A2, A3,$$

Where *A1* is the head of rule - scheme of sentence A1;
A2 is scheme A2, defining some file, or list {A2};
A3 is a logical function defining the conditions of transition.

The relation (*A1*, *A2*, *A3*) represents an inverse rule. If ***A*** has more than one term, the expression is being treated as the check on existence (or search) of data of file *A2*, which variables accept values corresponding to the relation *A1*. The search can be completed immediately after finding the first variant, satisfying the criteria of the data search, or be fulfilled cyclically for all possible values. In the latter case A2 is enclosed in curly brackets. At transition without check on existence *A2* and *A3* are absent.

B in a general view can be represented as a sequence

$$B1, B2, \ldots, Bn.$$

Here each of the constituent relations of level 2 is a sentence, either scheme, or list containing the unique scheme. The list {Bi} in this case is an outcome of exhaustive search of all possible values of uncertain variables or their combinations for the non-executable relations; for the executable relations it means the recurrence of operation.

As a result of executable relation the control is being transmitted sequentially to expressions *B1*, *B2*, etc. Normal return code is code 1. The interpretation of the sequence can be stopped, if one of *Bi* is ended with a return code 0 or -1. -1 is treated as interruption. For the executable relations the interruptions of the derivative relations are analyses by the executed unit itself. For non-executable lists {Bi} the completion of one of the components with code -1 results in leaving the list with the same return code.

Each of Bi relations can initiate the process of search of rules, in which A1 corresponds to Bi. And, for cutting the review of possible variants of prolongation, the search is started only in the case if Bi defines the non-executable relation or accesses to the subroutine/function completing by the code >= 0410[*] (initially 0411-0427 were treated as function keys codes of the Unix-terminal).

C represents the logical expression

L(C1,C2,...,Cn),

in which *Ci* is a sentence or a scheme, and the logic operations AND, OR are set by brackets:

AND - ( ) or **< >**,
OR - [ ] or { },

and in the case of usage of brackets **( )** or **{ }** the procedure for conditions testing is being determined by the order of record of sentences. The negation NOT is being set by the function of the 2-nd level **!** or **#Not**.

Transmission of values of variables. At the relations' interpretation the transmission of values of variables to the following relation is one of the key moments defining the form of algorithm record with the help of the language described. From one relation to another the values of variables are being transmitted as tables of variables. For each of processes two types of the tables are generated: the table of global variables TBLVAR and the tables of current variables TBLVar. TBLVAR is always unique - it allows transmitting values of variables from relation to relation irrespective of their enclosure degree. The tables of current variables TBLVar are generated for each executable relation separately.

The modification of the table of global variables or creation of a derived table of current variables happens during the interpretation of a relation. For global variables the changes are brought in the same table, further the updated variant is to be used, for current variables the changes have concern only the tables generated (or derived).

Depending on the location of an executable relation in the relation specifying the rule, there are two ways of filling in the tables derived:

1-st, when the relation is the constituent of sequence Bi; the derived tables are generated only on the basis of the parent table irrespective of outcomes of execution of other relations Bi.

2-nd, when the relation is the constituent of sequence Ci; in this case the derived table is unique and coincides with the initial table. All changes, which have been brought in the table at execution of other Ci relations, influence its current state.

Note. During the search the variables are stated according to the search relation A1 and are being updated by values, which they accept in file A2.

Subroutines / functions. Every 1-st term of sentences written as **#xxx**, is interpreted as a call to the subroutine (function) with name **xxx**. If the name of the subroutine starts with a

---

[*] Certainly, the concrete values of constants depend on realization, but are brought to not lose integrity of presentation.

large character, it is considered global (or standard) and is being searched among functions executing by the system kernel.

For more complete representation I shall bring, not pressing in details, enumeration of subroutines/functions of system level realized by the author in the prototype of the system. Some of them are functions of two arguments (#Belong, #Dec, #Eq, #Fix, #Ge, #Grtdat, #Inc, #Le, #Ltldat, #Move, #Ne, #Part, #Spawn), others have one argument (#Date, #List, #SystemR, #Time, #Tstdat), there are subroutines/functions not having arguments (#Break, #Delete, #Exit, #Not, #Save).

Such subroutines/functions as #Delete, #Not, #Save have no arguments too, but play the role of functions of the 2-nd level. Their operation spreads to a sentence, standing in sequences Bi or Ci immediately after these functions. These functions are represented respectively as:

#Delete:
! or #Not:
#Save:

Functions #Dec, #Eq, #Fix, #Ge, #Inc, #Le, #Ne besides the standard form #xxx (z1 z2) can also be written also respectively:

```
#Dec (z1 z2)   as   (z1 -= z2) ,
#Eq (z1 z2)    as   (z1 == z2) ,
#Fix (z1 z2)   as   (z1 := z2) ,
#Ge (z1 z2)    as   (z1 >= z2) ,
#Inc (z1 z2)   as   (z1 += z2) ,
#Le (z1 z2)    as   (z1 <= z2) ,
#Ne (z1 z2)    as   (z1 != z2).
```

The return codes of subroutines/functions accept one of three values: 1, 0 and -1, and 1 is treated as an execution of a logical condition, 0 and -1 - as a failure, -1 is considered besides as an interrupt return code.

The absence of outcome of search is treated in model as negation. At the same time there is a possibility to treat negation as result of inference with the help of rule, belonging to the special file of rules. So at simulation of constructions of the natural language belonging to the file of rules *RuleFalse* speaks that the result obtained with the help of this rule is negative.

For more visual representation about an exterior form of algorithm record with usage of the language for record of rules I shall bring an example.

We assume that it is required to organize a record in a text database, using as a key the attribute 'number of article', and sampling data from base on a key value or in ascending order of attributes values, if the key is not given. The file of rules can look as:

```
param = (art+ {s});
T = (param);
QUERY = 0413;
```

```
SAVE = 0423;
DELETE = 0424;

                    /*** Writing in file "Text" ***/

-> (Flag :=0), #win3a(Art), (Flag ==0), $query3b()
                              | (key == QUERY),(Art :=' ');

#win3a(Art) -> $query3a(art+) | (Art !=' '), (art+ :=Art);

#win3a(Art) -> { $query3a(art+),} | (Art ==' ');

$query3a(art+), T -> (Flag :=1), (Old := param), #win3b(param);

$query3b() -> (Old :=" "), #win3b(param) | (Art !=' '),(art+ :=Art);

#win3b(param) -> #Save: T, (Old := param) | (key == SAVE),
                                            (Old ==" ");

#win3b(парам) -> $query3d(), $query3c(param)
                    | (key == SAVE), Old !=" "), (param != Old);

$query3d() -> #Delete: T | (param := Old);

$query3c(param) -> #Save: T, (Old := param);

#win3b(param) -> #Delete: T, #Break() | (key == DELETE);
```

One of the major features of algorithm representation with usage of the language of inference rules is that there is no necessity of the external description for data structure in base. The first five sentences of the given text set substitutions and are introduced only with the purpose to the greater readability of algorithm, and substitution T = (param); underlines that the structure of the scheme of storage is identical to the structure of parameters of the window win3b.

Setting the system variable key should be provided by the programmer at realization of functions processing events on pressing corresponding keys with the usage of resources of DBMS program interface. (The creation of the interface units easily gives in to automation. In variant for Unix V.3 the possibility of creation of units with the usage of extended text editor was realized.)

In the given text the first rule states that immediately from the head program, at pressing the key QUERY with simultaneous assignment of value ' ' (empty) for global variable Art, the following sentences become active sequentially:

(Flag :=0) - reset of global variable Flag in 0;

#win3a(Art) - control transfer to the unit (subroutine/function), realizing the program interface with the window (form) win3a;

(Flag ==0) - check of Flag on 0;

$query3b() - non-executable sentence generating transition to derivative rules.

The 2-nd rule defines the transition from the unit of window interface win3a to non-executable sentence $query3a(art+). The condition of transition is nonblank value Art, which is stated at fulfillment of unit win3a. Simultaneously this value is assigned to the local variable art+ (presence of the sign + means that the inverse references of appropriate paradigm are ordered on increasing of values of variable).

The most essential for understanding of logic of DBMS functioning are the 3-rd and the 4-th rules.

The construction {$query3a (art+),} means initiation of transition to derivative rules sequentially for all values art+.

$query3a(art+), T is the inverse rule realizing the search of sentences on the value of variable art+ according to the scheme of storage T (in view of substitutions (art+ {s})).

It is necessary to remark, that the field *Text* is described as {s} that is the list of values of s (that in the given example is not necessary, as the search on the contents is absent).

The functions of saving and deleting are carried out with the help of functions of the 2-nd level and are being written accordingly as #Save: T and #Delete: T .

The standard function #Break() returns the code -1 to unit win3b in case the deleting is produced.

4 Integrity Part

By reviewing problems of data integrity let's limit us to integrity of the direct and inverse references for each of the relations that in many aspects is sufficient condition of integrity in the language model of data. We shall understand integrity of the references as not only correspondence of values of sequences to the defined range and nature, but also correspondence of the direct references to the inverse references of the composite relations. Except for codes (and types) of relations the structure of information of the model has double reserve on the data, i.e. at loss of the data of some relation the information on its direct and inverse references can be restored on direct and inverse references of other relations. This property of data structure allows speaking about stability to external effects caused by failures of the equipment. Moreover, as shows experience, even heavy refusals that are not reducing to loss of blocks the virtual storage can be corrected. The truth in this case part of the data can as though be ‘forgotten’, but the serviceability of the system as a whole is kept and allows for restoring of information to use procedures of logical level of integrity, it is unconditional, if similar were stipulated by a database designer.

In the prototype of DBMS, realizing main feature of language model of data, the author implemented the mechanism of rollback (any degree of enclosure), using journal data about writing, deleting and change of the relations and the feature of data structure, that the information on the references in working regime from the system is not erased at deleting (setting to zero) of the relation. Besides as additional tools the procedures of integrity check and compression (exception of the remote relations and their references) of data were worked out.

5 Realization

The features of realization are defined by necessity of solution of the task of effective processing and information retrieval from storage medium, in which the data are represented in implicit form and less compactly in comparison with traditional ways of organization. And, as a rule, all algorithms of search and interpretation of the relations on the nature are recursive and from execution time of each of steps not only the time of common response of the system depends, but the expediency of usage of similar way for representation of information does also.

Perhaps, a main feature of implementation of a DBMS constructed by principles of language model of data is usage of the mechanism of shared segments of memory (SHM) for operating system Unix or the File Mapping mechanism for operating system Windows as storage medium of information.

This mechanism realizes the idea of non-volatile virtual storage with the characteristics of access, being the best, as a rule, in comparison with access to the file system, that allows to refuse completely from the input-output system calls at programming of DBMS kernel functions. Besides, the process connecting a shared segment, allocates it in the limits of 4 Gbytes range of addresses for Unix or 2 Gbytes range for Windows NT. When programming the system kernel the addresses can be stipulated and fixed beforehand. In the prototype of DBMS based on principles of described data model the memory address simultaneously fulfills the function of the relation code or the type of the array. So, for example, in implementation for Unix the relations of the database are allocated always on the negative semi axis of addresses and the references to the positive one, herewith the relations of more high levels having smaller addresses.

The similar system solutions have allowed obtaining more high-speed load modules realizing basic functions, at the expense of primary usage of the computer instructions with direct addressing instead of indirect.

Taking into account inevitable multiple searches at usage of recursive algorithms, the procedure of search of the relation and in particular of search under scheme is key for language model in the problem of efficiency of data processing. The data structure of model assumes mandatory ordering of the direct references on values of relations' addresses, that in a finite case allows to reduce procedures of search to the search in the ordered sequences, to as most effective one [4]. The model allows also introducing rescheduling on probability at the expense of change of location of the relations (naturally with external utilities outside of a running cycle) with the purpose of improvement of the temporary characteristics of access. At the expense of structural solutions of model, and also careful improvement of multiply used program units the author managed to receive the temporary characteristics of data access, as a rule, best in comparison with modern relational DBMS even without additional rescheduling.

Concerning compilation of files of rules. The programmer writes the rules realizable in the system in one or several text files. The filename is specified as the parameter at call of the application. The records of this file are translated in the relations of the database. The translation of records is made at initialization of application under initiative of the system and only in case the temporary characteristics of creation/modification of the rules' file or the load module of application have varied.

6 To Problem about Natural Language

The language model of data representation has independent value, but it has arisen first of all from attempts of realization of retrieval systems of information represented on natural language, therefore features of representation of constructions of the natural language in the model have a special value.

In [7] the author entered treatment of natural language as a system of inference rules. In the present paper the problems of teaching and retrieval of information represented on natural language are considered in more detail certainly from positions of the language model of data.

So, we shall consider possible combinations, defined in some database between sentences of natural language, of sort:

<sentence> <question> <answer>

or

<condition> <consequence>,
<condition 1> <condition 2> <consequence>

as rules for the first case of sort:

$$q, s \rightarrow a; \qquad (1)$$

where s – some statement,

q – question,

a – answer.

(The inverse order q, s is defined by features of representation of information in the system, when the rule's head, on which the recursive search is carried out, allocates on the first place.)

For cause-effect relations are accordingly:

$$s \rightarrow a;$$
$$s1, s2 \rightarrow a;$$

Let's consider from positions of language model the possibility of implementation of algorithms of teaching on 'syntactical' similarity and of search.

Teaching

We admit, that the rule *(1)* is showed as a sample.

In the beginning the rule, similar sample, is searched in the system. This rule we shall present as

$$Q, S \rightarrow A \mid C; \qquad (2)$$

Here Q, S, A are schemes having the same amount of terms, as appropriate sentences q, s, a.

C requires explanation. ***C*** is the scheme, playing role of conditions of transition and containing pairs of paradigms and allowed combinations of their terms.

$$([c_1][c_2])\begin{bmatrix}(c_{11} & c_{21})\\(c_{12} & c_{22})\\ & \dots & \\(c_{1n} & c_{2n})\end{bmatrix}$$

c_{1n}, c_{2n} represent, as a rule, in the natural language (in particular Russian) the forms of the same word.

The new rule *(1)* supplements the rule *(2)* in that and only in that case if each of sentences of sample *(1)* contains no more than one word, not inhering to the respective paradigm of rule *(2)* in view of execution of conditions ***C***. For example, for:

$$s_1\ s_2\ \dots\ s_k\ \dots\ s_n$$

$$S_1\ S_2\ \dots\ S_k\ \dots\ S_n$$

for all $s_{i\neq k}$ $s_{i\neq k} \in S_{i\neq k}$ or $s_{i\neq k} = S_{i\neq k}$, but $s_k \notin S_k$ and $s_k \neq S_k$, whether depending on that is S_k a paradigm, it is supplemented by term s_k, or created new paradigm, containing S_k and s_k. Here $s_1, s_2, \dots s_k, \dots s_n$ is words of sentence ***s***, $S_1, S_2, \dots S_k, \dots S_n$ is the making terms (word and paradigms) of scheme ***S***.

In case the rule, similar to the sample, is not retrieved, the latter supplements the file of rules *RuleTrue* and thus is fixed in the system. The deleting of the rule is carried out as deleting of a relation or at impossibility of such deleting at the expense of reference of the rule to the file *RuleFalse*.

Search of the answer

We admit, that the information is being stored as set of records {s} and the question *q* is showed. The task of the system is the search of the answer *a* (or set of the answers), such, that

$$q,\ S \rightarrow a;$$

or being a direct corollary of *a*. *S* is the scheme being a recursive inference of sentence (or combination of sentences) from {s} provided that the variables accept values according to sentences {s}. The answer can be retrieved naturally only, if the system contains enough inference rules obtained during preliminary teaching. And during search the rules, inhering to the file of rules *RuleTrue*, participate and the rules from *RuleFalse* are leaving out.

On the language for record of inference rules the fragments of algorithms of teaching and search look as:

```
QUERY1 = 0411;
SAVE = 0423;
DELETE = 0424;
                                        /*** Teaching ***/

    -> #win11(s1 q1 a1) | (key == QUERY1),
                                   (s1 := "Tom read ( a book ) ."),
                                   (q1 := "who read ( a book ) ?"),
                                   (a1 := "Tom read ( a book ) .");
#win11(s1 q1 a1) - > #winR() | (key == SAVE), #add_rule0(q1 s1 a1);

#win11(s1 q1 a1) -> #winQ () | (key ==DELETE), #del_rule0(q1 s1 a1);

                                             ......

T = (art+ {s});
QUERY4 = 0414;
SEARCH = 0427;

                                    /*** Semantic search ***/

-> #win4a(q) | (key == QUERY4), (q := "who read a book ?");

#win4a (q) -> (Flag :=0), #trans4(q s),
            (Flag ==0), #win2b ("I do not know." " ")
                                          | (key == SEARCH);

#trans4(q s), { T,} -> (Art := art+), (Q :=q), #trans3 ({s} s1);

#trans3 ({s} s1) -> #trans2 (Q s1 a);

#trans2 (Q s1 a) -> (Flag :=1), #win2b(a Art);

                                             ......
```

Here variable s1 corresponds to the entered sentence, q1 - to the question, a1 - to the answer to the question. The values assignment for variables s1, q1, a1 is made for visualization. The parentheses select the steady collocations at teaching; it gives more large generalizations at modification of the schemes. The subroutine/function #add_rule0(q1 s1 a1) realizes the search of similar rules, creation or modification of the schemes of rules and addition of paradigms values. This subroutine creates also direct references (references of belonging) of created schemes to the rules file *RuleTrue*. The subroutine/function #del_rule0(q1 s1 a1) deletes the relations corresponding to the rule entered, and at impossibility of their deleting from the generalized schemes of rules, sets the given rule into the file *RuleFalse*.

#trans4(q s) realizes a search of sentences satisfying the condition of search, that is a search of sentences s, which together with a question q correspond to any inverse rule. And not only sentences, directly responding to the inquiry, are taken into account, but also sentences them generating.

#trans3({s} s1) selects the sentences immediately contained in the article retrieved, and also generates sentences being derivative from the article sentences and their combinations.

#trans2 (Q s1 a) searches the rules, satisfied by pair Q s1 (here Q is the initial question, s1 is the sentence generated by subroutine/function trans3) and forms the answer.

Once again I shell underline, that the system allows to generate not only direct answers, but also answers being derivative as for the questions (at the expense of the analysis of inverse rules) and for the answers as well (using direct rules). And at teaching, as in the example above, the generalized rules, including not only presented samples but also the rules similar to them, can be formed [see 7].

As the conclusion I want to state two reasons.

First that from the point of view of object-oriented programming the database responding criteria of the language model can be consider as the active environment of interaction objects.

And second that the experiments, which have been carried out by the author with the prototype of a DBMS, realizing main idea of language model of data, direct involuntarily on thought, that essence links of objects of the real world the model can represent as links of points of space of recursive rules.

References

[1] Aho A.V., Ullmann J.D. “The theory of parsing, translation and compiling”, Mir, Moscow, 1978.

[2] Codd E.F. "A Relational Model of Data for Large Shared Data Banks", CACM 13, 6 (June 1970). Is repeatedly published in "Milestones of Research-Selected Papers 1958-1982", CACM 26, 1 (January 1983).

[3] Codd E.F. "Derivability, Redundancy, and Consistency of Relations Stored in Large Data Banks", IBM Research Report RJ599 (August 19th, 1969).

[4] Knuth D.E, “The art of computer programming”, v.3, Sorting and Searching, Mir, Moscow, 1978.

[5] Kuznetsov S.D. “Foundations of modern databases”, informational - analytical materials of Center of Information Technologies, URL=http://www.citmgu.ru/.

[6] Nilsson U., Maluszynski J. "Logic: Programming and Prolog (2ED)”, 1995. Available from URL=http://archive.comlab.ox.ac.uk/logic-prog.html.

[7] Novikov V.M. “File mapping Rule-based DBMS and Natural Language Processing”, 2001. Available in the Computer Science archive under cs.CL/0106016 URL=http://xxx.lanl.gov/list/cs/0106.

In: Artificial Intelligence and Computer Scienceh
Editor: Susan Shannon, pp. 217-233
ISBN 1-59454-411-5

Chapter 9

DECISIONS, DELIBERATION, AND AGENT TYPES CDT – QDT – BDI – 3APL – BOID

Mehdi Dastani*
Utrecht University
Leendert van der Torre†
CWI

Abstract

In this paper we investigate the relation between decisions, deliberation and agent types. In particular, we are interested how deliberation leads to decisions, and how agent types classify patterns of deliberation. We therefore consider Classical and Qualitative Decision Theories (CDT and QDT), the Beliefs-Desire-Intention (BDI) model, 3APL systems, and Belief-Obligation-Intention-Desire (BOID) systems. The first two are based on a decision rule which expresses a notion of rationality, whereas the latter three are based on deliberation processes and agent types.

1 Introduction

In recent years the interest in models of decision making for autonomous agents has increased. A reason for this growing interest is the notion of agent autonomy which is often defined as the ability of agents to decide which actions to perform at any moment in time. Different proposals have been made, rooted in different research traditions and objectives. Each proposal explains the decision making behavior of agents in terms of different sets of underlying concepts. For example, classical decision theory [22] explains the decision making behavior in terms of a probability and a utility function, and a decision rule. Other approaches criticize the representation of classical decision theory as being non-practical

*E-mail address: mehdi@cs.uu.nl
†E-mail address: torre@cwi.nl

and unrealistic. According to them it is hard to translate all factors that influence the decision making behavior of an agent in terms of two functions that assign numbers to actions and states. In contrast, they aim at explaining the decision making behavior of agents in terms of qualitative concepts such as preference and likelihood ordering, or cognitive concepts such as beliefs, desires, intentions, and obligations. These concepts are claimed to be intuitive and easily accessible. In these approaches, the problem of deciding an action to perform is split into two problems. The first problem is to decide which goal should be achieved, and the second problem is to decide which action to perform to achieve the selected goal. The first problem is called goal selection and the second problem is called planning. The problem with these approaches is the lack of a clear formulation of decision rules that combines the underlying qualitative concepts to decide which action to perform at any moment in time.

There are many conceptualizations and formalizations of decision making. In [8] we compare classical decision theory with qualitative decision theory, knowledge-based systems and belief-desire-intention models developed in artificial intelligence and agent theory. They all contain representations of information and motivation. Examples of informational attitudes are probability distributions, qualitative abstractions of probabilities, knowledge, and beliefs. Examples of motivational attitudes are utility functions, qualitative abstractions of utilities, goals, and desires. Each of them encodes a set of alternatives to be chosen from. This ranges from a small predetermined set, a set of decision variables, through logical formulas, to branches of a tree representing events through time. Moreover, they have a way of formulating how a decision is made. Classical and qualitative decision theory focus on the optimal decisions represented by a decision rule. Knowledge-based systems and belief-desire-intention models focus on a model of the representations used in decision making, inspired by cognitive notions like belief, desire, goal and intention. Relations among these concepts express an agent type, which constrains the deliberation process. We also consider the relation between decision processes and intentions, and the relation between game theory and norms and commitments.

In this paper we are interested in the relation between decisions, deliberation and agent types. In particular, we are interested in the question:

> How does deliberation based on agent types lead to decisions?

This question breaks down in three sub-questions:

1. What is an agent decision? To answer this question we discuss different approaches and concepts used to explain the decision making behavior of agents. The first is classical decision theory [15, 22] and the second it qualitative extension (QDT) [1, 17].

2. What is agent deliberation and how does it lead to a decision? To answer this question we discuss two other approaches. The third approach we discuss is based on an abstract model of the mental attitudes of an agent: beliefs, desires and intentions (BDI) [2, 5, 19]. The fourth (3APL) is similar to BDI except that the decision rules is

replaced by a process called the deliberation process. It is this process that determine which actions should be performed for a given set of underlying cognitive concepts.

3. How do agent types classify patterns of deliberation? The fifth approach we discuss to answer this question is also based on mental attitudes extended with obligations (BOID) [3].

The layout of this paper is as follows. First we discuss decisions in classical and qualitative decision theory. Then, we discuss the BDI approach, 3APL systems and deliberation process. In the last section we consider the role of agent types in Rao and Georgeff's BDI approach and the BOID approach.

2 Decisions

2.1 Classical Decision Theory

In classical decision theory, a decision is a choice made by some entity of an action from a set of alternatives. It has nothing to say about actions – either about their nature or about how a set of them becomes available to the decision maker. A decision is good if it is an alternative that the decision maker believes will prove at least as good as other alternative actions. Good decisions are formally characterized as actions that maximize expected utility, a notion involving both belief and goodness. See [12] or [15, 22] for further explanations.

Definition 1 *Let A stand for the set of actions or alternatives. With each action, a set of outcomes is associated. Let W stand for the set of all possible worlds or outcomes. Let U be a measure of outcome value that assigns a utility $U(w)$ to each outcome $w \in W$, and let P be a measure of the probability of outcomes conditional on actions, with $P(w|a)$ denoting the probability that outcome w comes about after taking action $a \in A$ in the situation under consideration.*

The expected utility $EU(a)$ of an action $a \in A$ is the average utility of the outcomes associated with the alternative a, weighing the utility of each outcome by the probability that the outcome results from the alternative a, that is, $EU(a) = \sum_{w \in W} U(w)P(w|a)$. A rational decision maker always maximizes expected utility, i.e. he makes decisions according to the MEU decision rule.

Decision theory is an active research area within economics, and the number of extensions and subtleties is too large to address here. Several other decision rules have been investigated, including qualitative ones, such as maximin, minimax, minregret etc. Finally, classical decision theory has been extended in several ways to deal for example with multiple objective, sequential decisions, multiple agents, distinct notions of risk, etcetera.

Decision theory has become one of the main foundations of economic theory due to so-called representation theorems. Representation theorems, such as the most famous one of Savage [22], typically prove that each decision maker obeying certain innocent looking postulates (about weighted choices) acts *as if* he applies the MEU decision rule with some probability distribution and utility function. Thus, he does not have to be aware of it, and his utility function does not have to represent selfishness. In fact, exactly the same is true for altruistic decision makers. They also act as if they maximize expected utility; they just have another utility function.

2.2 Qualitative Decision Theory

Qualitative decision theory relaxes the assumption of classical decision theory that the decision making agent is able to weigh all possible alternative courses of action before choosing one of them. In realistic situations decision making agents are resource bounded in the sense that they have partial information and do not have resources to compare the utility of possible states. The research on qualitative decision theory aims therefore to develop representation and reasoning schemes for partial information and generic preferences to represent probabilities of states and generic preferences over those states [12]. Typically qualitative orderings are introduced that represent the likelihood (probability) and desirability (utility) of states. In contrast to classical decision theory where a decision rule such as maximum expected utility determines the course of actions, in qualitative decision theory and in the presence of incomplete information, the course of actions are decided based on various strategies such as maximize potential gain or minimize potential loss [1].

According to Doyle and Thomason [12, p.58], quantitative representations of probability and utility and procedures for computing with these representations, do provide an adequate framework for manual treatment of very simple decision problems, but they are less successful in more realistic cases. For example, they argue that classical decision theory does not address decision making in unforeseen circumstances, it offers no means for capturing generic preferences, it provides little help in modeling decision makers who exhibit discomfort with numeric trade-offs, and it provides little help in effectively representing and reasoning about decisions involving broad knowledge of the world.

Doyle and Thomason argue for various formalization tasks. They distinguish the following new tasks: formalisms to express generic probabilities and preferences, properties of decision formulations, reasons and explanations, revision of preferences, practical qualitative decision-making procedures and agent modeling. Moreover, they argue that hybrid representation and reasoning with quantitative and qualitative techniques, as well as reasoning within context, deserve special attention. Many of these issues are related to subjects studied in artificial intelligence. It appears that researchers now realize the need to reconnect the methods of AI with the qualitative foundations and quantitative methods of economics.

Some first results have been obtained in the area of reasoning about uncertainty, a subdomain of artificial intelligence which mainly attracts researchers with a background in reasoning about defaults and beliefs. Often the formalisms of reasoning about uncertainty are re-applied in the area of decision making. Thus, typically uncertainty is not represented by a probability function, but by a plausibility function, a possibilistic function, Spohn-type rankings, etc. Another consequence of this historic development is that the area is much more mathematically oriented than the planning community or the BDI community.

A typical example is Pearl's qualitative decision theory, in which decisions are based on abstractions of probability functions, and which is extended with a model of causality. Boutilier's logic of qualitative decision theory formalizes decisions as a set of controllable propositions. However, he introduces another concept in his logic, which makes the logic closer to the kind of logics we consider in the following section on deliberation and agent types. This new concept is the concept of goal. This is explained in the following section.

2.3 Introduction of Goals in Decision Theory

Goals serve a dual role in most planning systems, capturing aspects of both desires toward states and commitment to pursuing that state [10]. In goal-based planning, adopting a proposition as a goal commits the agent to find some way to accomplish the goal, even if this requires adopting some sub-goals that may not correspond to desirable propositions themselves [9]. In realistic planning situations goals can be achieved to varying degrees, and frequently goals cannot be achieved completely. Context-sensitive goals are formalized with basic concepts from decision theory [1, 9, 13]. In general, goal-based planning must be extended with a mechanism to choose between which goals must be adopted.

Boutilier [1] proposes a logic and possible worlds semantics for representing and reasoning with qualitative probabilities and utilities, and suggests several strategies for qualitative decision making based on this logic. His semantics is not quantitative (like CDT), but purely qualitative. Consequently, the maximum expected utility (MEU) decision rule is replaced by qualitative rules like Wald's criterion. The conditional preference is captured by a preference ordering (an ordinal value function) that is defined on possible worlds. The preference ordering represents the desirability of worlds. Similarly, probabilities are captured by an ordering, called normality ordering, on possible worlds representing their likelihood.

Definition 2 *The possible worlds semantics for this logic is based on models of the form* $M = \langle W, \leq_P, \leq_N, V\rangle$ *where* W *is a set of worlds (outcomes),* $\leq_P$ *is a transitive and connected preference ordering relation on* W*,* $\leq_N$ *is a transitive and connected normality ordering relation on* W*, and* V *is a valuation function.*

In Boutilier's logic, conditional preferences can be represented by means of ideal operator I. We have that a model M satisfies the formula $I(\varphi|\psi)$ if the preferred or best or minimal ψ worlds are φ worlds. For example, let u be the proposition 'agent has umbrella' and r be the proposition 'it rains', then $I(u|r)$ expresses that in the most preferred rain-worlds the agent has an umbrella. Similarly, probabilities are represented in this logic by means of a normative conditional connective $\Rightarrow$. For example, let w be the proposition 'the agent is wet' and r be the proposition 'it rains', then $r \Rightarrow w$ expresses that the agent is wet at the most normal rain-worlds. Its semantics is derived from Hansson's deontic logic with modal operator O for obligation [14].[1] A similar type of semantics is used by Lang [16] for a modality D to model desire. An alternative approach represents conditional modalities by

[1] In default logic, an exception is a digression from a default rule. Similarly, in deontic logic an offense is a digression from the ideal.

so called 'ceteris paribus' preferences, using additional formal machinery to formalize the notion of 'similar circumstances', see e.g. [11, 13, 23, 24].

In general, a goal is any proposition that the agent attempts to make true. A rational agent is assumed to attempt to reach the most preferred worlds consistent with its default knowledge. Given the ideal operator and the default conditional, a goal is defined as follows.

Definition 3 *Given a set of facts KB, a goal is any proposition* φ *such that*

$$M \models I(\varphi \mid Cl(KB)) \tag{1}$$

where $Cl(KB)$ *is the default closure of the facts KB defined as follows:*

$$Cl(KB) = \{\varphi \mid KB \Rightarrow \varphi\} \tag{2}$$

We assume (for simplicity of presentation) that Cl(KB) is finitely specifiable and take it to be a single propositional sentence.[2]

3 Deliberation

We discuss the BDI approach and a cognitive agent system called 3APL that aims at developing computational specifications for more concrete agents. They illustrate how deliberation can lead to decisions.

3.1 Belief, Desire and Intention (BDI)

A criticism to classical and qualitative decision theory is that they are inadequate for real time applications in dynamic environments. In such applications, the decision making agent should select and execute actions at each moment in time. As the dynamic environment changes either during the selection or the execution of actions, the decision making agent need to deliberate to either reconsider the previously decisions, also called intentions, or continuing the commitment to those decisions (intentions). This deliberation process is argued by Bratman [2] to be crucial to realize stable behavior of decision making agents with bounded resources. This approach has led to BDI systems [19] that extends decision theory with the additional deliberation component called intention.

In BDI systems, the partial information on states is reduced to dichotomous values (0-1); the propositions are believed or not. This abstraction is called the beliefs of the decision making agent. Similarly, the partial information about the objectives of the decision making agent is reduced to dichotomous values (0-1); the propositions are desired or not. This abstraction is called the desires of the decision making agent. Finally, the partial information about the previous decisions, to which the agent is still committed to, is represented by dichotomous values (0-1); the proposition are intended or not.

[2]A sufficient condition for this property is that each "cluster" of equally normal worlds in $\leq_N$ corresponds to a finitely specifiable theory. This is the case in, e.g., System Z.

3.2 3APL

3APL is a computational specification for cognitive agents. The specification language consists of two parts: the object-level and the meta-level specification language. The expressions of the object-level language specifies the cognitive attitudes of agents such as beliefs, goals, and plans (intentions), and additional ingredients such as actions that can be performed by the agent and reasoning rules that it can apply. The expressions of the meta-level language, also called the deliberation language [6, 7], specify the deliberation process that determines which actions should be performed at each moment in time. These expressions specify many decisions such as which goal to select, which reasoning rules to apply, which plan to execute, if and which goal to revise, and if and which plan to revise.

The deliberation language is a many-sorted language [6, 7]. It includes sorted terms that refer to object-level entities such as beliefs, goals, actions, plans, and rules, predicates that express relations between terms, and statements that selects goals, plans, reasoning rules, and generate plans or examine the consequences of the plans. For now it is important to illustrate only the statements of the deliberation language through which various types of deliberation activities can be implemented.

Definition 4 *Let s be any sort, t_s be a term of sort s, and V_s be a variable of sort s. The set of basic statements of the deliberation language is defined as follows:*

- $V_s := t_s$
- $selgoal(t_{sg}, f_c, V_{ig})$
  $selint(t_{si}, f_c, V_{ii})$
  $selplan(t_{sp}, f_c, V_{ip})$
  $selrule(t_{sxrr}, t_{sx}, V_{ixrr})$ *for* $x \in \{g, i, p\}$
- $update(t_{sx}, t_{iy})$ *for* $x, y \in \{b, g, i\}$
  $reviseplan(t_{ip}, t'_{ip})$
- $plan(t_{ii}, t_N)$
  $replan(t_{ip}, t_{spr}, f_c, t_N)$
  $btplan(t_{ip}, t_{spr}, t_N)$
  $explan(t_{ip})$

The set of deliberation statements is defined as follows:

- *Basic statements are deliberation statements*
- *If $\varphi \in DF$ is a deliberation formula, and α and β are deliberation statements, then the following are deliberation statements:*
  $\alpha ; \beta$,
  `IF` φ `THEN` α `ELSE` β,
  `WHILE` φ `DO` α

The first statement $V_s := t_s$ is designed to assign a sorted term t_s to a variable V_s of the same sort. The following statements are all selecting some item from a particular set of those items. The statement $selgoal(t_{sg}, f_c, V_{ig})$ selects an individual goal from the set of goals denoted by the term t_{sg}. The term denoting the selected individual goal is assigned to variable V_{ig}. The function f_c maps goals to boolean values indicating whether the goal formula satisfies the criterium c. The statement $selint(t_{si}, f_c, V_{ii})$ selects an individual intention from the set of intentions denoted by the term t_{si}. The term denoting the selected individual intention is assigned to variable V_{ii}. The function f_c indicates whether the intention satisfies the criterium c. The statement $selplan(t_{sp}, f_c, V_{ip})$ selects an individual plan from the set of plans denoted by the term t_{sp}. The term denoting the selected plan should satisfy criterion f_c and is assigned to the variable V_{ip}. The statement $selrule(t_{sxrr}, t_{sx}, V_{ixrr})$ selects a rule from the set of (goal, intention, or plan) reasoning rules denoted by the terms t_{sxrr} and assigns the term that denotes the rule to the variable V_{ii}. The selected rule should be applicable to a formula from the set denoted by the term t_{sx}.

The criterium c used in the selection functions can be used to define a preference ordering between the goals, intentions, plans and rules. So, in fact this is the place where a relation with qualitative decision theory can be made. The same argument can be made for the other selection functions. The main advantage over the classical decision theoretic approach is that the deliberation uses several independent preference orderings over different concepts. The combination of all these orderings leads to a decision on which action will be performed next. However, unlike decision theory where all factors have to be combined into one function that determines the best action, we explicitly program this combination. Besides this advantage of having all factors explicitly available (and thus easily adjustable) the combination of these factors into a decision can be made situation dependent, therefore allowing for an adjustable preference ordering of the agent.

The statement $update(t_{sx}, t_{iy})$ updates a mental base (belief, goal, or intention base) denoted by the term t_{sx} with the formula denoted by the term t_{iy}. The statement $reviseplan(t_{ip}, t'_{ip})$ removes the plan that is denoted by the term t_{ip} from the plan base, and adds the plan that is denoted by the term t'_{ip} to it.

The final set of basic statements are all related to updating the plans of the agent in some way. The statement $plan(t_{ii}, t_n)$ generates a plan expression with maximum length t_n to achieve intention t_{ii}. The generated plan expression is assigned to the plan base of the agent. The statement $replan(t_{ip}, t_{spr}, f_c, t_N)$ uses the set of planning rules t_{spr} and generates a new plan expression to replace the plan expression t_{ip}. The new plan expression satisfies the criteria f_c and has maximum length t_N. The statement $btplan(t_{ip}, t_{spr}, t_N)$ does the same as replan except that $btplan$ uses an order among planning rules and generates the next plan expression according to that order. Finally, $explan(t_{ip})$ executes the individual plan expression denoted by the term t_{ip}. We assume that the execution of a plan has some external effects. The internal mental effects should be realized using the update statement explicitly.

In this paper, we do not consider the formal semantics of this deliberation language since we are only interested in the implementation of the deliberation process and how autonomous agent properties related to the agent's decision making ability can be implemented. The semantics for this language is an extension of the semantics of the meta-language already presented in [6].

4 Agent Types

Agent types are patterns of deliberation. The most famous ones are the realism and commitment strategies defined in BDI systems. Agent types that are introduced in the BDI tradition can be considered as specification of abstract decision patterns that determine which state can be chosen as the goal state. These decision patterns can be extended in two directions. The first direction is to consider additional cognitive concepts that influence the decision making behavior such as obligation and norms. The goal state can then be chosen not only from desires, but also from obligation or norm states since obligation and norms are external motivational attitudes. Like in the BDI tradition, the set of goal states can be constrained by a number of axioms that determine which states can be chosen as the goal state. Another direction to extend the specification of abstract decision patterns is to consider the specifications of more concrete decision patterns or agent types. The latter extension results in what is called the specification of deliberation process which is usually formulated as a iterative procedure that repeats itself infinitely.

4.1 BDI-CTL

As a typical example of a BDI model, we discuss Rao and Georgeff's initial BDI-CTL logic [19]. In this rather complicated semantics of the BDI-CTL logic, the belief, desire, and intention of decision making agents are represented by the relation $\mathcal{B}$, $\mathcal{D}$, and I, respectively. In BDI-CTL, the formalization of mental states (belief-desire-intention) is extended with Computational Tree Logic CTL and CTL* in order to represent how the mental states of the decision making agent change through time. Time is considered as an abstraction of actions that the agent can perform.

Definition 5 (Semantics of BDI logic [19]) *An interpretation M is defined to be a tuple $M = \langle W, E, T, <, U, \mathcal{B}, \mathcal{D}, I, \Phi \rangle$, where W is the set of worlds, E is the set of primitive event types, T is a set of time points, $<$ a binary relation on time points, U is the universe of discourse, and Φ is a mapping from first-order entities to elements in U for any given world and time point. A situation is a world, say w, at a particular time point, say t, and is denoted by w_t. The relations $\mathcal{B}$, $\mathcal{D}$, and $I \subseteq W \times T \times W$ map the agent's current situation to her beliefs, desire, and intention-accessible worlds, respectively.*

BDI does not involve an explicit notion of actions, but instead models possible events that can take place through time by the branching time. The branching time structure models possible sequences of events and determines the alternative cognitive worlds that an agent can bring about through time. Thus, each branch in the temporal structure represents an alternative the agent can choose. Uncertainty about the effects of actions is not modeled by branching time, but by distinguishing between different belief worlds. In effect, they model all uncertainty about the effects of actions as uncertainty about the present state, a well known representation from decision theory [22]. This translation is discussed at length in [18].

The consequence of the fact that we no longer have pre-orders, like in Boutilier's logic, but only an unstructured set, is that we can now only represent monadic expressions like $B(\varphi)$ and $D(\varphi)$, no longer dyadic expressions like $I(\varphi|\psi)$. We have that a world at a time point of the model satisfies $B(\varphi)$ if φ is true in all belief accessible worlds at the same time point. Since there is no such ordering on the possible worlds in BDI, each desire world can in principle be chosen in BDI as the goal world which need to be achieved. It may be clear that it is not an intuitive idea to select a desire world as the goal world in a random way since desire worlds can be in principle not belief worlds. Selecting a desire world which is not believed results in wishful thinking and thus suggests an unrealistic decision. Therefore, BDI proposes a number of constraints under which each desire world can be chosen as a goal world. These constraints are usually characterized by some axioms called realism, strong realism or weak realism [20, 4].

In particular, the realism constraint states that agent's desire should be consistent with its beliefs. Note that this constraint is the same as in QDT where the goal worlds should be consistent with the belief worlds. Formally, the realism axiom states that the set of desire accessible worlds should be a subset of the set of belief accessible worlds, i.e.

$$B(\varphi) \to D(\varphi)$$

and, moreover, the belief and desire worlds should have identical branching time structure (the same alternatives), i.e.

$$\forall w \forall t \forall w' \text{ if } w' \in \mathcal{D}_t^w \text{ then } w' \in \mathcal{B}_t^w$$

The definition of realism includes an additional axiom to reduce the set of desire worlds and to guarantee that chosen desire world is consistent with the worlds that are already chosen as the goal worlds. Formally, this axiom states that the intention accessible worlds should be a subset of desire accessible worlds, i.e.

$$D(\varphi) \to I(\varphi)$$

and, moreover, the desire and intention worlds should have identical branching time structure (the same alternatives), i.e.

$$\forall w \forall t \forall w' \text{ if } w' \in I_t^w \text{ then } w' \in \mathcal{D}_t^w$$

In addition to these constraints, which are classified as static constraints, there are different types of constraints introduced in BDI resulting in additional agent types. These axioms determine when intentions or previously decided goals should be reconsidered or dropped. In BDI, choosing to drop a goal is thus considered to be as important as choosing a new goal. These constraints, called commitment strategies, involve time and intentions and express the dynamics of decision making. The well-known commitment strategies are 'blindly committed decision making', 'single-minded committed decision making', and 'open-minded committed decision making'. For example, the single-minded commitment strategy states that an agent remains committed to its intentions until either it achieves its corresponding objective or does not believe that it can achieve it anymore.

These static and dynamic properties determine the type of decision making behavior. Thus, in contrast to QDT, where the decision rule is based on the ordering on the possible worlds, in BDI any desire world that satisfies a set of assumed axioms such as realism, can be chosen as the goal world, i.e., BDI systems do not consider decision rules but they consider agent types. Although, there is no such issue as agent type in classical or qualitative decision theory, there are discussions which can be related to agent types. For example, in discussions about risk attitude, often a distinction is made between risk neutral and risk averse.

4.2 BOID

In the BOID approach [3] the actions are decided by first generating the goals that should be achieved, and then planning them. The goals are generated based on the derivation of so-called extensions in default logic [21]. Default logic extends the inference rule modus ponens with two new mechanisms. First, there is a consistency constraint on the inference process, such that rules are applied only if they do not lead to an inconsistency. Second, the application of defeasible rules may result in conflicting outputs and thus in conflicting goal sets. They lead to alternative sets of logic formulas. However, to resolve the conflict we have to consider the whole extension, because agents should consider the effects of goals before they commit to them. In the BOID approach, goal generation is based on prioritized default logic. The specification of goal generation process - the instantiation of a default theory - contains the specification of a set of facts, a set of rules, and the specification of a priority function ρ on the rules. To keep the formal details in this paper to a minimum we assume that individual extensions do not contain disjunctive information, that is, we assume that extensions are sets of positive or negated atomic formulas called literals.

The specification of goal generation process is given in Definition 6. The goal generation process starts with a set of observations *Obs*, which cannot be overridden, and initial sets of default rules for *B*, *O*, *I*, and *D*. The procedure then determines a sequence of sets of extensions $S_0, S_1, \ldots$. The first element in the sequence is the set of observations: $S_0 = \{Obs\}$. A set of extensions S_{i+1} is calculated from a set of extensions S_i by checking for each extension E in S_i whether there are rules that can extend the extension. There can be none, in which case nothing happens. Otherwise each of the consequents of the applicable rules with highest ρ-value are added to the extension separately, to form distinct extensions in S_{i+1}. The operator $Th(S)$ refers to the logical closure of S, and the syntactic operation $Lit(b)$ extracts the set of literals from a conjunction of literals b. In practice not the whole set of extensions is calculated, but only those that are calculated before the agent runs out of resources.

Definition 6 (Generate goal process) *Let $\Delta = \langle Obs, B, O, I, D, \rho \rangle$ be the specification of the goal generation process for propositional logic L, and let an extension E be a set of L literals (an atom or its negation). We say that:*
- a rule $(a \hookrightarrow b)$ is strictly applicable to an extension E, iff $a \in Th(E)$, $b \notin Th(E)$ and $\neg b \notin Th(E)$;
- $\max(E, \Delta) \subseteq B \cup O \cup I \cup D$ is the set of rules $(a \hookrightarrow b)$ strictly applicable to E such that there does not exists a $(c \hookrightarrow d) \in B \cup O \cup I \cup D$ strictly applicable to E with $\rho(c \hookrightarrow d) > \rho(a \hookrightarrow b)$;
- $E \subseteq L$ is an extension for Δ iff $E \in S_n$ and $S_n = S_{n+1}$ for the following procedure:

```
i := 0; S_i := {Obs};
repeat
  S_{i+1} := ∅;
  for all E ∈ S_i do
    if exists (a ↪ b) ∈ B ∪ O ∪ I ∪ D strictly applicable to E then
      for all (a ↪ b) ∈ max(E,Δ) do
        S_{i+1} := S_{i+1} ∪ { E ∪ Lit(w)};
      end for
    else
      S_{i+1} := S_{i+1} ∪ {E};
    end if
  end for
  i:=i+1;
until S_i = S_{i−1};
```

Agent types are used to distinguish, classify and compare agent decision making behavior. In this paper, we consider agent types that are defined in terms of goal generation process. These agent types are based on overriding, such that in realistic agents beliefs override other mental attitudes, and in social agents obligations override desires. Agent types based on goal generation are conflict resolution methods. An agent has a conflict if the goal generation process in Definition 6 derives multiple extensions. A conflict is resolved if the priority function is adapted such that no alternative extensions are generated. A mental attitude conflicts with another mental attitude if two rules from different attitudes are applicable, but applying both leads to an inconsistent set. A rule overrides another rule if it has a higher priority. Finally, agent types based on goal generation are formalized in Definition 7 as constraints on the set of available priority functions. When the process starts the selected priority function obeys the constraints corresponding to the agent type. An agent type is called primitive if it contains only one constraint, and complete if it induces a total strict ordering on the components.

Definition 7 *An agent type based on goal generation is a consistent set of constraints on priority function ρ of the form $X \succ Y$ with $X, Y \in \{B, O, I, D\}$ defined as follows: $\forall rule\_x \in X\ \forall rule\_y \in Y\ \rho(rule\_x) > \rho(rule\_y)$*
A primitive agent type contains a single constraint. A complete agent type is a maximal

consistent set of constraints.

There are twelve primitive agent types, which are listed in Table 1 together with the corresponding constraint. They are ordered in six pairs, each agent type A together with its inverse $\{X \succ Y \mid Y \succ X \in A\}$. An agent type is a set of primitive agent types. For example,

Constraint	Agent type
$B \succ O$ ($O \succ B$)	Realistic with respect to obligations (dogmatic)
$B \succ I$ ($I \succ B$)	Realistic with respect to intentions (over-committed)
$B \succ D$ ($D \succ B$)	Realistic with respect to desires (wishful thinker)
$O \succ I$ ($I \succ O$)	(Un)Stable with respect to obligations
$O \succ D$ ($D \succ O$)	Social (selfish)
$I \succ D$ ($D \succ I$)	(Un)Stable with respect to desires

Table 1: Twelve primitive agent types

the realistic agent type is $\{B \succ O, B \succ I, B \succ D\}$, the stable agent type is $\{I \succ O, I \succ D\}$, the social stable agent type is $\{I \succ O, I \succ D, O \succ D\}$, etc. Moreover, agent types can be derived. For example, since orderings are transitive we can derive that an agent which is unstable with respect to obligations ($O \succ I$) and stable with respect to intentions ($I \succ D$) is social ($O \succ D$). There are twenty-four complete agent types, of which the six realistic ones are listed in Table 2. The definition of agent types leads to a simple way in which agent types

Constraints	Agent type
$B \succ O\ O \succ I\ I \succ D$	Realistic, unstable-O, stable-D, social
$B \succ O\ O \succ D\ D \succ I$	Realistic, unstable-O, unstable-D, social
$B \succ I\ I \succ O\ O \succ D$	Realistic, stable-O, stable-D, social
$B \succ I\ I \succ D\ D \succ O$	Realistic, stable-O, stable-D, selfish
$B \succ D\ D \succ O\ O \succ I$	Realistic, unstable-O, unstable-D, selfish
$B \succ D\ D \succ I\ I \succ O$	Realistic, stable-O, unstable-D, selfish

Table 2: Six complete realistic agent types

can be compared. Agent type A is at least as general as agent type B if all the priority functions that respect constraints of agent type A, also respect the constraints of agent type B. The generality relation between realistic agent types forms the lattice visualized in Figure 1 if we add a top element. This figure should be read as follows. The level in this hierarchy indicates the generality of agent types. The bottom of this lattice is the realistic agent type. Each higher layer adds additional constraints resulting in more specific agent types. The top of this lattice is the falsum which indicates that adding any additional constraint to the ρ function results in an inconsistent ordering. Just below are the six complete realistic agent types.

There are also other constraints on priority functions. One of them is the following unique extension property, which says that ρ associates with each rule a unique integer. It induces a strict total order on the rules.

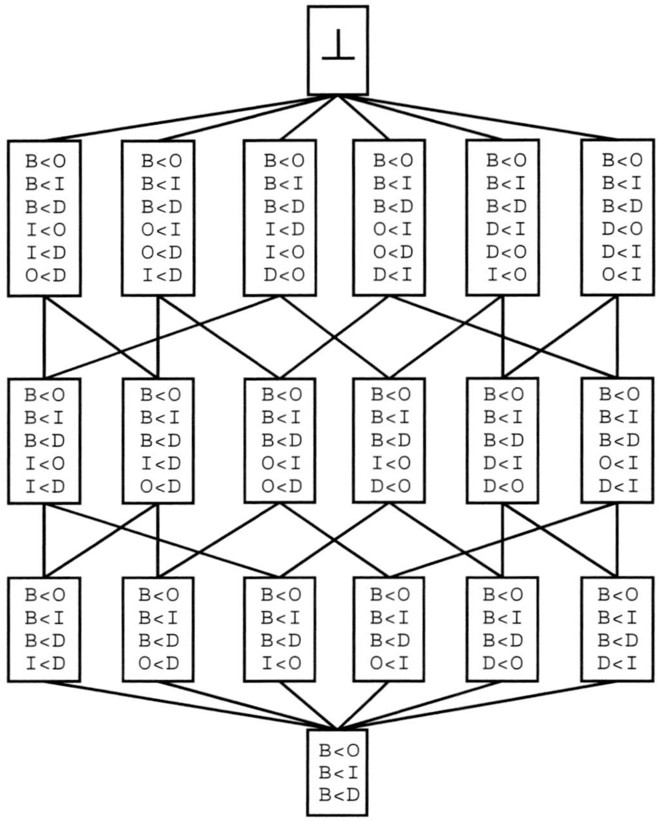

Figure 1: The lattice structure of realistic agent types.

Definition 8 (Unique goal set) *A goal generation process that generates unique goal sets is specified by a tuple* $\langle Obs, B, O, I, D, \rho\rangle$ *with* ρ *a function from* $B \cup O \cup I \cup D$ *to the integers such that* $\rho(x) = \rho(y)$ *implies* $x = y$.

Another constraint on priority function ρ is the following attitude order property.

Definition 9 (Attitude order) *A goal generation process specified by a tuple* $\langle Obs, B, O, I, D, \rho\rangle$ *induces a strict attitude order when* ρ *is a function from* $B \cup O \cup I \cup D$ *to the integers such that for all* $X, Y \in \{B, O, I, D\}$ *with* $X \neq Y$ *we have either* $X \succ Y$ *or* $Y \succ X$.

The only agent types that satisfy the attitude order property are the complete agent types. Lack of the attitude order property is illustrated by the realistic agent. It starts with the observations and calculates belief extensions by iteratively applying belief rules. When no belief rule is applicable anymore, then the set of either O, the I, or the D rules are chosen arbitrarily. The chosen set is called the active set of rules. If a rule from the active set of rules is applicable, then the rule is selected and applied. When the rule is applied successfully, the belief rules are attended again and belief rules are applied. If there is no rule from the active set of rules O, I, or D is applicable, then another set of rules becomes the active set of rules. If there is no rule from any of the *O*, *I*, or *D* applicable, then the process terminates – a fixed point is reached – and extensions are calculated.

5 Summary

We consider a range of systems, which are concerned with decisions, deliberation or agent types. We ask ourselves the following question:

> How does deliberation based on agent types lead to decisions?

This question breaks down in three sub-questions. First, what is an agent decision? To answer this question we discuss theories which define what a decision is, so-called decision theories. The first is classical decision theory [15, 22] and the second it qualitative extension (QDT) [1, 17]. In all these theories, a decision is the best option among a set of alternatives. We also illustrate that classical as well as recently proposed qualitative decision theories do not explain how decisions can be found, but in Boutilier's decision theory the concept of goal plays a central role. This is also a crucial concept in the three theories of deliberation studied in this paper.

Second, what is agent deliberation and how does it lead to a decision? To answer this question we discuss two other approaches. The first approach we discuss is based on an abstract model of the mental attitudes of an agent: beliefs, desires and intentions (BDI) [2, 5, 19]. The second (3APL) is similar to BDI except that the decision rules is replaced by a process called the deliberation process. It is this process that determine which actions should be performed for a given set of underlying cognitive concepts. The discussion on BDI systems and 3APL illustrates how deliberation finds decisions. The deliberation process is based on cognitive concepts like beliefs, desires, goals, intentions and plans. The system generates goals, and thereafter finds plans to achieve these goals.

Third, how do agent types classify patterns of deliberation? The fifth approach we discuss to answer this question is also based on mental attitudes extended with obligations (BOID) [3]. The discussion on BDI-CTL and BOID illustrates how agent types classify deliberation. The deliberation process in BDI and BOID has been characterized in terms of agent types or deliberation patterns. In BDI-CTL the agent types represent how beliefs, goals and intentions are related, and when goals are maintained or dropped. In BOID the agent types represent how the agent resolves his conflicts. For example, a selfish agent lets its desires take precedence over his obligations. Using cognitive concepts and formulating the decision rule in terms of deliberation patterns makes the later two approaches cognitive theories of decision making.

Acknowledgments

Thanks to Jan Broersen, Zhisheng Huang and Joris Hulstijn for many discussions on related subjects.

References

[1] C. Boutilier. Towards a logic for qualitative decision theory. In *Proceedings of the Fourth International Conference on Knowledge Representation and Reasoning (KR'94)*, pages 75–86. Morgan Kaufmann, 1994.

[2] M. Bratman. *Intention, plans, and practical reason.* Harvard University Press, Cambridge Mass, 1987.

[3] J. Broersen, M. Dastani, J. Hulstijn, and L. van der Torre. Goal generation in the BOID architecture. *Cognitive Science Quarterly*, **2**(3-4):428–447, 2002.

[4] J. Broersen, M. Dastani, and L. van der Torre. Realistic desires. *Journal of Applied Non-Classical Logics*, **12**(2):287–308, 2002.

[5] P. Cohen and H. Levesque. Intention is choice with commitment. *Artificial Intelligence*, **42** (2-3):213–261, 1990.

[6] M. Dastani, F. de Boer, F. Dignum, and J.-J. Meyer. Programming agent deliberation: An approach illustrated using the 3apl language. In *Proceedings of The Second Conference on Autonomous Agents and Multi-agent Systems (AAMAS'03)*, Melbourne, Australia, 2003.

[7] M. Dastani, F. Dignum, and J.-J. Meyer. Autonomy and agent deliberation. In *Proceedings of The First International Workshop on Computational Autonomy - Potential, Risks, Solutions (Autonomy'03)*, Melbourne, Australia, 2003.

[8] M. Dastani, J. Hulstijn, and L. van der Torre. How to decide what to do? *European Journal of Operations Research*, to appear.

[9] T. Dean and M. Wellman. *Planning and Control.* Morgan Kaufmann, San Mateo, 1991.

[10] J. Doyle. A model for deliberation, action and introspection. Technical Report AI-TR-581, MIT AI Laboratory, 1980.

[11] J. Doyle, Y. Shoham, and M.P. Wellman. The logic of relative desires. In *Sixth International Symposium on Methodologies for Intelligent Systems (ISMIS-91)*, volume LNAI Volume 542, pages 16–31, Charlotte, North Carolina, 1991.

[12] J. Doyle and R. Thomason. Background to qualitative decision theory. *AI magazine*, **20**:2:55–68, 1999.

[13] J. Doyle and M. Wellman. Preferential semantics for goals. In *Proceedings of the Tenth National Conference on Artificial Intelligence (AAAI'91)*, pages 698–703, 1991.

[14] B. Hansson. An analysis of some deontic logics. *Nous*, **3**:373–398, 1969.

[15] R. C. Jeffrey. *The Logic of Decision*. McGraw-Hill, New York, 1965.

[16] J. Lang. Conditional desires and utilities - an alternative approach to qualitative decision theory. In *Proceedings of the Twelth European Conference on Artificial Intelligence (ECAI'96)*, pages 318–322. John Wiley and Sons, 1996.

[17] J. Pearl. From conditional ought to qualitative decision theory. In *Proceedings of the Ninth Conference on Uncertainty in Artificial Intelligence (UAI'93)*, pages 12–20. John Wiley and Sons, 1993.

[18] A. Rao and M. Georgeff. Deliberation and its role in the formation of intentions. In *Proceedings of the Seventh Conference on Uncertainty in Artificial Intelligence (UAI-91)*, pages 300–307, San Mateo, CA, 1991. Morgan Kaufmann Publishers.

[19] A. Rao and M. Georgeff. Modeling rational agents within a bdi architecture. In *Proceedings of Second International Conference on Knowledge Representation and Reasoning (KR'91)*, pages 473–484. Morgan Kaufmann, 1991.

[20] A. Rao and M. Georgeff. Decision procedures for BDI logics. *Journal of Logic and Computation*, **8**:293–342, 1998.

[21] R. Reiter. A logic for default reasoning. *Artificial Intelligence*, **13**:81–132, 1980.

[22] L. Savage. *The foundations of statistics*. Wiley, New York, 1954.

[23] S.-W. Tan and J. Pearl. Qualitative decision theory. In *Proceedings of the Thirteenth National Conference on Artificial Intelligence (AAAI'94)*, pages 928–932, 1994.

[24] S.-W. Tan and J. Pearl. Specification and evaluation of preferences under uncertainty. In *Proceedings of the Fourth International Conference on Knowledge Representation and Reasoning (KR'94)*, pages 530–539. Morgan Kaufmann, 1994.

INDEX